AF605840

EXPERIENCES OF PASSAGE

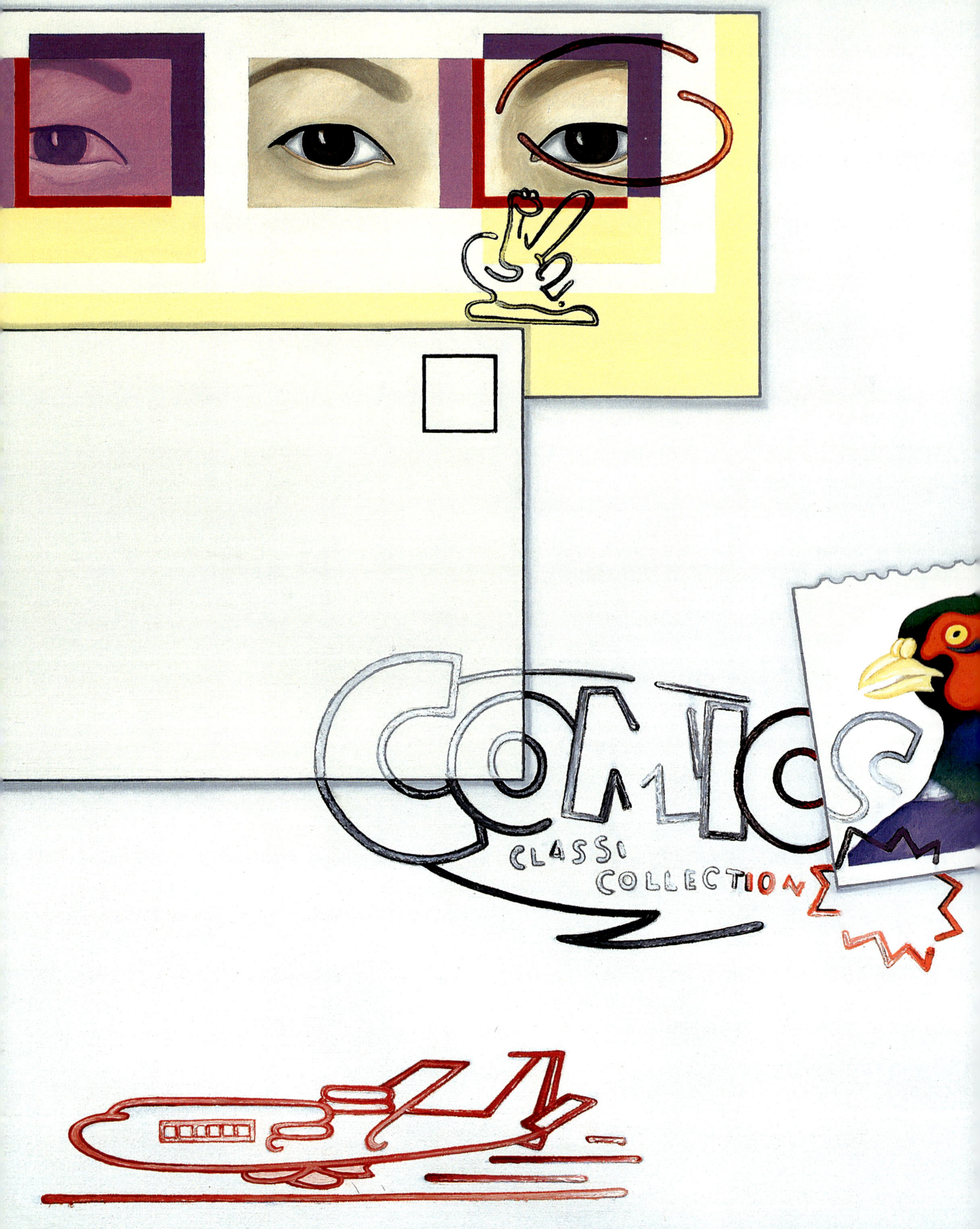

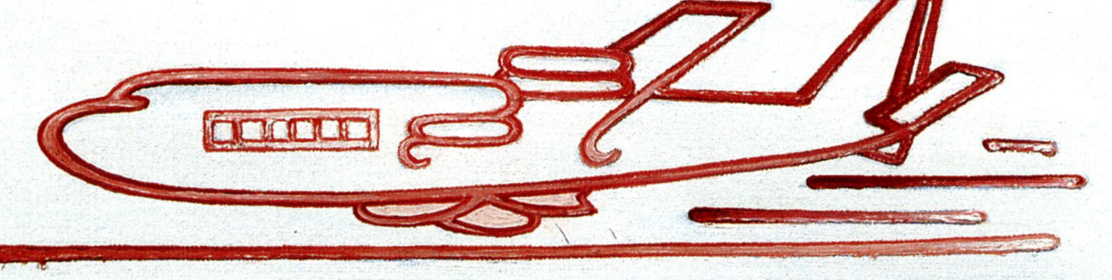
COMICS
CLASSI
COLLECTION

Experiences of Passage

THE PAINTINGS OF YUN GEE & LI-LAN

JOYCE BRODSKY

University of Washington Press Seattle and London

Generous support for the publication of *Experiences of Passage: The Paintings of Yun Gee and Li-lan* was provided by Victor Ma.

Printed in China
Designed by Ashley Saleeba
Typeset in Sabon and Helvetica
12 11 10 09 08 5 4 3 2 1

University of Washington Press
P.O. Box 50096, Seattle, WA 98145 U.S.A.
www.washington.edu/uwpress

Cataloging-in-Publication Data is available from the Library of Congress.
ISBN 978-0-295-98775-0

The paper used in this publication meets the minimum requirements of American National Standard for Information Sciences—Permanence of Paper for Printed Library Materials, ANSI Z39.48–1984. ∞

This book is dedicated to Li-lan,

to my daughter, Shara,

and to the late Stephanie Terenzio

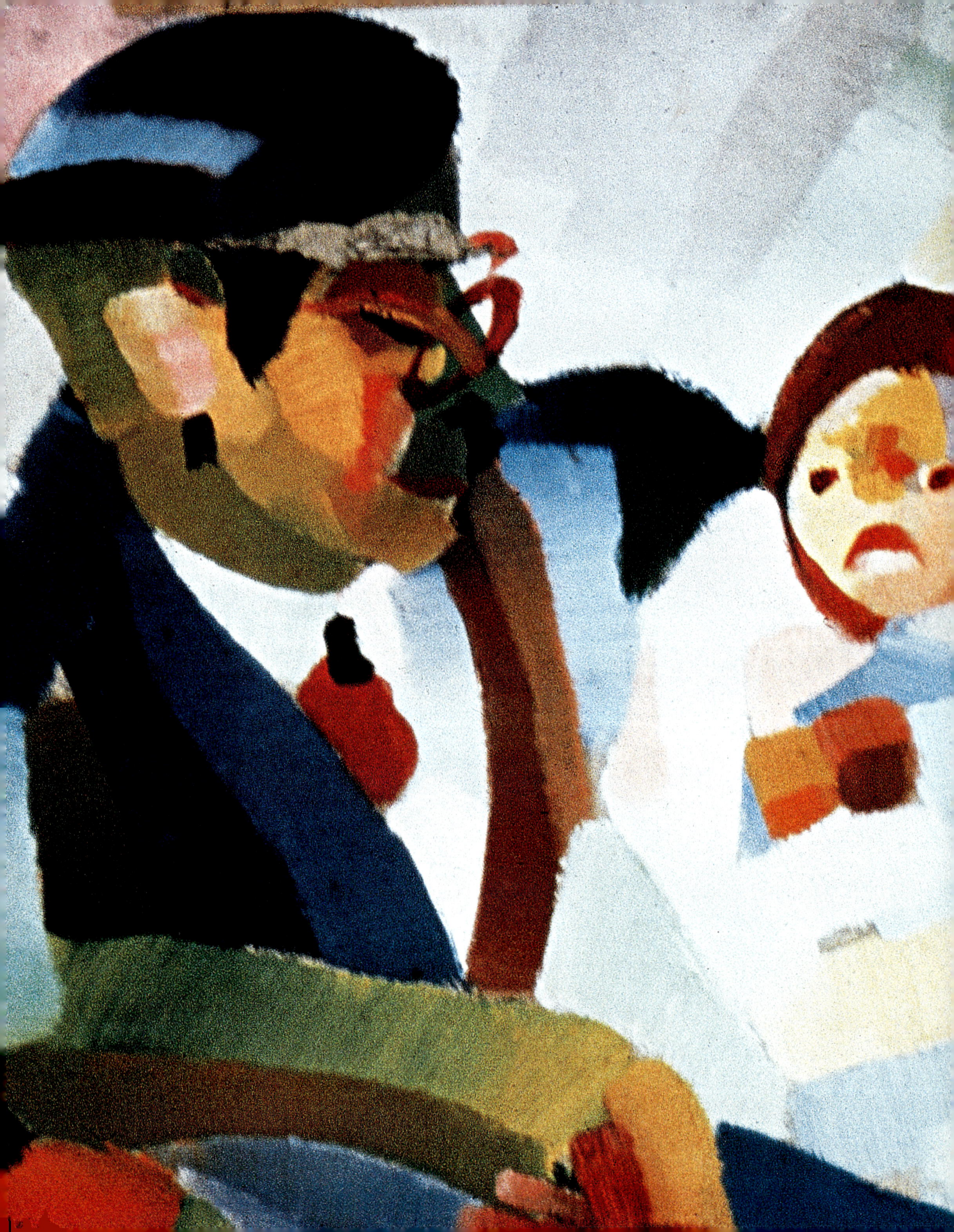

CONTENTS

ILLUSTRATIONS

Plates

YUN GEE

LI-LAN

Figures

PREFACE

It is difficult to acknowledge that this may be the right time for me to be engaged in this project. For one of the first times in my life, I can be more responsive to the feelings of despair that Yun Gee mentions many times in his autobiographical writings and in his poems. His moment in history was darkened by World War II and by racial prejudice that was particularly virulent against Asians; and while the early life of Li-lan, his daughter, seemed to take place in more peaceful times, the Vietnam War was soon to follow. The present dark moment of another war is one of all against all, and many of us go about our lives with dejection shading our psyches. I am a child of the New Deal, and I remember having come to political awareness watching President Franklin Delano Roosevelt riding in an open motorcar past my apartment building on Washington Avenue in Brooklyn. My memory pictures me waving a tiny American flag and sharing in the feelings of joy that swept over the crowd around me. Those were the 1940s, the World War II years, and I was about ten years old. In spite of the war, there was hope. I came to personal maturity in the 1960s, in a time of shared optimism about the global bettering of humanity; now, seven years into the twenty-first century, the post-national dream embraced in this book is, sad to say, rooted in our shared anguish for the future of the human species that inhabits this soiled planet. If any hope remains, the experiences of passage of transnationals like Yun Gee and Li-lan may provide one kind of model for a possible future.

How did I come to be writing about two painters of Chinese background? I want to tell two short stories that may partially answer the question.

The first story is about a kind of self-awareness. I was recently driving along with two close friends, and we all decided to name, in one or two words, what each of us believed to be our most intrinsic characteristic. When it was my turn, I said, without thinking, "Detachment." I had just finished co-curating an exhibition whose theme raised analogies to the human displacement that is at the heart of this book.[1] At about the same time, I had finished writing a short introduction to the catalogue for an exhibition of Li-lan's work.[2] As I began to write this book, I felt a connection between these two projects, on the one hand, and, on the other, my self-description as detached. A book review I read at the time, of Joseph Berger's *Displaced Persons: Growing Up American after the Holocaust,* ends this way:

> Berger knows that no matter what goes unsaid in the lives of Holocaust survivors, Auschwitz is always in the room. . . . This is the ultimate misfortune of the displaced person. You might have a roof over your head, but inside your head you still have that spiraling feeling of detachment, where there is no sense of place anywhere in particular . . . the refugee condition is one in which housing is beside the point; often it's the psyche that needs shelter.[3]

I am not a Holocaust survivor, nor am I aware of relatives who are, but I am Jewish. What does being Jewish mean in light of the Diaspora, and of the fact of the Holocaust?[4] As I write, anti-Semitism is on the rise worldwide. Do past and present history partially account for my sense of detachment (homelessness), or is that just a New Yorker's sensibility, or perhaps a factor in my particular makeup? Yun Gee was Chinese; he was born in Guangdong Province, China, and immigrated to the United States when he was fifteen. What kind of shelter did he need and receive? Li-lan is biracial and was born in New York. She was estranged from her Caucasian mother—Yun Gee's second wife, Helen—who died in 2004. We talked at a time when Li-lan was worried about the adversarial position of the United States toward China and Asians in general. As my work on this book began, China was being wooed by the Bush Administration, and as I revised the manuscript, attitudes had shifted again, in light of the U.S. invasion of Iraq: Muslims and Arabs are out of favor at the moment, and *all* "others" are suspect. Does that make Li-lan more anxious? What sense of place does she have? And how does her anxiety differ from the more ordinary feelings of strangeness that almost all of us experience in our lives at one time or another, feelings of strangeness that are now so pervasive?

The second story is about the role of serendipity in a person's life. In 1979, when I was teaching at the University of Connecticut, I organized an exhibition of Yun Gee's work at the university's William Benton Museum of Art and wrote the catalogue for it, at the request of the late Stephanie Terenzio, then the museum's curator of modern art. Through Helen Gee, Stephanie had become acquainted with the paintings, and she asked for my involvement because she thought that an art historian and theoretician like myself, with roots in painting, would be best suited to the task.

I had always liked Chinese art—and Chinese food, since it had been my first contact with things Chinese; as a child, I ate a most diluted form of it with my parents almost every Sunday in Brooklyn—and I have always wanted to visit China. Nevertheless, I am only beginning to know about the country and its art, although I am better informed about its cuisine. I took the exhibition and the catalogue on because I was intrigued by Yun Gee's early paintings, and because doing so would afford me an opportunity to learn more about China. I met Li-lan briefly at the opening; later, in 1990, we met again, when she had her own one-person exhibition at the same museum. I think the seeds of this book grew from that second meeting.

A few years ago, I had dinner with Li-lan in a wonderful Japanese restaurant in Soho. We were talking about her father, and she was reminiscing about the times she had spent with him in his studio apartment when she was a child. He loved to cook for her, and when he did, his rooms filled up with smoke from the Chinese cooking oils he used. All that smoke and grease had left a yellowish film on the surfaces of his paintings; but when I worked on the exhibition and catalogue, my lack of knowledge about Chinese art made me think that he had used some kind of Chinese yellow as a glaze! Most of the paintings have been cleaned since then, and my ignorance has been unveiled. I write now in part to correct some of my previous errors (not all of them related to the surfaces of Gee's paintings).

These stories may be illuminating, if obliquely, but they do not fully address the original question of why I decided to write this book. One of my reasons has to do with the fact that I am now living on the West Coast, where there are large groups of people of Asian background. It seems appropriate to root myself here by engaging with matters that are obviously related to this part of the country. I am also interested, both theoretically and politically, in transnational and postnational issues, and the paintings of Yun Gee and Li-lan, apart from evoking my aesthetic empathy, are replete with signs of such content. Gee still strikes me as an example, unique in the first half of the twentieth century, of someone who easily embraced several cultures; and I have had the good fortune to find in Li-lan someone of the next generation whose life and work are a response to that embrace. My connection with both painters, father and daughter, also affords me the opportunity to understand the similarities and differences between their experiences of passage.

Moreover, I am a lover of cities and think of myself as a cosmopolite, just as Yun Gee was, and as Li-lan is. A cosmopolite can be defined, perhaps rather too simply but nevertheless pragmatically, as someone who takes the whole world for his or her own country, a person who is not limited by nationalism or nationalistic attachments, one whose characteristics are suited to or arise from his or her experiences of many countries. At the same time, from within a postmodern perspective, writing about a culture, a society, a race, or a gender different from one's own could be considered politically incorrect. I consider myself to be a political postmodernist and a feminist; so, again, how do I justify this undertaking? I believe that there are many viewpoints, many forms of "situated knowledge,"[5] and it is in the layering of stories, told by all sorts of people at different times and in different places, that something like a full picture emerges. Each story may contribute a perspective that rounds out our knowledge about subjects and past events and, perhaps, prevents us from obfuscating historical actualities. The question of which version or versions should have more weight is complicated by particular moments and contexts, but keeping several versions in mind is probably the most edifying approach. My own version is of course "situated," but it was necessary for me, as it would have been for any other writer doing research, to study as much as possible about the chosen subject. That would have been the case if I had been writing about the Jewish painters R. B. Kitaj, Lucian Freud, or Philip Guston, as it was the case in my engaging with the Chinese artist Yun Gee and the biracial artist Li-lan. Trinh T. Minh-ha sends out a challenge that I have tried to engage:

> Assumptions [about] the role of art in communities of people of color are naturalized to [such an] extent that Caucasian critics never hesitate to claim that they find it difficult to conceive of Black, Chicana, Asian, or Native American women's experiences. They maintain that they can't presume to speak for them (under the pretext that they are not familiar with the latter's histories), thereby patronizing these artists with the latter's original "you-have-to-be-one-to-know-one" strategy.[6]

Even though I did painstaking research for the catalogue that accompanied the 1979 Yun Gee exhibition, errors still resulted from problems with verbal sources and from the fact that I did not then know Li-lan. Other errors were of the kind that any writer makes in forming a story—in this case, a story about artists' lives and creative endeavors. This story will also suffer because of yet different kinds of omissions and faulty inclusions. As I just said, we continue to dig into past subjects in the hope that overlying versions may yield something approaching the actual events. My primary interest here is to focus on both artists' lives and works, but I also feel an obligation, particularly to Li-lan, to correct, insofar as I can, the faulty inclusions that found their way into the catalogue essay on Yun Gee that I wrote more than twenty-five years ago.[7] This book, then, is rooted in the particular experiences of Yun Gee and Li-lan, as filtered in part through the perspective on those experiences that my own life has fashioned.

As for the organization of the book, the introduction has briefly suggested an appropriate model, one that situates the lives and works of Yun Gee and Li-lan in terms of their being transnational citizens—citizens, that is, in the "middle passage of contemporary culture."[8] The first chapter explores Yun Gee's social and political milieu and serves as background for the second, which is about his paintings and drawings and the artistic environment in which he performed. That format is repeated in the third and fourth chapters, which present the different experiences of passage that constitute Li-lan's life and work in the second half of the twentieth century and the beginning of the twenty-first.

The chapters on Yun Gee are based on my previous writings, on recent publications by Anthony Lee, and on essays by David Teh-yu Wang, Jane C. Ju, Chia Chi Jason Wang, and Paul Karlstrom, among others, that cover Gee's life in a manner close to that found in some of my own more recent observations. The chapters about Li-lan's life and work are less related to particular texts than to my conversations with her, and I think that those chapters may be richer in tone because of these interchanges, and because of the currency of the research. I brought these two artists, father and daughter, together in order to compare experiences of passage, in part because of their familial tie. It was also my concern to deepen my understanding of the impact that each artist's life has had on the work of the other, or on the reception of that work. Li-lan was exposed to Yun Gee's paintings and his cultural sophistication when she was a child, and this exposure was crucial to her artistic being. In turn, she has broadened and deepened the audience for his art through her archival work, the care she has taken with his paintings and drawings, and her efforts to encourage exhibitions of his work. If Yun Gee's influence on Li-lan's life and creative output is in the realm of the expected, her influence on his artistic fortunes and legacy is a more rare form and most noble.

One usually begins or ends any list of acknowledgments by letting those mentioned off the hook for any errors committed by the author; in keeping with this tradition, let me state that the responsibility for any errors is mine. Where the good ideas are concerned, however, responsibility lies with my friends, other authors I have read, and the artists with whom I have engaged. First, I wish to thank the members of my dear family for their constant support: Shara, Stephen, Michael, Susan, and my marvelous mother, Rose, who, though she lived to the age of ninety-six, did not live to see this book finished but was nevertheless with me all the way. I lost my father, Chick, many years ago, but his goodness, nobility, and tolerance provided a model that I still emulate (but to which I often fail to conform).

Second, I thank my friends. I have dedicated this text in part to Li-lan because she has been a joy to work with. Over the years, she has not only been the devoted archivist of her father's life and work but also has been honest and open with me about her own. I could not have realized this project without her. Zarina Hashmi is the quintessential transnational and cosmopolite, and in knowing her I have learned to understand something about the profound state of homelessness. She lives in that situation every day, and her stunning work, deeply rooted in her experiences of passage, has inspired me over the past decade.[9] I also wish to thank my mentor and dear friend Nathan Knobler, who recently died, but whose support and keen editorial eye kept me on the right track throughout my entire teaching and writing career. He was a great teacher, and many students found their lives changed because they had known him. Lois Knobler is a friend as well as an artist whom I admire; her perseverance is constant in spite of adversity, and as a result she provides an important model. The same can be said of Betty Antrim, who, like a good sister, keeps me honest.

Third, I thank my colleagues. Anthony Lee gave me the manuscript of his essays for a book for which he served as both editor and contributor.[10] I want to thank him for allowing me to read his writings; reading them helped me avoid redundancy and distinguish some aspects of my reading of Gee's life and work from his own. His collaborator Paul Karlstrom, with whom I had lunch several years ago, was very encouraging about this book, and I wish to acknowledge his support for it as well as his contributions to the book edited by Anthony Lee. Very special thanks are due to Tunghsiao Chou, whose meticulous work on the Yun Gee archives enabled me to refine my thinking about him; her article on Yun Gee was also important for my work.[11] She was more than helpful in accommodating my all too frequent requests, giving me editorial advice on the first two chapters and taking on the onerous task of compiling the index. In the final stages of getting this book ready for publication, Gene-Manuel was as meticulous in preparing the illustrations for reproduction as he was in completing other tasks. The late Helen Gee worked with me on the catalogue for the 1979 exhibition of Yun Gee's paintings, and I gratefully acknowledge her and the staff of the William Benton Museum of Art for their help.

Fourth, special thanks are extended to Pat Soden, director of the University of Washington Press, who has been very supportive. Jacqueline Ettinger, an acquiring editor at the Press, worked with me to prepare the manuscript for publication; her excellent suggestions have made this a much better book. I also appreciate the good suggestions of copyeditor Xavier Callahan and am grateful to Ashley Saleeba for the fine layout of the book. Special thanks as well to the three anonymous readers of the manuscript, who helped me rethink and rewrite sections and, I think, vastly improved the book. I also thank my former colleagues at the University of Connecticut, Storrs, and at the University of California, Santa Cruz; I was privileged to belong to two art departments whose members provided the kinds of stimulation necessary to continued creativity. I owe my gratitude as well to my colleagues at the Camargo Foundation, in Cassis, France, for the inspiration they gave me to do this kind of work during my two fellowship stays, and to Michael Pretina, who was director while I was there and who set the stage for hard work and wonderful play.

Fifth, I am more than indebted to the great generosity of Victor Ma, a major collector of Chinese art in Taiwan who has supported many other projects like this one, in order to enhance understanding of Asian art. Without his unstinting financial support, it is doubtful that this book would have seen publication in its present form.

Finally, it was my good fortune to engage with two artists who were not particularly well known, but whose careers are now entering the mainstream as issues of transnational modes of thinking and creating come into play. This is an exciting event, and I hope that my participation has helped, in some small way, to bring attention to their important contributions.

EXPERIENCES OF PASSAGE

INTRODUCTION

Transnationals in "In Between" Spaces

Old certainties—never certainties for everyone in any case—are wearing thin.

—SMADAR LAVIE AND TED SWEDENBURG

This book is dedicated to the critique of old certainties about culture, place, and nation, in light of transnationalism.[1] As father and daughter, Yun Gee and Li-lan provide the opportunity to study these issues in two very different cultural and historical contexts. While transnationalism is now often identified with globalization, these artists are examples of the desire to live and work free of national restrictions, and openly responsive to diverse cultures, not as a result of art-world trends but because they have embraced these issues in their very lives, and that is embodied in their paintings. Gee was somewhat unusual for his time, not only because he chose to become transnational but also because in his desire to explore many cultures and embrace aspects of them in his painting he can be compared to many contemporary artists (I have brought closure to this book in the epilogue by briefly discussing some of them who came originally from China). It is also important to underscore that Gee's ability to absorb, in a novel manner, aspects of cubism and School of Paris post–World War I painting resulted in important works that should be acknowledged in discussions of the history of modernism. Li-lan, who might be considered transnational in the flesh, as the biracial offspring of a proclaimed world citizen like Gee, was well prepared to explore her historical moment in the world of globalization almost before it produced what is being described as a transnational style.[2] This suggests that having a global sensibility is not directly tied to electronic or economic globalization.

In the cultural production of many biracial and emigrant artists, the notion of hybridity is often introduced in discussions of their work as a way of focusing on the different parts of such artists' dislocations.[3] With respect to artworks, the term "hybridity" has become a postmodern cliché in the critical practice of deciphering bits and pieces of each national or ethnic part and, at the political or social level, reinforcing "hyphenated subject" positions. In a short essay that Jane C. Ju wrote for a major exhibition of Yun Gee's paintings at the Taipei Fine Arts Museum in 1992, I was struck by her understanding that hyphenation is often politically loaded, in reaction both to the artist and to the works. Talking about his Paris period, she writes:

> From the materials concerning this period of Yun Gee's life, I found something that puzzled me. Although his paintings were clearly modernistic in expression, i.e., in the mode of Synchromism or Cubism, many writings on his art often describe them as expressing "Chinese" or "Oriental" sensibilities. Since I could not see any "Chineseness" in most of his works (except for those clearly depicting Chinese figures, or those inscribed with Chinese characters), I wondered whether his being a Chinese American had influenced the perception of these writers.[4]

This book explores the lives and works of Yun Gee and Li-lan and is not primarily theoretical, but ideas about hybridity, transnationalism, and cosmopolitanism do inform the work.[5] I call attention briefly to a few of these ideas while remaining aware of the necessity for a fleshed-out study of the relations between theory and practice pertinent to these issues. Such a study would examine, for example, the works of the transnational scholar Homi Bhabha, who is central to this discourse. From within the field of cultural studies, Bhabha has formulated a strong notion of the hybrid as an issue that concerns the individual's response from the inside to the various outsides, as opposed to the hybridity that exploits the fragmentation stemming from dislocation. Lavie and Swedenburg agree with Bhabha that in the realm of the political the notion of the hybrid is crucial in the sense that "all cultures turn out to be, in various ways, hybrid. Intercultural creations and miscegenations expose as a hoax the modernist and colonialist discourse concerning homogeneity of cultures—a myth sustained chiefly by the center's stranglehold on the global economy."[6]

Hybridity, then, turns out to be a very complex notion, with many critical issues emerging from the growing literature that explores the ramifications of mixed cultures and ethnicities. In relation to the task at hand—the study of transnational artists—two problems emerge as particularly consequential. In a broad social, political, and cultural sense, the superficial recognition of hyphenation and hybridity as difference not only may perpetuate a subtle level of discrimination but also may result in deflection from the necessary commitment to change that actually supports diversity. Moreover, transnationalism can aspire to a simpleminded desire for universality or transcendence that results in blindness to local differences and conditions and can sometimes support a dangerous return to essentialist notions. At a more personal level, in the lives of the artists I am discussing, these overriding concerns play out in the daily negotiation between the acceptance of their hybrid nature, even in the face of hostility, and the desire for a harmony that is inclusive of that diversity. What may emerge from the struggle is constitutive of the stronger notion of the hybrid embedded in a different kind of vision that forges coherence from the cultural parts. This may materialize from what Homi Bhabha labels being in "the third, or in-between, or transnational space."[7] It is this more profound notion that is decisive in understanding the life and works of Yun Gee and Li-lan.

Bhabha also writes that critique itself is effective because it "opens up a space of translation," a "place of hybridity," which allows for the creation of something new that is "*neither the one nor the other.*"[8] Bhabha's essay is dedicated to the creative and political role of theory as such in its interaction with practice, but it can be applied to the life and work of artists like Yun Gee and Li-lan, who reside in their respective transnational spaces.[9] While seemingly fraught with the anxieties of exile that Edward M. Said so poignantly describes as "the unhealable rift forced between a human being and a native place, between the self and its true home," such that "its essential sadness can never be surmounted," it is none the less true that "both the new and the old environments are vivid, actual, occurring together contrapuntally."[10] That sadness may characterize the past and present exilic situations of the many, but in the hope for a future in a postnational world such passages may be less burdensome. In the meantime, the contrapuntal may be the rub that stimulates new kinds of perceptions embodied in original works. I think that critical energy is what characterizes the work of many transnational artists like Yun Gee and Li-lan.

Now that almost every place in the world is inhabited by immigrants or biracial persons, what does it particularly mean to be a cosmopolite or a transnational? I use those designations for persons who embrace their multinational, multicultural, and multiracial experiences and, as a result, combine them intrinsically, sometimes in spite of the pain that this complex passage may entail. This approach often contrasts with that of those who migrate but who choose, for all sorts of complex reasons, to remain rooted in the structures of their social, cultural, racial, or ethnic origins. People in the former group, just because of their desire to be inclusive, often gain a special awareness of others and an acceptance of diversity in the life lived and the work produced. Irit Rogoff has lived the life of a transnational, and she explores the ramifications in an excellent study where she writes about herself:

> It seems important to say in this context that I am currently on my fourth country and third language; none of my displacement has been the least tragic, like the plight of those forced to leave homelands for political and intellectual reasons. My movement has had to do with a restless curiosity, opportunities, and the making of certain choices, not much more. . . . Nevertheless, my own displacement entails complex daily negotiations between all the cultures and languages and histories which inhabit me, resulting in the suspension of belief in the possibility of either coherent narratives or sign systems that can actually reflect straightforward relations between subjects, places, and identities.[11]

These ruminations are particularly apt for discussions about the lives of Yun Gee and Li-lan. If I qualify Rogoff's comments in any way, it is to suggest that for these two artists there is a kind of coherence that emerges from the "complex daily negotiations between all the cultures and languages and histories" that inhabit them. I hope to show that there is a wholeness to their lives and to their work that ought to be the focus of inquiry, replacing the emphasis on their being Chinese Americans. While the term "Chinese American" is descriptive in different ways of both Gee and Li-lan, as such terms are for many "hyphenated" persons, racial implications may be at play.

In the case of Yun Gee, how does the artist's being a transnational cause his situation to differ, in terms of creative production, from the situation of any other émigré artist in any time frame?[12] If I considered only the twentieth century and restricted my question, for the moment, to Europeans who emigrated to the United States, I would be considering hundreds of artists who escaped poverty and persecution, the latter predominantly occasioned by Fascism. They took with them the social and cultural experiences of their home countries, as did Gee. I think the difference lies both in the forced nature of their exodus and in the artistic ambiences of their native countries. For the most part, European artists brought the avant-garde modernist experiences of the late nineteenth and early twentieth centuries here and continued to explore them. They were already formed as artists and, at first, were not particularly interested in the art of their adopted country. While some of them did engage aspects of American culture, for the most part they provided the new creative direction that would change the art of the United States; Willem de Kooning is a prime example of such an artist.[13] Most Asian émigré artists were trained in what were considered to be the more traditional styles of the countries from which they came, or in a form of Western art deemed provincial and academic in the West. Even if, as may have been the case for Gee, they were aware of some of the latest forms of Western art, they had to learn to create works in the adopted country's idioms of the time if they wanted to compete on the national scene.[14]

While Gee had a more difficult time living and working in the first half of the twentieth century, and particularly during the war years, he had much in common with many contemporary transnational artists who are not driven from their native countries because of obvious repression or poverty but often move around in order to engage other contemporary ideas and audiences.[15] As Gee did, many of them live for periods of time in several art centers and are conversant with the "international" styles practiced there.[16] They seek out these spaces and often produce work that embodies their complex cultural experiences. Yun Gee may seem to differ from them somewhat because international institutions like biennales did not exist in the early twentieth century, nor did such media of mass communication as the World Wide Web, and traveling to faraway places was still difficult; moreover, Gee was poor. He also faced a form of racism that is less overt today for artists who move to major cosmopolitan centers. As a creative intellectual, however, he adopted Western modernism very quickly, just as his contemporary counterparts embrace global art forms. Although he found his stylistic vocabulary first in the United States and later in Paris, from his early years he had effortlessly been absorbing other social and cultural milieus.[17] Gee was fully engaged with the social, political, and artistic environments in which he lived at any given time. He probably learned about the art and culture of other countries, perhaps Japan and France, through his education in China because he spent his childhood during a revolution that introduced many Western ideas, often by way of Japanese examples. He painted some important works with Chinese themes, but particularly when he went to Paris, and later in New York, such themes became infrequent in his work, as did Christian themes. His work was primarily secular in content—genre scenes, cityscapes, portraits—and he shares with many recent transnational émigrés a unity of vision that in his best paintings is more than just a blending or synthesis of different cultures. As Gee wrote in a short article,

> When I visited the Louvre day after day, the Masterpieces there spoke to me in a language which was neither French nor Chinese but which transcended time and place. Here was something universal which had meaning for every man regardless of race or state. A painting by Cézanne or Courbet became as close to me as any of the scrolls by the Chinese masters with which I was so familiar. And I realized that East and West were not so far apart, for in their finest creative effort, there was something very much akin.[18]

The chapters in this book about Gee's life and work examine the particular factors that enabled this person from a provincial village in southern China to live and work in what we now label a transnational mode.

The situation of Li-lan is obviously another matter. She is the daughter of parents who both participated in the cultural world of New York City, and her experiences growing up biracial in the second half of the twentieth century constitute a different kind of passage from Yun Gee's. She is an American of mixed parentage, as are growing numbers of people born in the United States, but in spite of their numbers, isolation plays a part in many of their stories. In her early years, Li-lan felt cut off from her peers, partially as a result of being perceived as "an Oriental," and she felt abandoned because she did not receive the emotional support she needed from her mother, with whom she had a more than complicated relationship. Li-lan functions in a manner different from that of her father, but still in the kind of "in between" space that can also be related to transnationalism. While living with her mother, Li-lan writes, "I visited my father in his top-floor walk-up from the time my parents separated, and subsequently divorced, when I was two, until he died, when I was twenty. During those years, my father's paintings inhabited my visual world."[19] Her artistic foundation was her early experience in her father's studio, where she absorbed elements of Chinese art and culture alongside his "Western"-style painting and his knowledge about Western philosophy and literature and, later on, international surrealism and New York's pop art and minimalism. She acquired firsthand knowledge of Japanese art when she married the printmaker Masuo Ikeda and lived in Japan for many years. More recent encounters are subtly changing her work as she exhibits in Taiwan and travels in China, and to the village where her father was born. She is at ease in Eastern as well as Western environments, and although she produces work with a different form of unity from that which characterizes Yun Gee's painting, she also circumvents the fragmentation that is so characteristic of facile hybrid practices.

As previously indicated, discussions of hybridity and transnationalism are fraught with pitfalls. While I am claiming for Yun Gee and Li-lan a different kind of vision, one that seems to bypass acknowledgment of the various components of their cultural heritages in a mode I call "transnational," it is none the less obvious that the elements forming that complexity can be identified. I have discussed aspects of both artists' lives and works that point to influences that can be characterized as Eastern or Western. What I am suggesting, however, is that it is the desire to create a different kind of unity that is most compelling in both of their endeavors, and that emerges from and in spite of the difficulties of the experiences of passage. Discussions about what is constitutive of this new approach are only now taking place, and my contribution to the dialogue is in the formative stage. First it is necessary to study in depth how Yun Gee and Li-lan have created images of negotiation between both the hybrid and the transnational aspects of their lives, and that is what this book is about.

Underlying these issues—in this case, issues about being Asian—are the problems associated with the "marked body" as the site of both stereotype and critique.[20] I will refer to particular instances of these issues in discussing both artists' lives. It is interesting, however, that Yun Gee's habit of always wearing Western dress except in music and dance performances, and his desire to look like an artist and a bohemian in San Francisco and New York, were adornments of the body that he adopted not to disguise his being Chinese—which would have been impossible anyway, given his features—but to declare his modernity and his freedom from the stereotypical Chinese body. Li-lan grew up biracial, and Western dress was normal attire for her. What is fascinating in her case is her withdrawal from her Chinese body when she was young, so much so that she detested the Chinese costumes her mother had her wear on certain occasions. Recently some of her paintings include Asian eyes, and her attire is styled in part by Asian designers; she also sometimes wore kimonos while living in Japan. Their willingness to use the body freely to assert mastery was probably a factor in the life and work of both father and daughter that helped to alleviate the suffering caused by racist stereotyping.

In this connection, I am reminded of the marvelous image of the fragile Maya Lin before a committee of congressmen and military veterans. She was being ruthlessly impugned over her design for the Vietnam memorial, partly because she is Asian. She wore a flowing dress and a huge hat that called attention to her difference from all the others, who were wearing suits or uniforms. She spoke softly, but some of her power resided in her daring to parade a highly feminine costume in that setting rather than one that would have blended in with the mostly male bodies surrounding her. She was in control of "othering" all the others.[21] Biracial artists like Maya Lin and Li-lan and transnational artists like Yun Gee may be burdened by the effects of racism and bigotry, but the perceptions they gain from their location in the "third space" may provide them with insights that strengthen their resolve and enrich their art practice. I hope to show that this is true for both Yun Gee and his daughter, Li-lan.

1 EXPERIENCES OF PASSAGE IN THE LIFE OF YUN GEE

The cultural materials analyzed through the modalities of the "third" [time-space] . . . have tended to be highly stylized domains of knowledge, framed as dramatic, literary, artistic and musical texts. Bridging ethnography, cultural studies, and minority discourse will be possible if we incorporate the primary daily realities from which such textual representations emerge. . . . A reconceptualization [is necessary], from the standpoint of lived identities and physical places as well as the texts of expressive culture of the multiplicities of identity and place. —SMADAR LAVIE AND TED SWEDENBURG

The ideology of modernism precluded most considerations of the impact of social and political realities on the everyday lives of artists and the works they produced; Lavie and Swedenburg, quoted in the epigraph to this chapter, reinstate these contexts as crucial. In the same manner, Anthony Lee opens his essay on Yun Gee in this manner: "Political revolutionary, cultural radical, social visionary, teacher, inventor, opportunist, and relentless self-promoter, the American modernist painter Yun Gee was all of these and more."[1] Lee then proceeds to discuss all these aspects of Gee's life in relation to the political and social context of the second quarter of the twentieth century. Gee had both the fortune and the misfortune to have been a transnational in the chaos of the twentieth century; that disorder in China was positive in its implications for Gee's life and work in his early years, but in his later life in New York the disarray of the times worldwide, including the early hopes for China, had negative consequences for him as well as for so many others. Some were able to circumvent these events; for Gee, the mounting personal and world crises were often nearly insurmountable, and yet he persevered. I think it is crucial to understand that Gee's desire to triumph over what separates peoples and cultures from each other was

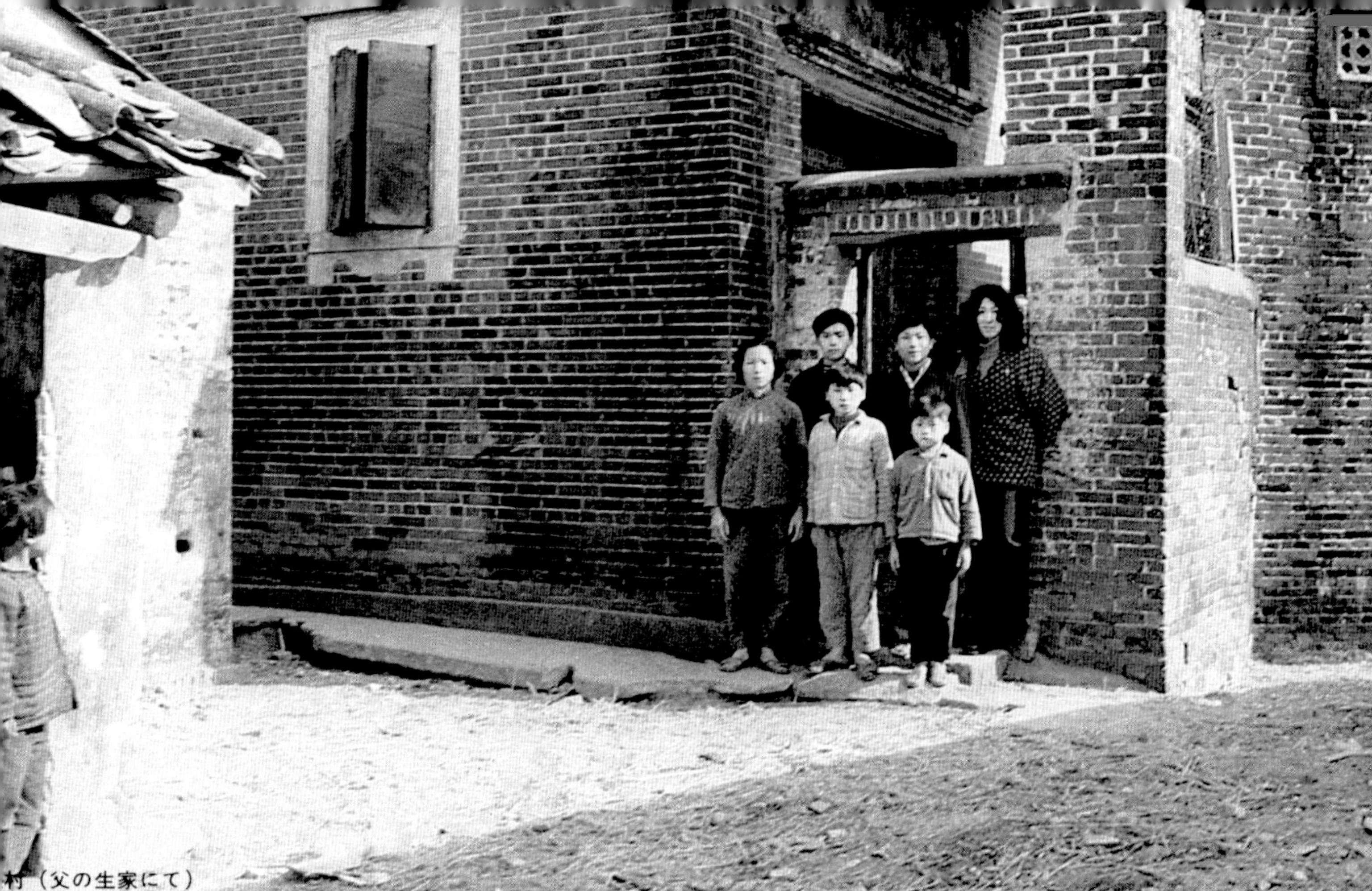

1.1 Li-lan visiting with family and friends in front of Yun Gee's house in Chu Village (formerly Gee Village), 1980.

constantly frustrated, but his identity as Chinese enabled him to sustain that hope. Often the commitment to one's native tradition preempts regard for others. But Gee's belief in the power of culture emerged from his deep roots in his own, and I think it was an important factor in his persistent receptivity to other traditions. The story of his life unfolds as a constant battle between his desire to be an inhabitant of the world and the desire of others to force him into a simplistic orientalism.

Yun Gee (Gee Wing Yun was his Chinese name) was born in Gee Village (now called Chu Village), Yanglu Town, Kaiping County, Guangdong Province, China, on February 22, 1906, the second son of Quong On Chu and Wong See.[2] The year of his birth is significant because his father, working in San Francisco under the Exclusion Act, convinced the authorities that he was (and so his son was as well) a citizen of the United States whose birth records had been lost in the great earthquake and fire of 1906. Yun Gee emigrated to the United States as a fifteen-year-old with an American identity and took up the study of painting at the California School of Fine Arts (now the San Francisco Art Institute) in 1924. He soon established himself in the city's art community. In a few short years, he absorbed some aspects of Cubism from his friend and teacher Otis Oldfield that enabled him to paint genre scenes, portraits, and a few allegorical works in a unique modernist style, an offshoot of Cubism that Gee later theorized as Diamondism.[3]

In 1927, Yun Gee traveled to Paris under the patronage of the Prince and Princess Achille Murat and quickly situated himself in Parisian artistic life, exhibiting at the famous Galerie Bernheim-Jeune, among other venues, and meeting his first wife, the poet Paule de Reuss. Paradoxically, Yun Gee describes his first trip to Paris as a homecoming, even though while he was there he painted his self-portrait as that of an isolated Chinese man.[4] He moved to New York in 1930, and after spending six years there he returned to Paris, and to continued acclaim, until World War II broke out; he returned to New York in 1939. He married Helen Wimmer in 1942, fathered their daughter, Li-lan, and was divorced in 1947.

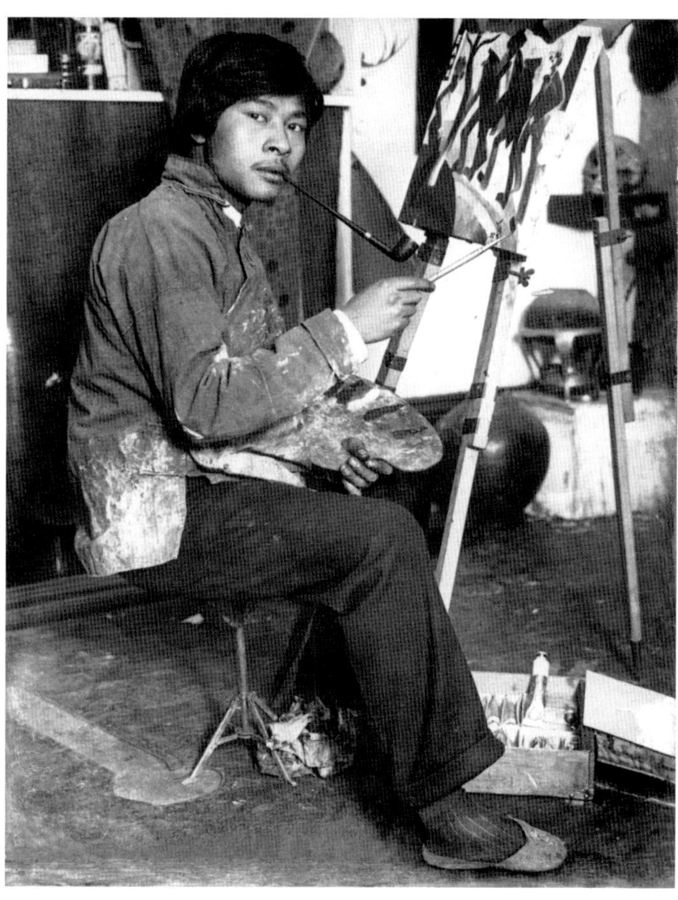

1.2 Yun Gee painting *Big Robbers and Little Robbers*, 1926 or 1927.

Falling on hard times as the buildup to World War II progressed, Yun Gee returned to New York to face a society that was fundamentally hostile to aliens, interested in a regional and social realist kind of painting, and soon to turn to abstract expressionism. While subsequently producing significant paintings, some on a monumental scale, and a notable series of political cartoons created to support relief efforts, Yun Gee fell into relative obscurity. This was no doubt partially fueled by his lifelong addiction to alcohol. It may also be attributable to the international flavor of his work at a time when, artistically, the United States was individuating from the early modernist tradition that Yun Gee had so successfully incorporated into his own style. He tried to emend his work to fit the times; however, he was unsuccessful in that endeavor. He died in 1963, at the age of fifty-seven, of stomach cancer, having been cared for by the devoted Velma Aydelott, whom he met in 1950.[5] From the late 1970s and sporadically through the 1980s, his work appeared in one-person and group exhibitions, and in 1992 Yun Gee was finally recognized with a major retrospective of his paintings and drawings in Taipei, where he was credited as an early cultural emissary to the Western world.[6] The honor accorded to the painter in Taiwan has stimulated critics and historians in this country, as well as in others, to actively engage his work.[7]

These aspects of his life have been established, and it is not my intent in this chapter to replicate the information provided in my previous writings or in more recent works.[8] I am exploring the social and political milieu in which

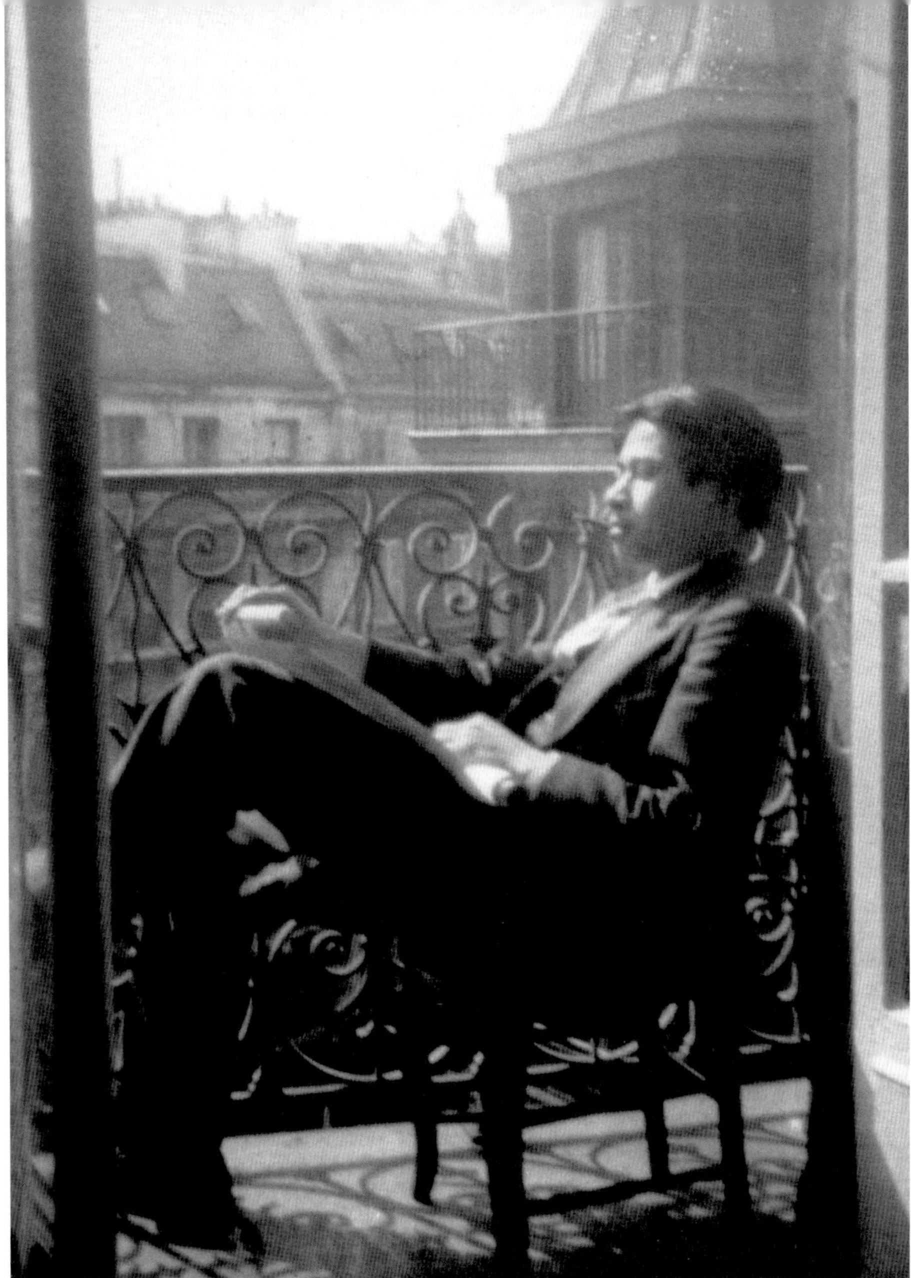

1.3 **Yun Gee in Paris, 1928 or 1929.**

Gee practiced from a somewhat different perspective. Anthony Lee, for example, writes as a "Chinese American" (an appellation that he justifiably detests), and the understanding that Gee was perceived as one is, Lee believes, crucial to an understanding of Gee's failure in New York in the 1940s and 1950s, if not earlier. More important, Lee highlights the racist element as the determining factor, and he argues that Gee faced its ugliness every moment of his life.[9] There is no doubt that Gee had periods of despair as poverty and lack of recognition plagued him, particularly in the last twenty years of his life. He was also an alcoholic, and one might argue that this was in reaction to racism; in part, it probably was. However, Li-lan was told on a trip to his village in China, and by some of his relatives in the United States, that Gee started drinking at a very young age.[10] In the preface to a poem called "The Garden,"

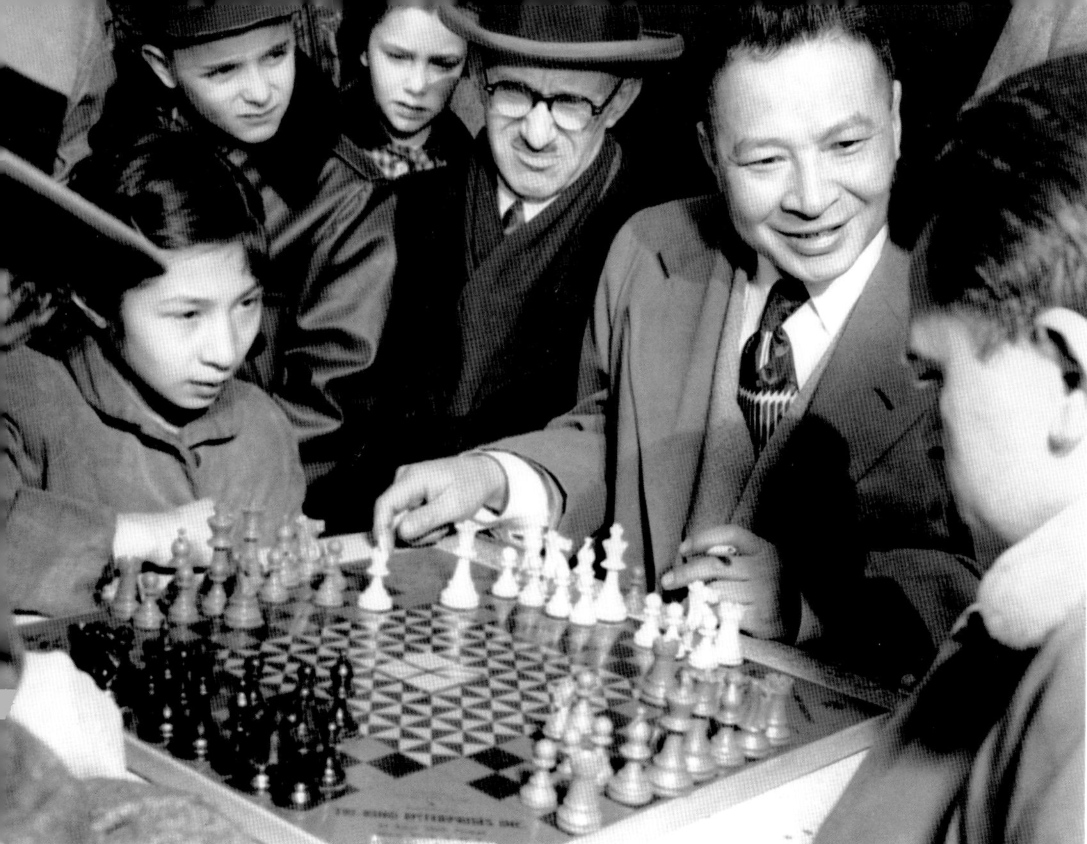

1.4 Yun Gee playing four-dimensional chess with Li-lan, Jay Hood Wright Playground, New York City, 1954.

probably written in 1935 or 1936, Gee writes, "When I was eight years old I was already quite a good drinker. Usually I sipped my wine beneath the trees where the birds drank their water."[11] Li-lan recalls that a bottle of sauterne was never out of reach. While the pain of racism must remain paramount, I want to focus on other aspects of Gee's amazing life.

While Gee himself, as well as Helen Gee and Li-lan, note periods of Gee's depression, his ambition and his belief in his talent, along with his spirituality, his empathy with all living creatures, and his extremely creative mind, allowed him to be productive and basically optimistic in spite of continuing racist oppression. Helen Gee describes her husband as playful by nature, although also serious.[12] Li-lan reminisces about the times he shared with her—painting, going to the park, playing chess, and so on—while she speaks about his moods that she, as a child, could not really understand. Gee painted, pursued exhibitions for his work, taught art, collected traditional paintings and tried to sell them, marketed his four-dimensional chessboard under the label Tri-King Enterprises, worked for causes, wrote poetry, gave performances of music and dance, wrote and directed a marionette show for which he also produced the puppets, and worked on inventions while always trying to promote himself.[13] In spite of poverty and career setbacks, he was active and involved almost to the end of his life.

Where Gee's radicalism is concerned, I acknowledge its part in his very early life, but I don't believe that Gee was really an active political radical except for a few years in San Francisco; in my view, he was more a social thinker and humanitarian. His political beliefs centered on democratic ideals and Confucian and Taoist principles, and his later loathing of Communism is obvious from his writings. Like many other intellectuals, he turned away from Communism primarily because of Stalin and Fascism, which he and his peers equated. Gee became more conservative as he grew older, but I am not convinced that this was entirely due to racism. Gee was very complex, and interpreting the causes of his feelings and actions is always partially guesswork and must remain hypothetical, as it would be for anybody else. That he was radical in his thinking about many things in general is beyond doubt; his political radicalism in particular, however, is open to question. Most important, his life and work attest to his sensitivity to and easy absorption of aspects of several cultures, and to his amazing responses to many views and diverse attitudes in the people and artists he engaged wherever he lived. He was also able to reflect on his own position from the standpoint of a cosmopolitan citizen of the world whose hope for universal harmony was a constant desire, even during the worst periods of his life.

I want to focus in this chapter on the social and political environment he faced when he left his place of origin to live in San Francisco, Paris and New York, and on particular intellectual and political interests that derived from his study of philosophy, science, political and social theory, poetry, and music, some of which disciplines he practiced alongside painting. These pursuits enabled Gee to profit from a life lived as a transnational.

Life in China (1906–1921): Preparation for a Transnational Life

Anthony Lee suggests that Gee's involvement in revolutionary causes was probably related to the fact that "he was raised in the same hotbed of Han Chinese nationalism that produced Sun Yat-sen," and his founding of a revolutionary artists' group in San Francisco, the Chinese Revolutionary Artists' Club, probably stemmed from his having observed the Chinese Revolution at first hand and quickly become an "avid, frontline supporter of the radical Kuomintang, Sun's nationalist party."[14] Lee's contextual reading of Gee's youth in Guandong accords with my suggestion that this ferment in Canton seems to have had an impact on Gee in terms of the predisposition for political radicalism that he demonstrated in his early years in San Francisco.[15]

Several short and longer versions of an unfinished autobiography remain, and these can be used, with the discretion advised with respect to such documents, for crucial insights into Gee's own story about his life, his work, and the way he thought about the world.[16] Penned at different times in his life, they attest to his strong belief in his genius; he never hesitated to promote this belief. He describes his childhood as very happy and his association with his family and his brothers as very nurturing; he writes that he was the star of the family. He had two brothers and a sister: Rung-zhi (Edward), Rung-zhang (Winston), and Ruei-lan.[17] On April 11, 1995, Li-lan traveled to Chu Village with an interpreter and spoke with a few of her father's remaining relatives and friends. They told her that there had been no school in the village until 1917, and so Gee seems to have studied in Guang-zhou (Canton), but what he studied is not known. They also said that the family had some money, although they were not wealthy, and as a result did not have to do farm work themselves, and the children could go to school. In a telephone conversation with Li-lan, the daughter of Gee's brother (she was then living in California) confirmed that the family had some money and had built a house three stories high, as Gee had written, and that Gee had been born in the one that was still there; Gee's niece described the house as having a garden and a river on one side, but she also contradicted the story about Gee's father and his birth as written in Gee's autobiography.[18] Gee wrote:

> When the last flames of the San Francisco fire had burned themselves out, one Quong On Chu, a Chinese gentleman[,] left the Western City and returned to his native land. There was great rejoicing in the village of Wing-on-Li when he returned[,] for he was a learned scholar, one who had passed the imperial examination with great honors, and as such was a man to be revered. As if to complete the happiness of his home coming, his wife[,] Wong See, begot him a little boy child, Wing Yun Chu.[19]

But Nga Lai told Li-lan that Gee's father had worked in a grocery store and had also been a chef in Mississippi and San Francisco, working for wealthy families in their homes. Gee's Chinese relatives knew nothing about Gee's education but thought that his parents had been able to support him when he was young. She also suggested that Gee's mother, Huang Ji-li, loved all her children equally and that Gee was not the favored one, or star; hence the need to use Gee's autobiography with care. Gee went on to write that he was also proud of the fact of his having been expelled from school because at thirteen he had written a radical essay titled "The Morality of the Chinese in the Times of the Three Kingdoms."[20] If this claim is true, that act of defiance dates to 1919, two years before Gee emigrated to the United States. Could the revolutionary fever in Canton, particularly that perpetrated by artists active there, have engaged Yun Gee even at that early age?

The Cantonese artists of the Lingnan School—Gao Jianfu; his younger brother, Gao Qifeng; and Chen Shuren—lived in Japan between 1905 and 1908 with thousands of other Chinese studying there.[21] There they joined the Alliance Society, an anti-Manchu revolutionary group and forerunner of the Nationalist Party, which had been formed in Tokyo by Sun Yat-sen in 1905.[22] Jianfu returned to Canton in 1908 to found a branch of the Alliance

Society. His painting activity was a cover for his revolutionary concerns, and the headquarters was a paint store. Jianfu was actually involved in the bombing assassination of the Manchu Tartar General for Guangdong and other highly dangerous activities, including the Alliance Society's attempt to seize Canton in 1911.[23] In 1912, both Gao brothers left for Shanghai to pursue their painting careers, and they returned to Canton in 1918. Chen was politically active for a much longer time and did not return to Canton until 1927, but he left again to continue his political work, and his painting became more of an avocation.[24] While the Lingnan School flourished after Yun Gee left for the United States, the artist's activities in the province had been well known at least a decade before. Gee mentions the Gao brothers only once in passing, and it seems probable that in his autobiography he would recall encountering them or, more important, that he would recall studying with them. Even if he did not really know them, but only about them, they were part of the ferment that influenced Gee's youth.

In his autobiography, Gee wrote that before departing for San Francisco he spent six months in Canton "listening to spoken English and practicing that language, learning the modern system of democratic ideas, enjoying the sights of the big city." This may be the educational experience in Canton that a family member cited. He also wrote of his good fortune in that his Uncle Won Foo was a close friend of Dr. Sun Yat-sen, and he said that he had been introduced to many people around him as well as to the new, democratic methods practiced by Dr. Sun and his followers. His two brothers joined him in Canton, and then they went to Hong Kong. From there, he and one brother boarded a Japanese vessel for America.[25] Gee wrote that the "incident impressed [me] with the strong nationalist tendency of the Japanese." This observation remained with Gee all his life and erupted in his political drawings against the Japanese occupation and persecution of the Chinese before and during World War II.

What do we know about Gee's intellectual pursuits at this time? What had he read in his early years? He wrote that his first schooling

> was from a private teacher who bestowed upon Yun the 'scholar name' of Chih, meaning angelica, for the rare flower that grew by the Yuan River. Quong Tang, instructor, and two special teachers instructed Little Brother in fencing, sword dancing, and breathing exercises, in the Chinese characters which Yun quickly learned to write with great beauty, and in Chinese instruments of music like the lute.[26]

He seems to have been involved in self-promotion from the very beginning. He mentions studying Confucius' "Philosophical Dialogues" and his "Doctrine of the Mean," and "through his own initiative he studied also the literature of the great prophets and poets of China."[27] He also mentions Laozi (Lao-tze, Lao-tzu) and, in a poem about him written in Paris in 1927, his doctrine of the Three Treasures—kindness, economy, and humility—as inspirational. He also refers to the works of Sun Yat-sen in the same vein. In relation to religious beliefs, Gee writes that he and his brother were baptized Protestants in San Francisco, and he later painted a few works with Christian subject matter (as he also did with Chinese themes). He studied several religions and seemed more interested in ethics and spirituality than in institutional religious practices. In his writings and poetry he is constantly questioning the acts of an all-powerful but often unloving God. While his intellectual and political concerns were unusual at that time for a young man from a small provincial farm town, it was the continuation of these interests, and his desire to learn about other countries and pursue a variety of cultural activities, that further set him apart from the norm. And, of course, there were his ambition and his strong belief in his own intellect and creative abilities.

This is all we really know about his life in China, and we can only surmise, from his later comments, what experiences may have influenced his early ideas about social, political, and artistic matters. It was Gee's good fortune to have enough family support to enable him to pursue his desires and realize many of them; it was also his fate to have been born in a radical time in modern Chinese history that helped engender those desires. Ralph Croizier ends his excellent study of the Lingnan School in a manner that may provide the social and artistic context for the early life of Yun Gee in Guangdong:

> As artists and revolutionaries the founders of the Lingnan School reached higher than most. Though they could not ultimately grasp their goals of remaking Chinese art and Chinese society, they contributed to both. In art, they started the longer process of accommodating the great tradition of Chinese painting to Western influence and modern needs. As revolutionaries, they participated in the rise of the Guomindang but were not involved in its downfall. Their "failure" came from striving for goals beyond the immediate reach of their generation.[28]

It was this kind of striving that dominated all aspects of Yun Gee's life. He was doomed to failure, not because he strove for goals beyond his reach, but rather by the racism that was endemic to American society in the first half of the twentieth century and by the fact that his painting was seemingly out of step with the prevailing styles practiced in New York from the 1930s on, in part because it was rooted in multicultural forms. The striving in life and work didn't stop until a few years before his death.

Life in San Francisco (1921–1927): The First Leap into the World of the Transnational

Gee writes in the outline page of his autobiography, "Returning to her office to write an article headed; 'Is Glory Awaiting This Steerage Passenger?' Mrs. Salinger recalled the first time she had seen Yun, when she had been sent to 'cover' his first exhibition. She had found him far from prepossessing,"

> a young man with long black hair, thick and stiff covering his head and forehead like a wig, his coat pulled in all directions, his shoes full of wrinkles, probably because too big. But what a difference when you meet him! Not that anything about him appears any different but it then takes such a meaning that you like it for there is about that boy something which speaks of more [than] ordinary personality. A light shines in his eyes and flows over his yellow face which tells of his inner beatitude which cannot be bought with dollars. The signs of intelligence, goodness, and genuine confidence are on him and his whole being conveys the impression that the word "greatness" can be used when referring to this young Asiatic.[29]

In contrast to Gee's youth in Guangdong, we know a fair amount about his life and work in San Francisco. His father was a cook and perhaps worked for a merchant, and while he helped Gee somewhat, Gee lived in poverty in San Francisco as he did for most of his life. Given that fact, Li-lan learned on her visit to his village that he still was a hero to the people she met there for always having sent money home to his family. In the several fragmented versions of his autobiography, he says he worked in a saloon run by a Mr. Ryder, but Prohibition closed it down, and he was out of a job. He also writes that he used that time to attend public school with his brother to learn English, and that they were baptized Protestants. He became interested in Christianity and made copies of old masters' religious paintings. None of them survive.[30]

These years between 1921 and 1927, and the few following in Paris, were among the most productive and exciting times in his life. His enthusiasm resulted in a time of experimentation—artistic, social, and political. He embraced the most avant-garde mode of painting practiced by teachers who had recently returned from Paris, and he put it to use in the service of the Chinese community by picturing everyday life in Chinatown. He brought the revolutionary zeal from his early years in China to young artists in San Francisco by actually forming a revolutionary art club to teach modern concepts and revolutionary ideas to young Chinese students.[31] In a photograph from those days, Gee appears with his long-stem pipe in his mouth, carving a bust of himself that the students seem to be using as a painting model.[32] The walls are covered with what look like student paintings in the cubist style and one Chinese scroll. The latter has been identified as a reproduction of a hanging-scroll landscape by the famous artist Ni Tsan.[33] It does not show those aspects of Lingnan painting that would have nicely supported Anthony Lee's thesis about that school's impact on him. It would be easy to deduce from what is hanging on the wall that Gee's work would be hybrid, in the weak sense described in the introduction: a pastiche of obvious elements of East and West. His work will tell a different story.

San Francisco in the third decade of the twentieth century was a hostile environment for Chinese immigrants. The Chinese Exclusion Act of 1882 was particularly venomous between 1924 and 1952, when it was finally revoked. Anthony Lee writes that the Chinese, whether immigrants or native-born, were ghettoized, and the racism directed against them was more virulent during this period than at any time before or after.[34] While Chinatown provided a base for the embattled Kuomintang, it was obviously restricted to that part of San Francisco, and few Chinese, even radical ones, ventured out of the Chinese ghetto.[35] Gee formed the Chinese Revolutionary Artists' Club there in 1926, perhaps in emulation of the Lingnan School, or through contact with the Lingnan School revolutionary artist Chen Shuren, who had traveled to San Francisco to raise money for Sun Yat-sen. The club members invited Diego Rivera to visit in 1930 or 1931, but Gee had departed by then; perhaps his legacy lived on.[36]

Many years later, Gee wrote that he had "entrée to the very center of activity in Dr. Sun's quarters," but there is no information on Gee's direct involvement with the Kuomintang.[37] He also wrote in an unpublished essay that Lee dates to 1927, "We must make art become [a] real value and to be in step with Dr. Sun's Three Principles. . . . Is this not what Dr. Sun said, 'To save the world with art?'"[38] While these are all indications of Yun's sympathies, they do not allow us to jump to Lee's conclusion: that "when he founded the Revolutionary Artists' Club, Yun Gee was beginning to see it as a potential ally of the [Communist Party] and thought optimistically of a nationalist regime that would incorporate theories and organizational skills from the Soviet Union."[39] Lee, in his enthusiasm for Gee's revolutionary spirit, may be painting a picture of Gee's political thoughts on the basis of a few comments that Gee may have made in undated and unpublished manuscripts written in recollection. Most of Gee's later comments are quite negative vis-à-vis Communism.[40] There is, however, enough information to paint a fairly vivid portrait of an unusual, daring, and ambitious young man and artist who had arrived in a new country and almost immediately made a mark in the art world and in political society. His dynamic optimism seems to be reflected in his early painting.

In spite of the awful restrictions imposed on the Chinese, it is amazing that Gee not only attended an art school outside Chinatown but was also befriended

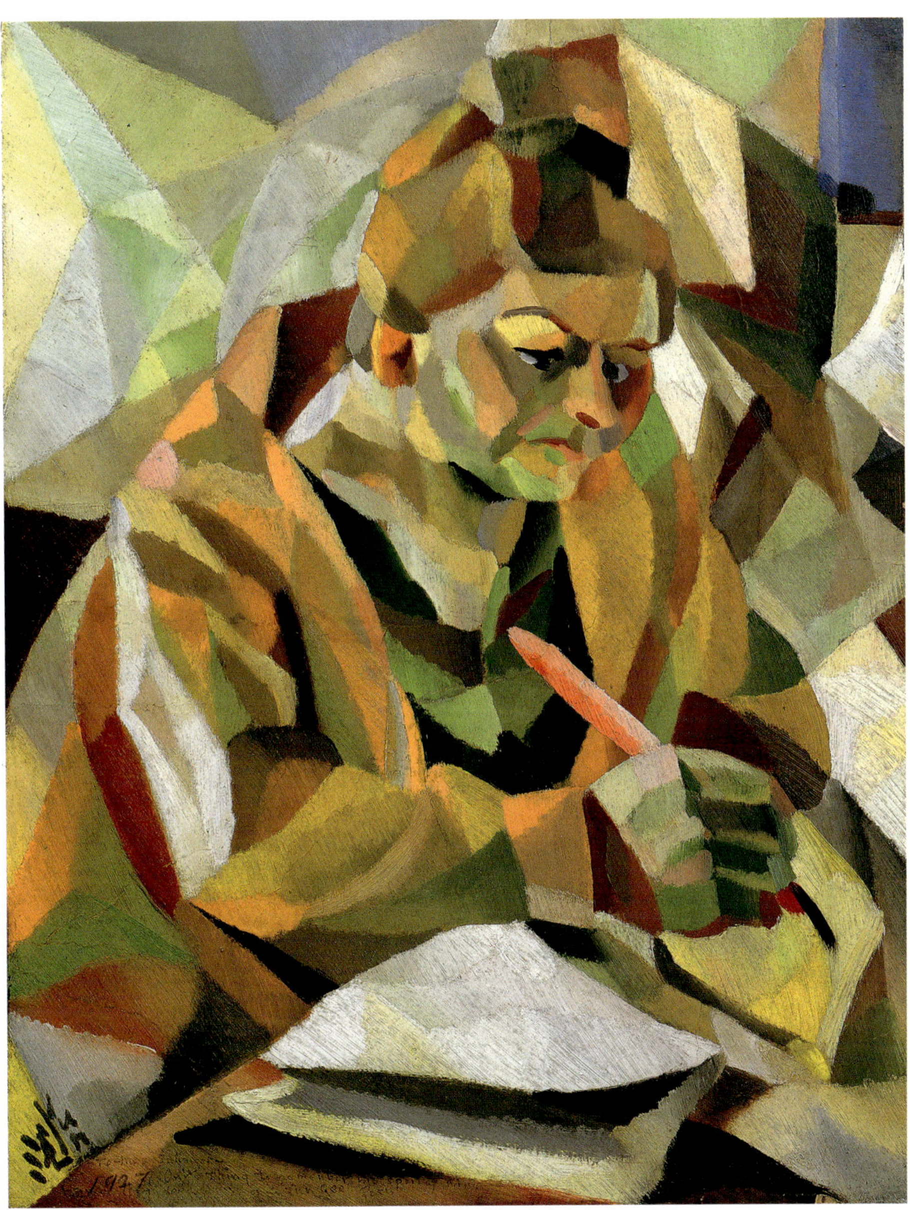

Plate 1 Yun Gee, *Untitled* (*Mrs. Salinger in Paris*), oil on paperboard mounted on wood panel (19 7/8 in. x 14 15/16 in.), 1927. Photo credit: Kevin Ryan

by Caucasians like his teachers Gottardo Piazonni and Otis Oldfield (the latter remained a lifelong friend). In a parting letter to Oldfield written on June 16, 1927, the broken English cannot hide Gee's deep feelings for his friend and teacher.[41] His first patrons, the Prince and Princess Murat, supported his voyage to Paris in 1927 after they saw his exhibition at the Modern Gallery, of which he was a founding member, and after Jehanne Biétry-Salinger bought and wrote about his work. Among his acquaintances were the writer Kenneth Rexroth and the painter Victor Arnautoff, both active Communists. As we shall see in chapter 2, Gee's work was exhibited in galleries outside Chinatown and was reviewed in local newspapers that were not Chinese. All that for a twenty-one-year-old immigrant whose English was very poor! In spite of the hostility toward the Chinese, a small but enlightened art community celebrated Yun Gee's accomplishments. What remains undocumented is what motivated Gee to matriculate at the California School of Art and to take classes from artists like Otis Oldfield, who taught the most advanced international style of the day.

While it is obvious that a good deal of his time was devoted to his painting and his career, and to political and social activity, Gee also had time to write poetry, which he continued to do seriously all his life. What was quite remarkable was his ability to write poetry in English, and to write in the most modern poetic format of the time. This is apparent in the poems recently published in *Yun Gee: Poetry, Writing, Art, Memories*, edited by Anthony Lee; Gee's poems are as radical as his paintings. Several essays in the book suggest links between his painting and his writing; nevertheless, even though a few poems are directly connected to specific paintings, such as the marvelous *Where Is My Mother* (pl. 2), it was not Gee's usual practice to write about his pictures. The poem "The Phoenix," dated February 5, 1927, refers to elements like the eagle and the airplane that appear later in a few of Gee's paintings and drawings (and are also found in Lingnan painting), but it neither relates nor refers to any particular painting.[42] The poem, written before Gee left for Paris in July of that year, is a possible reference to the end of Sun Yat-sen's revolution and the 1927 takeover of the Nationalist Party by Chiang Kai-shek, another demagogue who purged China of all dissent.[43] Sadly, Gee supported him in his later life, in all probability to curry favor, and particularly when Madam Chiang Kai-shek was in New York.[44]

There is also a poem about a cat—a text that is as matter-of-fact as some of Gee's San Francisco paintings—and there is a short love poem that is both sad and playful, a combination often found in his later poetry. The most touching poem is the aforementioned "Where Is My Mother," dated May 31, 1926, which is directly related to the painting of the same name. It ends with elements seen in the painting: the mother looking out the door, and ships on the sea.[45] One can feel Gee's sorrow in both works.

Anthony Lee is right to emphasize that Gee's poetry was quite modern and in some ways comparable to that of the beat poets.[46] He is also correct to disengage the relationship between poetry and painting that is so ubiquitous in the Chinese tradition. While there are a few examples of Gee adding written statements to his paintings, his poetry and his paintings are separate endeavors, the former more introspective, spiritual, and philosophical and the latter primarily depicting everyday events. In chapter 2, I will suggest that it was probably Gee's intention in his early work to disengage from the Chinese "literati" tradition and leave words out of most of his painting, although he often signed his name in both Chinese and English. In a few instances, as when he painted Chinese themes in Paris, sometimes writing was included.

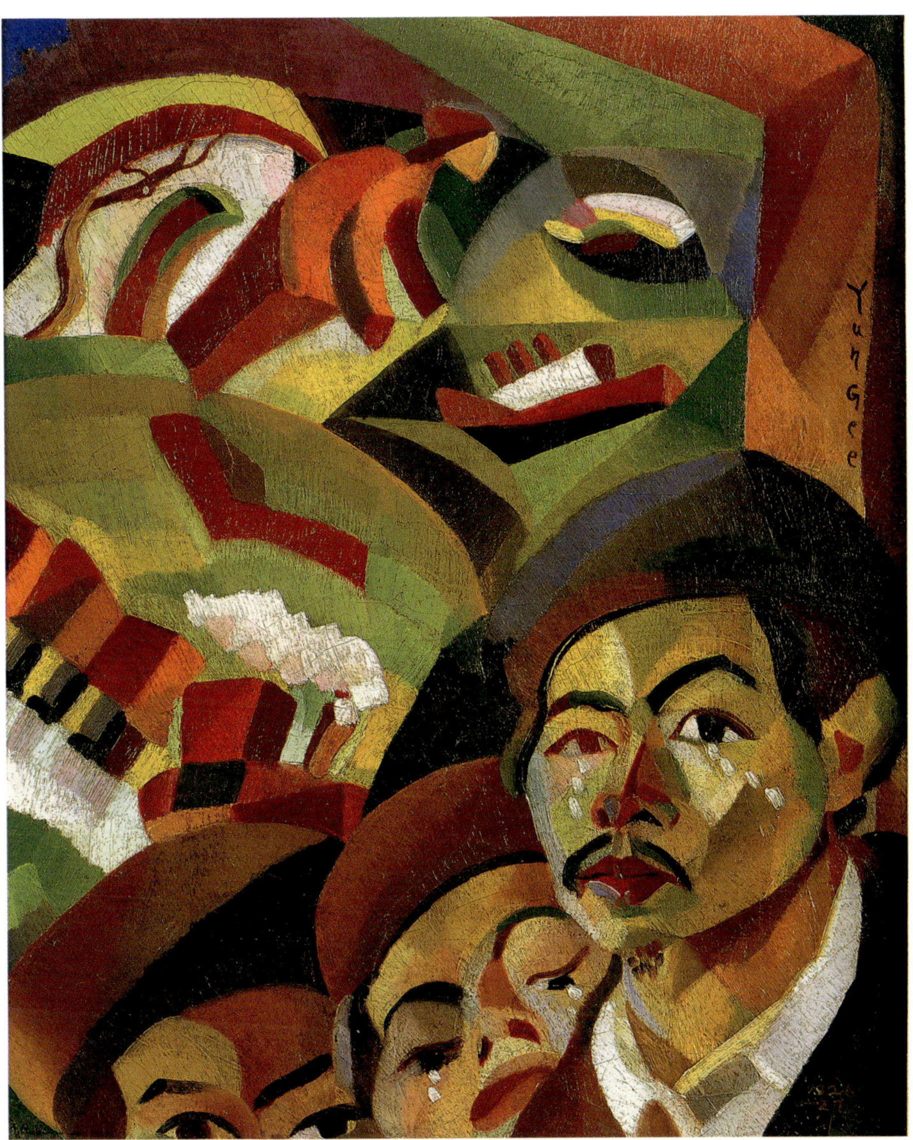

Plate 2 Yun Gee, ***Where Is My Mother***, **oil on canvas (20 1/8 in. x 16 in.), 1926–27. Photo credit: Kevin Ryan**

Gee's intention in San Francisco was seemingly to pursue the latest forms of Western art, unencumbered by Chinese traditions, and he accomplished that goal with astonishing success. While some wrote about his work as a blending of motifs from the East and the West, that is a trope used in dealing with "hyphenated" persons. Like contemporary transnational artists, Gee practiced an international style, essentially synthesizing aspects of modern art, and that probably accounts for his success in San Francisco and even more in Paris. But Gee never tried to conceal the fact that he was indeed Chinese, and many of the subjects in his early painting were Chinese people engaged in ordinary activities in their neighborhood streets and parks. His desire to help his fellow Chinese students cultivate openness to modern ways of living and working also reveals his concern for his compatriots. Most important, his embrace of the most modern form practiced in San Francisco already indicates that Gee refused to relinquish the complexity of his experiences, and to profit from the particular acuity developed through living in the "in between" space.

While Jehanne Biétry-Salinger did call Gee a Chinese artist—as did many others throughout his life, even if his typical work was grounded in the vocabulary of modernism—in her July 1927 newspaper article about him, written immediately after his departure for Paris, she wrote about this twenty-one-year-old artist in glowing terms. She particularly underlined his adventurous spirit, his deep longing for and love of his mother, and his potential greatness:

> What is going to be the reception given to this artist in Paris? He himself does not seem to have given thought to this question. He is on his way, that is probably all he knows at the present; all he cares. He does not understand a word of French. He does not have the least conception of what a city like the French capital may look like. He does not know a single person there, and his childlike helplessness gives the impression that he will never be able to get there. Yet he does not worry.[47]

She then goes on to describe the trunk that he took with him, filled with books and paintings.

> The inside of the cover offers a strange sight indeed. All kinds of handwritings, all kinds of characters are on it. This was an idea of Yun. He wanted all his friends to write some lines. . . . And there are beautiful lines, in English, in French, in German. Some good-looking words in Islandic [*sic*], in Italian and very odd Chinese characters written there.[48]

The First Trip to Paris (July 1927–July 1930), and the Second Leap into the World of the Transnational

Gee arrived in Paris in the summer of 1927 with that marvelous trunk of books and paintings. Biétry-Salinger need not have worried; Gee was even more of a success there than he had been in San Francisco. There were many factors in play, including the support of his patrons, the Prince and Princess Achille Murat, who introduced him to artistic society. There was also Gee's ability to engage what was then the Parisian penchant for genre subjects in painting, as well as the soft touch of postcubist brushwork, which Gee quickly absorbed in what he called his lyrical period. He was also extremely handsome and self-assured. In Paris, a city that he admired, just as he did the language and the culture, he had several important exhibitions, and he met and married his first wife, the German-French princess and poet Paule de Reuss. He learned to write and speak French, and in an unpublished essay he painted his artistic life in Paris as almost ideal. His most vivid memories were of the cultural life and the art talk with his newfound friends:

> My orientation to [the city's] atmosphere was immediate, due, perhaps, I often think, to the temperamental similarities of the French and Chinese peoples, to their individualism and their cultivation of the art of living. . . . Perhaps nothing welds peoples together more closely than a common understanding and respect for each others culture.[49]

One can imagine the impact that this handsome young man had on the artistic circle that embraced him. Dressed in Chinese costume, as in the photograph taken in New York in 1933, and dancing and playing the flute or the mandolin or the other Chinese instruments he had mastered, he would have been a sensation.[50] He painted Princess Murat in costume in her Chinese library in 1927.[51] In one of the few poems that actually describe a painting, he writes:

I haven't seen beauty since long
Now I paint the Princess Murat in her Chinese Library
in her Chinese costume lying on her sofa.
Strange it is to me no voice, no colors like
flying. This makes me happily remember Known
and Look (two masters who live in the Song Dynasty) poem
She with the beauty of art in a western palace
Her costume with original coloring, Chinese.
Since I came to Europe, keeping Chinese eyes is
difficult. She the only one here that makes me
remember China and now I can follow
the wind now I can travel in Tong
in Sung.[52]

Does this poem mean that only in Princess Murat's presence, or among her circle of friends, was Gee allowed to be Chinese? In one of his most revealing and poignant paintings, *How I Saw Myself in a Dream*, Gee pictures himself in a Chinese scholar's robe, hunched over and wandering alone in the streets of Paris—the other side of his life, no doubt, perhaps reflecting the racist treatment he may have received from the average Parisian, or the loneliness that many people feel in a foreign country, unless this image is simply an assertion of the artist's being Chinese.[53] In 1931, a year after he returned to the United States and settled in New York, he wrote:

> Paris is a liberal city. Only that liberality is limited to certain nations among which are not the United States and China, countries whose people are unable

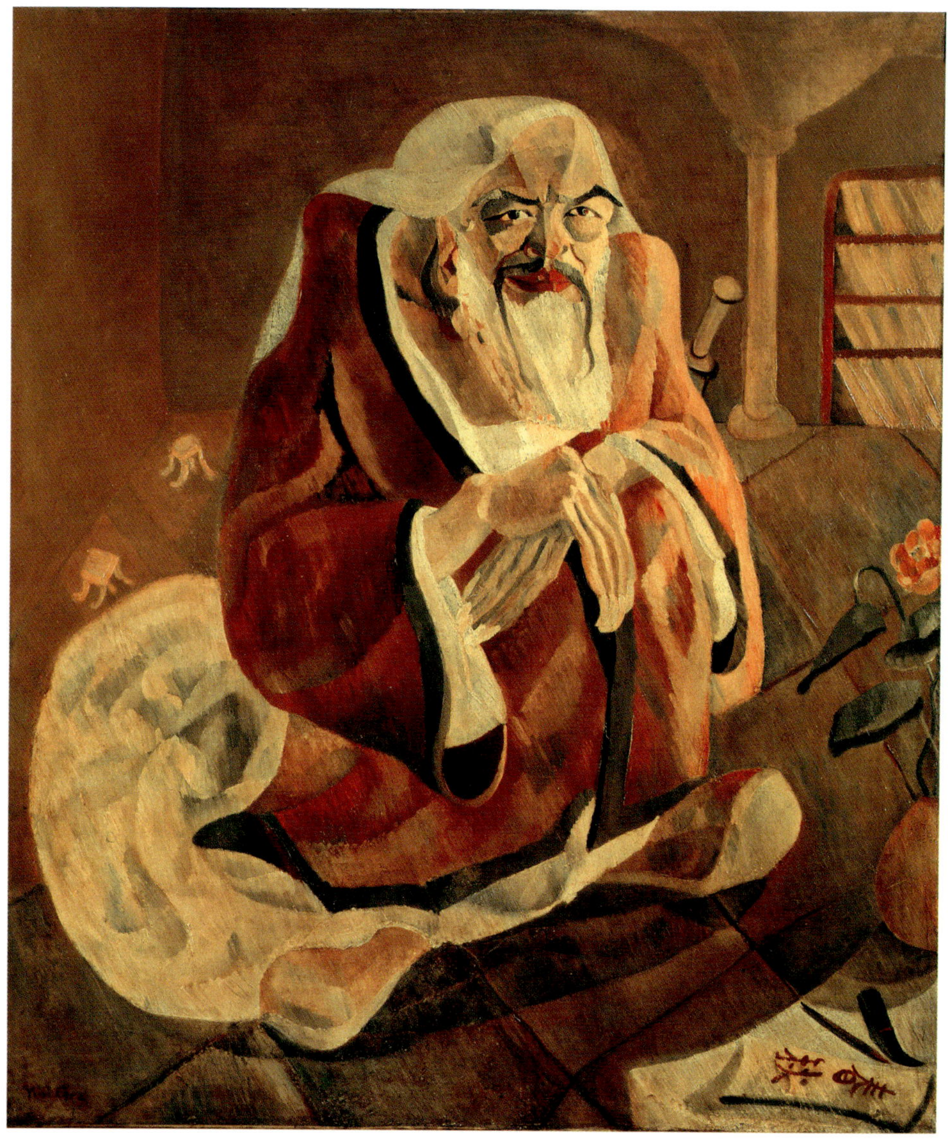

Plate 3 Yun Gee, *Confucius (Chinese Sage)*, oil on canvas (48 3/8 in. x 40 3/8 in.), ca. 1928.

> to flatter the exacting demands of an egotism and especially a foreign society. Besides one feels that the French are afraid of America because of its wealth and materials, and of China because of its wealth of spirit.[54]

Gee hit Paris just as the love for the exotic was coming fully into play there. Josephine Baker, who arrived in Paris in 1925, was sought after as an exotic primitive and was already starring in the Folies Bergère in the 1926 and 1927 seasons. One might expect Gee to have been courted as an exotic Oriental; after all, these were the Roaring Twenties, and Paris was the center of it all. If it profited Gee to belong to this era in Paris, the benefit was probably limited to the circle of his patrons and artistic friends; his street encounters seem to have been a different reality. *Le Nègre* may have been tolerated, but Orientals were not.

It is probably correct to assume that euphoria, depression, and avowals of being Chinese were feelings and impulses that Gee experienced in Paris, and that they are reflected in some thirty paintings that he produced during those years. These paintings include the first of his very few pictures with Chinese themes.[55] No paintings with Chinese motifs survive from his San Francisco period, but Gee says in his autobiography that he burned more than two hundred paintings in a ceremonial bonfire, and such subjects may have been among the works that were destroyed. After his first Paris trip, he painted only a few such images that we can identify, although there are several drawings and watercolors with Chinese themes. Perhaps he turned to these themes because of the "orientalism" favored by the elite.[56] But his use of these motifs may also have derived from the prejudice that caused him to strongly affirm being Chinese, or such themes may have reflected subjects dear to his heart, since some of them are related to his philosophical and spiritual interests. The Chinese costume in *How I Saw Myself in a Dream* perhaps encapsulates both affirmation and rejection. It is difficult to fully understand Gee's image of himself in this painting; nevertheless, he associated with people who were very sophisticated and cultured, and he not only attracted but married a wealthy French-German poet, facts that attest to what was special about him. His being Chinese may have made him exotic, but I think it was his intellect and his ability to absorb new cultural environments that made him a sought-after member of the cultural elite.

In 1928, while all this was going on, Gee traveled to Spain and stayed for a few months. (That trip seems to have made an impact on his painting, one that I shall discuss in chapter 2.) If his self-portrait *The Blue Yun* was painted there, and if he was dressed in that soft, wide-brimmed hat and fur-collared coat while traveling, then he must have made quite an impact, just as he had done in Paris. In a photograph taken in Paris in 1929, he is wearing that hat, and he seems to have exaggerated its size in the painting; his longish hair, his mustache, and his tiny goatee are the same in both the painting and the photograph.[57] In the preface to "Madrid," a poem written in 1935, he writes:

> I lived opposite the palace. The sleepy-eyed soldiers I passed held guns in their hands and the taxicab drivers often refused me a ride, so busy they were with drinking. There was royalty in the big cafes. But most of the population sat in the boulevard cafes and listened to open-air concerts. It was here, where I sat much too often, that I felt Spain's civilization still remains.[58]

Although he was born in a small village in China, Gee seems to have been a natural cosmopolite, even a flaneur.[59] He never lived outside a major city. But Gee also experienced the kinds of negative things that are frequent in cities (such as, later on, being snubbed in a New York subway). That he was able to slough off such insults without rancor is a tribute to his good nature, his humor, and his humanitarian predilections.

What Gee seems never to have mentioned is how he supported himself in Paris, and how he could even afford to travel. Were his patrons generous? Did Paule de Reuss have money? We know that her family cut her off in 1928, when she married Gee. Did he sell his paintings? Gee's financial situation was already dire when the worldwide economic collapse forced him to return to the United States. Thus any financial support that he may have enjoyed probably ended with his departure, and it would have been next to impossible for a Chinese alien to find work in Paris at that time. He had to leave his wife, and although he fully expected to bring her to the United States later on, he never did. They divorced but remained friends, and they corresponded until Paule's death, a year or two before his own.[60] At any rate, Gee landed in New York in the summer of 1930, with high expectations because of his triumph in Paris. In a newspaper article published a few months after his return to the United States, Gee is quoted as saying, "Paris can no longer give me what I want. It has been kind to me, but I must go to America where I hope to find more than kindness—a sincere cooperation of West and East between my fellow youths of both races."[61] Thus he headed for New York, the most cosmopolitan city in the country, and already home to a very diverse population. But after a few years of being noticed, what he encountered was a form of resistance wherever he turned.

While it is not my intention to repeat the work of Anthony Lee and his colleagues,[62] it is important to engage briefly the few poems that can be dated to Gee's Paris years. They are thematically diverse but may reflect the emotional complexity of Gee's life in Paris. The prose poem "Confucius" is a diatribe against "the vanity of this city, its women and wine and its temptations . . . at so much shamelessness I could not help crying out, 'Civilization, and withal savagery, can I tolerate this?' . . . Accordingly I locked my door and gave myself to be impressed with the force of his [Confucius'] dignity and I seem to hear his voice, that call of heaven."[63] Gee says he hadn't painted for almost a year and in his loneliness turned to Confucius for inspiration. His large painting titled *Confucius* (*Chinese Sage*) (pl. 3) dates from 1929 and was painted in Paris. Gee also wrote a poem—an homage to Laozi, dated July 25, 1927 (apparently soon after he arrived in Paris)—and in this poem he mentions a painting of Laozi that may also have been completed before July 1930, when Gee returned to the United States. He takes solace in the humble spirit of the man whose philosophy "is a mighty doctrine with the power of moving men."[64] The sad poem "Poetess," from 1927–28, seems to have been written after Paule was cut off by her family and separated from her friends because of her relationship with Yun; he urges her to continue writing poetry.[65] Figure 4 in Lee's essay "Solitary Proposals" shows the original album page and the poem written in French, Chinese, and then in English.[66] That page alone is a visual metaphor for Gee's embrace of cultural plurality.

"Rat," dated July 25, 1927, is a short poem on the hard life of the animal living in darkness—perhaps a metaphor for aspects of Gee's life in Paris. Gee loved animals and birds of all sorts, and he wrote about them frequently; they are also subjects in some of his paintings and drawings. "Falling Leaves" (1928) is so abstract and staccato in style as to be almost incoherent.[67] It is important to read it out loud, particularly because the words are like musical sounds. Out loud the poem sounds like ruminations about death and rebirth, entertained while the poet walked along some body of water (a frequent theme in his poetry). "Resurrection (Ascension) Messiah," dated April 28, 1928, is written in the voice of the resurrected Christ and ends with Christ lifted to heaven in a

trolly sent by Father
fast as a horse
speedy as automobile
swift like airplane
drawn by God's angels
grasped in God's hand
who offers me a triumphant song
flutes
drums
troops
guns
cannon
bombs
    electricity . . .

A modern resurrection if ever there was one! Gee's spiritual beliefs were complicated, and in this case his depiction of Christ and God included what might be considered beneficial gifts, like airplanes and automobiles and electricity, as well as horrific ones, like guns and cannons and bombs.[68]

Gee was also very modern in his philosophical questionings, and his painting *Chinese Man in Hat* (probably painted in 1928) bears witness to this attitude. It is one of the few paintings that Gee made of Chinese people—in this case, the author and actor Fu Chau Fa, who lived in South America, traveled to Spain in the fall of 1928, and probably met Gee there.[69] He was the one who composed the poetry that appears on the left and right sides of the portrait.[70] Gee must have approved of the poem, since he ruminated over issues like this one throughout his life, and the poem's modernist style was similar to his own:

I am thinking, thinking of me, I am thinking of me;
I am worried, I am happy, I am at once worried and happy;

I have nothing, I have something, I have at once nothing and something;
I am dreaming of myself, I am dreaming of myself.
Who creates, creates whom, who creates whom;
Who is alive, who is dead, who is both dead and alive;
Who knows, who is enlightened, who knows and is enlightened;
Who changes whom, who changes whom.[71]

In a different fashion, the 1929 painting *One Who Loves Himself* teases out different aspects of Gee's intellectual and emotional life. In this work, Gee painted "a crane holding a fan in his beak, . . . standing on a ball-like object which appears to be a globe, . . . confronting a gentleman in traditional Chinese dress. The painting is related to Taoist philosophy of preserving one's physical body and prolonging one's life. The crane is the symbol of longevity in the Taoist tradition."[72] Gee signed it "Lan Wu-chou Gee Yun," which literally means "Blue Five Continents, Gee Yun." David Teh-Yu Wang interprets this as follows: "Obviously Gee regarded himself as a cosmopolitan man who belonged to, or at least wandered around, the world."[73]

What do we make of the first word, "blue?" A clue may exist in one of the four large scrolls painted in Paris in 1929 or 1930: *Yang Kwei Fei at Her Bath,* a Chinese theme in a Chinese landscape; *The Resurrection*; the portrait titled *The Poetess (Paule de Reuss)*; and a self-portrait, with Gee wearing a Chinese robe and playing the mandolin, titled *The Charm of Music*. The last of these paintings had a date, and a poem in the right-hand corner that Gee effaced in 1951; he also painted over aspects of other works and seriously defaced them.[74] In the poem, which the painter was to remove years later, the world traveler, still in his twenties, is disillusioned and retreats into creative solitude:

When I was young, the poet relates, I made a craft of my curiosity and sailed out upon the sea of human happenings. I sailed until I reached the portals of the dawn and found that the sun, whose Light I had followed, was long since dead. So I returned a man, and wandered though the desert lands, finding many Gods and many saints, but though I saw their shadows grow to the heavens, I could not discern their substance here on earth. Now I have returned to the solitude of my own cell and content myself to play a melody of longing upon my instrument. And the music, whose notes are visions sent by God, opens the eyes of my soul so that I see what I vainly sought for throughout my wanderings.[75]

In the Yun Gee archives, there is a long poem titled "Charm of Music," dated 1928; another copy is dated 1930. The poem is a cry of despair for the plight of humans and animals, yet the poem ends with belief in a tarnished image of God (or gods). One line is almost a description of the painting *Charm of Music*: "I am in my studio, playing the crying and laughing piano / While all these [animals we see in the painting] fly and walk and crowd about." And some lines later, we find this:

> *Just as the god of us who are also gods . . .*
> *Where has my sermon gone? I cannot*
> *Face that golden bottle from which my*
> *Heart bids me drink—*
> *You know that the tiger, too, has a god:*
> *Tigers pray to Heaven before they eat men*
> *If all this is against God*
> *I kneel before you*
> *Forgive me.*[76]

Like his paintings, Gee's poetry reveals many aspects of his complex life in Paris but is more personal in how it gives voice to the small pleasures and many anxieties, the constant questioning, undergone by a person sensitive to human suffering. Gee probably did not intend in the beginning to publish these poems but changed his mind later on and had them typed up; however, they were never published in his lifetime. He seems to have used his writing to express private sentiments while painting professionally for public exhibition. Each of these creative forms is a testament to Gee's desire and ability to respond to the cultural environments surrounding him, and to absorb aspects of those environments, not only in how he lived but also in the works he produced. His responses were both cultural and expressive of his feelings for humanity as a whole.

Life in New York (1930–1936): The Weary World Traveler Tries Again

> In 1931, still floating from the reception and kindness of Paris, I came to New York. . . . Here the scene changed to indifference. . . . I was no longer an Artist. I was an Oriental from China Town . . . and I suppose the interpretation of such a person was that he was only a Launderer or a Restauranteur [*sic*]—Facil in a concoction . . . they call Chop Suey . . . and this was hardly the reception I expected in my own country. . . . The name for Chinese in this city was "Charlie," an unfair interpretation of the many distinguished Chinese families who aided in making America grow. . . . After dragging through this moral muck for five years I decided To return to Paris. . . . [77]

It is obvious that New York was a miserable place for Gee in many ways, and in his autobiography he mentions periods of depression and loneliness more intense than those he experienced in Paris. If his criticism of the French had to do with their cultural snobbery, in America the focus of his criticism was essentially racism, as described in the foregoing quotation. When he first arrived, his expectations were high, given his success in Paris and his marriage to Paule de Reuss. He had several one- and two-person exhibitions, was included in two very important shows at the Brooklyn Museum and the Museum of Modern Art, and received a commission for a large painting of the Last Supper for a Lutheran church in the Bronx. Starting in 1931, he was very active on behalf of Chinese people who were experiencing the horrors resulting from severe floods and from the Japanese invasion of Manchuria; he painted and drew political cartoons to raise money for the Chinese and publicize their plight after the 1937 Sino-Japanese war. He staged concerts, dance recitals, and puppet shows and wrote poetry. He also participated in the WPA art programs.[78] His divorce from Paule, in 1932, was devastating, but in 1935 he met his future second wife, Helen Wimmer, and he married her in 1942, several years after returning from his second trip to Paris. It is interesting that the women he married and lived with (the ones we know about) were all Caucasians, including his last companion, Velma Aydelott. His portrait paintings and his drawings from models depict Asians, Caucasians, and Africans. Gee's openness to all races and cultures was as evident in his personal life as it was in his moral and philosophical commitments. While it is easy to suggest that exoticism may have played a part in his being attracted to white women, his life and his work attest to the total lack of prejudice with which he engaged others in spite of the racist attitudes he suffered.

Gee tried in every way to make a life in New York and to pursue his painting career. David Teh-Yu Wang and Anthony Lee describe Gee's years in New York, and although the racism there was less extreme than it had been in San Francisco, it was still virulent. Gee's own writing, cited earlier, tells it all. The Depression wrecked New York City's Chinatown, and 3,000 workers lost their jobs; the 1920 census recorded only 5,793 Chinese living in all of New York State.[79] It is obvious that Chinatown must have been even more decimated in the 1930s. It is an amazing testament to Gee's endurance and his belief in his abilities that he was able to exist at all in those years on the odd jobs that seem to have supported him while still finding time to paint and be socially and politically active. It is also noteworthy that Gee lived in Greenwich Village and not in Chinatown.[80]

In "Yun Gee: A Reminiscence," Helen Gee describes the beginning of her relationship with Yun Gee. They were introduced by Helen's art teacher when Helen was a sixteen-year-old art student. She describes Gee's small studio in Greenwich Village as "two irregularly shaped rooms crammed with paintings, bird cages, plants, books Chinese musical instruments, and numerous works

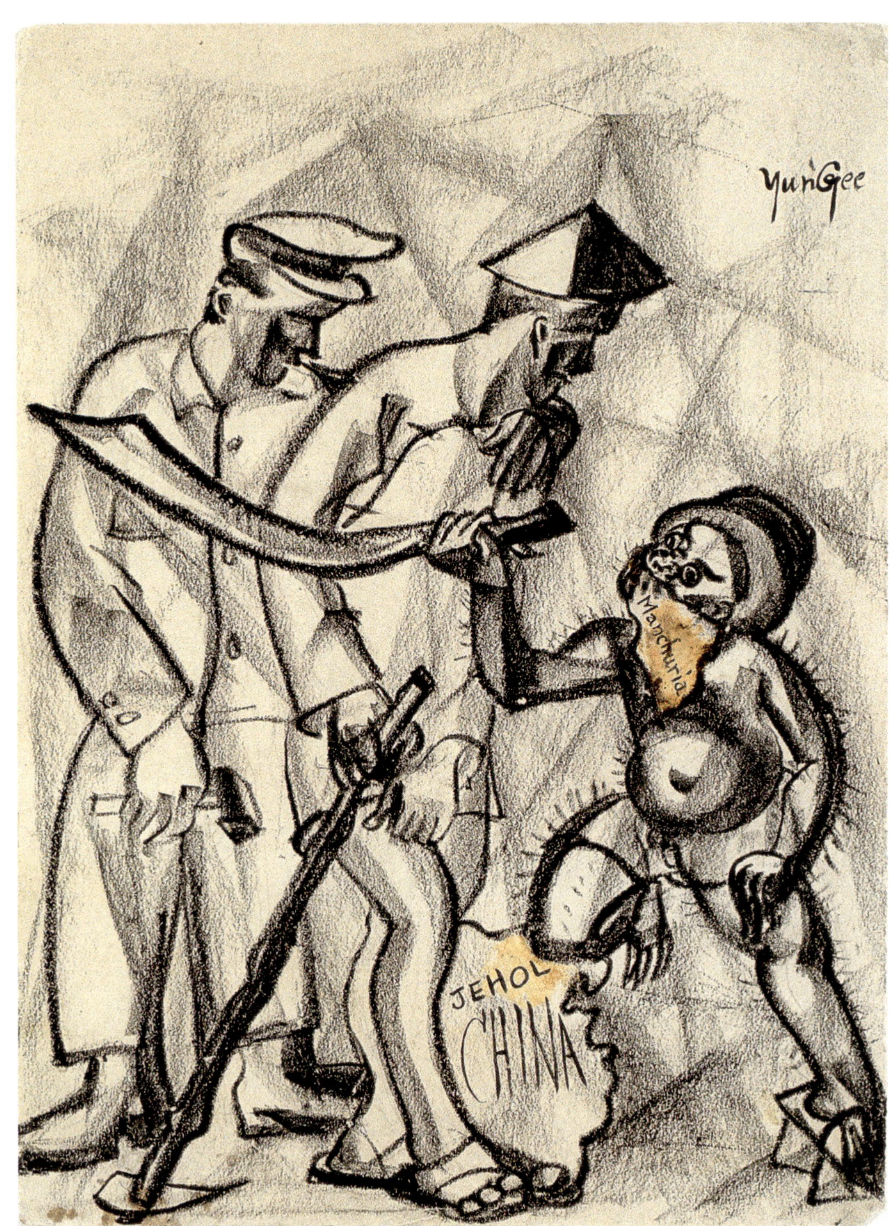

1.5 Yun Gee, *China and Manchuria*, political cartoon (18 1/16 x 12 13/16 in.), c. 1926.

of art. . . . Despite the crowding there was a sense of order and it was in this setting—the most beautiful I had ever seen—that I came to know, and eventually marry, one of the most creative and fascinating human beings it was my privilege to meet."[81] She goes on to describe Gee's prodigious intellect and lists the books, aside from the many on art, that she saw there, including the *Analects of Confucius,* Kropotkin's *Modern Science and Anarchism,* Freud's *Outline of Psychoanalysis,* and *The Tales of Edgar Allan Poe* as well as Gertrude Stein's *Three Lives* and the Bible. Gee mentions his love of Poe in his autobiography, and his flirtation with the macabre may have reflected that influence; as for Stein's revolutionary form of writing, he seems in his own poetry to have pushed it sometimes to the point of incoherence. Helen Gee mentions Gee's diverse intellectual pursuits but also stresses his commitment to his Chinese heritage: "Yun remained essentially Chinese. He felt contempt for those 'rice bowl Christians' who, in an effort to adapt to Western ways, sacrificed their racial identity."[82] Occupying that third, "in between" space—aware of so many different points of view, without rejecting being Chinese—Gee was a world citizen centered in his acceptance of his heritage. As mentioned earlier, I think this grounding was a crucial factor in his ability to immerse himself in other cultures. From his early years in San Francisco, he wore being Chinese easily, and he never confined himself to a ghetto, physically or psychologically. His self-confidence and his pride in his heritage provided him with a base that in his best times prevented the fracturing, in life as well as in work, that many immigrants experience. His life of passage expanded his vision, and this is evident in many of the paintings he produced, especially in a primary work created during this period, *Wheel "Industrial New York"* (pl. 4).

Gee's life seems to have been full and active. Despite the first rumblings of war in Europe, he left the miseries of New York and his faltering career to return again to Paris—perhaps to repeat his earlier success, or to escape the racism of New York, or to be with his former wife, Paule. Gee was only thirty, but he had easily absorbed the philosophies and cultures of parts of three continents. His belief in his creative abilities was as strong as ever, even if the art world and racist New York frustrated their development, as is evident in the major paintings he produced then, such as *Wheel "Industrial New York,"* and in what we can tell about the now lost *The Last Supper* (fig. 1.6, p. 37).

What I can glean from the many poems written in New York and dated 1935 and 1936 is that, as in Gee's poems written in Paris, ordinary subjects often serve as metaphors for spiritual and philosophical ruminations, and the poems often feature a staccato rhythm. This is something of a contrast to the subjects he was painting at the time and seems related more to his earlier painting in San Francisco and Paris. The poems are sometimes plainly humorous, as are "Picnic Party," "Conference," and "Heat" (in which people are sweating all over the world as in a New York summer); "Heat" ends as follows: "If I were you, my God, I'd make a big fan, to release the people, beneath you."[83] "Stopping Machine" is an attack on industry, which produces the traffic that causes his model to be late, and "Sensation" describes an awful incident—people baring their teeth at him on the subway and the bus—but he turns that around by doing the same back to them and makes them laugh.[84] "The Mandolin," like several other poems, is about music,[85] and Gee's pairing of color and sound suggests that he may have known about the music and color theories of Klee and Kandinsky. His response to the sounds of the world was amazing for its time. He was open to it all, and perhaps the repeated "Alas" in the poem alludes to the "sounds" of pain felt in his fingertips, and to his empathy for the suffering of people all over the world:

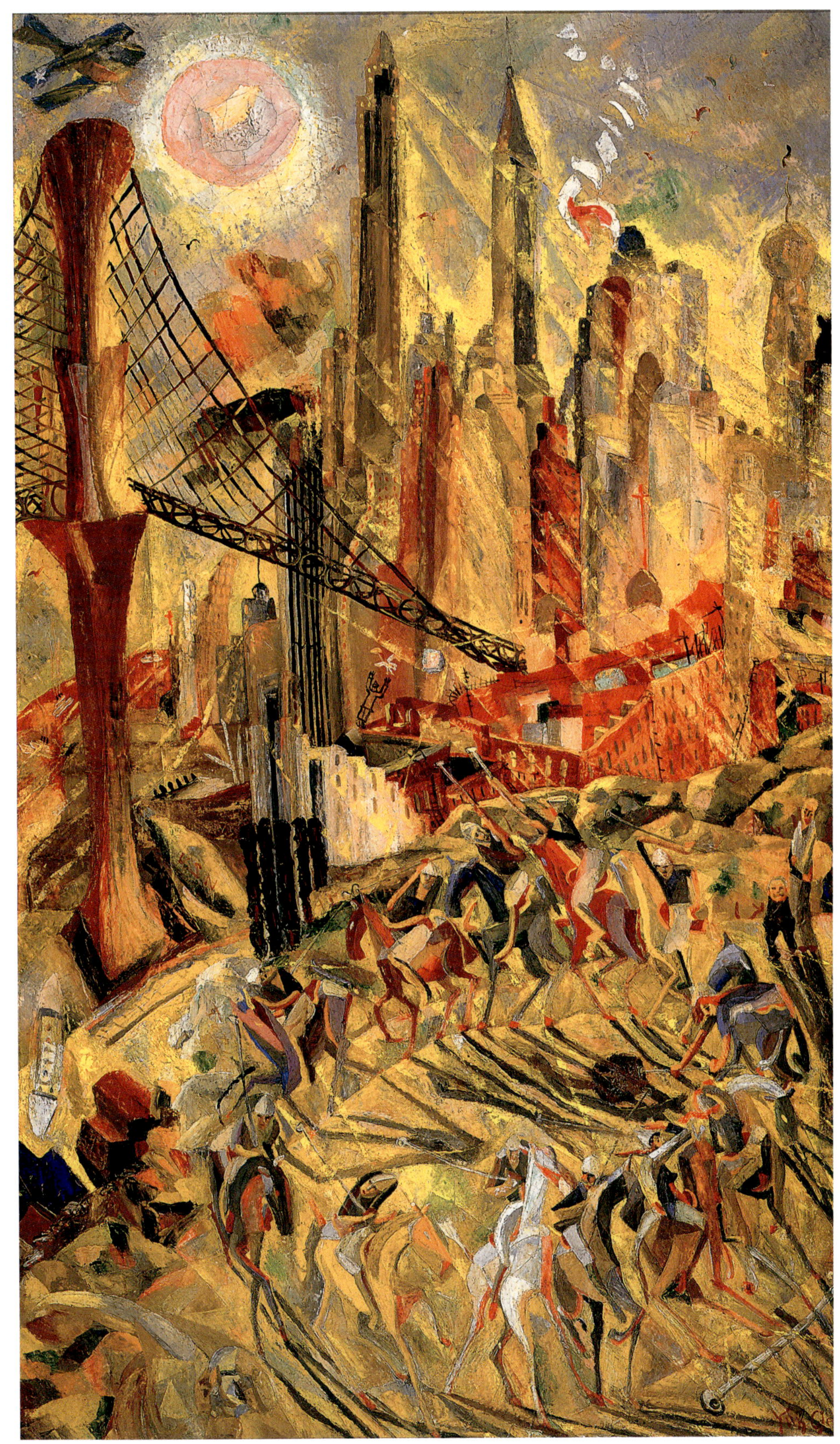

Plate 4 Yun Gee, ***Wheel "Industrial New York,"*** oil on canvas (83 ½ in. x 47 ¼ in.), 1932. Photo credit: Kevin Ryan

Listen
the sound is blue
is yellow
is red
Listen
the sound
like the wave
against the rocks
and the growing hands
are pale
Each finger-tip
aches
Alas—the sound from Africa
Alas—the sound from America
Alas—the sound from Asia
Alas—the sound from Europe

It is clear that Gee embraced the world. He not only wrote letters on behalf of the Chinese but also wrote one to President Harry S. Truman in the interest of protecting India.[86] The poem "Pigeon" shows Gee at his empathetic best, in his love of animals and of particular birds (Helen Gee mentions his having had canaries, nightingales, skylarks, finches, and a mynah that sang in both English and French).[87] In the long poem "My Speaking Bird's Death," Gee cries out with ambivalence toward an all-powerful God who has taken his beloved mynah bird, as God has also taken and caused great suffering to millions of people.[88] In several other poems and writings, Gee voices his uncertain feelings about what he often perceives as an all-powerful but sometimes inhuman God. His own humanity shines forth in these poems; often they serve as allegories of his own life and of the questions he raises about life, death, and spiritual beliefs.

The poem "Blood," dated 1936, was probably written before Gee left for Paris, since it pictures aspects of his Greenwich Village apartment. I quote all of it because I think it is one of his best, and when I read it, I feel Gee's loneliness and, what is perhaps more poignant, why he had to leave New York:

The red wine passes my lips
and warms this dim room
all is so still
but the rain
The red wine warms my throat, my body
The room is so dim
so cold
all is darkness
Till one flash of lightning brightens

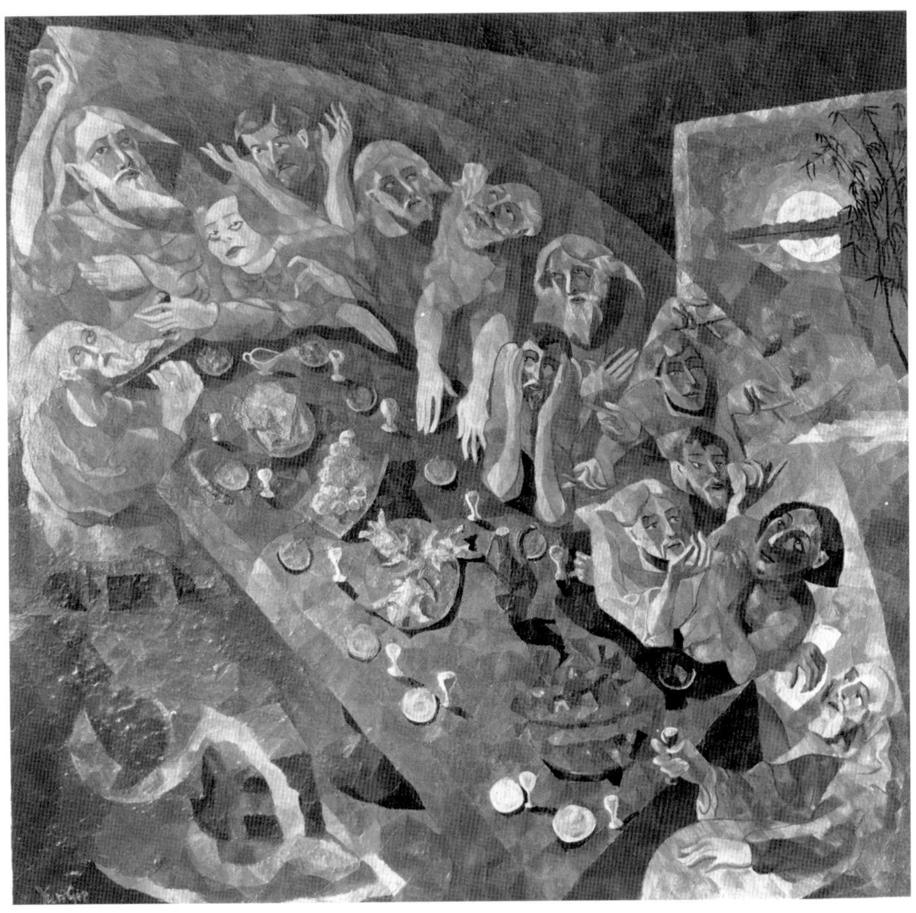

1.6 Yun Gee, *The Last Supper* (ca. 5 x 5 in.), 1933.

the night
and the memories return
like a knife
There is an empty pipe, a stuffed bird
a lonely room
and through this
this cutting white knife
I taste of the red wine, the blood of my heart
from this bottle that
knows no time
I am alone in my dining room
One canary in each cage
looks at me
the lightning that lights the room
bothers them not
They love the smell of wine, too
but they have no memories
how can wine
paint the wound
of that cutting white knife?[89]

Second Trip to Paris (1936–1939): The Transnational Tries to Find a Permanent Home

Perhaps the poem titled "Paris" was written soon after Gee landed once again in that city; if so, what a euphoric beginning, in contrast to the situation depicted in "Blood":

> *Paris is one of the beautiful cities of the world*
> *The people there, on the street and in the cafes,*
> *Are active.*
> *Compared to elsewhere, they have more of an actor's attitude.*
> *Most are so happy and so delightful.*[90]

And then the mood changes: the next line reads: "Except myself so long in suffering." The rest of the poem is about the poor and weak and old people who sleep along the Seine and "live long lives without taking. / And no doubt they are the vanguards of those non-propertied." Thus a political moment, perhaps nostalgia for past radical beliefs, closes the poem. In spite of his ambivalence, however, Gee might have stayed in Paris if the war had not made that impossible. Many years later, perhaps in the late 1940s or early 1950s, Gee wrote:

> Paris welcomed me again. . . . A welcomed relief from the darkness of New York's apathetic coldness. . . . It was in this period that I met DR. SIGMUND FREUD and other notables. . . . It was here that I discovered the HERALDED SCHOOL OF DIAMONDISM. . . . It was here in fabulous Paris that I regained the title of master. . . . There I remained in comparative happiness until the clouds of war began to close over the world. . . . [91]

Again, there is no mention of how Gee earned a living or of whether he sold any paintings, but he seems to have found some initial contentment. He exhibited in one-person and group shows with frequency and received positive critical reviews from his former friends. He was now divorced from Paule de Reuss, but they seem to have remained close, and she is quoted in "Yun Gee Speaks His Mind" as a French expert commenting on his painting. But France was an economic mess in these early war years, and the group of friends he had made was also in dire straits; some were leaving for America and other countries. As I will discuss in chapter 2, some of the reviews he got seemed to belittle his being Chinese, in contrast to his earlier reception. It will become evident that his more "realistic" genre painting, which had developed in relation to the social realism and regionalism favored in New York, was not synchronous with the pseudocubist, dadaist, and surrealist forms of painting practiced by most Parisian artists in the early years of the war. While Gee pursued his theories about Diamondism, his studio practice was far more conservative than his work had been during his first sojourn in Paris. He seems to have been thrashing about to find his own voice again, and it came to the fore in several exciting works.

It is more difficult to tease out Gee's thoughts and feelings from the poems that he may have written in Paris. So many are undated, and the structure of the poetry is often so abstract, that meaning yields to rhythm and meter. Even reading them out loud does not seem to be helpful in decoding the content.[92] Many poems titled "Abstraction" are undated but seem to have been written in those years. Several of the poems seem to have been influenced by concrete poetry, particularly by the works of Guillaume Apollinaire, who died in 1918. Although they are not calligrams, or visual poems that take the form of what is being described, the poem "Abstraction Color," as one example, lists the colors that Gee was using at the time in an abstract pattern. Gee continues his experimentation with sounds and complex rhythmic structures, and the diversity of moods, from playful to despairing, is similar to that of his earlier poetry, although at times these poems become even more impenetrable. In some of the poems, Gee writes about drinking; a few seem to be about love, and some are about the war; life and death are also frequent subjects. It is interesting that as Gee's paintings became more realistic, his poetry became more abstract. Because his poems were a private matter, Gee could experiment to his heart's content. But painting was his public profession, and there, perhaps, Gee made the mistake of trying to be in fashion. Nevertheless, he needed to sell work in order to live; circumstances provided no other way out.

What is interesting about the phases of Gee's work up to this time is the manner in which they may have been an early reflection of a contemporary concern among artists who practice in a transnational manner. If cubism and its offshoots constituted an international style through the early 1930s, then transnational artists like Gee suffered as the result of the artistic changes that occurred when countries became nationalistic, partly because of the social and political vicissitudes of war. Nationalism is again on the rise in many parts of the world today, and it may be engendering similar problems; nevertheless, the vast numbers of people who are of mixed nationality, race, and culture may act as an alternative force.

The Final Return: New York (1936–1964)

Periods of depression and Gee's alcoholism affected the later years of his life, but it is erroneous to account for that life from this time on as colored by continual mental illness or severe nervous breakdowns. In "Yun Gee: A Reminiscence," Helen Gee describes his home life and the wonderful food he cooked when he was entertaining, but she does not mention his drinking, and she attributes an incapacitating illness in his later years to his "lonely position in the art world" and to the social and cultural pressures he endured because of being Chinese.[93] Writing of the same period, Li-lan says:

> I now understand the moodiness that confused me then. The sauterne bottle was always within his reach and was the source of the erratic behavior that sometimes scared me. He drank day and night, with meals and without, and his ability to function became seriously impaired as time went on.[94]

But Li-lan also remembers the pleasure she had in visiting her father, the smells of his Chinese cooking and their hours together,

> filled with sounds of both French and Chinese as he struggled to teach me those languages. I wrote Chinese character after Chinese character but, regretfully, I didn't learn them. . . . We had better luck when we painted together. . . . Sometimes we would leave our easels behind and go on an outing around New York City. He took me to the Zoo, the Botanical Gardens, and our favorite, Central Park. He painted many scenes of the park in the '30s and '40s, but when we were together he would rent a rowboat and take me out on the lake. I cherish the memories of those special times in which my father shared with me his love of language, music, color, painting and the out-of-doors.[95]

Accounts of the last twenty-five years of Gee's life in New York often sound as if he accomplished nothing and was basically incapacitated. I, like other authors, dispensed with engaging those years in my past writing because they seemed so sad, and I saw little of the work that has been judged inferior. I still think that in those years Gee only sporadically painted works that were as exciting as those from the previous two decades or so, yet he was very active, in spite of bouts of depression, until he was truly incapacitated by stomach cancer. The list of his activities was long, apart from his continuing to paint and draw prolifically and promote himself in spite of poor reviews and infrequent exhibitions after the 1940s. He tried to establish his own Diamondism School of Art but was unable to get it licensed. He taught painting for the WPA at the Museum of the City of New York. He amassed a collection of "old master" paintings, which he tried to sell, but although some were authenticated at the time, they were later found to be inauthentic. He worked in a factory, making searchlights for the army and the War Department as a research engineer. He was the creator of several inventions—for example, a four-dimensional chess game so complicated that few could play it (but Li-lan could). He also worked tirelessly on behalf of the Chinese and the

Allies' war relief—donating paintings, writing letters, giving concerts, and speaking.[96] Helen Gee also describes his life, particularly in the 1940s, as very social:

> Dinner at Yun's studio was a forum for the lively give-and-take that was part of Greenwich Village life of the early '40s. Yun, essentially a loner, belonged to no clique or "scene," yet he attracted a stream of visitors interested in his paintings, his ideas, and his tales of Chinese history and legend, as well as the culinary miracles which emerged from his wok and a battered and beloved old rice pot.[97]

She goes on to describe the often heated conversations, with Gee reaching into a pile of books that included Chinese classics, as well as writers like James Joyce, Emma Goldman, Sigmund Freud, John Dewey, and Karl Marx, to make a point. His guests were both Chinese and Caucasian, and they often listened with doubt to his many advanced ideas: that future overpopulation would lead to famine and environmental depletion, that alienation was an American illness, that soybeans were part of the future American diet, that acupuncture and tai chi would become commonplace in the West, and that the destiny of China was to be a leading power economically able to solve its devastating problems. What perspicacity! I think it was the result of Gee's sophistication about world events, in contrast to the isolationist perspective that dominated awareness in the United States in the prewar years.

But what was it really like for anyone who was poor to live in New York during the war years, and what would it have been like if one had been born Asian? While the New Deal and the war helped to end the Depression, they did not bring an end to racism; and, obviously, the Japanese attack on Pearl Harbor increased racist attacks. Gee wrote that he had been obliged to shave off his moustache because wearing one was identified with being Japanese, and Americans were unable to differentiate.[98] According to Helen Gee, she and Yun often had to walk on different sides of the street in order not to be leered at or attacked. Lee, writing about the last fifteen years of Gee's life, which were lived in obscurity, says that they coincided with the rise and apotheosis of abstract expressionism, and that Gee's paintings—mostly figurative and often clinging, in New York, to a mild form of the social realist aesthetic developed in the 1930s—did not please the tastes of dealers or attract the interest of critics. Also during those years, Gee's best efforts as a painter, which had always been in dialogue with key cultural and international political events, were not finding the same kinds of historical material to sustain them. Gee's complex internationalism ran up against the American Cold War effort to simplify an East-West divide and demonize all those who professed even a whiff of radicalism, and in this atmosphere of simpleminded nationalism it was enormously difficult for Gee to find a place in the political

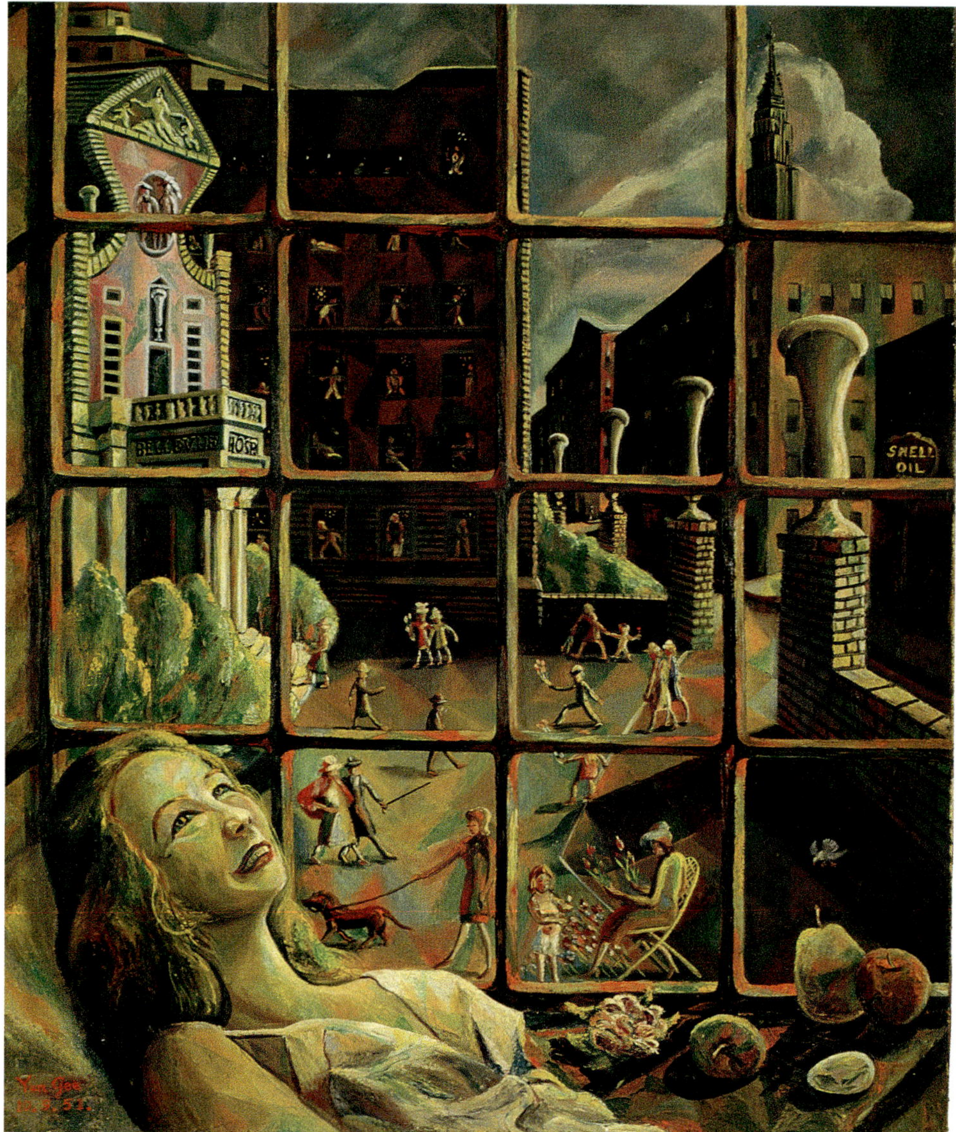

Plate 5 Yun Gee, ***Hospital Court***, **oil on canvas (41 $^{7}/_{8}$ in. x 36 in.), 1951.**

landscape, let alone garner regular support among politically conservative museums and galleries.[99]

But by this time Gee's work was not radical in any sense, and while Lee is certainly correct in accounting for aspects of Gee's difficulties, I disagree with the association of the paintings with political ideology. Gee's work was consistently rooted in genre themes, cityscapes, and portraits, and although the manner of painting them changed, the content was not really social realism. In light of what Erika Doss has to say about social realism and regionalism, Gee's work remained free, for the most part, of the political meanings of those "isms."[100] And if the modernism of the late 1950s—rooted in the reification of the alienated and isolated self—should have appealed to Gee, he rarely used his painting for such kinds of expression. It is also the case that Gee was politically in sync with the growing disdain for Communism that was linked with Fascism after Stalin.

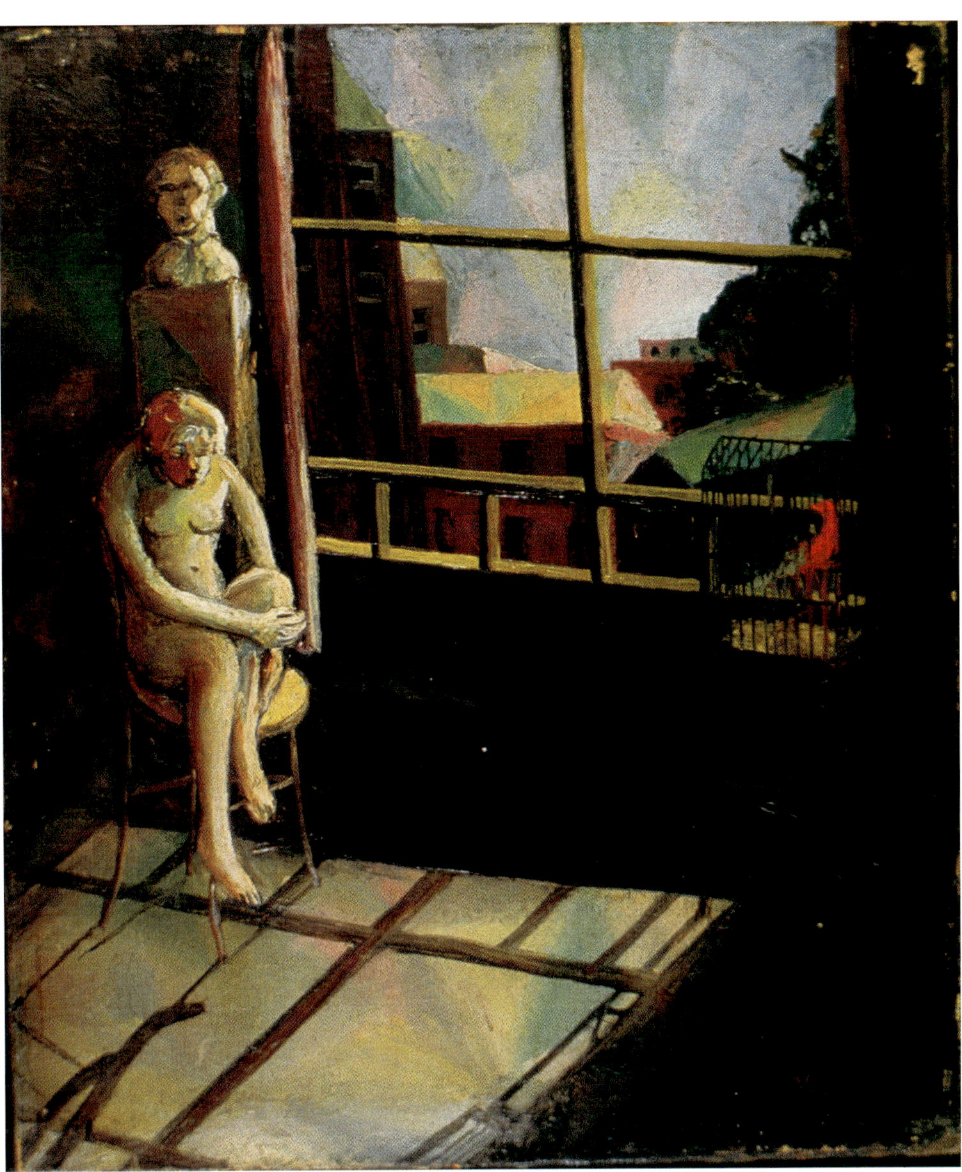

Plate 6 Yun Gee, ***Untitled* (*Nude in Studio*)**, oil on canvas (21 ¾ in. x 18 in.), 1950s.

The last ten years of Gee's life became more and more difficult. As late as the early 1960s, Li-lan told me, the immigration authorities were calling Gee and members of his family regarding his status as a citizen. Family members were told that if they confessed to not being citizens, they would not be deported; some family members wanted to confess, and others, including Gee, did not. Nothing came of it, but the threat indicates how prevalent fear and anxiety could be after all those years. Perhaps Gee's decision not to visit China was in part related to such fears. Added to this strain was the fact that his professional life as an exhibiting artist came to a halt; he had no exhibitions of his work from the late 1940s until a year before he died. Yet what I find exciting is that some of the paintings of the 1950s suggest a new, more complex direction in subject, composition, and brushwork. *Hospital Court* (pl. 5), *Untitled (Nude in Studio)* (pl. 6), and *Untitled (Nude)* (pl. 7), from the early 1950s, alongside *Wanamaker Fire* (pl. 8) of 1956—one of the very few expres-

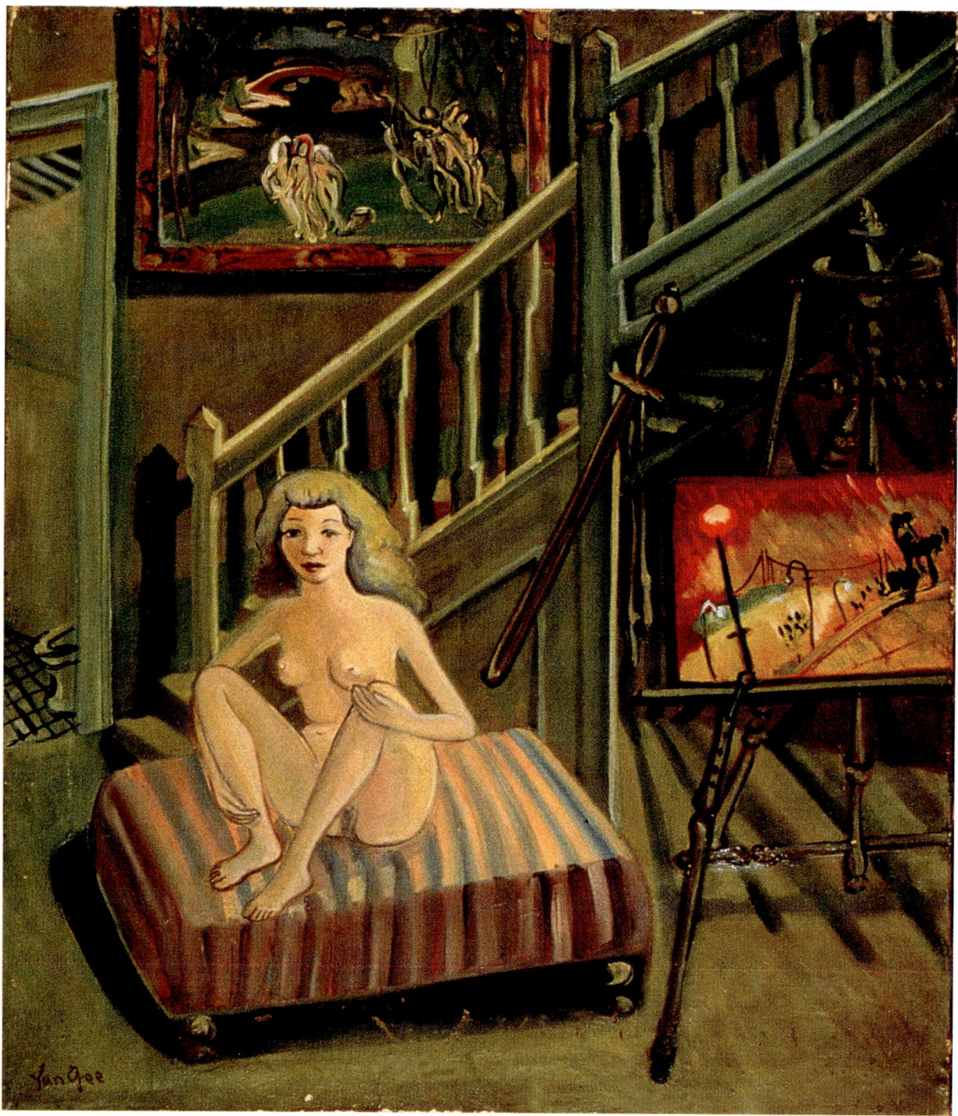

Plate 7 Yun Gee, *Untitled* (*Nude*), oil on canvas (25 5/8 in. x 21 ¼ in.), 1950s.

sionist paintings that succeed—are strong works, and in some of them Gee makes use of Diamondism in a very sophisticated manner. There are also some wonderful portraits, such as the large painting of Velma Aydelott. While Gee tried in a few paintings to be an expressionist in the late 1940s, expressionism seems to have been an uncongenial mode for him. Interestingly enough, it would later be the same for Li-lan. In the 1950s, Gee apparently found his way once again, but that new phase met with no success, in part because he was out of favor with the growing trend to abstraction that had started in the late 1940s and swept everything else aside. It is only fair to consider that many of Gee's works from the 1940s on did not carry the visual authority of his earlier work.

There are fewer poems to help us understand Gee's private feelings during those years. The dated ones include "Wo Woo Wooo" and "Hoping for Peace," an homage to Pierre Mille and to one J. B. Powell, who had been interned in a concentration camp by the Japanese because of his defense of China.[101] Many

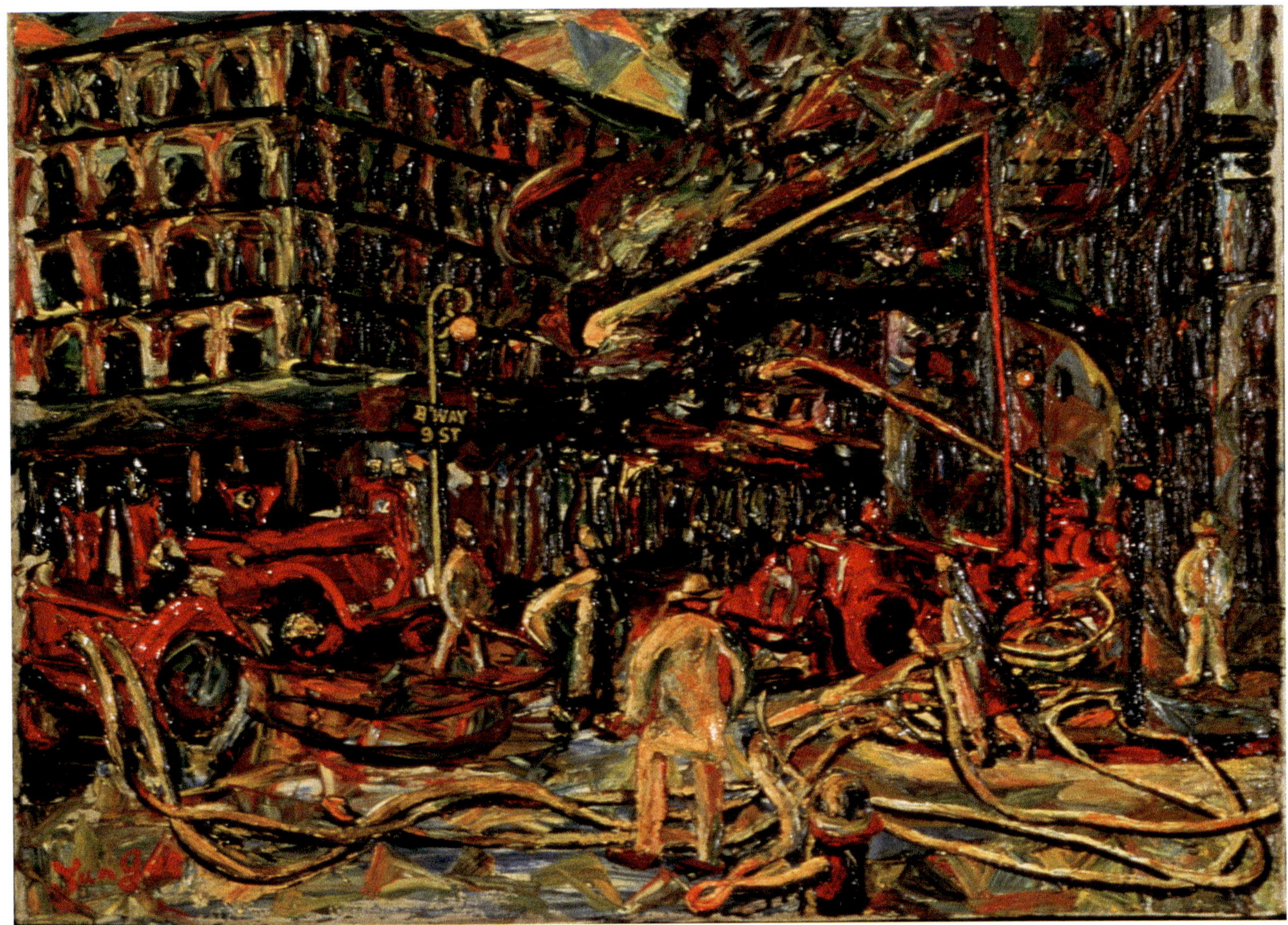

Plate 8 Yun Gee, ***Wanamaker Fire***, oil on canvas (21 1/8 in. x 29 in.), 1956.

of the poems are, again, very difficult to understand, but "The Bend of the Hour" is one of the few uplifting verses, and it is fitting to end this chapter by quoting it. It is a signal to me that this poet and painter never stopped being the incomparable Yun Gee:

The bend of the hour
Has formed a point
Where I and my true heart
Are singled out against the universe—
Here we part with all the past.
We cannot pierce the mystery
of the future.
We only have this tiny point of time
Unpartitioned.
Where we are one with the Eternal
Though flesh and time
Define our limitlessness
We are an area of bliss
And its destiny of freedom.[102]

2 YUN GEE'S PAINTINGS

"How People Look at Things and at What"

This synthesis of East and West held no contradictions for Yun. But to some it seemed an anomaly, and I sensed his irritation when asked "Why don't you paint like a Chinese? Why don't you paint flowers and birds?" "Because I'm living in a modern industrial society," was his usual reply. " . . . I'm not contemplating nature on a mountain top." —HELEN GEE

Gee lived the life of a transnational, embracing the various cultures that informed it. How did that way become the form and content of his painting? I think it did so first through the way he integrated his experiences of passage into a unity of vision. He did not accentuate the separate parts of his complex existence, because his ideals were universal in scope, and in his best work the "populist" subjects were wedded to the most advanced forms of expression that were practiced internationally, and that he directed to a global audience.[1] He crossed national boundaries with seeming ease and open-mindedness; and, in contrast to the work of many other artists, who believed their own national styles to be preeminent, what informed all of Gee's work was—in part—the spiritual, philosophical, and ethical dimensions that he had inherited from being Chinese, and that motivated the humanitarian concerns evidenced in his painting.

Gee rarely produced works with easily identified elements of Eastern and Western painting, but most of his works were realized in a modern mode. When he painted Chinese subjects that were clearly recognizable, he often rendered them with fully integrated modernist elements. While Gee's training in calligraphy can be cited, particularly with respect to his many ink drawings

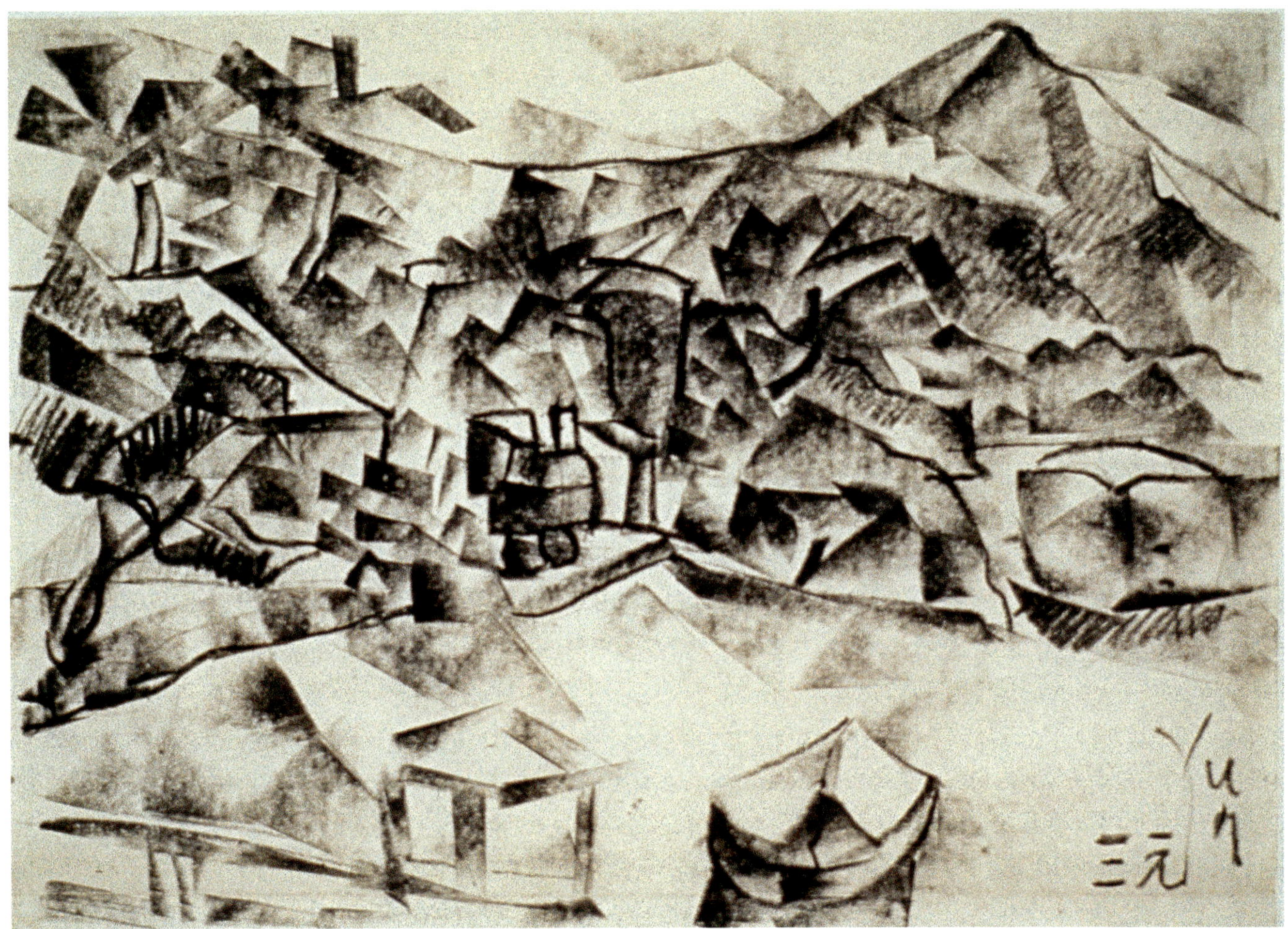

2.1 Yun Gee, *Landscape*, pencil drawing (8 7/16 x 10 15/16 in.), 1927.

of the nude model, his way of rendering is not easily distinguished from the ways of many Western artists. His drawings can be compared to those of Matisse, for example, and are much less given to "Oriental" exotica than are many works of that artist. His early "cubist" pencil drawings are filled with dynamic "Cézannesque" passages unlike anything found in most Chinese ink-and-brush paintings, although some of these drawings' density might be referenced to that tradition. Gee was a modernist, influenced by the offshoots of cubism in the 1920s, by Cézanne and some of his School of Paris followers from the 1930s on, and he showed a tendency to be somewhat more of a realist in the 1940s and even a surrealist in the 1950s.

In spite of Gee's modern attitude, it has been both fascinating and disconcerting for me to view his painting from George Kubler's perspective.[2] I have been particularly interested in Kubler's view of fame and recognition as central to the making of a good or a bad entrance into the game of art history—so much for the concept of the genius free from institutional practices. Gee engaged cubism in San Francisco, and its more representational and lyrical form in Paris in the 1920s and 1930s, as did many other artists. When Gee entered the artistic scene in San Francisco and Paris, as a very young man, his short period of fame resulted from the fact that his style was in harmony with the most current painting practiced in both cities and was transnational in its reach. In New York, from the 1930s through the late 1950s, he was off center, still working at first with references to cubism, while recognized artists were practicing regionalism and social realism; and as he changed his style somewhat, to accommodate that shift by returning to more representational forms of genre painting, portraits, and cityscapes, major artists in Paris had become surrealists, and in New York were shifting to abstract expressionism. He tried painting in a more expressionist style in a few instances, but it was contrived and seemed contrary to his temperament. If Kubler's model is an appropriate guide to Gee's work, then Gee was doomed to fail from the start, and if we add the issues of racism, discussed earlier, it is almost amazing that he succeeded at all. I often wonder what he would have produced if he had been able, with the appropriate support, to develop his remarkable blending of everyday subjects with his particular form of a modernist vocabulary. Sadly, the picture I have painted of his life makes clear some of the reasons for the thwarting of that development. What was not thwarted, and what intersects with Kubler's "art world" theory, was his personal determination to picture the neighborhoods and daily activities of ordinary people, whatever the prevailing attitude, and often in spite of his ambitions. In the early 1950s he wrote, "Every sincere painting tries to find an adequate expression of its time. In expressing *how* people look at things and at *what*."[3]

I will argue that Gee, as a transnational, had no part in the "regionalism to modernism" issue that dominated discussions of painting, particularly in New York, in the 1940s. He was neither a regionalist nor an abstract expressionist, and those particular American modes, and the discourses surrounding, them touched him in adverse ways just because he was not involved in the battle but only, like many other artists of the time, a victim of it. For most of his life, Gee painted genre subjects, in a modernist mode, centered on the everyday activities of ordinary people pursuing work and pleasure in the streets and parks of the city; perhaps one could call his style a "universal populism."

In a review of a book about photography, Richard Woodward takes the author to task for proposing that photography in New York is a Jewish practice, but he writes that this proposition "shouldn't be entirely discounted," and that the book's author "is clearly on to something when he writes that photography allowed Jews to express 'a vigorous populism that suited their evolving ambition. . . . Most movements within modernist art required that you give up your ethnic credentials and adopt a utopian platform.'"[4] Indeed, Gee did develop a kind of "utopian platform," and if it was not also a "vigorous populism," it was rooted in democratic ideals and humanitarian principles, and he was able to wed them to a modern form. Although a private teacher gave Yun Gee a scholar's name when he was very young (Yun Chih Chu), and although he received a traditional education, he practiced a

Western form of genre painting all his life, as seen in many of the paintings that have survived. He maintained this practice while retaining his ethnic credentials, sometimes signing his paintings with the Chinese form of his name, Gee Yun, and sometimes with his scholar's name. While his training may not have prepared him for the direction he ultimately took, the political and intellectual concerns of his youth in southern China were probably crucial to his artistic formation.

Gee's parents were not in any sense wealthy, but they understood how important an education was, and so Gee, like his brothers, was given a "gentleman's" education. In his only mention of his art training, Gee wrote that he studied traditional painting with master Chu in 1918–19, and that his first painting was a portrait of Kuan Kung, a deified warrior active in the Three Kingdoms. He also mentions, once, the paintings of the Gao brothers, both of whom studied in Japan and were founders of the Lingnan School of Painting, in Guangdong.[5] This school was noted for having introduced elements of modern Japanese, Westernized painting into traditional work. As discussed in chapter 1, Gao Jianfu, the elder brother, was also a political revolutionary. Harrist is correct that there are no elements of the Lingnan School in the work that Gee produced in San Francisco.[6] No paintings survive from Gee's early years in China, so it is not possible to tell if modernist aims had an impact on his work. Croizier, in his excellent study of the Lingnan School, defines its contribution to modern Chinese art as "Western realism . . . translated by Japanese artists into ink painting, and combined . . . with strong emotional expressionism . . . two strains—realism and romanticism—often coexisting if in an uneasy tension."[7] But neither realistic depictions nor romanticism, often realized in Lingnan landscape and animal painting, has much to do with Gee's painting. At that time in Gee's life, in fact, it may have been a revolutionary decision on his part to forswear the landscape and animal and flower subjects that constituted so much of Chinese painting in Guangdong, as they did elsewhere in the country.

Gee wrote later on that in 1926 he had burned more than two hundred paintings in a bonfire because he considered his previous work to be academic; this act, he wrote, was symbolic of his dedication to modern art.[8] It may have been the revolutionary spirit of the Lingnan School's artistic commitments that inspired him; he certainly seemed prepared to pick up the semi-abstract color style that Oldfield was teaching at the California School of Fine Arts, and he did so with seeming ease in the less than two years he spent there. There is no indication of direct influence from the Lingnan School on the form or content of Gee's work, but it is a wonderful coincidence that in 1932 Gao Jianfu painted a scroll in ink and watercolor called *Flying in the Rain*, which imaged biplanes flying over a misty landscape, and that Gee, in the same year, painted *Wheel "Industrial New York"* (pl. 4), a major painting exhibited at the Museum of Modern Art, with a biplane in the right-hand corner.[9] Gao had exhibited other paintings featuring airplanes in 1927, in Canton.[10] How could Gee have seen them? In each painter's case, the plane was probably a coincidental sign of a modernist propensity. Gee was always interested in modern industry and in modern means of transportation, particularly airplanes. His brother, who was an aviator in Philadelphia, may have had something to do with that interest. Perhaps Gee was more directly impressed by the depictions of lions and tigers that were prominent in Lingnan ink painting and symbolic of revolutionary power: Gee's ink drawing *The Chinese Lion Is Aroused* of 1931 shows the same kind of ferocity that Gao Qifeng portrayed in his *Roaring Tiger* of 1908.[11] In an essay written in the 1930s, Gee echoes the spirit of the Lingnan School:

> The strongest hope for reviving a once great but now jaded and worn art lies with those painters who are making a serious endeavor to combine the old with the new. The aim of this school is not to cultivate merely an art of compromise, nor a safe, middle-of-the-road art, but to create an art that is vital and alive that will contribute to the development of Chinese painting techniques. This is no easy task. But, since the republic is young and art is long, time will be an ally in the successful development of the new style.[12]

The Lingnan School may not have accomplished that goal, and it became more conservative in the 1930s and 1940s, as did Gee, but the artists connected to it may have had profound meaning, in another direction, for a creative intellectual like Gee—that is, with respect to Gee's very early stand on notions of orientalism. He once condemned Eastern artists like Tsuguharu Foujita for pandering to Western desires for orientalia.[13] Gee himself did paint some Chinese subjects, but he rarely capitulated to orientalism.

I have already written a great deal about the works Gee created in San Francisco, in Paris, and in his first sojourn in New York.[14] The paintings made in San Francisco and Paris, and those made in New York through 1932, are always discussed because they are the ones upon which Gee's reputation as an exciting modernist is based. In this chapter, I also want to address his later work, and to discuss it in light of social realism or regionalism and the emergence of abstract expressionism in the 1940s. I argue here that Gee remained primarily a genre painter to the end, and that he was always more attuned to French painting, his experience of it having been formed when he lived in Paris in the late 1920s and 1930s, than to American art of the same period. Elsewhere I have suggested that further work needs to be undertaken in order for us to understand the role of Gee's teachers, or of the institutions that he attended, as well as the political, cultural, and social contexts that nourished or inhibited Gee's achievements.[15] I began to investigate the question of teachers and institutions in connection with Otis Oldfield and the California School of Fine Arts in the 1978 catalogue.[16] The following section, which briefly summarizes my previous writing on this topic, is a synopsis of Gee's art education in San Francisco but reflects additional research that I and others have undertaken to correct earlier omissions.

Painting in San Francisco: American Primitive (1921–1927)

To begin, the pictures of Chinatown and the portrayals of his friends that Gee made in his "primitive" years are unique,[17] both because they were painted by a young immigrant Chinese artist and, more important, because they diverge in such a personal manner from images made of that part of San Francisco by others in the first and second quarters of the twentieth century.[18] In his very interesting study of photographs (and some paintings) made of Chinatown by Caucasians and Chinese, Anthony Lee uncovers the different degrees of exoticism that determined the perspectives of the photographers.[19] For the most part, the photographers reinforced the stereotypical views of Chinese life that tourists formed even before visiting Chinatown. In light of these images, Lee rightly considers Gee's works radical, but I think for questionable reasons; he may be underestimating the paintings' uniqueness by overdetermining their political meanings. Gee's small pictures on paperboard concentrate on the everyday activities of workers or people in the park with their children, or they are portraits of friends, teachers, and fellow classmates. In Gee's cityscapes, it is the neighborhood architecture that intrigues him along with the spatial environment activated by his newfound system of abstract color shapes. In several paintings there are no figures at all, but Gee pictures the telephone poles and wires of communication that accentuate the growing modernization of Chinatown. In the photographs that Lee reproduces in his book, even the most casual views seem posed to accentuate the Oriental other. In Gee's paintings, however, nothing exists of the exotic aspect of Chinatown, and his figures of Chinese inhabitants are never dressed in native Chinese clothes; they are always pictured in Western dress. Lee is surely correct to see in this feature an aspect of Gee's desire for all things modern, and the absence of Chinese themes in his work from this period is symptomatic.

Sometimes Gee's favored stick figures—an echo of calligraphy—are actively engaged in construction. The glimpse of goings-on in the street appeals to him; the glance of the flaneur is ever present. A girl sits on the edge of a bridge while a man puffs on his pipe in a nearby automobile. In his portrayal of single subjects, quiet matters often predominate: a man tenderly holds a baby, a woman reads a book, a man huddles over his painting, people sit next to each other on a park bench; and the wonderful tints and shades, bright in some works and luminous in others, result from Gee's special gift as a colorist. Yet

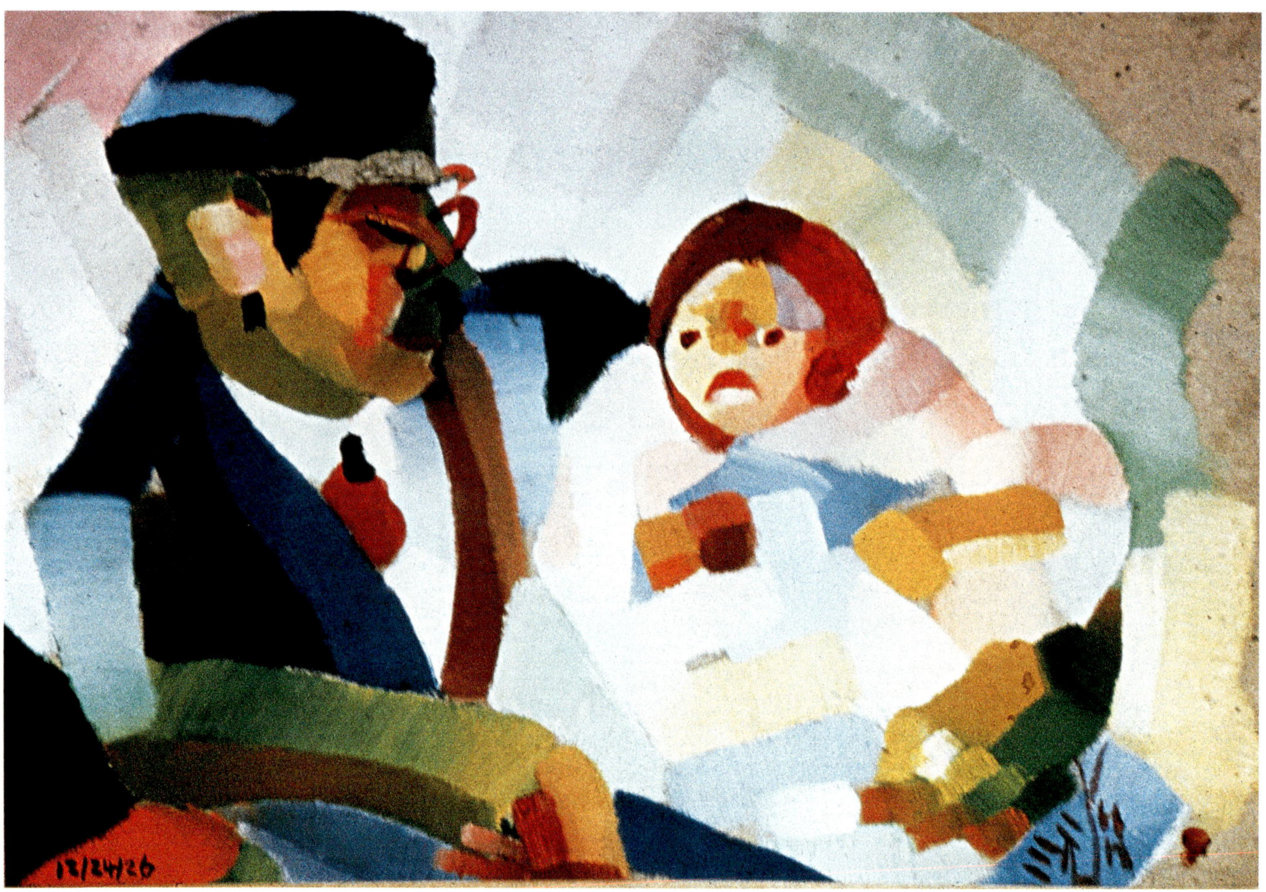

Plate 9 Yun Gee, *Man Holding Baby*, oil on paperboard (11 ¼ in. x 15 ½ in.), 1926.

Lee seems to want read some of these works as reactions to the horrible racism practiced against the Chinese and, in so doing, to establish racism as one of Gee's motives for leaving San Francisco and moving to Paris. For example, Lee writes of *San Francisco Street Scene with Construction Workers* (pl. 11), "We see the cavernous mouth of the tunnel at the bottom center, just beyond the crest of the subtle rise that is the intersection of Stockton and Sacramento Streets. The location is significant because it is the very southwestern edge of Chinatown, the extreme boundary of the policed quarter beyond which, through the tunnel, an entirely non-Chinese San Francisco begins."[20] Lee then spends some three pages suggesting that the picture is not only full of racial pathos but also badly painted in relation to other street scenes, such as *San Francisco Chinatown* of the following year, which shows a "self-sufficient view of a contained artistic presence."[21]

But Gee did get out of Chinatown with some frequency, as mentioned in the previous chapter, and seems not to have been confined by that tunnel. Moreover, the figure in *San Francisco Street Scene with Construction Workers* that Lee describes as a stand-in for Gee, showing "pathos in the carefully measured step of the surrogate, who traverses a boundary that the painter could rarely cross," is similar in gait to the many other humorous, cartoonlike

(opposite)
Plate 10 Yun Gee, *Park Bench II*, oil on paperboard (16 in. x 11 ¼ in.), 1927.

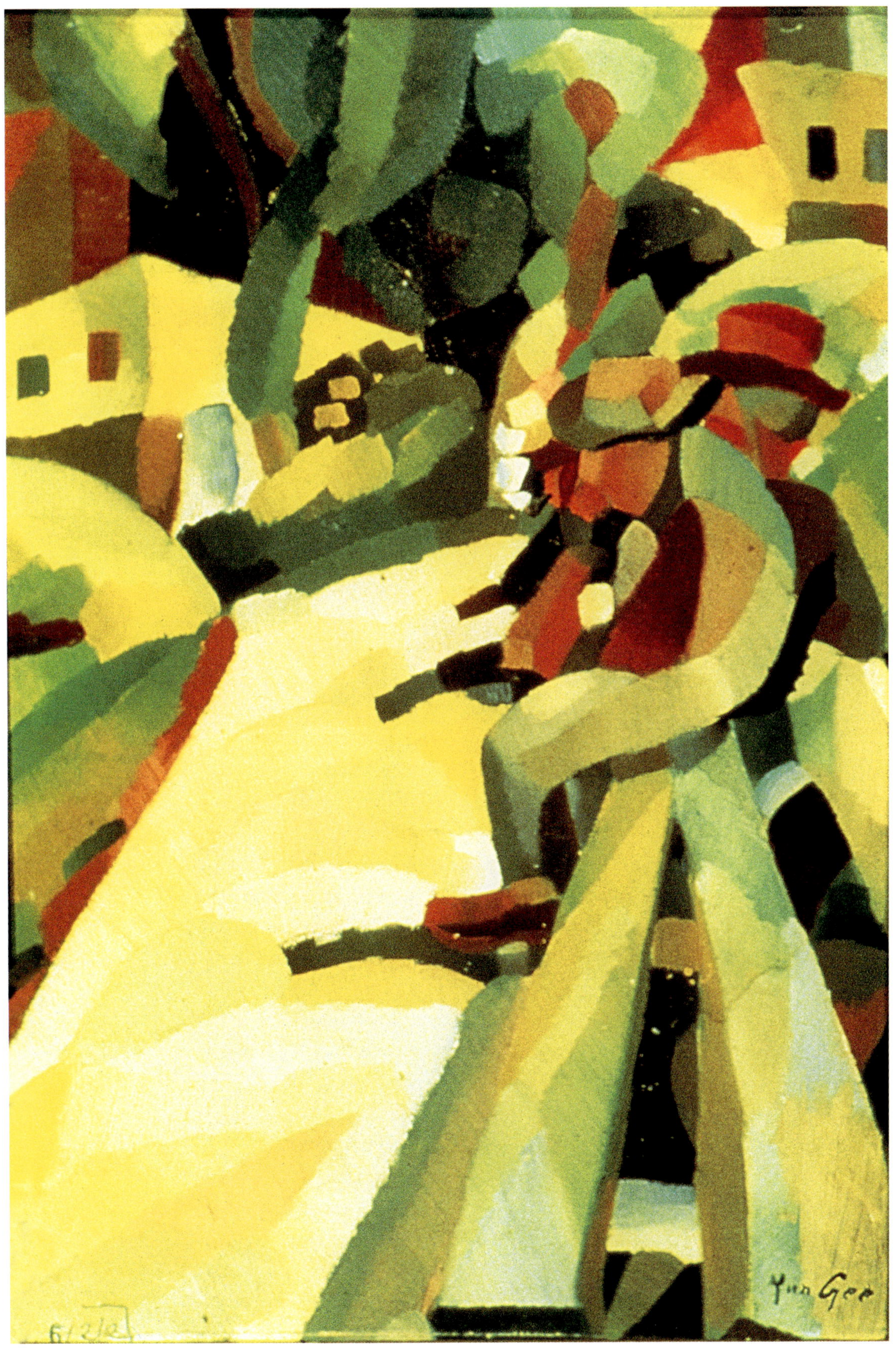
Yun Gee

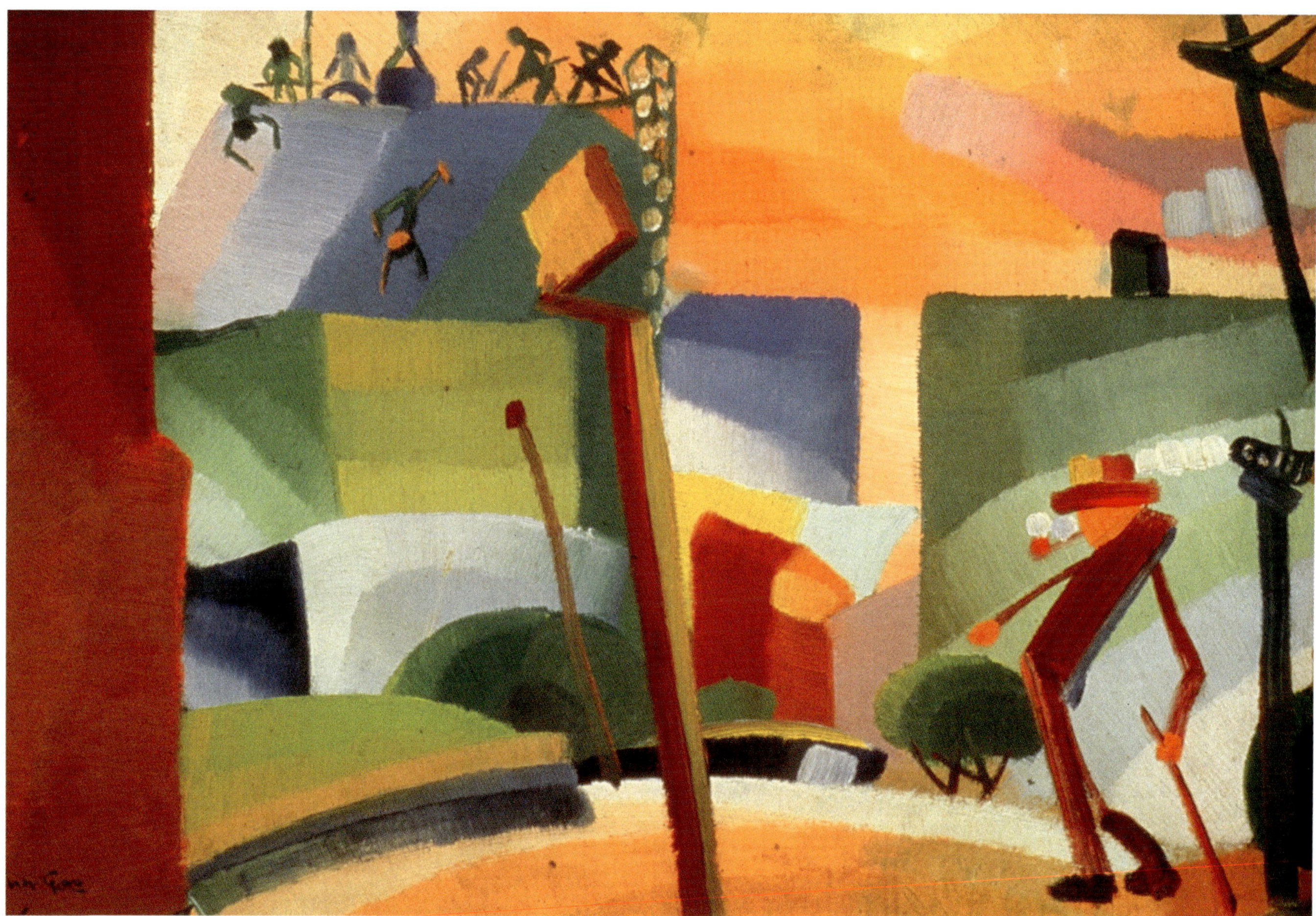

Plate 11 *San Francisco Street Scene with Construction Workers*, oil on paperboard (11 5/16 in. x 16 11/16 in.), 1926.

figures that were almost the artist's signature. As for this work's being badly painted by comparison with the later painting, in 1926 Gee's work was less systematically fragmented than in 1927, but this painting is just as lively in its use of color, and it shows the amazing development of Gee's work in the latter part of 1926 by comparison with his paintings made earlier that year. Where the cavernous tunnel is concerned, it is a very small part of the painting and is framed in green, with only a small circle of shadow. It seems to me that this is simply one of many wonderful small paintings on paper that Gee produced after wandering the streets of Chinatown and elsewhere in San Francisco, delighting in the ordinary; it does not seem to me that Gee, "at Chinatown's borders, . . . was most acutely aware of the meaning of his physical presence to the city outside" and was therefore "required [to] encode that knowledge in the figure of his convulsed stroller and, indeed, in the painting's awkward construction."[22] Lee is interpreting the work of a very young art student who is intent on learning his craft. Aside from Lee's overlooking the unique quality of Gee's painting, it is an overdetermination on his part, to say the least, that he imposes so deep a political and psychological reading on a lively, playful, empathetic depiction of the ordinary activities of city life. One of the personal enjoyments that Yun Gee shared with his daughter was love of the act of painting, and of rendering ordinary things special. Lee's stress on racist politics is disconnected from Gee's penchant, rooted in his humanitarian and populist beliefs, for depicting everyday life. I agree with Lee that the main figure in this painting is a stand-in for Gee, but it is a visual metaphor for modernity and for the cosmopolitan sensibility of the flaneur.

Otis Oldfield, Gee's primary mentor in San Francisco, was instrumental in teaching Gee the ways to express that sensibility through the most advanced international style. Oldfield had spent fifteen years in Paris and returned to San Francisco in 1924. He was aware of every change in the art world, from impressionism through cubism and futurism to dada, while his own work remained essentially realistic. When he returned to San Francisco, his painting had become more Cézannesque, and the French "soft" cubist André Lhote was much admired by him. Applying triangles of color, he painted landscapes, still lifes, portraits, and cityscapes, and he taught color theory to his students in a manner that influenced Gee's work and his theory of Diamondism.[23] Oldfield's later painting was quite impressionistic and included scenes of everyday life around his studio on Telegraph Hill, seascapes, and rural landscapes.[24] In contrast, Gee was never enticed to paint rural landscapes or seascapes.

Gee was a willing student, however, and Oldfield's lessons stayed with him all his life. Two wonderful photographs, taken on a camping trip, show Gee's adoration of his teacher; he is dressed exactly like Oldfield.[25] In a letter found in the Yun Gee archives, Oldfield tells Gee about a painting trip he has taken and says he wants to take the same trip again, this time with Gee. The tone of the letter is one of deep friendship. There are others, written to Gee in Paris, that sound almost like the letters of a father to his son and encourage Gee to pursue his career in spite of setbacks. These letters suggest that Gee, at first, was having a tough time in Paris, and this tone continues in letters that grew more infrequent but were written until almost the end of Gee's life. In some of these letters, Oldfield complains about his own stalled career and his financial problems. Helen Oldfield, Otis's wife, paints a picture of Gee that is even more telling, as Anthony Lee cites her. Gee,

> out on a stroll with Oldfield, . . . "had fitted himself out to be a Chinese carbon copy [of his teacher]; he'd gotten a beret; he had a suit made that was as close as it could be, identical to the one that Otis wore most of the time; he'd gotten a cane and pipe. . . . The beret stuck up on top of his wiry Chinese hair; it wouldn't fit down on his head at all."[26]

Lee rightly calls Gee a flaneur, yet he wants to suggest that Gee was awkwardly covering up his being Chinese: "The costume is ill-fitting and suspicious, seeming not to accord with underlying life. Its vulgar explicitness makes

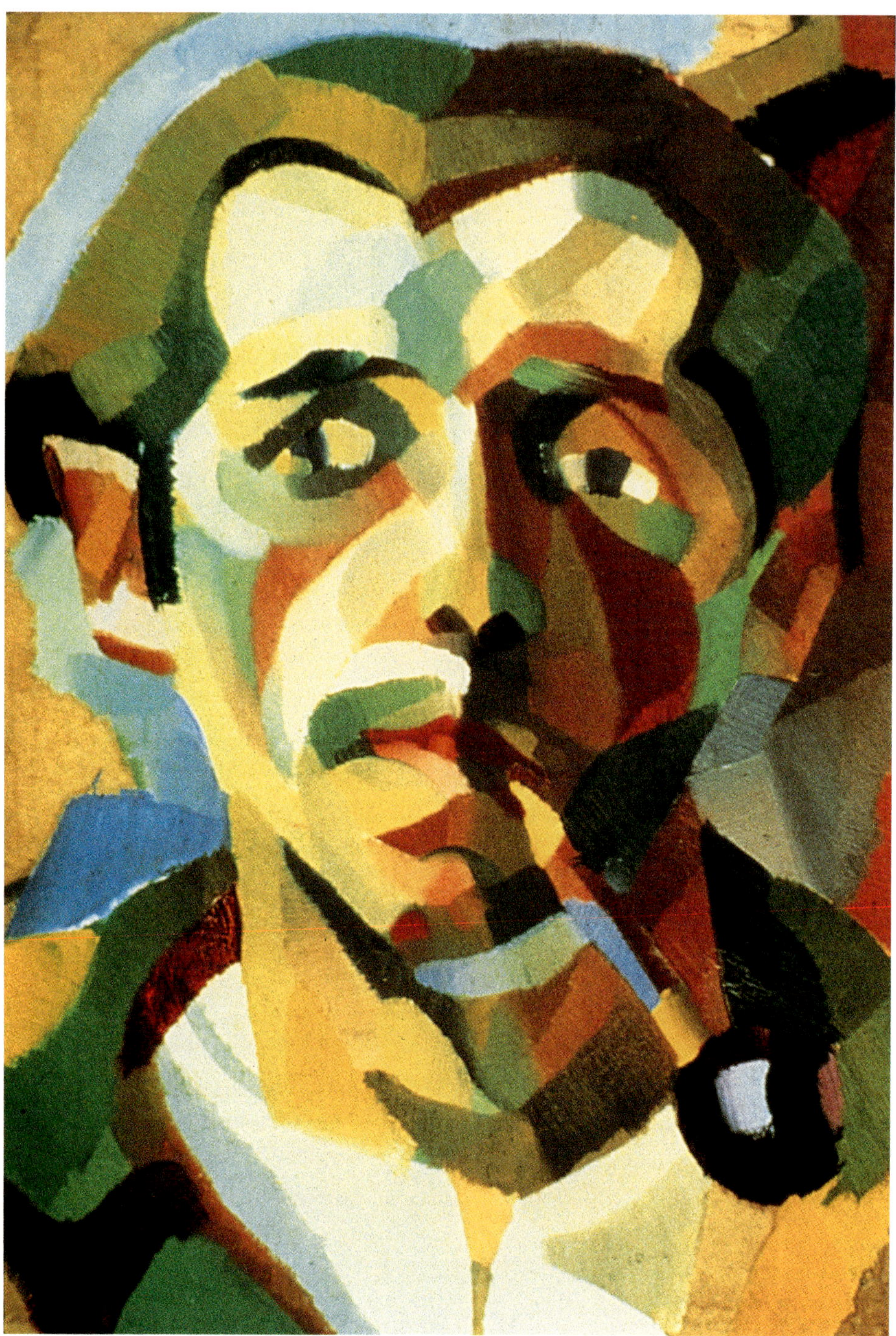

Plate 12 Yun Gee, ***Man with Pipe* (*Otis Oldfield*)**, oil on paperboard (15 5/8 in. x 11 in.), 1926–27.

it parodic or even self-parodic."[27] But why, for Lee, is Gee not doing what almost any young artist type does, trying to be bohemian, copying the mentor's style, "twirling his cane, jauntily stepping past the tourist shops and beneath the colorful canopies, disguised as the Francophile Oldfield"?[28] Gee was a Francophile in spirit before the fact, and a flaneur, and a cosmopolite, and, as Lee paints him, a radical.[29] Several times during these years, Gee also painted himself in the modern style that he was absorbing; a telling photograph from about 1927 shows him in that old suit, painting his self-portrait. *Head of Man in Cap* is another painting with Gee apparently in the same suit, sporting his famous mustache.[30] Then there is *Where Is My Mother* (pl. 2), first discussed in the previous chapter, and to be discussed further in this one. There are several drawings and paintings made by friends, and they picture Gee in just that way, as he himself does in a wonderful drawing. In all these works, he paints himself in Western clothes, and in the modern way he was learning from Oldfield.

Gee was certainly close to his teacher at this time, since he was the only one mentioned when Oldfield was interviewed for a Works Progress Administration (WPA) monograph series published in 1937.[31] I don't know how much of what follows is the writer or Oldfield himself, but in a section titled "Creation of the San Francisco Art Center" we find this:

> In the 1928 Spring semester at the California School of Fine Arts there was enrolled a Chinese student named Yun. Oldfield became interested in him and sought to train the oriental mind in occidental ways of art. At the vacation season, the two decided upon a painting tour through the Mother Lode Country to portray this picturesque section modernistically, a thing completely foreign to Yun's Celestial background and training.[32]

Aside from the insipid, patronizing tone, the date is wrong, since Gee was already in Paris in July 1927, and he had totally absorbed the modernist format by the time he and Oldfield went on that trip. At the bottom of the next page, ambiguity reigns. A portrait of Yun, produced by Oldfield, had been criticized in the *Argus* of July 27:

> The portrait of Yun by Otis Oldfield is an excellent canvas from the standpoint of color, proportion, depth and perspective, but it does not show the genuine young Chinese painter as most people know him. It represents him as a mature and stern man, which is a respectable viewpoint, but an altogether different conception to that which most persons who know Yun have of this young artist.[33]

I am not sure whether the author is chiding Oldfield for making Gee look too respectable, perhaps too important, or for not picturing him as a true bohemian. To give him the benefit of the doubt, perhaps the author is making the same sorts of comments I heard some forty years later about Yun's playfulness, dynamic spirit, and bohemian presence.[34] At any rate, in 1926 Oldfield did a drawing of Gee in flat crayon, in a cubist style, and did capture Gee's dynamic intensity.[35]

While his emulation of Oldfield is obvious, what is startling is that Gee's paintings show a more personal vision, and a more consistent use of abstract color and form, than can be found in his mentor's work. Gee's work also differs from that of artists practicing in the synchromist or orphist styles. Gail Levin writes that although many synchromists used subjects, it was the color relations that dominated; the subject was only a springboard.[36] In the catalogue for an exhibition of Yun Gee's work mounted in 1968 at the Robert Schoelkopf Gallery in New York, John Ferren, a friend of Gee's in San Francisco, wrote as follows about such color experimentation:

> The first sign of an emerging artist is that he recognizes the ground current of his time. From Paris came the ground swell and Yun's 20s production grasped the color-structure implicit in the painting being done there *at that time*. They were not done after the fact. This is remarkable. He had no direct contact. De la Fresnay, Lhote, etc., did it no better nor with more mastery. He began full fledged. . . . MacDonald Wright was somewhere about, but he was painting sexy Orientalia.[37]

The press release for the show features the same theme: "The remarkable thing about Yun Gee is that his early work in the Synchromist style was done in San Francisco before he went to Paris and before he came into contact with Morgan Russell."[38] My research authenticates those claims, but I am less convinced that Gee was really a student of synchromism than that he was a student of Oldfield, whose knowledge of early-twentieth-century French cubist painting, and whose own color-zone theories, were a much more significant influence than synchromism may have been. Whatever the influences, Gee's uniqueness was determined by a *system* wedded to the *choice of subject*.

Other teachers at the California School, in particular Gottardo Piazzoni, taught aspects of modernism that they had encountered in Europe, or at the 1915 Panama-Pacific International Exposition in San Francisco, of some of the paintings that had been on view in 1913 in New York at the now infamous Armory Show, but their own works were rather traditional.[39] Some enlightened California artists were also influenced by that selection of paintings from the Armory Show. The 1915 show featured more futurist-style paintings than had been exhibited in New York. Several paintings by Picasso, Picabia, Matisse, and others were then exhibited at the Palace of Fine Arts. This exhibition influenced a group of expressionist landscape painters called the Society of Six.[40] Gee never mentions this group or its members, and they seem to have had little impact on his painting. Their subjects were essentially landscape; they did not paint city people in city environments. In California as a whole at that time, impressionist brushwork was often the preferred technique, and landscapes were the preferred motif. Gee was always a cosmopolite, and even at the very beginning it was people in the city and the city itself that became his consistent theme. Gee was using not only the most up-to-date Western style but also the most current choice of subject; how ordinary people looked in pursuing their daily activities had very broad appeal, and Gee practiced an international style modernism in a most sophisticated manner. What is also interesting is that when Gee wrote about the aims of his art—or what can be culled on this subject from his poetry—broad themes were stressed, yet his paintings depict ordinary people in concrete situations.

There are some thirty-five paintings, and several drawings, dated or titled in ways that identify them as surely being from Gee's years in San Francisco; others can easily be associated with these, since Gee's style often changed to respond to where he was at a given time. The development in Gee's painting from 1925 to the summer of 1927, when he left for Paris, is truly astounding. Not only did he learn to control his use of color and his brushwork and find a system for applying them, but the compositional structure in relation to the chosen subject also became very sophisticated. In the paintings that were probably done early in 1926 (and in two dated 1925), Gee tried out different kinds of brushstrokes and abstract shapes to form portraits, figures, cityscapes, and landscapes, groping as a student does to control the oils, the color, and the composition in forming some kind of coherent whole. Even in a painting from 1925, *San Francisco Landscape,* Yun was able to use consistent broad brushstrokes that changed direction as he painted land, sea, and sky. A comparison of *Head of Woman with Necklace,* undated but probably from early in 1926, with the later painting *A Woman Reading* reveals the differences emphatically.[41] The earlier painting is more expressive, in part because of its strong contrasts of orange, rusty red, blues, and browns applied in large areas that abut one another, but the latter is more luminous, and the softer color juxtapositions—lighter for the ground, the window scene, the head, the book, and the hands, and darker for the body that hovers over the book—are also more complex. *A Woman Reading* is still essentially a blue/orange painting, but Gee played with tints and shades of those colors, adding greens and eliminating the large passages of dark black or brown. What was gained is specificity through bodily gesture, created by juxtapositions of the right color passages. It is already an accomplished genre study, with all the aspects of Gee's mature style in place, if the word "mature" can be used to describe the work of a twenty-year-old painter.

The same comments are relevant to Gee's vibrant cityscapes: the one titled *Steps*, dated July 22, 1926, is somewhat darker than most, and the brushstrokes are thick and fill the shapes methodically, whereas *San Francisco Street Scene with Construction Workers* (pl. 11) is light in color, with thinner and more blended strokes—and those marvelous, active stick figures, Gee's signature drawing icon, are already in place. Again, a particular situation was observed and recorded, not as documentary, but as the product of empathetic engagement. If we move on to 1927, the developmental strides now appear enormous. From this year come a whole host of wonderful heads, including *Man with Pipe (Otis Oldfield)*, *Portrait of Gottardo Piazzoni*, and the beautifully painted *Female Portrait*, all formed of much smaller passages of color and illustrating Oldfield's Cézannesque method of applying paint, but with Gee's unique ability to synthesize the color elements and the subject. Oldfield taught his students by way of a program of "color zones" and the "law of simultaneous contrasts" of color:

> The program was confined to color-zones, organization of a surface and a rhythm. The students enjoyed the freedom of choice, even adding or subtracting portions of the subject. That was their business, their personal taste, which was scrupulously respected as was the choice of color. The application, being the trade part, was rigorously disciplined. Work was executed upon paper. The pigments were spread across the top. Palettes and their abusive mixings were eliminated, and the students painted directly by zones constructed in juxtaposition from the nucleus key-tone without preliminary sketch, and in pure color only. Cleverness and petty effects were automatically abolished by the stubborn surface of the absorbing paper, necessitating a new application at each stroke to the quickly dried matter.[42]

Gee took this program and applied it to a range of genre subjects. Some of them were classroom subjects, but paintings like the two versions of *Park Bench*, one with the figures close up and the other with them seated at the end of a long bench (pl. 10), were entirely his own motif. What he did follow consistently was the planar structure inherited from cubism and the tendency to concentrate the forms toward the center of the painting at first and then fill the whole plane, almost telescoping the move from analytic to synthetic cubism. Because of Gee's abiding interest in depicting real people whom he knew or had observed, they were always painted with their material substance intact. All his portraits are images of particular people, and if we do not know who they are, we know that each figure represents someone. Given its title, the stunning *Untitled (Mrs. Salinger in Paris)* (pl. 1), dated 1927, may have been painted in that city; if so, it is a carryover from the San Francisco paintings. Gee captured, through a complex network of forms and harmonic color passages, the intensity and concentration of the writer at her task. The small *Untitled (Audience)* (pl. 13), dated 1927, is a gem. For the backs of the heads of the viewers, who are focused on the bright figures onstage, Gee used contrasting dark passages. The paint facets are also more varied, larger in front and smaller at the rear; Gee created a sense of distance, having completely understood how scale and color make that possible, while preserving the plane. I wonder about the paintings by Degas he may have seen.

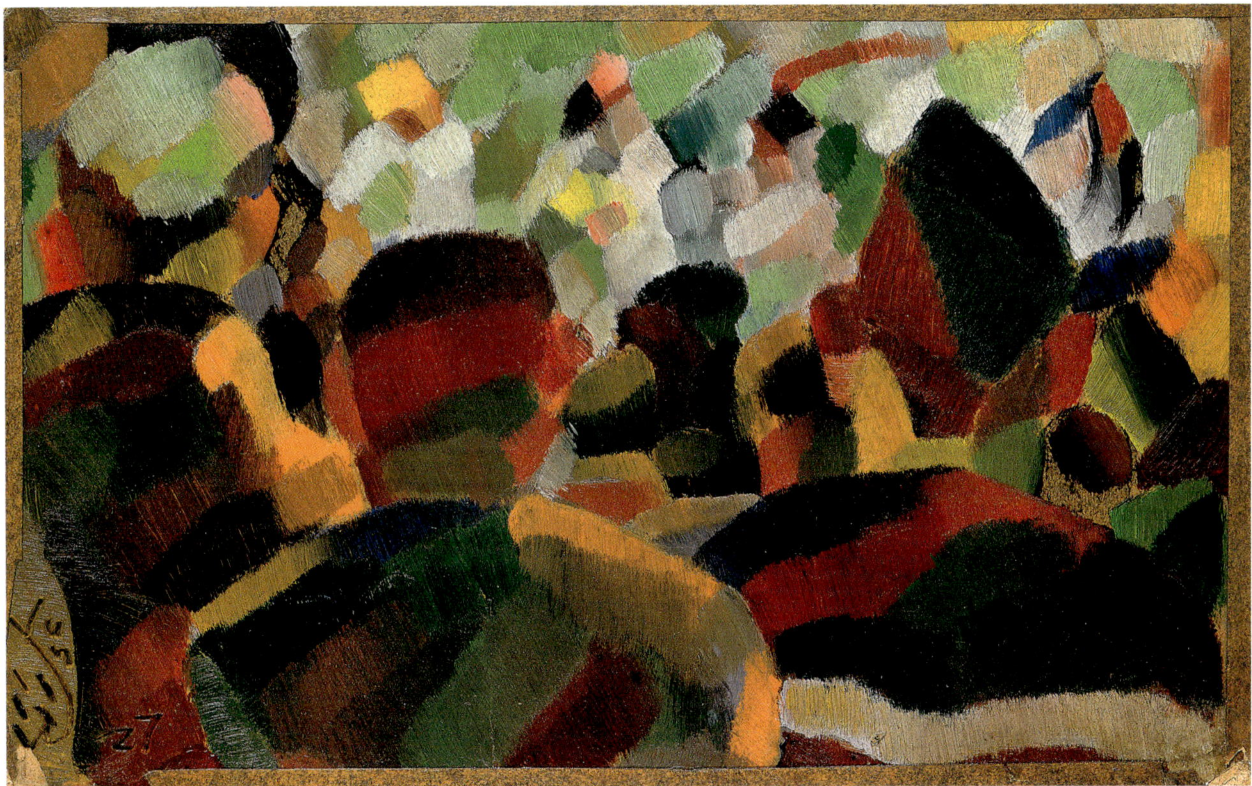

Plate 13 Yun Gee, *Untitled* (*Audience*), oil on paperboard (5 ½ in. x 8 ¾ in.), 1927.

In addition to these many genre pictures, Gee painted four subjects—*My Conception of Christ, Skull, Chinese Musicians,* and the aforementioned *Where Is My Mother*—that reveal the breadth of his attitudes and feelings, aside from his love of the everyday content he observed in the world around him.[43]

> [*Skull*] is a riotous but controlled symphony of cadmiums, ochers, earth greens, cobalts, crimsons, magentas, and black and white, producing a powerful image of energy emanating from the central cavity of the mouth. This is no decorative synchromy but an evocation of the radiant force residing in the human skull that bears comparison with the work of the American painters Arthur Dove or Georgia O'Keeffe, who give to natural objects mysterious powers and encapsulated energies.[44]

Chinese Musicians, even more than *Skull,* comes close to being almost completely abstract: a head and perhaps part of an instrument can be identified in the rhythmic shapes that sweep through the panel. Among all the other interests that Gee pursued, music was dominant, and rhythmic syncopations radiate from this painting as they do from other vividly realized works from these early years.[45]

Where Is My Mother (pl. 2)—another dynamic canvas, painted in darker shades—includes Gee's self-portrait with mustache, beret, and white tears running down the figure's cheeks. Two other, partial portraits rise from the bottom edge to meet Gee's full self-image. One can only guess at who these figures represent—perhaps brothers and a sister Gee left behind, but probably not Gee himself, as others have suggested, because there is no mustache on the face of the figure closest to his, and its features seem to be those of a woman. The heads repeat the formal strategy of repetition that Gee uses in another painting from around this time, *My Conception of Christ*, in which Christ's head appears three times; "because [Gee] believed that Christ was never static," rhythm was a means of showing the movement vital to this concept.[46] Gee's depiction of Christ is one that portrays Christ's active presence in a modern world. A few years later, he would paint Confucius in a similar way.

Where Is My Mother depicts the ship that took Gee away from his mother and the rest of his family in China, across the ocean to America; apart from one brother, the world traveler never saw his family members again. He did not return to China, as his father and his other brother had done, not even to visit, and yet he longed for his mother, and he revered China all his life. This complex painting combines, in harmonic unity, a futurist framework, abstract shapes, and a fairly realistic portrait of Gee. I know of few other modern paintings in the cubist mode with such heartfelt content, and this one was painted by a twenty-year-old with less than two years of art school. The organizational device that Gee used in this painting may be related to similar devices in Chinese landscape painting, or to artworks of the late medieval period and the early Renaissance, with the main subject below and close to the picture plane, and the narrative elements—in this case, the remembered image of the mother, left behind in the country from which the traveler departed—placed above and made smaller, to suggest distance.[47]

Gee's love of his mother may have made him responsive to other women as well, since he painted wonderful pictures of them all his life, from the aforementioned *Female Portrait* and *Untitled (Mrs. Salinger in Paris)* (pl. 1) to his paintings of Paule de Reuss during his first trip to Paris, *Madam Gabriel Perreux* (pl. 14) during the second, and Helen Wimmer in the 1930s and perhaps again in *Hospital Court* (pl. 5), dated October 9, 1951. The painting *Linda Darnell* is from the same year, and although the subject was imaged as glamorous, she was also painted as a real person.[48] Often Gee portrayed women as fully present, as people he admired; at other times, in his many drawings and watercolors and a few paintings of the nude, his depictions are more in keeping with the usual male studies of women that are on the edge of erotica. There is no denying that Gee loved women that way as well.

Women are often depicted in his many drawings, but there are all kinds of subjects, drawn in different linear modes. In San Francisco, Gee's cubist-style drawings in charcoal and ink wash, pencil, and colored crayon are at first a student's work from the model, and the earliest of these are dated 1925; then,

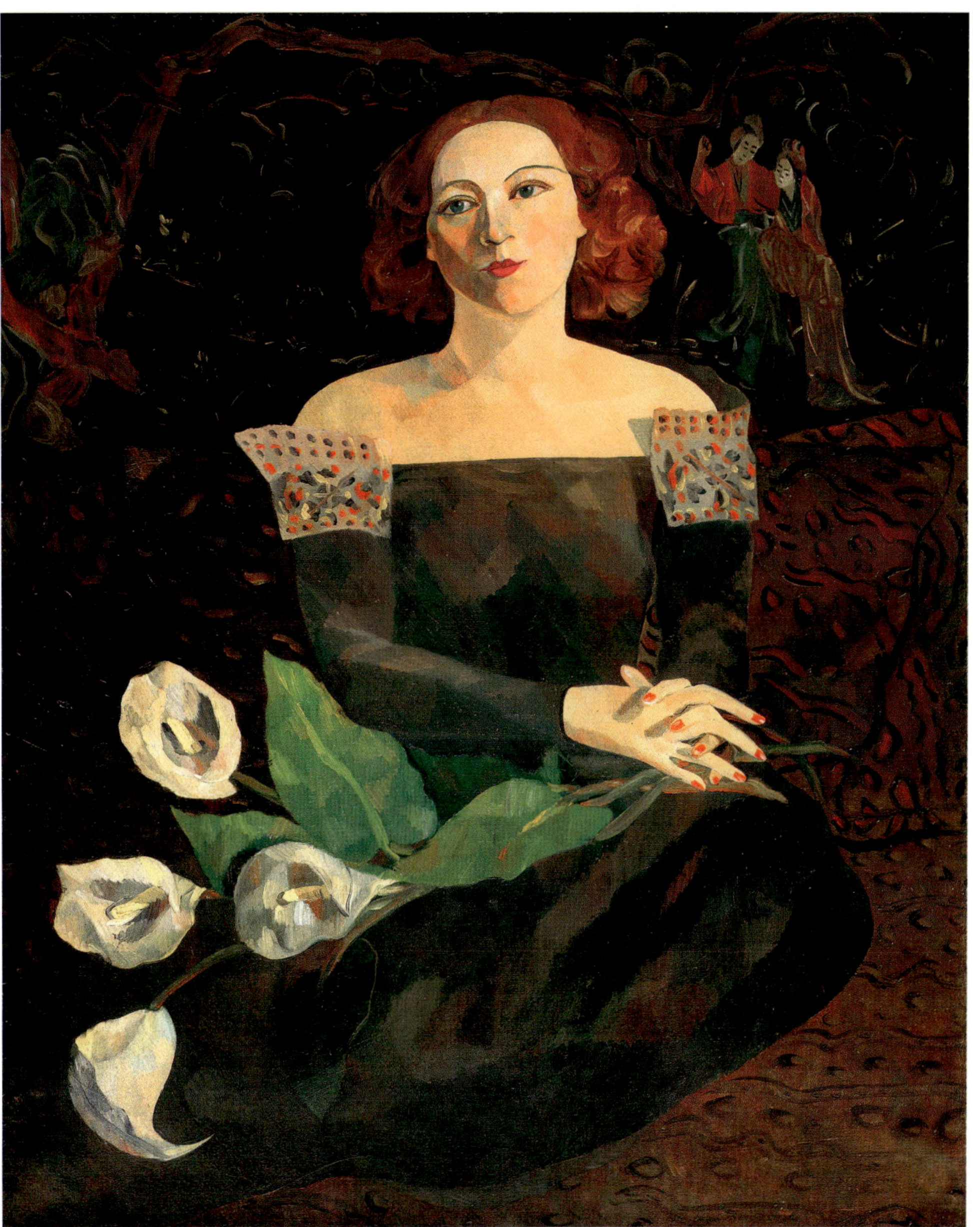

Plate 14 Yun Gee, *Madam Gabriel Perreux*, oil on canvas (36 1/8 in. x 28 3/4 in.), 1937.

in the latter part of 1926 and in 1927, come wonderful portraits and cityscapes, fully realized pictures by an artist in command of his drawing media. One drawing of an abstract walking figure—the figure repeated four times—clearly shows Gee's understanding of futurist structure. It may have been an exercise for the type of stick figures that appear in plate 11, *San Francisco Street Scene with Construction Workers.*

And then there is what might be the earliest of Gee's political drawings, *China and Manchuria* (fig. 1.5, p. 33). Executed in that semicubist style of the late 1920s, and different from the more linear drawings made in the 1930s, it seems to reference a particular event. As far as I can tell, it may have been a response to the desire of Sun Yat-sen, and then of the Kuomintang from 1927 on, to further absorb Manchuria and subdue the Mongols, already dispersed into provinces like Jehol that China had "normalized" as Chinese.[49] In the pencil drawing, a large figure holding a hammer, and dressed in a coat and hat like those worn by the Communists in Russia, has his arm over the shoulder of a Chinese peasant. A smaller, beastlike figure holding a sword may represent the hated Japanese.[50] "Manchuria" is written on a maplike form partially covering the face of the barbarian, and the words "Jehol" and "China" appear beneath the leg of the peasant. It is a very strong image, and whatever its specific meaning, it illustrates that Gee's commitment to political action was an aspect of his art from the beginning. He continued to produce such drawings through the 1930s and 1940s, although I think this very early example is one of his best.

Gee seems to have sold seventy or so of these works made in San Francisco in his first one-person show, which took place at the Modern Gallery on Montgomery Street in November 1926. With Otis Oldfield, he had helped to found the gallery, a cooperative venture involving ten artists.[51] Gee exhibited in the gallery's first group show, and his one-person exhibition was the gallery's first. It was there that he met the Prince and Princess Achille Murat, who encouraged Gee to go to Paris, where they owned a gallery. They obviously thought that Gee's work would be well received in Paris. Although he seems to have left art school in October 1926, he continued to paint and exhibit in San Francisco before following their advice.[52]

What a time for Gee to be in Paris, and to study with teachers who were familiar with the accomplishments of so many avant-garde artists, particularly in that city but also in the rest of Europe! Northern California, more than New York at that time, responded to the impact of the latest "isms" in European art. Given Gee's desire for everything modern, he was more than predisposed to embrace them wholeheartedly. It is quite an achievement that he did so, quickly and seriously, producing a body of work that could stand comparison with the best painting produced on the West Coast in the 1920s. What is even more impressive is that, although he was formally influenced by what was going on in San Francisco, his humane perception that people are people everywhere, and that the small things that comprise everyday life are what should be recorded, was never undermined. Perhaps he passed on to his daughter, Li-lan, his vision about the profundity of the quotidian, since it is the dominant content of her painting.

What was also remarkable about this stage of the young painter's creative work was his ability to absorb a foreign tradition, with few traces of his native culture apparent in his painting. He accomplished this while still rejoicing in being Chinese, and yet he rejected—at least while he was in San Francisco—the blending of elements of East and West. Yun Gee, at a very early stage, was able to achieve a coherence of subject and form through his understanding of international modernism, a level of understanding achieved by only a few other transnational artists, and by no one else from China of whom I am aware. He would show the same acuity in Paris as he took in other aspects of modernism.

Painting in Paris: The Lyrical Period (1927–1930)

By the time Gee was twenty-three years old, he had been given four one-person exhibitions in Paris, at major galleries: the Galerie Carmine, in November of 1927; the Galerie des Artistes et Artisans, in April 1928; the Galerie Ferme la Nuit (owned by the Princess Murat), also in 1928; and the most prestigious of the venues, the Galerie Bernheim-Jeune, in June 1929, an exhibition that Raymond Duncan reviewed for a Parisian magazine.[53] Almost all the paintings Gee showed at these exhibitions had been made in Paris, and they covered all his subjects and styles, from *Confucius (Chinese Sage)* (pl. 3) to cityscapes like *Houses in the Latin Quarter* and genre scenes like *Big Robbers and Little Robbers*.[54] Gee was also in important group shows like the Salon des Indépendants, and in a review from February 1929 his *Confucius (Chinese Sage)* was singled out as the most interesting painting in an exhibition.[55] Other reviews of Gee's work were quite positive, particularly the one by Lou Benoish, and many of them over emphasized the "blend of East and West" as the most important quality.[56] Although there are more than forty paintings (that we know of) that Gee made in Paris, only about ten are of identifiable Chinese subjects or have themes symbolic of China. In a few, Gee used cubist passages to build the painting; in others, he used a fluid linear style that could be associated with Chinese painting, but the way in which he rendered the subjects reflected his own inventions. Unfortunately, most of these were pictures that Gee repainted in the 1950s, and it is difficult to make out the original colors and subjects, although there are photographs of some of them. There are also drawings and watercolors with Chinese content, executed in the same fluid style, one that could be identified with calligraphy. It is easier to decide that Gee was a much more creative painter in the works showing the modernist style he developed in San Francisco and Paris than in the works he produced with Chinese subjects, but at least in the example of *Confucius (Chinese Sage)*, to which I will return, he successfully united Chinese content and Western modernism.

Why did Gee abandon his San Francisco style of painting so quickly after arriving in Paris? I think that a certain pressure to be "Oriental" may have come into play, since the intellectual and artistic group he traveled with was very interested in the art and ideas of the exotic East. The portrait of Princess Achille Murat, his patron, is quite significant in relation to this interest. The rest of Gee's work is indebted to some of the painters identified with the School of Paris, given Gee's renewed interest in Cézanne, whom he was studying very seriously in these years. It was also Gee's desire to absorb the latest ways of painting that he encountered in the cities where he lived, even if that meant doing work that at first sight seemed more derivative; a new emphasis on aesthetic refinement colored the best of his Paris paintings as he perfected his craft. Painting of this kind was among the preferred modes in Paris at the time, and it was a reaction to the more forceful and experimental nature of the years that had been dominated by cubism.

What was the Paris art scene that Gee engaged? From the first surrealist exhibitions, in June 1925, emphasis on the irrational, the internal, and the symbolic had been permeating the Paris art world. Also in vogue was a reassertion of the private, the domestic, and the introspective, which were characteristic of artists identified with the Nabis and with the symbolist and art nouveau movements from the turn of the century. A retrenchment from the dynamic advances of fauvism, cubism, and dada could be observed even among painters who had been some of the prime creators of these still resounding movements.

It was a wonderful coincidence to have looked again at these paintings in an exhibition held in New York at the Metropolitan Museum of Art while I was writing this chapter. I also consulted the Metropolitan's collection of School of Paris for an exhibition in 2000, to get a more recent feel for what Gee may have been looking at.[57] Matisse exhibited his sensuous nudes and hothouse interiors, filled with flowers and exotic textiles. The Met's *Reclining Odalisque* of 1926 is a prime example of the outrageous orientalism occasioned by Matisse's trip to Morocco. Picasso's monumental figures of women metamorphosed into complex images incorporating the physical and the psychological, often in one encapsulating curve. Bonnard painted his wife in seductive, obsessively observed interiors and garden views, and Vuillard's intimate scenes of domestic life were highly regarded; and then there were the languid nudes and portraits of Modigliani. Working in a lyrical mode were artists like Marie Laurencin, Jules Pascin, and Maurice Utrillo, who was painting his moody "tourist" scenes of Paris. André Lhote, the intelligent and perseverant painter and critic, had departed from his earlier synthetic cubist style to make still lifes, portraits, and scenes in a simplified Cézannesque manner. It was with these painters that Gee exhibited, and his work was often compared with theirs.

Chia Chi Jason Wang suggests that in Paris "Yun Gee settled down to explore the kinship between East and West," and he goes on to say, "Dreamscapes, memories, self-portraits and subjects drawn from traditional Chinese culture [became] prominent areas of thematic concern during the Paris period"; he then reads the painting *How I Saw Myself in a Dream* as a "depiction of Gee wandering the streets of a foreign land in a dream that hints at Freud's theories on the interpretation of dreams" and as "an attempt to engage in self-analysis or psychoanalysis through painting."[58] Although I agree with aspects of Wang's view of Gee's Paris paintings, I think that Wang may build upon too few of them, and that he may overdetermine the Freudian aspects of Gee's work. *How I Saw Myself in a Dream* is the only painting I know of from the Paris years that may conform to Wang's interpretation.[59]

I think that Gee responded as he did in San Francisco, and as he would do again in New York, to aspects of the prevailing currents, and that this reaction impinged on his usual subjects. His Paris subjects seem to be the same as they were in San Francisco—street scenes and portraits—but in Paris they were often painted on canvas or on a wood panel instead of on paper. Gee used a darker series of color tones, and the passages, while still somewhat cubist, are softened by a diagonal brushstroke that is repeated all through the canvas. I think that *Pantheon and Workmen*, for example, painted on paperboard, is transitional, a softer version of the more faceted paintings that Gee did in 1927 in San Francisco.[60] The view is from one of the narrower side streets, like the rue d'Ulm, and the painting still includes the busy stick-figure workman, but the color relations are more harmonious, and the diagonal brushstrokes are more insistent. They seem muted by the change in light from San Francisco to Paris. Then the signature workmen almost disappear, and the street scenes are often unpopulated. The mood is sober, as in *My First Impression of Paris*, where the populated street scene, painted from the artist's window, and his bottle of wine and his glass on the sill tilt as a segue into the kaleidoscopic view of the figures and buildings.[61] This genre scene suggests that a first encounter with this great cosmopolitan center is, to say the least, disorienting. Gee also depicted lovers embracing in public—too much sin for Gee, as he wrote in his prose poem "Confucius."

While Gee's paintings are primarily city views like *Place Maubert* (pl. 15), *Notre Dame* (pl. 16), *Rue Pétrarque* (*House with Gate*), and *Caretaker's Cottage,* a few are more like landscapes with buildings—a Cézanne motif—and several are interior views, like the beautiful *The Red Chair* (pl. 17), *Cat and the Rain,* and the justly famous self-portrait, *The Flute Player (Self-Portrait)* (pl. 18). These quiet scenes are meditative in mood; if a musical metaphor is appropriate, in Paris it is the sound of the flute that resonates, not the controlled cacophony of many instruments that seems to resound in the San Francisco works (*Chinese Musicians* is emblematic.) I do not believe that these scenes suggest deep anxieties; rather, they are in part a response to the painting that was practiced in Paris in the late 1920s and early 1930s. As for dreamscapes, memories, self-portraits, and subjects from Chinese traditional culture, I think that Gee was trying out different motifs in these paintings, but they constitute only a small fraction of his Paris work, and of his entire oeuvre; these are less frequent subjects than those used in the prevailing

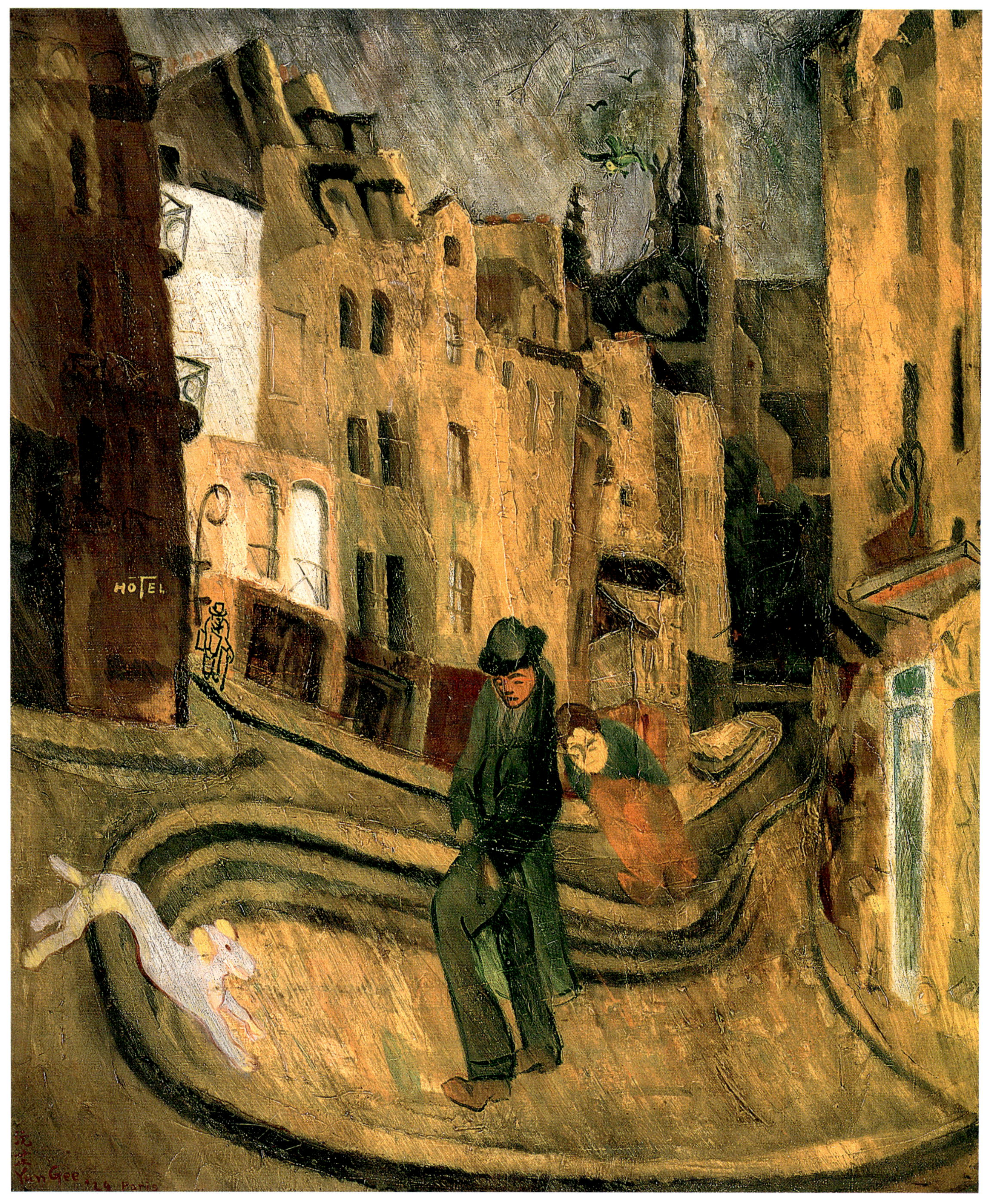
HÔTEL
沅芷
Yun Gee
Paris

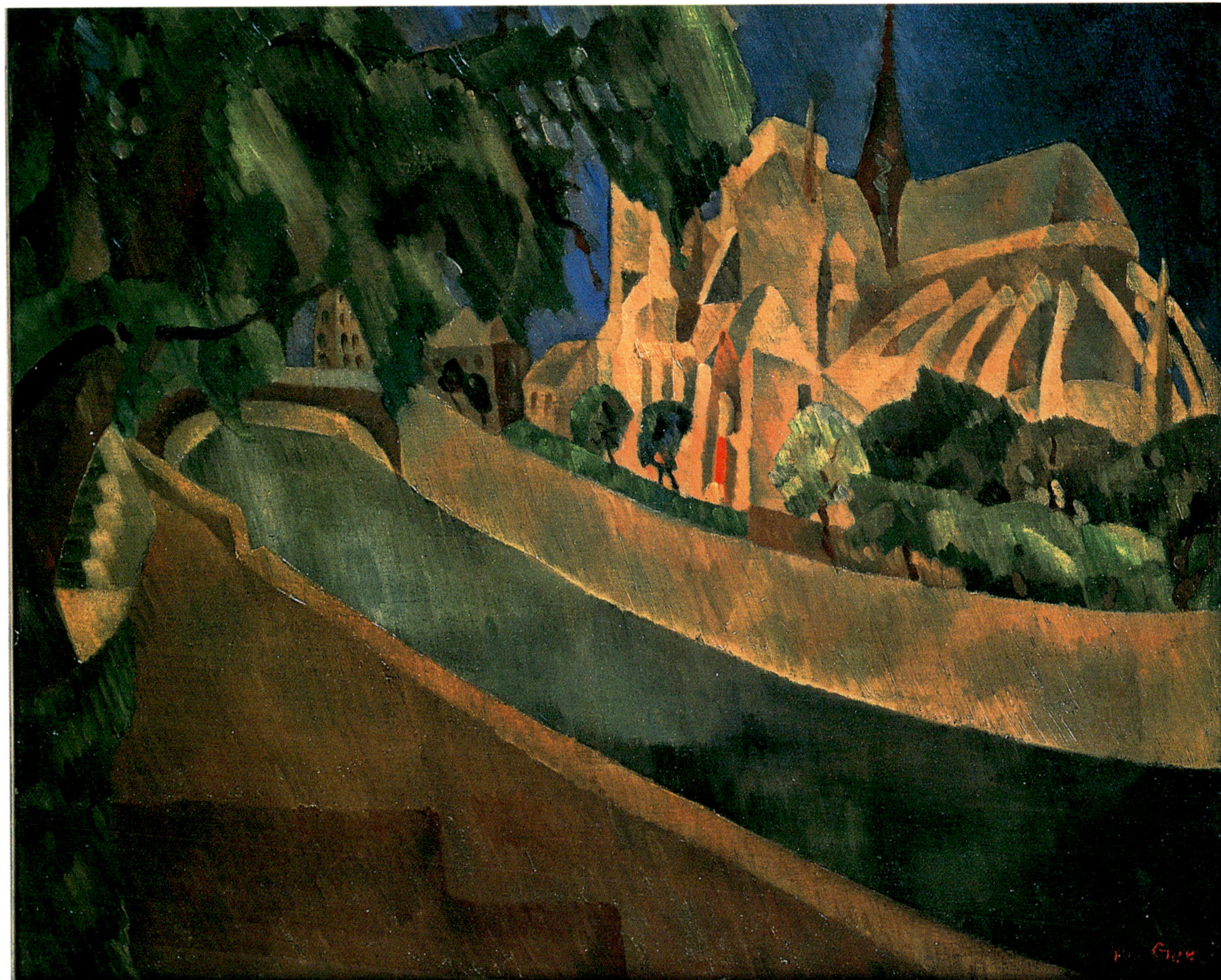

(opposite)
Plate 15 Yun Gee, *Place Maubert*, oil on canvas (28 ⅞ in. x 23 ¾ in.), 1929.

(above)
Plate 16 Yun Gee, *Notre Dame*, oil on canvas (23 ½ in. x 28 ½ in.), 1928.

cityscapes and landscapes. It is also true that some lost paintings, as well as sketches and watercolors, have titles indicating Chinese themes; new works by Yun Gee are being discovered as I write, and perhaps that fact will alter my understanding of this period of his oeuvre.

Although Gee was looking closely at Cézanne, his own paintings are gentler, more intimate, like those of Matisse and Bonnard. *Portrait of Paule de Reuss, The Red Chair*, and *Cat and the Rain*, all painted in 1928, evoke this personal note.[62] The first of these three was painted on paperboard, in cadmiums and ochers, and is a beautiful portrayal of Gee's wife captured in a mood of reverie. In *The Red Chair* (pl. 17), gently billowing curtains frame the gray-blue sky viewed through an open window, and a pair of slippers before a cadmium red chair references a departed occupant. The subtle handling of transparent planes recalls Delaunay's window series, while the air outside, in contrast to the intimate glow of the interior, is a softer and gentler version of those color evocations of the outside, in relation to interior privacy, that are among Matisse's finest work. Either as part of the curtain or as a

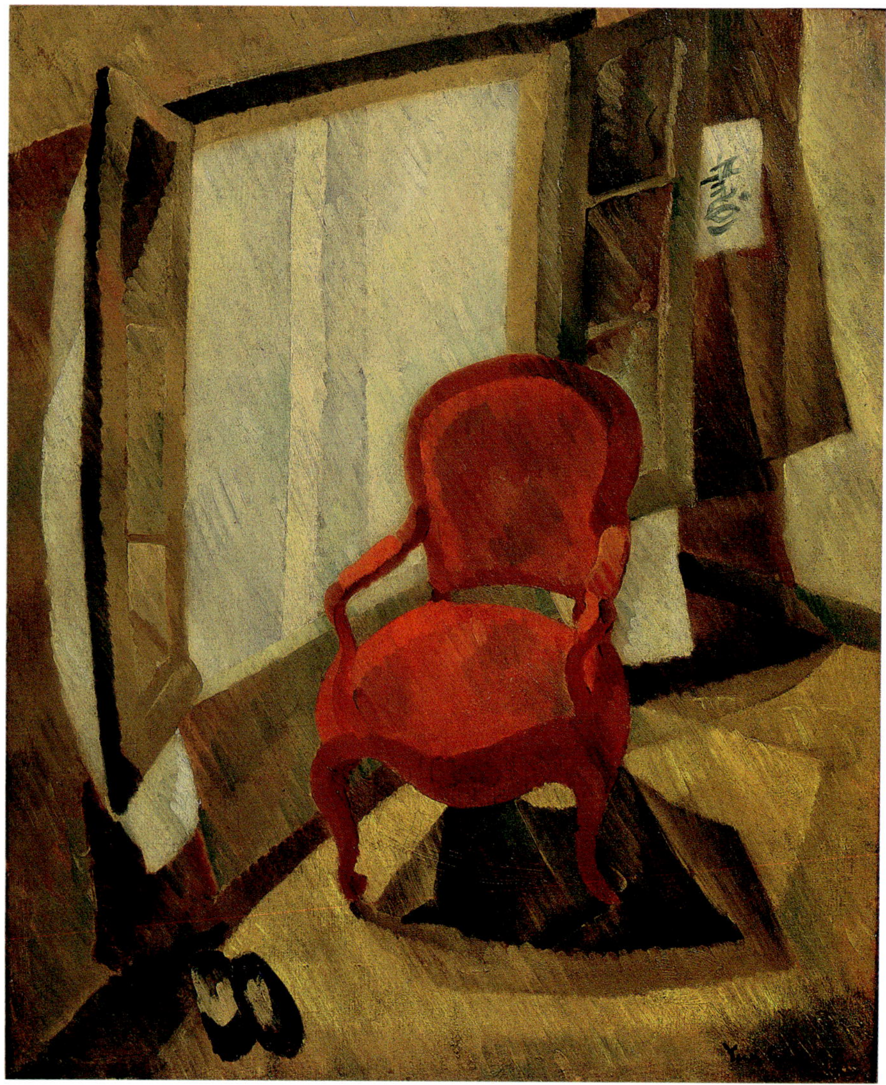

Plate 17 Yun Gee, ***The Red Chair***, **oil on canvas (28 $^{7}/_{8}$ in. x 23 $^{5}/_{8}$ in.), c. 1928. Photo credit: Kevin Ryan**

picture on the wall, Gee wrote "drawing" in Chinese characters, perhaps as a pun or as a subtle reference to the Chinese tradition that makes little distinction among calligraphy, poetry, and painting. *Cat and the Rain* is moodier, with muted colors and novel spatial complexities. In his cartoonlike manner, Gee drew a perfect cat grimace on the curled-up animal that looks out at the viewer. The apartment windows across the street are open, and one can barely make out a plant, or perhaps a person; there is an open book left on the sill, and a lingering sense of occupancy. The rain falls; it is very quiet.

The Flute Player (Self-Portrait) (pl. 18) is a picture about serene moments of internal harmony. The subject, in tints and shades of green and ocher, is seated in his red chair, playing the Chinese flute, with his brushes in a vase behind him and his pipes pegged on the wall. The flute is the dominant diagonal that all the other lines parallel, and it leads to the brushes: musician and painter united. There is a red jug on the table along with five small red

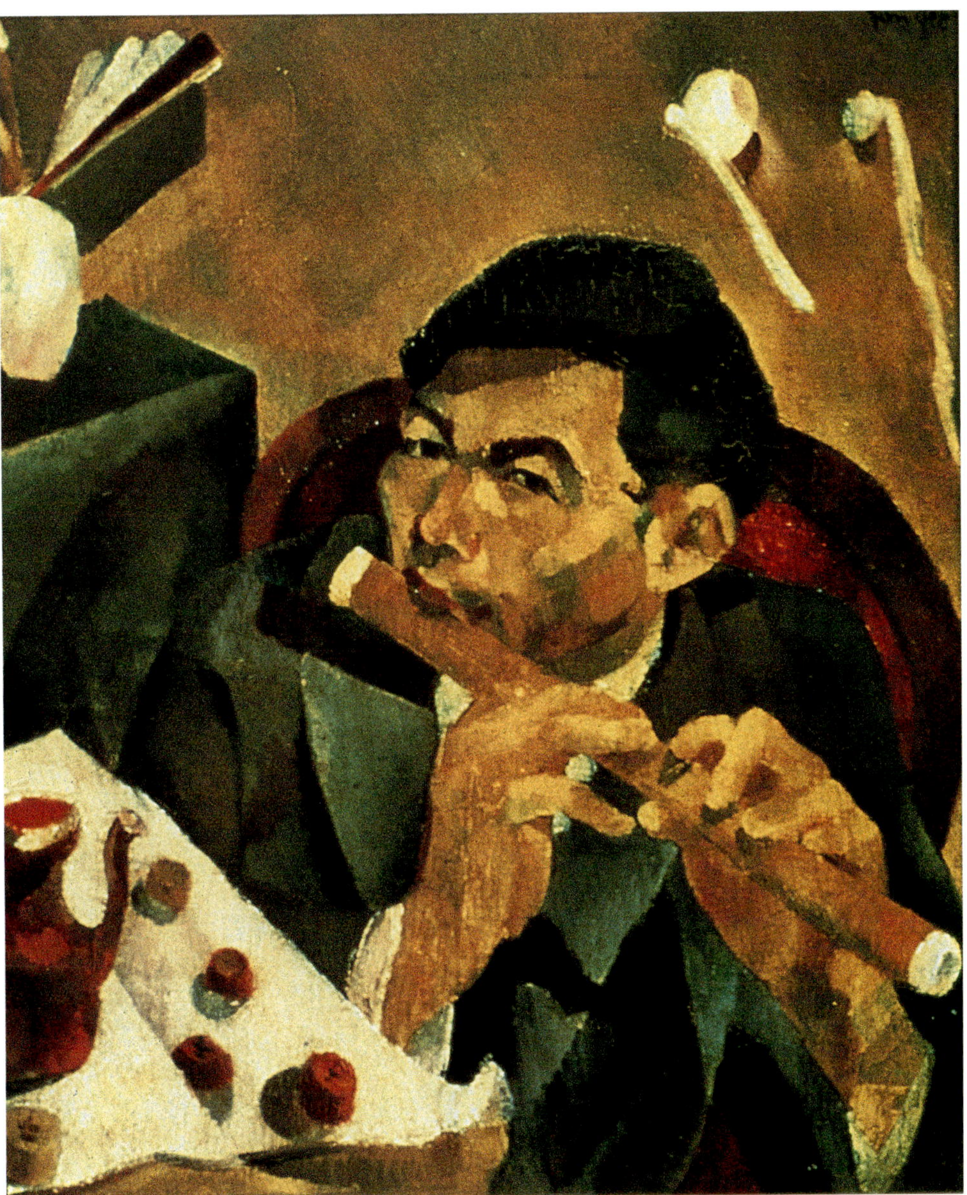

Plate 18 Yun Gee, ***The Flute Player* (*Self-Portrait*)**, oil on canvas (23 in. x 19 in.), 1928.

and ocher shapes, what some have described as apples (an homage to Cézanne?), or perhaps they are small candles. They are there in an almost harmonic counterpart to Gee's playing, like rhythmic notations. *The Flute Player (Self-Portrait)*, admired by a broad audience whenever it is exhibited, encapsulates Gee's humanistic desire to portray a harmony that would appeal universally by imaging an event rooted in the quotidian and the specific.

In a similar manner, but now using a scene observed from outside, Gee painted *Place Maubert* (pl. 15) in 1929, a neighborhood perhaps like the ones Gee lived in. At Place Maubert, a series of old streets come together in one of those particular French locations that still exist, although they are becoming rarer. The colors in this painting are somewhat darker, and the rhythmic, linear component is stronger than in the interior scenes. I used to think the painting was grim, but cleaning off the layers of varnish revealed a brighter scene, with yellow ocher predominating. Gee painted the life of the street with sympathy and humor. The three figures and the dog are pure genre, with Gee's signature cartoon man coming around the corner carrying a newspaper, and the large man in the foreground romping with his dog. There is a small figure behind him that may be a workman, a pickpocket, a beggar, or all three. Is the man with the dog pulling something out of his pocket to give to this ambiguous figure, is he searching for something that has just been taken from him, or is he pulling out a treat for his dog? If one can talk about an artist's arriving at a mature stage in the development of his painting, that stage is surely where Gee was when he painted these Paris works—and he was now only twenty-two years old.[63]

In contrast to the genre subjects, Gee painted a series of portraits and a few paintings with Chinese and/or symbolic subjects—unfortunately, some were painted over later on. *Chinese Man in Hat*, with its introspective, ambivalent lines of verse (quoted in chapter 1), may contain references to the literati tradition as reinterpreted in relation to a modernist portrait; it is close in color and form to *The Flute Player (Self-Portrait)* and was probably painted in 1928. A larger portrait, in oil on canvas, of Princess Achille Murat must once have been a wonderful work in the lyrical style, if the poem that Gee wrote about this painting can be referenced. This is one of the works that Gee later painted over with strong triangles, perhaps during his second trip to Paris, to bring it into relationship with his now fully formed theory of Diamondism. In so doing, he seems to have obliterated some of the subtle brushwork that is still visible in parts of the portrait, although this remains a compelling work. The princess wears an Eastern-style lounging robe and holds a fan in her left hand while her elegant right arm arches over her weightless but poised aristocratic head. *The Poetess* (*Paule de Reuss*), one of four paintings made on silk to approximate a scroll, is also elegant and very lyrical, like Gee's portrait of the princess, and it, too, was repainted, but probably in the 1950s, when Gee sometimes added strong outlines to the softer images he had painted earlier. In the upper right-hand corner of the original *Princess Achille Murat*, Gee made a small painting of a Chinese face with a long thin mustache. This figure may have represented Gee himself, or it may have been a stand-in, but Gee later obliterated the features, conceivably in a dreadful mood of self-denial.

And then there are the paintings with Chinese themes and symbolic content: *One Who Loves Himself*; *How I Saw Myself in a Dream*; *Confucius (Chinese Sage)*; *Harmonie Universelle (Lao-tzu)*; *Lao-tzu Taking a Sunbath*; *Butterflies: Dream of Chuang-Tze*; and *The Hundred Beauties*. There are also the four scroll-like paintings on silk, mounted on board: *The Charm of Music*, *The Poetess*, *The Resurrection*, and *Yang Kwei Fei at Her Bath*.[64] If Gee was truly a citizen of the world, what might have accounted for the emergence of Chinese themes in his painting at that time? I have already suggested that the interest of Gee's Parisian friends in things Oriental, in mysticism, and in Daoism may have encouraged Gee to express in his paintings aspects of being Chinese that seemed less compelling when he was a radical modernist in San Francisco. But Gee always maintained his love of his Chinese heritage and his belief in the depth of its revolutionary, spiritual, and creative accomplishments. David Wang is surely right when he says that Gee, "being Chinese and much versed in Chinese cultural upbringing," had "rooted his moral principles in Chinese culture."[65] As I suggested earlier, this grounding in his native roots provided the springboard for his ability to absorb aspects of other cultures. For the most part, however, Gee did not combine elements of East and West but painted populist images in an international modernist mode, and Chinese themes in an obviously "Chinese" manner. I also think that the resurgence of the Chinese-oriented work may signify that negotiations between what was native and what was transnational were part of a daily struggle, particularly at times when the pressure to be "Oriental" may have been overt. This possibility would also account for paintings containing certain themes that would be considered conservative for a radical, a child of the revolution, and a modernist. The revolutionaries in particular forswore Confucius and Laozi, just because their teachings could be considered responsible for the status quo in China.

What Gee did in his monumental painting *Confucius (Chinese Sage)* (pl. 3)—about four feet high and over three feet wide—was to envision a Chinese sage for modern times. In this work, he achieved something unique, but not only by synthesizing aspects of East and West, even if the painting was highly praised for just that reason when it was exhibited, particularly when it was shown at the prestigious Salon des Indépendants in February 1929. By that time, aspects of modernism were no longer the exclusive property of Western artists; in fact, modernism was practiced worldwide. Gee had been trained as a modernist, and if he applied modernist techniques to a traditional Chinese subject, the painting was none the less modern. This painting of Confucius—not as damaged as other paintings except for its layers of varnish and the removal of the calligraphic quotations from the pre-Confucian *Spring and Autumn Annals*—depicts the Chinese sage in his study, with his books and writing implements around him. Interestingly enough, according to Wang, the inscription was not "a mere passage" but "a shorter version of Gee's essay . . . that tells of Gee's understanding of Confucius' philosophy as an antecedent of modern Darwinism."[66] In that essay, Gee had written:

> Alas! The Scholars look upon Confucius as only a teacher of the past, but I recognize in him the teacher of all time. For him politics revolved itself into

Justice and Righteousness. His principle of the survival of the fittest has been necessitated by modern science. Thus his greatness was not only shown in his own time but has returned to this modern age.[67]

Instead of a more traditional depiction of the sage, Gee created a modern image through the use of encapsulating rhythmic contours and faceted planes that constructed the figure as a dynamic and present force. In theme and scale, this forceful painting is different from Gee's paintings of genre subjects, but in its embodiment of a universal ethics, as personified by Confucius, it expresses the same interest in the humble and the everyday.

Confucius (Chinese Sage) was probably painted in 1928, whereas many of the more symbolic works still to be discussed in this chapter seem to be from 1929, when Gee turned away from abstract facets to construct the figure in linear outlines, and with a much more restricted palette. It may be that these works also came after his trip to Spain and the awakening of his interest in the more somber palettes of the Spanish old masters that he saw there.[68] His self-portrait *The Blue Yun* was probably painted during or after that trip, and the absence of abstract color facets, and even of noticeable brushstrokes, is quite a departure from any of his previous methods.[69] In light and dark browns, with a background of blue-green, the figure of Gee is shown looking in a mirror and painting himself almost as an old master. Although this is a relatively small canvas, the presence of the subject is powerfully rendered, in part because of the shapely brimmed hat. And yet, in the wonderful *Madrid Landscape with a White Building*—a harmony of ochers, greens, browns, and reds, reflected in the white of the house—is so French (even though the canvas was probably painted in Spain) that Gee could have passed for someone who had been trained in Paris and painted there all his life; the small brushstrokes reveal that accomplished Parisian touch. Gee seemed to absorb, in the flesh, the cultural and artistic environments in which he lived at different times, in part because he was a creative intellectual with many diverse interests.

Thus some of Gee's other paintings with symbolic content may likewise be responsive to French Surrealism.[70] André Breton was writing a series of articles defending the surreal, and *The First Manifesto of Surrealism* was written in 1924, with *Nadja*, a lyric meditation on love, following in 1928. André Masson, among others, was painting his unconscious automatic gestures in an abstract, fluid style.[71] It seems probable that the surrealist movement would have stimulated exciting discussion in the intellectual group to which Gee belonged. He may have found this atmosphere inspiring for his paintings of symbolic and Chinese themes in a flowing, linear style. One such work, titled *One Who Loves Himself*, is dated 1929 in what seems to be Gee's handwriting on the back of a photograph of the painting. *Harmonie Universelle (Lao-tzu)* is also a painting in the curvilinear, lyrical style and was exhibited at the Salon des Indépendants in February 1929. A canvas of the same size as *Confucius (Chinese Sage),* it shows Laozi leaving Han Pass on a blue bull. Laozi preached the gospel of "intelligent inaction"; for this philosophy, and for his withdrawal from the capital because of its decadence, and his departure for regions unknown, he was an inspiration to Gee. Whatever intelligent inaction may actually have meant to Gee, I think it governed his political and moral life after his more radical days in San Francisco; it represented a culture that became the basis of the universal harmony that Gee always longed for. The search for peace and harmony is also the subject of another painting, *Lao-tzu Taking a Sunbath,* a large canvas that may also have been painted in Paris; an inscription on the painting tells about Confucius' visit to the philosopher. The canvas is also signed "Blue Five Continents Gee."[72] Gee wrote about Laozi many times and saw him as the greatest of the mystic philosophers. His conception of "the Way" and of "doing nothing" in order to achieve peace and relaxation was the basis of Gee's advertisement, written in the 1950s, to announce instruction in Laozi's methods of physical and mental relief.[73] In the second part of Gee's poem, he identifies with the sage as a model of perseverance:

He, going about the world alone
with the Three Treasures from ancient
times down to now when men
have chosen to live on-
ly with laughter and weakness, came forth out
of the cave, a hunter, and journeyed out-
side of things. Then I forgot heroes and
men full of power as
well as the model of
all thieves for one who obeys and is pure.
 I am not afraid to
 express this tiny thought in my picture.[74]

Christ was another sage for Gee, and in the one Christian-themed painting that I know of from Paris, the large *Resurrection,* for which there is also an ink drawing (fig. 2.2, p. 76), Gee renders transparent the elongated figures of Christ, one overlying the other, the repetition a device already used in the more abstract *My Conception of Christ*, which he had painted in San Francisco. Gee used abstract passages in *My Conception of Christ*, concentrating on the three heads of Christ close to the picture plane to stress Christ's material presence, whereas in *Resurrection* he emphasized transcendence. In the latter painting, the colors are again subdued and almost transparent, ocher being the most prominent, and there is a wonderful luminosity fitting the miraculous event. The sketch for this painting helps me understand the

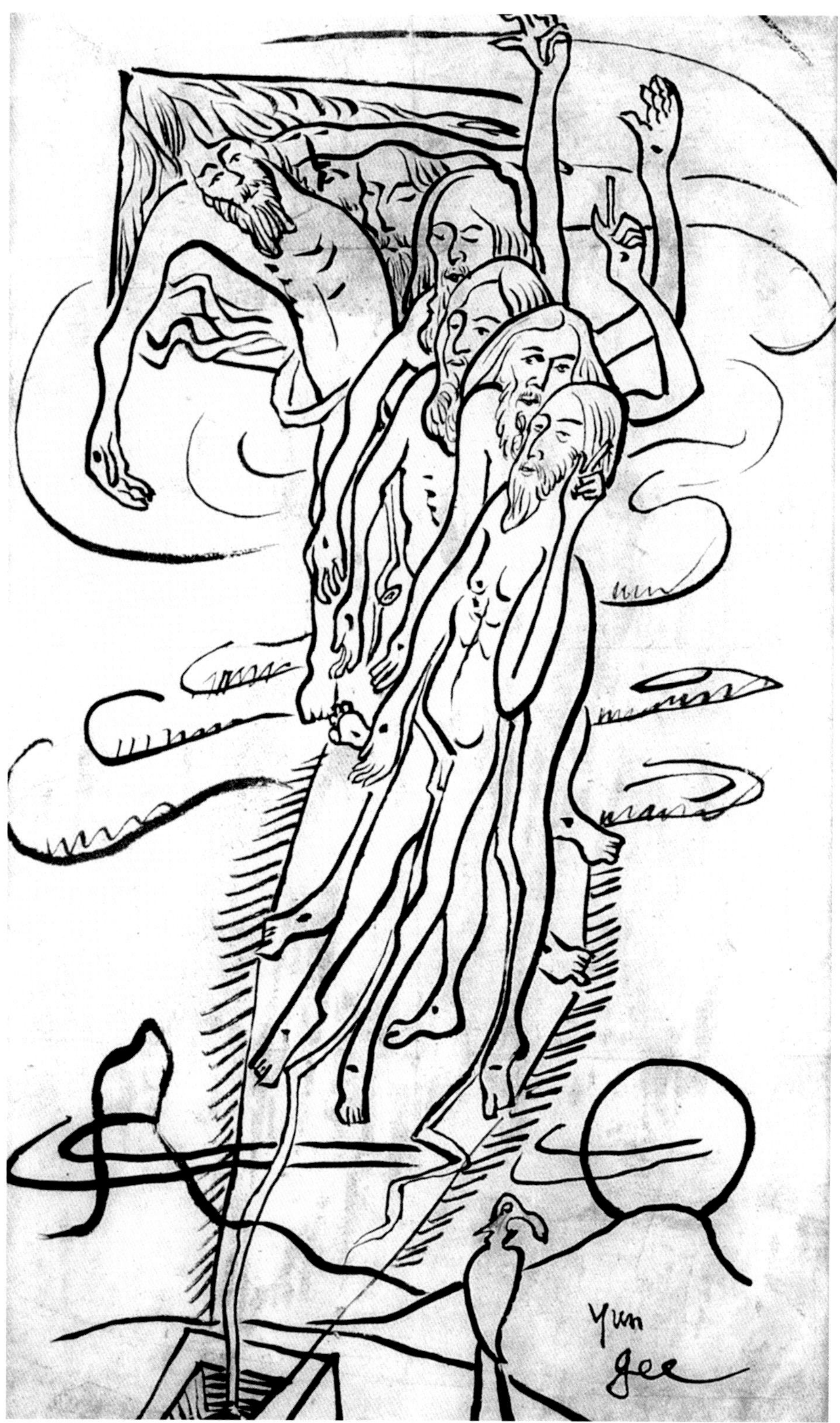

2.2 Yun Gee, study for *Resurrection*, ink drawing (12 3/4 x 8 3/4 in.), 1930.

complexity of Gee's idea because the rhythm of the figures can be read from the top down as well as from bottom to top. While the figures rise from the coffin below, the resurrected Christ above is depicted in the position of the crucified body. This is a singular treatment of the theme, as far as I can tell, but again it illustrates Gee's commitment to the human nature of Christ even in the moment of resurrection. This whole series of paintings is in keeping with Gee's later writings, which explore universal themes as an expression of the desire to create a new spiritual philosophy for modern times. It was in this sense that Gee approached the different cultures that became part of his lived experiences. This was a monumental task, probably more successfully achieved in his genre paintings than in the symbolic works.[75]

In his earlier work done in San Francisco, Gee's youthful enthusiasm for a "radical" modernism resulted in a coherence that makes the Paris work appear unfocused, but that may be the consequence of Gee's desire to explore the many facets of his experiences of passage afforded by his success in Paris and his growing maturity. Gee also had an uncanny ability to change his approach in view of the subjects he was painting. His formal strategies when he was painting genre subjects, portraits, and religious themes were different from those he used when engaging Chinese content. Nevertheless, a series of factors—the desire to be known, racial prejudice, economic pressure, and perhaps even his commitment to Laozi's philosophy—sometimes made him capitulate to the prevailing taste in the art centers of the cities where he lived. Thus Gee sometimes worked against his abilities, and in opposition to a vision that had emerged in San Francisco and continued to be expressed throughout his life in the production of some marvelous paintings. One painting from his first stay in New York, *Wheel "Industrial New York"* (pl. 4), exhibits the unity of subject and form that is characteristic of Gee's most exciting works, which were always portraits of people he knew and depictions of places where ordinary people live their everyday lives.

Painting in New York: The Power Period (1930–1936)

> We, today are not looking for still landscapes; we go to the street and paint the moving auto and what it symbolizes.[76]

Thus, although Gee obviously learned a great deal in Paris, the preceding quotation suggests that he was ready for a more dynamic environment, even if financial concerns were primarily what necessitated his leaving. Gee's success in Paris directed him to try his luck in New York instead of returning to San Francisco. New York, not yet the center of the art world—which it would become in the late 1940s and 1950s, partly because of immigrants after World War II—was none the less a thriving metropolis. It was where Gee, the cosmopolite, belonged, and in his early years there he found his "modern" voice on his own terms.

In the first few years, Gee was very active, not only painting and exhibiting but also working for the WPA. He also gave art classes as well as dance and music concerts to support war relief. Social realism and regionalism were in full swing, and Gee's somewhat more realistic paintings should have found a place in the New York art scene of the early 1930s. The problem was that he wedded recognizable subjects to a form of abstraction that was still too "European" for New York in that decade. It is nevertheless amazing that Gee used his knowledge to make major works that dynamically synthesized aspects of his more abstract San Francisco genre pictures with elements of the School of Paris. From this synthesis, in 1932, he painted *Wheel "Industrial New York"* (pl. 4), a major work often called his masterpiece. He did have a fairly full exhibition schedule at first, and *Wheel* was included in the mural exhibition for the 1932 opening show of the new Museum of Modern Art on Fifty-seventh Street, but the show as a whole was panned, and Gee received only a few positive comments. He had about seven solo exhibitions, which included the unveiling of his commissioned *The Last Supper* in June 1933 at St. Peter's Lutheran Church in the Bronx and several exhibitions in conjunction with benefits. He also participated in about eight group exhibitions, including one at the Brooklyn Museum and another titled The Social Viewpoint in Art at the John Reed Club in 1932. After 1934, however, he showed almost nothing but a few paintings in four of the annual exhibitions of the Society of Independent Artists. According to Helen Gee, as mentioned in chapter 1, Gee stopped painting from 1933 to 1935 and was in a serious state of depression, but there are several drawings from this period as well as many poems.[77] Toward the end of 1935 and the beginning of 1936, the artist painted three canvases of Helen (then still Helen Wimmer). They were painted in a manner that seemed to bode well for a fresh start. In 1936, he left for Paris again.

Gee made more than twenty paintings that can be dated to his first New York period, including preparatory drawings and color studies for *Wheel* and *The Last Supper*.[78] He also produced many drawings, most of them undated; some are political, others have Chinese themes and brushwork, and many are drawings and watercolors from the nude model done in a Pascin-like linear style that had come to the fore in Paris.[79] Other paintings may also be associated with this period, given their stylistic similarities, although the erratic nature of Gee's themes and painting styles sometimes makes dating almost impossible. When I look at the paintings that Gee was showing in New York in the early 1930s, I can better understand his inability to find a place in the art scene, then and later, although he kept trying.[80] A telling example of his problem was the reception of his oil studies and drawings for *The Last Supper* (fig. 1.6, p. 37) at the eighteenth annual exhibition of the Society of Independent Artists.[81]

The reviewer for the *New York Times* of May 7, 1933, began by saying that Gee's oil studies and drawings were the most ambitious pieces in the exhibition but went on to say that Gee's work was "frankly disappointing," adding, "The color indicates so feebly what this adventurous Chinese artist can do when he really wants to do something dazzling." I don't know what he was comparing these studies to—perhaps to *Wheel*—but Gee, in keeping with his subject, did use somewhat darker tones, although the color was still radiant. There was also a complaint about the difficulty of recognizing which of the figures represented in the studies was Christ. I think this reviewer did not understand that Gee's emphasis was on the humanity of Christ, and on the human reactions to the tragic news; in the composition, the oblique lines of the table all lead directly to Christ. The finished painting was positively reviewed when it was unveiled at St. Peter's Lutheran Church in 1933, but the congregation later rejected the work; it was removed and later lost.[82] Was it the combination of a traditional theme indebted to his knowledge of European art and presented in a modern manner that was unacceptable?

If I now try to make sense of what the art world may have thought about what they saw of Yun's painting, I can say that they certainly did not face a consistent body of work. Yun appeared to be all over the place, and little of his work was related to what most other artists were doing in New York. The Chinese paintings were ignored by all but Chinese reviewers, and the rest, like *The Last Supper*, were not considered to be realistic enough or to have content of redeeming social value—and Gee was still considered a Chinese artist. This was the Depression era, the 1930s; art needed to be relevant to American social needs, and American artists were the ones who should and would make it. Abstraction gave way to realism in the work of many artists, such as the supreme regionalist, Thomas Hart Benton, who nevertheless had studied in Paris in the first decade of the twentieth century and, like Gee, had been influenced by Cézanne and by abstract structure in his early work. Erika Doss wrote an excellent study of this period. She discusses the social and political scene that determined the art world's predilection for realism and its desire to retreat from "European" abstraction. But abstraction, of course, had not yet seeped into the work of more than a few artists: those who had traveled to Paris and other European art centers; some of their students, like Gee; the few artists who had been influenced by the 1913 Armory Show in New York; and those connected to Alfred Stieglitz's 291 Gallery.[83]

It was the New Deal and World War II that enabled the United States to turn away from regionalism, and any notion of a workers' society, toward a politics of liberalism, centered in nationalism, and of what was to become corporate capitalism. The regionalist desire to picture different aspects of the country, revitalized by what Benton called "producerism," was preempted by that change in the social and political direction of the country. And the art world, in tandem, began to move away from the concern to picture revitalized communities by representing working people in their daily lives and toward, of all things, European abstraction and abstract expressionism. Ironically, Jackson Pollock was to become one of the favored artists of corporate capitalism. Doss tells a wonderful story about how modernism of that variety became identified with the United States, particularly in the art made during the cold war.[84] Its triumph in the late 1940s eclipsed almost every other kind of artwork; realists were in the closet and remained there almost until the 1980s.

In the midst of all this, where was Gee? An answer can be found in the entries for the Museum of Modern Art's mural exhibition of 1932. The letter of invitation that went out to forty-nine artists from Lincoln Kirstein expressed appreciation for the contributions of the Mexican muralists but stressed that the artists should integrate their subjects with architecture to produce an indigenous American mural style.[85] Gee was one of the few contributors who did just that, combining abstraction, social realism, and the New York skyline. Joseph Stella, Stuart Davis, and Georgia O'Keeffe contributed a hard-edged form of city-scene painting that came to be known as precisionism. Ben Shahn, Stefan Hirsch, Benjamin Topman, and William Gropper were social realists; the rest were romantic realists, such as Reginald Marsh, who in *Post-War America* used many of the same elements that Gee used—bridges, planes, skyscrapers—and then united them with an arc of scantily clothed modern muses on horseback emerging from the smoke of a locomotive. Gee usually kept his muses away from industry. It is no wonder that most of the positive critical reviews went to photomuralists like Bernice Abbott, Charles Sheeler, and Edward Steichen for their views of New York's bridges, architecture, and industry. The show was attacked as too leftist, particularly because some of these artists were identified with Communism. Gee's work did not receive much attention, although a few reviews mentioned his work in positive terms; one reviewer remarked, "There may be those who will object that Yun Gee's gorgeous fugue . . . is conceivably a shade too warm."[86] It seems that the painting was still wet when Gee delivered it to the museum, and so it could not be photographed and never appeared in the catalogue. It could have helped to make his reputation; instead, its weak reception only added to his sense of isolation, and to his dilemma about what to do next.[87]

Aside from the power of Gee's mural, and its sophisticated meshing of many ideas, I linger over it because it is perhaps a key to some of the reasons for Gee's subsequent failure to attain the recognition he so deserved. It took Gee less than three months to finish the canvas (seven by four feet) and the three small panels that may have been preparatory studies. Glowing in reds and yellows, with planes of white, and those calligraphic black lines to delineate details, such as the man usually identified as falling from the Brooklyn Bridge, the panel moves in a rhythmic arc from the solid anchoring forms at the bottom to the light sky and gleaming sun above. Circles of energy spread from the discus thrower, at the bottom left, to polo players and then to the abstract structure of verticals and opposing diagonals in the bridge and skyscrapers above, to finally reach to the sun and the biplane in the upper corner. The dynamism of modern industrial energy, so common in the works of many artists, is here united with natural and human energy. But there is more: Gee roots the painting in concrete reality with several ironic twists. A woman and a small boy stand watching the wealthy playing polo—ironically, a game played in China as early as the Tang Dynasty. It was a sport immensely popular in metropolitan New York around 1930.[88] To add another level, tenement houses at the base of the bridge are juxtaposed with the soaring elegance of those needles of commerce in the financial district of Manhattan. The little man drawn in black, in Gee's signature style, may have just jumped from the bridge, but that reading—a tragic one, which might have been justified if the figure had been added later on, in one of Gee's periods of depression—is contradicted by a photograph taken at the exhibition, which shows that the figure was there from the beginning.[89] I think, instead, he is standing on a rooftop, trying to fly like the bird above him, perhaps exalted by his inclusion in the exhibition and by what it may bode for the future—the drawing for the painting makes that even clearer.[90]

How did Gee develop this accomplished work in only two or three months? A charcoal drawing of a merry-go-round, and a painting of the same subject at an oceanfront amusement park (one of the panel entries), seem to have been early ideas. Similarly, a pencil drawing shows a large Ferris wheel, possibly based on the one in Delaunay's *The Cardiff Team*. Instead of the Eiffel Tower in Delaunay's painting, Gee used vertical lines and rhythmic areas that may stand for skyscrapers and a bridge. In the second charcoal drawing Gee made, he changed the merry-go-round horses into polo players and treated them in a manner that seems related to the early stages of Jacques Villon's analytic horse-and-jockey studies of 1924. The fluid, linear horses and the figures of the merry-go-round in the drawing and the painting yield to the stronger planar structure of the polo players in the second charcoal. A final pencil sketch has everything resolved, and it includes the little flying man, who seems to be standing on the edge of a roof and reaching for or holding on to the legs of the bird, not falling from the bridge at all.

In the three entry panels exhibited with *Wheel*, several different approaches are taken. I don't think that they were painted as part of a triptych, but they were exhibited together, although the subjects are really unrelated except for their genre motifs.[91] In the first one, nude women are reclining on chairs on a roof overlooking a bridge, possibly on the New Jersey side of the Hudson River. The sunbathers are drawn with fluid contours, as in the Paris painting *The Hundred Beauties* and in some eighteen drawings that Gee may have made for it. *Merry-Go-Round* is in a similar style. In *Modern Apartment,* a blonde woman, who seems to be sewing, poses seductively in a flaming-red dress beside a large black telephone. The bridge and the night skyline of Manhattan are visible through the window while transparent angles and planes shoot out from a light that floods the interior. The languid beauty seems to be caught in the web of Diamondism. Who is she? Is she glancing at the telephone, waiting for it to ring? While these works have some relation to *Wheel* (pl. 4), it seems more likely that they reflect the different approaches to painting that Gee continued to pursue from that point on. He successfully integrated them in *Wheel* and produced a unique genre painting for the modern world.

Wheel may pay tribute to Robert Delaunay's *The Cardiff Team* and *Homage to Bleriot* and to de la Fresnay's *The Conquest of the Air*, all of them major paintings that Gee probably saw in Paris. His integration of European color abstraction with the concrete depiction of a social event was entirely in harmony with social realism, if not regionalism, and was as fully contemporary as any other painting of its time. If Gee's work was the one that actually answered the call stipulated in Lincoln Kirsten's letter, then why did Gee fail to become a leading painter on the New York scene? I think *Wheel* was too European and too cubist, particularly in the horse-and-figure group in the foreground. It was not "realistic" enough, even if the bridge and the skyscrapers were quite detailed. It was not precisionist enough, because the brushstrokes were painterly—another connection to the School of Paris. I think David Wang is right to emphasize that cubism "was yet to be properly introduced to New Yorkers," and that cubist works "were regarded as avant-garde by New Yorkers."[92] When modernism actually took hold, in the late 1940s, it was of a different kind; at first it was surrealism, not cubism, that influenced abstract expressionism.

The Last Supper, now lost, was another amazing mural-size painting that fully explored Gee's concept of Diamondism. If Diamondism was rooted in theories related to Oldfield's teaching, Gee fully developed and propagated it in his own teaching from the 1930s through the 1950s.[93] Gee was trying to formulate both a universal philosophical explanation of all the activities synthesized in the creative process and an art historical explanation of style in a diagrammatic form consisting of three intersecting triangles. The first triangle defined the work's physical properties of color, form, and light; the second, the work's psychological properties of mood, desire, and observation; and the third, the work's intellectual and spiritual components of time, morality (or philosophy), and purpose:

> All these nine matters are inevitably influencing, causing the creative process. Some painting schools deliberately ignored the presence of some of them. But they were there nevertheless. The different schools can thus be easily classified and explained when putting stress on one of the matters. Latins: Color. Anglo-

> Saxons: Form. Impressionists: Mood. Surrealists: Desire, Dislikes etc. . . . Cubism wanted to give the Inside Information too. Why was it a failure? Because they did not tune in all the matter.[94]

While art historically Gee jumps from race "isms" to art "isms," what is fascinating in this formulation is that Gee is au courant with modern theory—in this instance, perhaps with the implications of the crystal, an idea that engaged many artists and writers in the first quarter of the twentieth century. One writer has summed it up as follows:

> Cubists, Futurists, Expressionists, De Stijl artists, Bauhausler and Constructionists were concerned to find equivalents with which to express the physical truth of nature and the man-made worlds as well as the spiritual truths transcending material existence. For many the motif of the crystal, and its analogue glass, took on cosmic significance. . . . Such artists were passionately concerned with form and light. In their desire to give concrete visual expression to their perceptions, it seems as though they were attempting to reach to the heart of the formative principles of nature that could be seen as manifesting themselves in the process of crystal growth.[95]

This could not be a better description of what Gee was aiming at, and form and light were just as dominant in *Wheel,* a purely secular subject, as in *The Last Supper*, a commissioned altarpiece. What is different, beyond the subject, is the consistent use of planar facets of colored triangles throughout the painting.

From what I can tell, using black-and-white photographs and the three oil studies, it seems to be one of those places where Diamondism as a theory was appropriate for enhancing the meaning in the production of a powerful work. When Gee applied it randomly, particularly in overpainting earlier works, it was often disastrous, as was the added hard line with which he contained the more painterly aspects of his earlier work. In *The Last Supper*, Gee responded to iconographic and formal precedents in traditional paintings that he probably had seen in Paris and Spain and seemingly utilized the psychological grouping of figures in versions like Leonardo's, and Mannerist compositional features like Tintoretto's oblique tilting of the table. The table is bountifully laid—bread, fruit, chicken, and fish. It was a daring attempt, as in *Confucius (Chinese Sage)* (pl. 3), to paint a modern version of a traditional subject, and again an amazing achievement for a young painter. The head of Christ at the upper left-hand side of the canvas recalls the earlier *My Conception of Christ*, and on the right side Gee included a "landscape painting with bamboo rendered in Chinese manner; again, the free, calligraphic brushwork tells of Gee's autograph."[96] Once more, it was not that elements of Chinese art were blended with modernism but that the painting was totally integrated. Gee's inclusion of that landscape in a basically modern composition was a simple statement of who he was: modernist, Christian, and Chinese as well as immersed in the art of many traditions.

Aside from three other large paintings—*Temptation*, commissioned by two Chinese actors (Miss Leung Suk Hau and Mr. Lao Sou Chi) and painted in 1931, and two political paintings, *The Tanaka Memorial, Japanese Imperialist Dream*, painted in 1932, and *War Dance: Hitler and Hirohito*, painted in 1933—most of Gee's paintings that have survived are small oils, such as *Houses in the Bronx* and *Morning in the Bronx*, both painted soon after Gee returned from Paris in 1930.[97] Gee is at his best in these kinds of genre cityscapes, the architectural environment for the way people live in the dynamic present. They are quite different from the country landscapes that Cézanne painted, and that Gee emulated, in a few paintings he did in Paris. In 1943, he continued the theme in *Here's New York* (pl. 19). There are also many ink and colored-wash drawings of nudes that continue the fluid linear style of his Paris drawings as well as some washes with Chinese motifs, such as *Dragon*, *Snorting Dragon*, and *Landscape*. It is interesting that Gee continued to utilize an abstract vocabulary in many of his paintings, whereas in his drawings and watercolors the flowing line dominates to enhance symbolic subjects as well as Chinese stories or legends.[98] He applied paint with the full knowledge gained from Oldfield's theories and from his study of Cézanne and Parisian art; the fluidity of his drawing derives in part from his calligraphic studies in China, perhaps reinforced by his looking at the renderings of artists like Matisse and Pascin.

Gee's sensitivity to different media is particularly reflected in the twenty watercolors he exhibited in California, which seem to be symbolically united, in contrast to the genre paintings he exhibited in the same gallery in his first solo show in 1926.[99] In 1933, Gee wrote:

> The paintings at the art center deal with my new problem of watercolor, geometry and color theory. There are included eight sensations: four about dancing and four about travel impressions. The latter fuse sound and tone of modern industry, one object related to another through composition; the former fuse sound, air and water via rhythms of movement. Two—*The Octopus*, and *Living Stone*—are inspired by my wife's poem. . . . Beauty in art is valued according to its emotional expression. The great painter is he who can translate emotion, whether of things living or dead, on canvas. This principle dominates Chinese Art.[100]

Gee was still trying to bring theory into relation with practice, as in Diamondism, but now he seemed to attribute aspects of these works to Chinese art, and to equate their fluid lines with that tradition. Gee's theories about art were never logically consistent; rather, they were intuitive and related to the

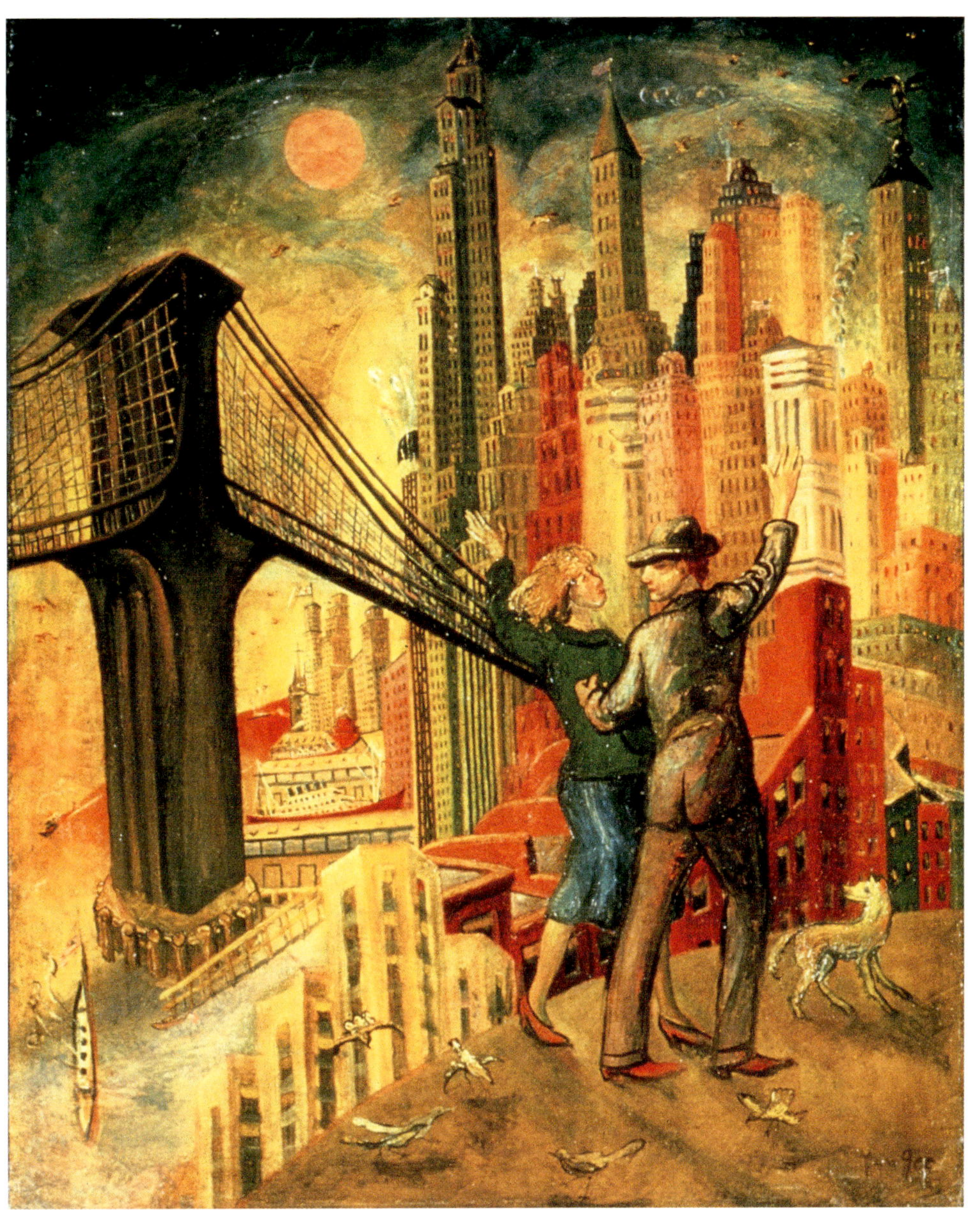

Plate 19 Yun Gee, ***Here's New York***, oil on canvas (36 ¼ in. x 28 ¾ in.), 1943.

body of work he was producing at the time, and this writing reflects his desire to unite modern industry with "natural" sensations in symbolic images that he believed he was rendering in a Chinese manner. Yet what these watercolors display is a clear dedication to modern abstraction. This may have been the only time that there was a desire on Gee's part to blend aspects of East and West in his writing, but in the paintings he blended a softened Diamondism with curvilinear rhythms in those works that contain floating figures that grew out of the technique of watercolor and perhaps also from his encounter with surrealism.

Then depression overwhelmed Gee, and he almost stopped painting altogether. All that remains from the last year or so before Gee left again for Paris are three small oils, two of them on silk and mounted on board: *Meditation (Portrait of Helen)*, painted in 1935; *Helen at Sixteen*; and, on canvas, *Girl in Mirror.*[101] In these soft, dreamy, meditative paintings of a young woman—elegant and languid in form, and painted in darker tones of reds and greens, with touches of brilliant red—the French mode is picked up again, but now, as in the ink drawings and watercolors, it is the poetic style of the figural painters of the School of Paris, such as Laurencin and Pascin.

It becomes more difficult to summarize these later phases of Gee's painting and drawing, as will become evident in connection with his return to Paris and his later years in New York. It is easy to say that Gee's working career ended with the wonderful paintings of the early 1930s, as I did in my earlier writing, and dismiss his later work as inferior because of racism, financial impoverishment, and alcoholism. In part, that was the case, but Gee did not stop working; in fact, he produced many paintings, drawings, and watercolors, some of which can be appreciated along with his earlier work. What is apparent to me is that in this New York period Gee continued to explore ways of painting for the modern world and to bring together the many aspects of his experiences. I also think that Gee increasingly embraced his Chinese inheritance, partially because of his foundering career as a modernist and perhaps also as a form of self-protection. Gee's ability to absorb aspects of several cultures in his life and work, when he emigrated from China to San Francisco, then to Paris, and at first in New York, served him well. Unfortunately, the battle to hold things together dominated the rest of his life. What is remarkable is that in some of his very last paintings he found a unique way of encapsulating his experiences of passage.

Painting in Paris Again: The Life Period (1936–1939)

Anthony Lee summarizes Gee's second venture in Paris this way:

> The awkward criticisms he did receive—some in fact trying to be laudatory—attest to the critics not finding a clear way to deal with him. They began to resort to cliché and increasingly to note how his Chinese-ness mattered in his art. (Never mind that he had not lived in China in nearly twenty years by that point. Never mind that he had developed nearly all his ideas about oil painting in San Francisco, Paris and New York.)[102]

While allusions to his Chinese-ness were fairly constant, Gee exhibited frequently in Paris, and although he did not paint major works, he did paint many portraits; there is a whole group of Pascin-like drawings of nudes, in ink with color wash, that I think were done during those years. Paule de Reuss was then living in Lausanne, Switzerland, and arranged for one work, *The Son of God*, to be exhibited at the Galerie Lion d'Or in December 1936.[103] His reputation from his first Paris trip followed him, and he seems to have fit right back into a place in the art scene he had before; it was therefore easy for him to have previously arranged a solo show at La Reine Margot in the same year.[104] Then, in 1937, he was included in three group shows; in one, called L'Enfant dans la Peinture Moderne, at Galerie Le Niveau, he seems to have shown *Man Holding Baby* (pl. 9) from 1926. (This tells me that Gee probably took all his paintings with him, and what he exhibited verifies that possibility.) A reviewer commented on this painting, "Yun Gee se fait remarquer pour ses couleurs délicates, et sa composition si personnelle" ("Yun Gee stands out for his delicate colors and his highly personal style of composition"). Gee exhibited *Wheel "Industrial New York"* (pl. 4) at the Salon d'Automne exhibition, and one reviewer was more than impressed: he called Gee Chinese but thought his painting was remarkable, a union of the metaphysical nature of his Chinese culture with a modern atmosphere.[105] In December 1937, Gee's work was in an exhibition at Galerie Pittoresque alongside that of André Lhote and others. The following year was a marvelous one for Gee, with more than fourteen group shows and a major solo exhibition—again at La Reine Margot—of thirty-seven works.[106]

Taking into account what I have been able to put together from the group exhibitions, I would estimate that Gee, in addition to the paintings just discussed, showed landscapes; street scenes; still lifes, such as *Under the Lamp*; portraits, such as *André Salmon* and *Paul Guillaume with Picasso's "Pure Joy"* (a photograph of the latter is signed on the back and dated 1938—this work was painted for the prestigious Paul Guillaume Prize at the Galerie Bernheim-Jeune in December 1938); fantasy subjects, such as *The Hundred Beauties*, in an exhibition that included Derain, Pascin, Picasso, Dufy, and others; Christian subjects, such as *The Last Supper*, shown at the Salon des Indépendants in 1938, where it received rave reviews); and a few with Chinese subjects, such as *Harmonie Universelle (Lao-tzu)*. If one adds the major exhibition, sponsored by the government, that was to have taken place in October 1939, one can conclude that Gee had a career in Paris, if not much financial support, and that he probably would have stayed there if war had not broken out.[107]

Gee continued to paint cityscapes and city scenes in several styles, ranging from soft and blurry brushwork (*Cluny at Night*) to heavily painted and more "expressionist" canvases (*Port St. Cloud*) to some more realistic ones with emphasis on architecture, such as *Sorbonne Square* and *Untitled (Woman and Child Walking in Park [Sorbonne Square])*. He had worked this way in the past and would continue to do so when he returned to New York. He may have begun that kind of practice even as far back as his time in San Francisco: *San Francisco Chinatown* was exhibited in 1927 at Galerie Carmine in Paris; unless it was repainted, it is almost entirely without abstract passages of color, and the oil paint is applied heavily; it does share the bright color vocabulary

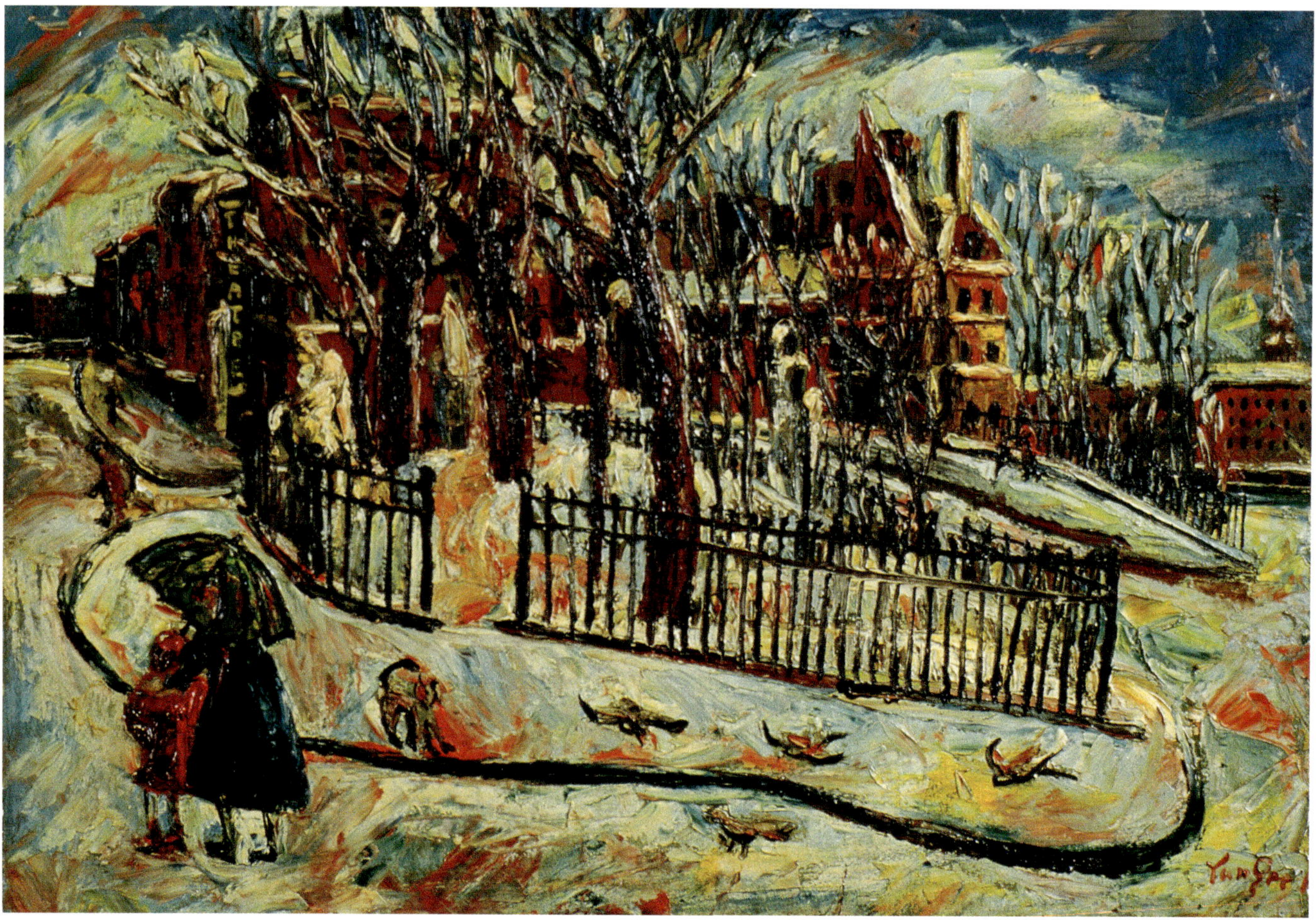

Plate 20 Yun Gee, *Sorbonne Square*, oil on canvas (22 in. x 32 in.), late 1930s.

that Gee was using in California. His portraits are also diverse, and Gee produced interesting renditions of personality, as in the portrait *Paul Valéry*.[108]

One of the finest portraits is *Madam Gabriel Perreux* (pl. 14). Her dress, her face, and the wonderful bouquet of calla lilies that rests in her lap are painted with the softened triangles that appeared sporadically in paintings from Gee's first Paris trip. The decorative pattern of the couch she sits on, and into which her dress blends, is harmonic, almost like Vuillard's figures that become one with the domestic ground. Her face, with its clear blue eyes and red lipstick, like her hands and polished nails, is clearly delineated from a Chinese-like tapestry or painting of two lovers under the sinuous branch of a fruit-bearing tree; the background looks like black velvet. It is a stunning portrayal of a beautiful redhead, painted in rich shades of blues and browns, and Gee frames her glowing shoulders on each side with what may be decorative embroidery painted in light gray, with red, yellow, and blue stitches. This is an image of a woman with impeccable taste. I single out this portrait in part because it was never repainted, as some of the others were, and because it may have provided critics and viewers with a reason to continue to refer to Gee's work as Chinese—in this case, because of the background.

When Gee painted portraits of women, they were always, like Madame Perreux, treated with great admiration for their particular sensibilities. His

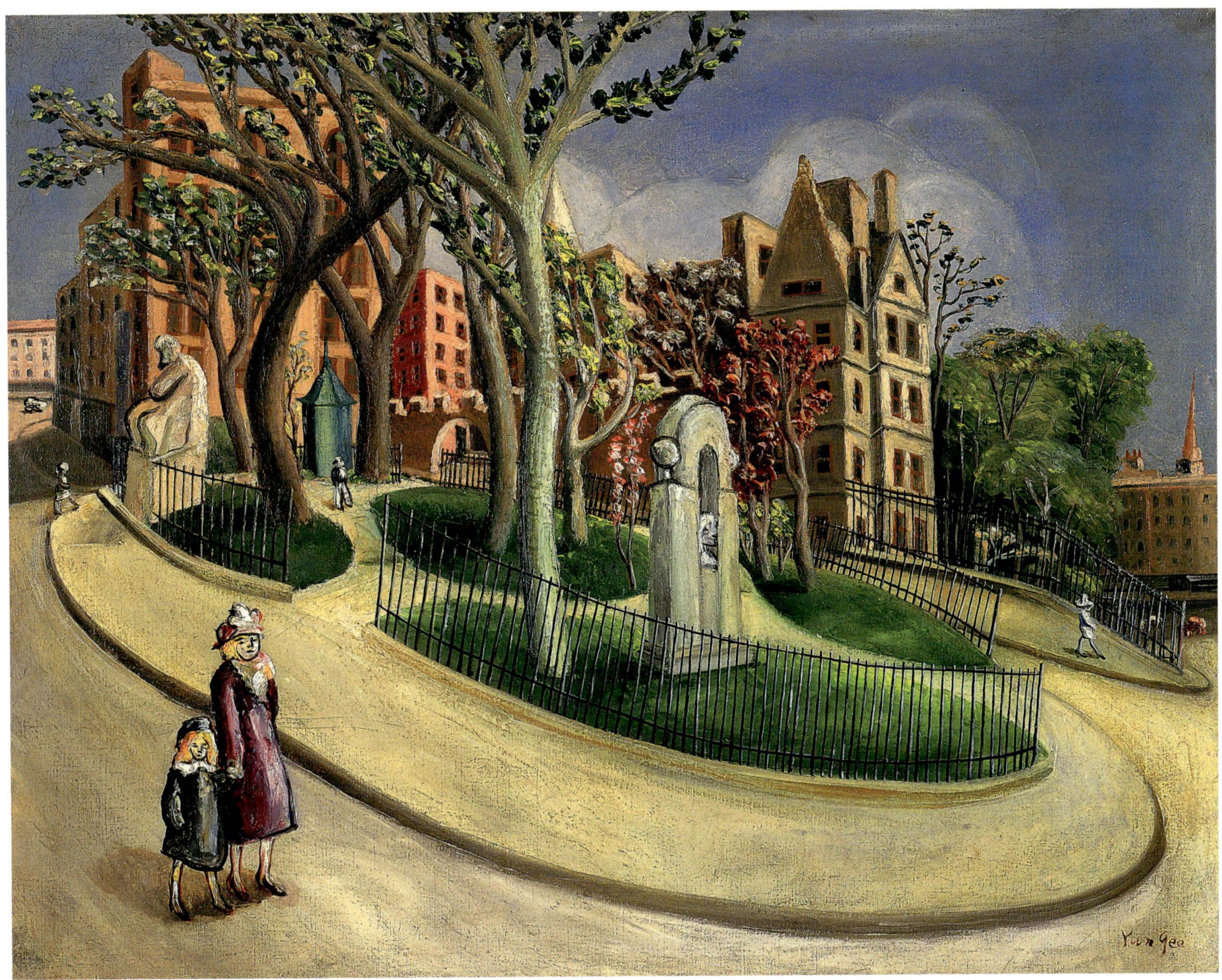

Plate 21 Yun Gee, *Untitled* (*Woman and Child Walking in Park [Sorbonne Square]*), oil on canvas (28 5/8 in. x 36 1/8 in.), late 1930s.

drawings from the nude model are something else again. There are a whole series of ink and watercolor nudes, some painted indoors and others in nature, perhaps inspired by Matisse and by Picasso's pink period. An ink drawing called *Paradise* sets the stage for the group. Gee wrote on the bottom, "Paradise This paint what I go to paint in Paris next," and at the bottom sits the painter with his sketchpad, observing naked beauties. Here Gee followed the usual stereotype of equating women with nature, or he drew them as objects of desire, but some of them are little gems in spite of that. Several of them show two nude women in each other's arms, sitting in a park. In one of them, the two nudes seen from the back are walking what looks like a tiny dog; even here, humorous genre motifs are included. Then there are nudes on horseback, and what is wonderful about them is Gee's use of the pen to search out the contours, different from his use of ink and brush that characterizes the lyrical fluidity of his nudes and studies of horses from the first Paris period and New York. He continued that way of working as well, and a group of linked nudes dancing in a circle, titled *Harmony*, is a brush drawing. Several of these drawings were made as studies for paintings, but *Nudes on Horseback,* like others, is probably a complete work in itself: Gee wrote on the bottom, "This painting finally succeeds to carry out what I want in 'The Knights' and is as successful as the '*Dancers*' during the day of declare war by England."[109] Two of them are complete as watercolors, *Nude* and *Nudes and Horse.* In the former, an elongated nude with her arms interlocked over her head sits in front of a window; in the latter, almost the same figure sits in front of trees, and another small figure in front of an elegantly drawn horse is curved to denote analogies. Gee's depictions of spatial contraction in both of them were done easily, since rendering planar space had simply become a part of the vocabulary of all modern artists. In spite of this, Pierre Mille wrote:

> It is said that the Chinese brought painting to Europe. But they only knew watercolor. In teaching them oil painting, we gave them as much as and more than they gave us, and even more than they think, that is, the possibility of restoring to an aged art a new sap with its racial character, if not its primitive force. That is what appears very definitely in the paintings of Yun Gee. He passed through London and New York and those influences are visible. His art has that stripped appearance of the English and American schools. But he came to France, where he found the richest and most varied impressionistic palette at the same time as he found Picasso's acrobatic simplification. He added to these the patience and thoughtfulness of his race—that taste for pure and honest color which has remained with the potters of his country. All art is summed up in the form of a varnished vase shaped like a fruit or breast, which is as agreeable to touch as to see. The Orientals have maintained the usual relationship of the sensitivity of the soul—the conductive wire of artistic emotion. That is why their painting, without clashes or hatchings, goes straight to its goal, which is the stable and intellectual transposition of our rapid and fugitive visions. . . . Among the Oriental and Chinese who have come to us, Yun Gee is one of the most remarkable because his race remains evident in his work, and because our Occidental gift flourishes there like a well planted seed. . . . Yun Gee is a remarkable and noted artistic agent de liaison.[110]

Mille was a friend, but his comments probably sum up the way in which Gee was understood in Paris. Mille's characterization is laudatory in a completely stereotypical fashion, but it is entirely without interpretive meaning in relation to Gee's work, if it has any meaning at all. It does suggest, however, that all these fluid works seem to have fit the prevailing art scene, and that the Parisians' love for the "Oriental" was still in vogue. Unfortunately, it also set the stage for the best kind of reception that Gee got for the remaining twenty-four years of his life in New York, since it was quoted several times in connection with Gee's exhibitions there, such as his 1945 solo show at the Lilienfeld Gallery. What is strange, given that Gee was a painter sensitive to political and social issues, is that his work, like that of so many other artists working in Paris, does not reflect any aspect of the rise of Fascism and the coming war. All Gee's nudes in nature—sometimes whimsically, humorously, or romantically rendered—are fantasy escapes from political events. No cartoons or paintings with political implications exist, although his return to New York in 1939 dramatically announced his awareness, and several works would be made with war as their subject.

To conclude this discussion of Gee's experiences in Paris, the artist was in tune with the life and the art of the city during the time that he spent there, and in many ways he could be considered a Parisian painter, but I think his best work was accomplished in the United States. Paris may have catered to what Gee could produce easily, in a fluid and languorous mode, since he could rely on his basic skills, but San Francisco and New York provided the dynamism that enabled innovation. Gee did some wonderful paintings early in his first Paris period, in response to the art scene there, but they were still partially shaped by his San Francisco experiences. *Wheel "Industrial New York"* (pl. 4), perhaps his most complex and most accomplished work, embodies the spirit of New York. Toward the end of his painting life in New York, he was again empowered to produce innovative works.

Painting in New York: The Expressive Period (1939–1963)

Gee came back to New York, perhaps unwillingly, to lead an active and productive life for quite a while, but he was essentially ignored by the art world for the last fifteen years of his life.[111] He had solo exhibitions through 1947 and then nothing until 1962, one year before he died. He was also included in half a dozen group shows, but even though he was still a working artist, he was no longer noticed for his art, and he did not appear in group exhibitions after 1944. In my previous writing about Yun Gee, relying on information from a single source, I formed the impression that Gee had suffered a severe mental breakdown and did not produce work after 1945. It is true that his public career was to be over in a few years, and that his productivity diminished as a result, but Gee continued to work in spite of adversity, and he produced some exciting paintings, such as *Hospital Court* (pl. 5) in 1951 and *Wanamaker Fire* (pl. 8) in 1956. He was doing other things as well, but it is still both difficult and very sad to write about this part of his career, and to have to admit that, as a result of all the negative factors in his life, he had lost his concentration, and that many of his paintings were poorly done. It seems that Gee pursued one direction after another, and that some of these may have been alien to his temperament.

At first his showings were frequent. It appears that in 1940 Gee had two solo exhibitions; the one at the Court Gallery featured one hundred of his paintings. One review mentions only his works with Chinese and Christian subjects, whereas another lists those works among many others from Gee's earlier stays in New York and Paris.[112] He also exhibited a mural, *The Spirit of Chinese Resistance*, at the Young China Club. At the Montross Gallery, at the end of the year, there were twenty-six paintings shown; once again, Pierre Mille's essay was in the exhibition catalogue and set the tone.[113] In that show there were several new works, three of them scenes in Central Park, a subject that Gee would continue to paint over the years; there were also several paintings from his first and second sojourns in Paris and several works related to the war. Gee included *San Francisco Chinatown* in several exhibitions—again, probably because it was painted more in the style of his loosely brushed Paris scenes than in the style of the more abstract planar works he had painted in California. He had two exhibitions at the Milch Gallery, one in 1942 and the other in 1943. In the latter showing there were twenty-three paintings, none of them with Chinese themes; many were still lifes and recent New York scenes, including several of Central Park. Some of them had been painted in Gee's first New York period, and it seems that Gee may have been trying to tailor this exhibition to the realism that was in vogue in the 1930s and early 1940s. Nevertheless, the exhibition catalogue reads as if Gee was essentially a Chinese painter. It starts by noting that he was an American citizen, since he was the son of an American-born Chinese, and goes on as follows:

> Yun Gee spent his boyhood in his native village near Canton, and it is natural that his art should have a distinct Chinese flavor. His painting combines Eastern vision with practical and vigorous American expression. Since he has spent most of his life in America, and has studied here, he consequently makes use of *our modern technique* in creating his original and highly individual paintings. He has not attempted to divorce himself entirely from his cultural heritage, but he has freely absorbed *our American way* of life and re-creates it in his paintings with enough *Oriental spirit* to form that delicate fusion of *East and West* which reveals itself between a pagoda and a skyscraper. . . . The current exhibition represents work . . . done within the last year.[114]

It is almost unbelievable that after all the time Gee had spent as a modern artist, and in spite of his American citizenship, however acquired, the patronizing use of "our American way" and "our modern technique" and the simplistic designation "Oriental spirit" should still mark how Gee and his work were received. It is hardly necessary to examine these stereotypical and covertly racist remarks, because the reasons for them are, sadly, too obvious: the artist must have Chinese elements in his work simply because his name is Yun Gee. But what would critiques of his work have been like if his name had been John Smith? No wonder Gee was frustrated and depressed!

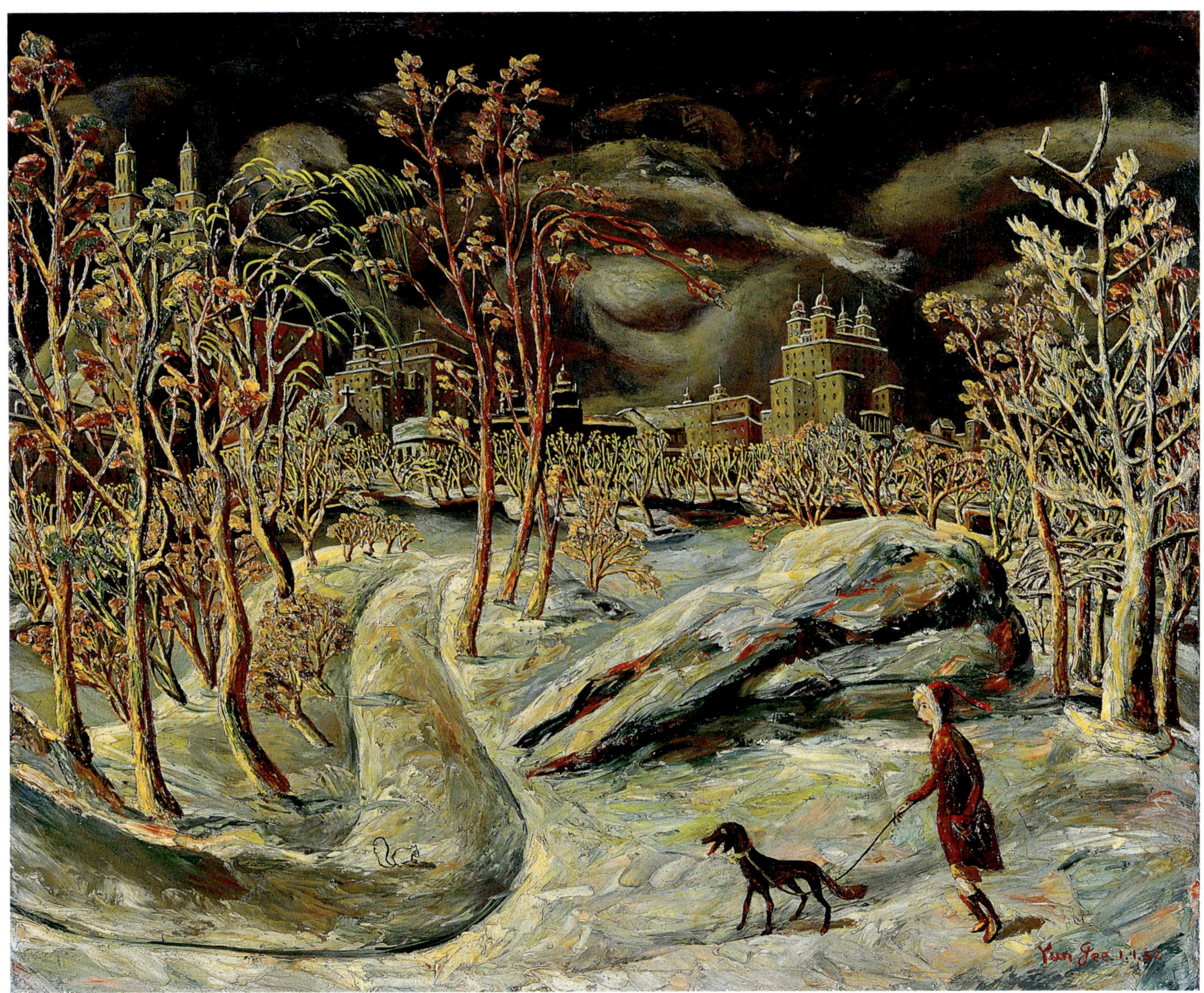

Plate 22 Yun Gee, *West Tower from Central Park in Winter*, oil on canvas (30 1/8 in. x 36 in.), 1952.

In a 1942 exhibition at the Milch Gallery, a benefit for the British and American ambulance corps, the thirty paintings Gee showed were varied in style and subject, but few were recent works. At the same time, in the 1940s, he was the only Chinese-American artist to be included in the *Portrait of America* exhibition at the Metropolitan Museum of Art, with a new painting, *Here's New York* (pl. 19).[115] In 1946, the Lucien Laubaudt Gallery in San Francisco showed twenty-nine of Gee's paintings. Gee had known Laubaudt, also a painter, from his San Francisco days, and Laubaudt, who had died three years earlier, had appreciated Gee's work.[116] The show was a miniretrospective and included several San Francisco paintings owned by Jehanne Biétry-Salinger, a portrait of Yun by Laubaudt from the San Francisco days, and recent works painted in New York. It may have been intended as an homage both to Gee and Lucien Laubaudt, whose widow probably curated the show and perhaps wrote the short essay:

> A prodigy artist, [Gee] held his first one-man show in 1926 at the Modern Art Gallery[,] . . . selling the 72 pictures shown. . . . Paul Guillaume, one of Paris's well-known connoisseurs, praised him immediately as one of the most talented young artists working in the French capitol. . . . An American citizen, Yun Gee has remained interested in his native China. Included in this exhibition is *The Spirit of Chinese Youth*, which the artist painted during the war to symbolize the spirit of Chinese resistance. . . .
>
> As an artist, Yun Gee has remained distinctly Chinese although most receptive to occidental gifts. French critics have pointed out that he has the patience and thoughtfulness of his race, a taste for pure and honest color kindred to the potters of his native country, and that he has retained an oriental sensitivity that penetrates deeply underneath art form[s]. He received his first impulse in San Francisco, has lived in Paris and tasted of French civilization, is now a New Yorker . . . and it [is] all [reflected] in his works, a highly personal transposition of his experience.[117]

In spite of the awareness of Gee's transnational experiences, Pierre Mille was still the authority on Gee's purported orientalism, even in San Francisco. The same note continued to be sounded in New York the following year (perhaps more understandably, given the venue) at the China Institute in America, at China House, with twelve Chinese, Christian, and political paintings, among them the now lost *Last Supper* (see fig. 1.6, p. 37):

> Yun Gee combines the styles of French impressionistic modernism with the American school, personified by our age of industrialization. But in all his paintings there breathes the reincarnated spirit of the Chinese aesthetic of the Ming Dynasty, giving his work the ageless, universal quality of great art.[118]

In his penultimate solo exhibition, Gee showed forty-five of his works and three paintings from his collection of old masters; seven of his works were sculptures that he had made at various times.[119] Again, this exhibition included a cross section of paintings from different periods, many of them recent scenes of New York; almost for the first time, little reference was made to his being Chinese except for mention of his having been born in Canton.[120] The catalogue for his last show, from December 1962 to January 1963 at the Gudenzi Galleria in New York, had a short essay by Jehanne Biétry-Salinger, who was the first critic to write about his paintings and the last to do so while he was still alive. He showed thirty paintings and two pieces of sculpture; again, the show was a miniretrospective of all the kinds of paintings Gee had done in all the places where he had lived.[121]

To summarize Gee's reception in New York, it seems obvious that the artist was unable to free himself from the French engagement with his work. Perhaps Gee thought that the French appraisal would stand him in good stead in the New York scene because it emphasized his reputation in Paris. Unfortunately, however, New York, even though it was still in its regionalist and social realist phase, was soon to become the center of abstraction, and many artists who had participated in the realist mode were soon to be left behind. How, then, could Gee, returning from years in Paris, have been able to predict the future of the art world? There were also issues concerned with integrity and with creating what was necessary to an individual's practices, and Gee referred to these issues several times in his writings. Gee did try to respond to the New York art scene in order to stay alive, but he was and would continue to be a painter of everyday life. His poetry, autobiographical writings, and philosophical ruminations suggest that his quest was spiritual, motivated by the search for universal, humanitarian solutions, but his painting remained, for the most part, rooted in the specific.[122]

Gee called this period his expressive phase, and many works are indeed painted in the gestures associated with expressionism, but Gee was already doing that—for example, in his portrait of Princess Achille Murat and in a self-portrait painted around the same time.[123] *Portrait of a Man,* dated 1940 in Chinese, is an excellent example of one painted in New York, as are many nudes in that style.[124] There are scenes in Central Park, mostly in greens and blues, of children playing, picnics on the grass, people in rowboats, and animals cavorting, in a looser and more linear manner also used in Paris.[125] A third style, found more in the 1950s, joins the painterly brushstroke with diamond facets, usually in the background. Two excellent examples are the 1951 portrait of the actress Linda Darnell and the marvelous *Hospital Court* (pl. 5) of the same year, which may portray the hospitalized Helen Gee. A fourth manner of painting unites painterly brushstrokes with architectural forms and sometimes rhythmic line, mostly utilized in scenes in Central Park, like the 1952 picture of a woman walking her dog on a dark winter's day, *West Tower from Central Park in Winter* (pl. 22). In the delightful portrayal of a squirrel that seems to be burying a nut, Gee's signature drawing returns as it does in the earlier *Swan Lake, Central Park.*[126] Gee seems to have also really loved the skyscrapers of New York, since they are in evidence in many of his New York scenes from both times he lived there.[127]

Gee's third mode—painterly, with diamond patterns used sometimes very gently to describe facial and body planes, but mostly set in the background—seems to have been reserved for portraits. It was used in one nude with a cigarette, painted in Paris, to structure both the subject's golden body and the green background; it was also used in the face and shoulders of *Madam Gabriel Perreux* (pl. 14) (1937). In the 1951 portrait *Linda Darnell* it is subtly united with a more painterly stroke in the subject's blouse, skirt, and hair. Gee presented her in the stereotypical woman-and-mirror theme, but he also subverted that by having her writing and smoking, not looking in the mirror as in the age-old *vanitas* portrayals. What Gee painted in the mirror is the other side of her profile. She is glamorous, but she is also present as a person, with a private and individual persona. The added touch of a candle casting its diamond-patterned light to the mirror is pure Gee, as is the linear white smoke that bifurcates the panel. I have grown to admire this painting almost as much as Gee seems to have admired the actress, both because of its treatment of the woman and because of its subtle use of Diamondism.

And then there is that fourth way, almost always reserved for paintings in which architecture predominates. *Bridge in Summer* seems to me to be the finest of this group, since it blends painterly water and sky with the hard edges of the planes of the buildings.[128] It is almost as if Gee had learned Cézanne's lessons so well that he could transpose the earlier painter's Provençal landscapes, with red-tiled buildings in the foreground and the Mediterranean behind, to industrial New York.[129] All the genre elements are here: a little dog plays, a woman is perhaps watering her garden, boats for work and pleasure sail the river, two or three tiny figures on the other bank dive in and swim, and birds and airplanes fly. Gee contrasted domestic living, on one side, with industrial and office buildings, on the other; a miracle of modern industry was painted as a simple fact of contemporary life.

Then there are a few paintings that suggest a new direction; although undated, they were probably done in the early 1950s. They combine genre, the nude, and portrayal in a complex manner. Although they are essentially realistic, Gee introduced spatial elements and objects that suggest mysterious relationships. In *Untitled (Nude)* (pl. 7), the figure with her legs bent up, exposing her genitalia, is seated on a striped hassock, and on the back wall Gee copied his earlier Paris painting *Seven Nudes in Central Park* in a manner looser than in the original. On an easel to the right sits a picture of a bridge in a landscape, a copy of one of his more expressively painted works, now stylized in keeping with the painting in which it is embedded; both pictures within the picture are similarly adapted.[130] A wonderful wooden staircase divides the canvas, and the bathroom—with only the toilet seat visible, drawn in his signature style—is to the left. In the middle of the painting, hanging from the staircase post, is a sword like the one that Gee used in his performances of traditional Chinese dance. It hangs there quite precariously, almost threatening the nude. The colors are dark, green and brown except for the areas of bright red. It is almost a summation of Gee's interests, lacking only poetry. The composition is essentially planar, with the shadows of the easel, the steps, the hassock, and the ceiling of the bathroom in abstract spatial juxtapositions echoed by the way the colors work. Gee seems to have wedded knowledge gained from his San Francisco "cubist" format with a more realistic but spatially complex environment to house his objects of desire. It is also a kind of collection of various ways of painting, from the linear to the more painterly, which Gee may have wanted to picture here.

Untitled (Nude in Studio) (pl. 6) is painted very differently; it is all about light and dark, and Gee introduces his diamonds to signal the former. Most of the painting is keyed to the window, which shows buildings and sky, opens onto a wonderful little city scene, and reflects back into the studio through a pattern of diamond lights on the floor. A nude sits with her head bent and her arms around her legs, and above her on a pedestal is a portrait bust. Could it be Gee himself? He did make a stone bust that was exhibited in the Jersey City Museum show of 1948, but it looks more like a plaster portrait made of him by someone else.[131] To balance this, on a diagonal across the room is a brilliant red bird in a cage. The juxtaposition of the privacy of the interior with those particular objects and the ordinary buildings outside the window suggests that more than what one sees is intended. Most compelling is that there is nothing left here of the influence of Matisse; this is a work at least as original as Gee's early paintings.[132] In these two works he weds his continuing interest in the ordinary—in this case, the painter's studio—to a level of complexity and mystery that denotes a very mature phase of Yun Gee's creative output.

The largest and most spatially complex canvas of them all, *Hospital Court* (pl. 5), is dated October 9, 1951, as already mentioned, and that date serves as a focal point for this group of works, and in particular for *Untitled (Nude)* (pl. 7), because they are both painted alike. The scene is a room in Bellevue Hospital, but most of the attention is drawn to the view outside the window. A beautiful smiling woman (Helen Gee?) reclines near a table with flowers and fruit, all worked in painterly diamond shapes. The paned glass window fills almost the whole canvas, and what I see outside the window is an amazing genre scene akin to Breughel's paintings of daily life. Over the smiling woman's face are green bushes that frame the hospital entrance, facing a courtyard. A large dark building closes the courtyards in the back, and in each window there appears to be a figure in an almost puppetlike position. Is this the psychiatric ward of Bellevue? In total juxtaposition is the courtyard filled with little figures: children playing, a woman walking her dog, a man with flowers walking toward the entrance, people leaving the building, and a child buying flowers directly beneath the table with fruit inside the room. The street on the right, in front of the courtyard, disappears into the distance, and I can see the Empire State Building in the distance. To top it all off, a Shell Oil sign from across the courtyard meets the name of the hospital at the entrance. Strong contrasts of dark and light triangles produce, alongside the activities, a cacophony of the everyday. Does the smiling woman—radiating life, fecundity, and pleasure—contrast with the dark building and its occupants in their pain and misery? That's what Gee saw there, down to every detail, but he combines what he saw to create a mystery of life that in the end may be the most lucid interpretation.[133]

Wanamaker Fire (pl. 8) was painted in 1956 on the spot of the disaster. Lilan remembers that her father told her about being there in a letter he wrote to her in 1957, while she was away at camp. The brushstrokes are expressionist in style and completely suited to the frenzy depicted. This is also a genre scene that encapsulates the more threatening dynamics of city life, in contrast to all the halcyon scenes that Gee painted of Central Park. The glow of the heat is intense, and the subtle use of triangles skillfully stabilizes the raucous red gestures that cover the canvas. It is a small panel that almost explodes with dramatic vibrancy. Undated paintings from the 1940s and 1950s, like *Old Broadway in Winter, Harlem*, and *Street Scene at Dusk, New York*, attest to Gee's continued search for appropriate means of painting how people lived, and where; the "where" was now all over New York City.

I think that Gee, in these last paintings, found his way to a mode of working that was entirely his own. These works seamlessly unite many of his experiences of passage, from his early training in China to his absorption of cubism in San Francisco, of lyricism and surrealism in Paris, and of the more realist and populist style occasioned by his New York life. This unity developed from his interest in genre, which had emerged during his student days and was never abandoned. They are complete paintings in which the personal, the everyday, and perhaps even the meaning of life for Gee seemed to come together. He was now forty-five years old and could have begun the most important part of his creative work. These paintings were rarely shown in his lifetime, as far as I can tell, and there was almost complete silence about Gee's later work until the 1990s. In the first posthumous showing, in 1968, there were no paintings exhibited that had been made after 1932; almost all the works were genre subjects, and many were abstract. I followed suit in the exhibition I curated in 1979. As late as 1992, all the paintings shown in the Taipei Fine Arts Museum exhibition had been made before the 1940s, with the exception of some drawings that were done a few years later.

From the late 1990s on, things began to change, and I think that there are several reasons for the earlier exclusion and recent inclusion of these late works. For one thing, taste matters, in relation to both time and place. Earlier showings emphasized Gee's modernity, whereas the later showings, under the umbrella of postmodernism, have allowed for a wider range of Gee's styles and subjects. This is true of the taste of New York, whereas recent exhibitions in Taiwan, as well as sales there and in Hong Kong and southeast Asia, tend to reflect less interest in the earlier work and more interest in the nudes, the landscapes and animal studies, the scenes in Central Park, the symbolic works, and the works with Chinese themes. This painter of the many styles and subjects that he garnered from his experiences of passage is now being discovered and exhibited in many countries, and the work of one of the first truly transnational artists is crossing the borders between East and West. Not only transnational artists but also Chinese artists are particularly courted at this moment. After all the years of neglect, it seems that Yun Gee is finally in sync with the times. Nevertheless, his recent success still probably owes much to his being considered a "Chinese artist."

3 THE LIFE OF LI-LAN

An Experience of Passage in Reverse

Li-lan belongs in the same way as I do to that increasing number of the not exactly belonging people. I understood her sense of isolation and escape to Europe soon after I met her in Tokyo or New York where she traces the steps I know so well. How fortunate are those of us who have gained the constancy of art to guide and welcome us. Li-lan has found that blank page of our school notebook which we may all claim as our own. Upon it we can write our thoughts freely, beyond race and without prejudice.

—ISAMU NOGUCHI, *LI-LAN*

Engaging the life and work of a living artist is an endeavor quite different from writing about someone who is no longer alive, and whom one has never met. The latter task involves encountering the works and interpreting written texts (although, in this case, verbal interviews with Helen Gee and Li-lan about Yun Gee have been extremely important). The challenge is to test the accuracy of the written material, and to try to make sense of competing views; memory is also risky in the interview process. The challenge in the face of the living artist is both the same and different: similar in the sense of facing the works and dealing with the memory issue, but different in the sense of having the artist's comments on her own life and paintings. I have spent many hours over the past five years or so talking to and recording conversations with Li-lan, the latter particularly in March 2003 and April and May 2004; this chapter and the one that follows are, in part, the result of this form of interactive research.[1] Nevertheless, the discussion of her paintings centers on many hours of looking, and sometimes on my understanding aspects of her work differently from her own perceptions. There was abundant written material to support my research for the chapters on her father; by contrast, although Li-lan is and has been much exhibited as a painter, and although there have been many short essays in catalogues as well as many reviews of her showings in the United States, Japan, Taiwan, and elsewhere, this is the first extended study of her life and work, and so this chapter and the next have provided me with the additional rewards that emerge from a fresh approach.[2]

Most of Li-lan's early life and education took place in New York City in the second half of the twentieth century. If her father's life is without doubt transnational, how is this an appropriate appellation for hers? Scarlet Cheng, commenting on an exhibition by Li-lan, wrote, "Transnational and multicultural, caught up in journeys between countries and borders, these works reflect a kind of thought diary."[3] It is the crossing of countries and borders—literally and, more important, conceptually—that is most significant, along with Li-lan's being biracial, and that gives rise to an unexpected perspective. In an interview that I conducted with Li-lan in relation to one of her visits to China, I asked her about the impact of that trip, and she remarked that she had lived in too many places to have had an epiphany when she finally visited her father's village in China.[4] Yun Gee was born and educated in China, and China remained a prime component of his worldview, even as he embraced other cultures, whereas Li-lan discovered the Chinese part of her identity later in life, and yet it constitutes one of the most compelling parts of her story. As her father did, Li-lan has absorbed aspects of several cultures, and in their fusion she has created a body of work that is even more consistently transnational than her father's. Her life is a kind of reversal of the experience of passage that was her father's voyage. If he courted new environments and experiences very early in life, Li-lan, departing from a self-protecting youth, embraced cultural diversity as a young woman and is still embracing it. More important, I hope to show that the nature of Li-lan's conception of life and what her paintings explore justify the designation "transnational," as does her living in the "in between" state that is intrinsic to her history as a biracial woman.

Growing Up in New York City

Li-lan was born into a biracial family in New York in 1943, the only child of Yun Gee and his second wife, Helen Wimmer, a highly independent woman who later developed her own career in the arts.[5] Helen's marriage to Gee only lasted three years; they separated when Li-lan was two years old, and subsequently they divorced. Because Helen had to work, Li-lan went to a preschool, the Church of all Nations, until she entered public school. Although she lived with her mother until she was seventeen, Li-lan has positive memories of her father, with whom she often spent weekends in his studio. Other than her father and some friends and family members whom she met in his apartment,

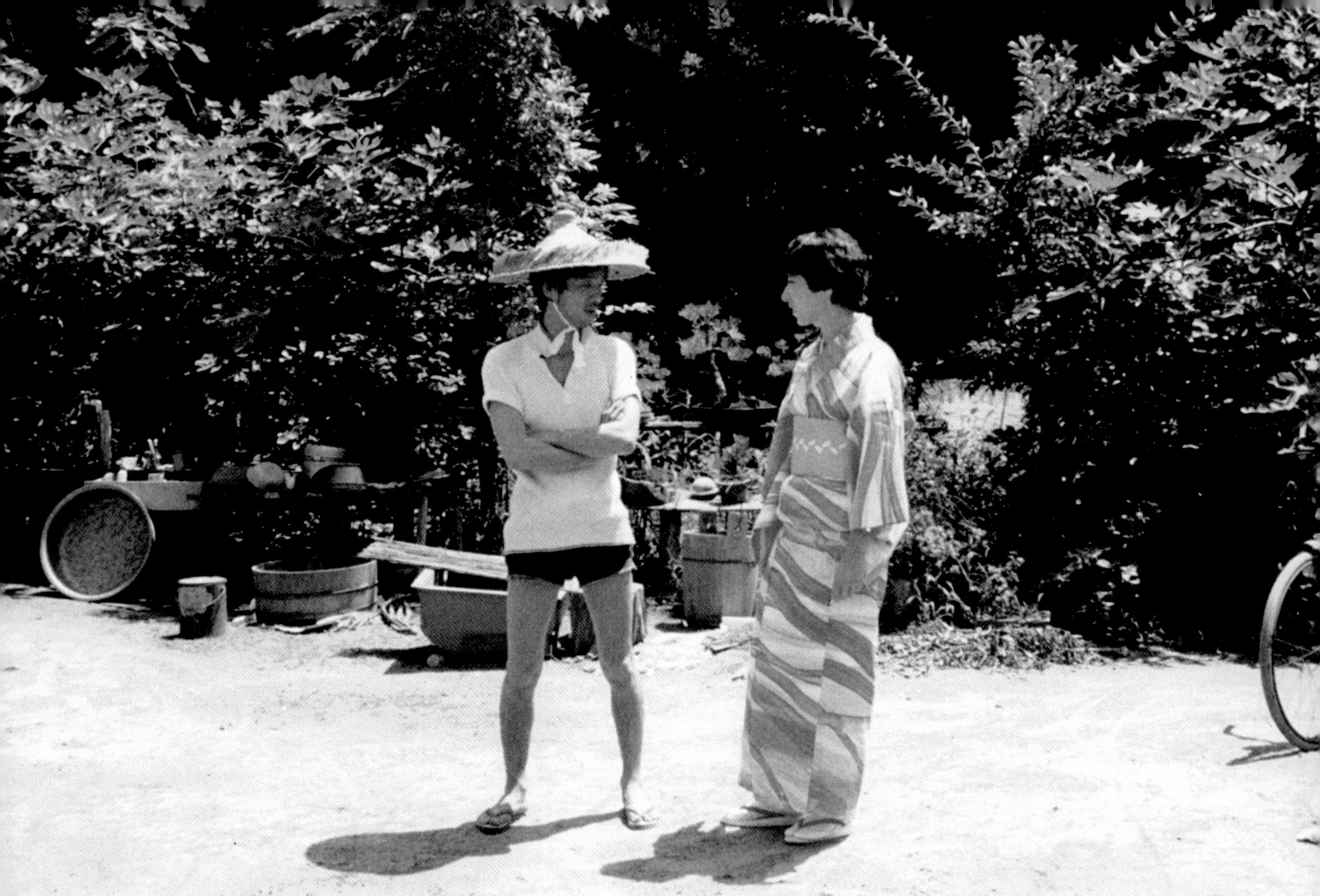

3.1 Li-lan with Masuo Ikeda, Nagano, Japan, early to mid-1970s.

she had almost no contact with Chinese persons or other Asians and people of color until she went to the High School for Performing Arts in Manhattan to study acting, and even then, few students in the drama department were Asian. Her first real encounters came when she left home after graduation at seventeen and supported herself by working at Takashimaya, a department store in New York. That was her first really positive experience in a non-Western environment—interestingly enough, on Western soil. She fell in love with all things Japanese and slowly began to discover and embrace the Asian part of herself. It is particularly revealing that it was her immersion in Japanese culture, many years before her encounters with China, that had the most profound consequences for Li-lan's acceptance of the Asian part of her heritage. She is much more knowledgeable about Japanese culture because she lived in Japan for many years, whereas her firsthand knowledge of China came only through two short trips, through her immersion in literature and the other arts, and, of course, through the experiences she shared with her father. For the past decade or so, she has been involved with Taiwan because she has a gallery affiliation and exhibits there frequently—many of her friends are now Chinese.

Li-lan speaks about her childhood in sad and sober terms. She felt alienated and lonely a good part of the time and was very unhappy in her preschool and public grammar school. She describes her mother as caring but self-involved, quite moody and away a good deal of the time. Helen Gee tried very hard to support herself and her daughter by working in a factory, then retouching photographs at home, and, in 1954, added to this she opened the first gallery for photography in a coffeehouse called the Limelight. There are some wonderful photographs of young Li-lan helping to refurbish that run-down Greenwich Village space. In those photos, and in others taken when she was young, Li-lan looks very withdrawn; only in one or two of them does she smile.[6] When Helen opened the coffeehouse and exhibited the work of major photographers, Li-lan was too young for their work to make an impression on her; instead, the gallery competed with her desire for her mother's presence. Helen writes in a motherly fashion about her relationship with Li-lan, whom she describes as sometimes difficult, but Li-lan's own memories of those days always stress that she was lonely and afraid a good deal of the time.[7] She obviously had a very volatile and complex relationship with her mother, whom she cared about, and whose love she sought, but she also had to deal with what she felt were her mother's complicated feelings toward her. Helen was a very ambitious woman, and raising a child alone was a responsibility that must have interfered with her aspirations.

Li-lan was also not totally at ease with her beloved father, who was temperamental in ways different from her mother, and the constant drinking and disillusion about his career were additional factors that provoked long periods of silence. But every day when she was little her father walked her to school and picked her up there, and she spent every Sunday with him.[8] He did sometimes tell her about his home in China, among other stories of his life. Li-lan told me that he still had a strong accent, and that may have inhibited conversation with his English-speaking daughter, although he wrote English fairly well, as his letters and poems testify. The two of them were often quiet together. Li-lan was surrounded by her father's paintings, his musical instruments, and the many birds he acquired. They also did many types of things together—painting, taking trips to Central Park, listening to music, and playing his invented four-person chess game. Gee tried to teach her the Chinese language and calligraphy, but to no avail. I wonder if Li-lan's inability was really an act of refusal.

3.2 Li-lan, early to mid-1950s.

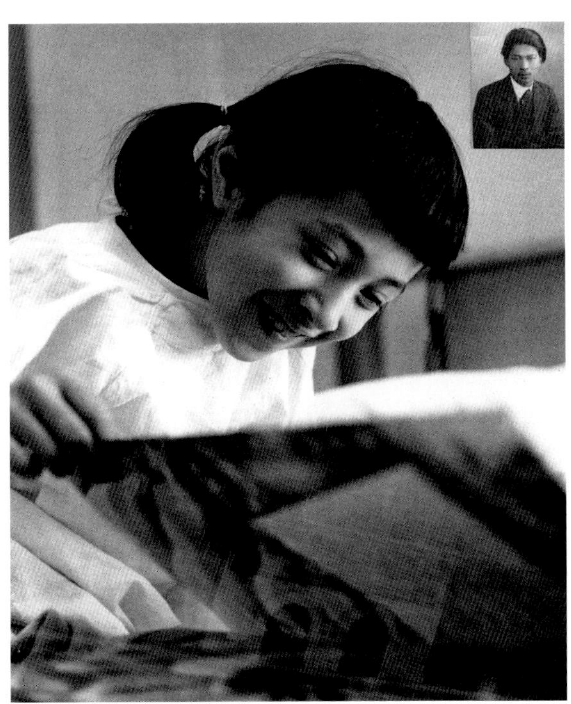

In her early years in school, Li-lan desired to be Caucasian, like her friends and classmates; she rejected all things Chinese and was particularly upset when her mother dressed her in Chinese costumes for some occasions. She suffered enough because she looked different from other young girls, with her "Oriental"-shaped eyes. She was taken for pure Chinese, and people thought she was adopted. Li-lan was usually the only Asian or even minority student in her school. We talked about how this affected her, and even today Li-lan's shyness and sense of apartness results in her keeping a kind of silent space, a quietude that others often erroneously describe as her "Oriental" self and project onto her painting. One of the reasons for her divorce from Masuo Ikeda, a well-known Japanese printmaker (now deceased) whom she married in 1969, was his movie-star fame, both in Japan and New York, which upset her need for anonymity and privacy. Thus something about being the "other" has followed her from her childhood to the present moment, although she now feels more herself than ever before.

In contrast to her father's written memories of a happy childhood in China, his daughter's early life experiences growing up in New York were anything but that. If Gee was outgoing and social, constantly promoting himself, and with deep beliefs about the quality of his artistic abilities, Li-lan still suffers from self-doubt. In many ways Li-lan has been deeply affected by racism, if more subtly practiced, just as her father suffered from the overt bigotry that he endured. He was finally undone by it, whereas she has been able to live a rich life on many levels, but the scars are there. Yun Gee, in his younger days, had a resiliency and a humor that allowed him to triumph over the worst kinds of hatred. It was only in his later years—unfortunately, those years when Li-lan was growing up—that poverty and lack of recognition took their toll. In contrast, Li-lan's early years did not provide the kinds of nurturing that would wipe away the anxieties about not belonging. Neither her mother nor her father was able to provide stability, and their estrangement was of a kind that furthered her feelings of dislocation.

One of the most poignant writings of hers that I came across in her scrapbooks is an essay about her very early years that she wrote for a special issue of a feminist magazine; the theme of that issue was "Third World Women: The Politics Of Being Other."[9] She describes what she thinks she remembers about being so young that she was still sleeping in a crib at her parents' studio on East Tenth Street, and about overhearing the fights between them. Helen left Yun Gee after three years of marriage and moved out with Li-lan because she considered Gee's behavior irrational and sometimes violent, although she also describes leaving as the most difficult thing she had ever had to do in her life. She attributes his actions to the beginning of a mental disorder, which she later called a form of schizophrenia.[10] Gee was very broken-up about the divorce, and so, with trepidation, Helen allowed Li-lan to visit him on Sundays. Li-lan writes, "I remembered my fear and I remembered chilling fights

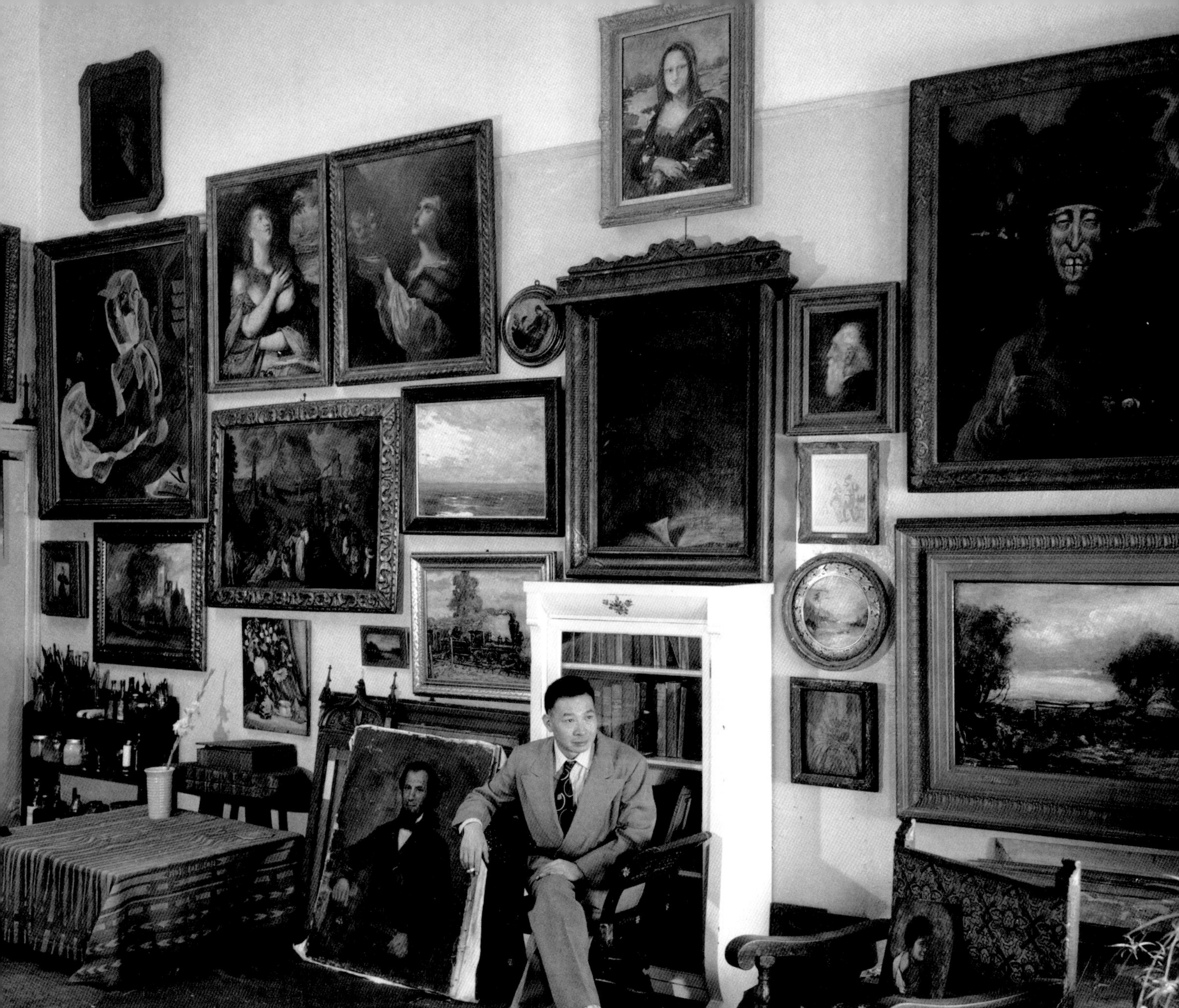

3.3 Yun Gee in his Tenth Street apartment with his collection of "masterpieces" and some of his own paintings, 1950s.

[that is, between her parents, when she was barely two years old and still in her crib], but I couldn't understand why we suddenly left the studio on East Tenth Street, and why I only saw my father on Sundays from then on," and she notes her father's remarkable ability to be self-sufficient and to hold himself together during her visits with him.[11] She later wondered about this behavior if he was really so incapacitated.

Li-lan was in her midthirties when she wrote this, and later she began to question Helen's interpretation of her father's illness and his seeming total mental incapacitation. Finding Gee's later work, speaking with members of her family, and questioning what seemed illogical elements of the story, Li-lan has been led to question parts of the past she had written about that may have been influenced by Helen's interpretations of events. A most touching exchange of letters in 1957, when Li-lan was fourteen years old and at summer camp in Vermont, not only attests to her love for her father and to her need to have his love in return but also indicates that Gee was fully capable of running his life even then, after years of drinking and failure to be recognized. Writing to his daughter, Gee described all the work he was doing in relation to the business he had organized, Tri-King Enterprises, for advertising and selling his chessboard, and there are also letters related to his marketing of his collection of supposed masterpieces of traditional art. Gee also talked about his excitement in starting to paint *Wanamaker Fire* and said how sad he was that the building had burned to the ground. In 1958, writing from San Francisco as he attended his dying father, he shared his experiences and his feelings about the city of his youth, which he still loved. Reading these letters when she was older was also a factor in Li-lan's determination to know the truth about her father.

It is partially this feeling that her mother took her father away from her, not only physically but through distorting aspects of his life, that left her with a damaged image of him that she so resents. This, among other issues, led to her estrangement from Helen for a large part of her adult life; in a deeply affecting way, she lost both her father and her mother.[12] To add to the tension, she was privy to battles between her mother and her father as a constant factor in her youth, and living as biracial, particularly in an environment of familial discord, heightened her fear and loneliness and exacerbated her sense of being different. Nevertheless, Li-lan has fought to keep her father close all her life, in part through her tireless efforts to bring his work, including the later paintings, to their rightful place in the history of modern art. She has archived Yun's life and work and kept his paintings close—many hang on the walls of her homes in Manhattan and East Hampton—and her father's presence is everywhere. Her feelings about her mother are extremely complex, and perhaps they have enabled Li-lan's preference for her Asian part, although her friends and her interests are as diverse in relation to race and ethnicity as were Yun Gee's.

After Helen left Gee, she and Li-lan went to live at the back of a an apartment on West Fourteenth Street, the home of Helen's sister; in Li-lan's description, "the two long, narrow windows opened onto a narrow courtyard facing a high brick wall which blocked air and light from reaching our room. I had tormenting daydreams of being trapped in that dead-end labyrinth, or of running into that impenetrable brown brick wall."[13] Li-lan goes on to talk about watching her mother hunched over a table, painting an endless number of roses—she was painting colored flowers on porcelain boxes in a factory all day, and she was painting them on the lids that she took home to work on at night. It was as a result of this work that Li-lan, at the age of two, had to be

Friday August 2, 1957

Dear dad,

Thank you so much for the clipping. That's really wonderful. I folded it so just your picture shows- in my wallet. But, I keep taking it out and showing it to my cabinmates as I'm real proud of it. And why shouldn't I be- I have a great father.

The Saranac canoe trip was just great! We had a fabulous time. We didn't paddle that much.. actually. It rained quite a bit- but we didn't get wet till the hail storm. Yes.... a hail storm in the middle of summer. That was the day before we were supost to go home. I the truck came to pick us up- cause the counselers didn't want us to sleep in wet sleeping bags- and one girl was sick! So we missed a day of our trip.................... but- just the same we had a grand old time. And for dinner we cooked steaks one night- chops another- ummm boy! ~~Charcoal~~ Charcoaled potatoes and corn- slurp. We had wonderful food on the trip.

I'd love to write to you all day- but I've got to go to dinner now and I want to mail this. So tra la. don't work too hard. Try to take a vacation. And- Good Luck again with your masterpieces.

Love,

Lilan

P.S. don't worry about the top of the (over)

3.4 Letter from Li-lan to her father in San Francisco, August 2, 1957.

sent to a preschool, where she stayed every day from eight in the morning until six in the evening:

> I vaguely remember feeling abandoned, being frightened of the children. I clearly remember them sitting me on a chair in front of the class and shooting me with rifles while laughing hilariously; I remember them chasing me down long, dark, mysterious, winding corridors, and down steep, cavernous stairwells. The recurrent nightmare was as real to me as the long days at school. Once I ran away from school and I remember my mother's frantic worry turning to anger when I was discovered late at night crouching down in the bottom of a telephone booth where I had hidden for hours. I don't remember it but I am told that I refused to talk at school—they thought I couldn't. They told my mother I was mute.[14]

July 30

Lilan Darling

I am so glad you are having so much wonderful time in the camp, the way you describe it to me, make me feel I were there myself - please tell me more of it. it certainly make young & feel like the kid again too. And further more I wish you write me more of it. As you know how I work, about 16 hours a day, not only have no time thinking about the nature not even have time to sleep or eat. Except you are alway with me. Now I have to make enough money to pay the Tai-King loan. when now not enough money come in to pay any thing yet. So you must understand why am slow answer your letter too. every minute I say to myself: I must write to my dear daughter, than the work take me away from it. so-so you must excuse me by not write more & faster.

Thank God, since I finish my Nativity 2 years ago. now I was greatly inspired by the Wanamaker fire! I paint

3.5a Letter from Yun Gee to Li-lan at summer camp, July 30, 1956.

Her early childhood was indeed bleak, as is often the case for children who look different or behave differently from the so-called norm. It is probable that the issues of absence and the complexities that surround communication, both ubiquitous in her work, are related to the experiences that colored her younger years. Many of the stamps she uses are about the failure to find the other; one of the most poignant is "return to sender." In spite of this, her work is also permeated with humor and a playful dimension that often mingles with the sobriety. Her letters to her father in 1957 also show the playful side of her—her love of swimming and canoeing, and all the trips she took and things she did with the other campers. They are letters from a typical kid who loved camp and was completely involved with all the activities. They are the usual kinds of letters kids write to their parents except that they are longer, ask for replies with urgency, and are perhaps more frequent.

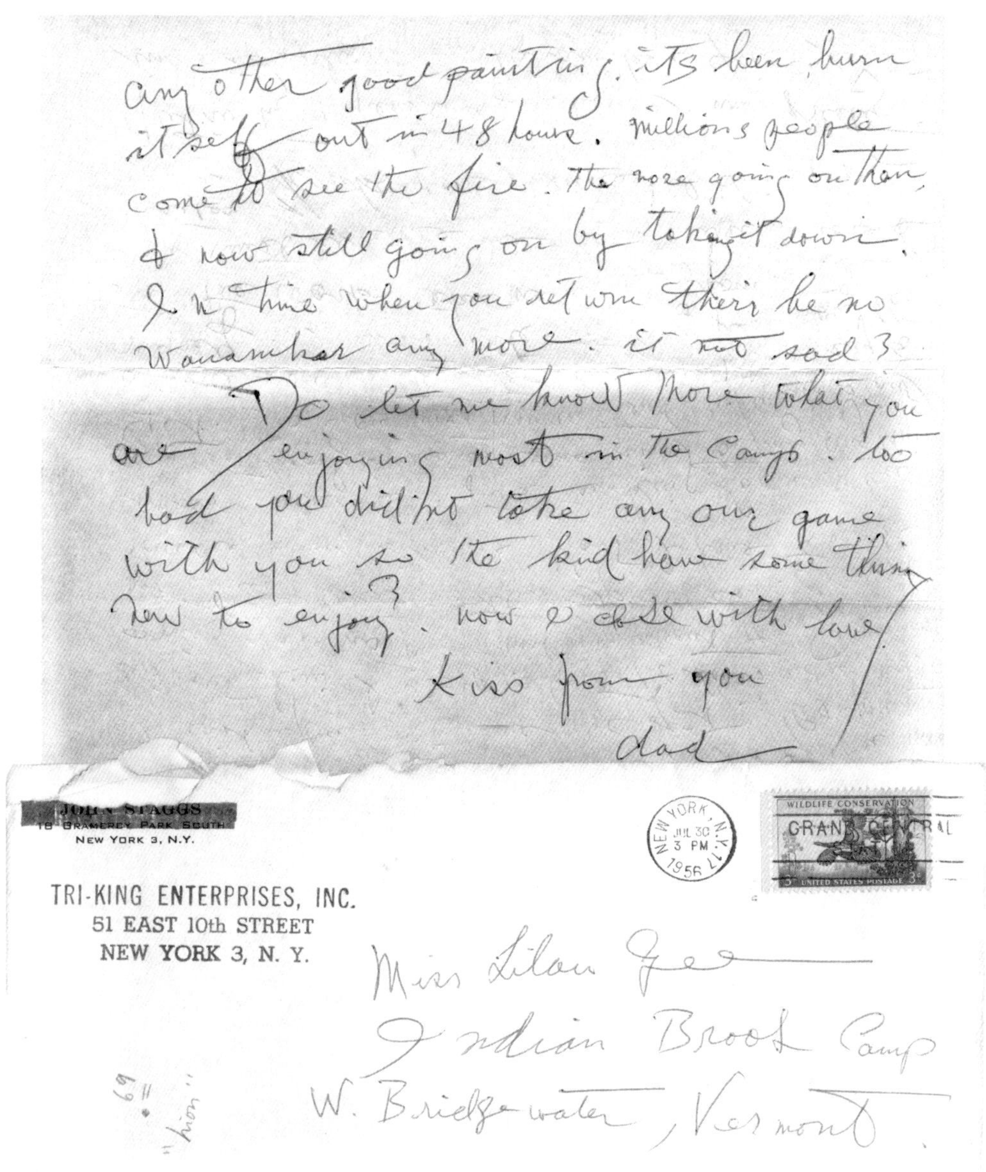
any other good painting. its been burn
itself out in 48 hours. millions people
come to see the fire. the noise going on then,
& now still going on by taking it down.
In time when you return there be no
Wanamaker any more. it not sad ?
Do let me know more what you
are enjoying most in the camp. too
bad you didn't take any our game
with you so the kid have some thing
new to enjoy. now I close with love
kiss from you
dad

JOHN STAGGS
18 GRAMERCY PARK SOUTH
NEW YORK 3, N.Y.

NEW YORK, N.Y.
JUL 30
3 PM
1956

WILDLIFE CONSERVATION
GRAND CENTRAL
UNITED STATES POSTAGE

TRI-KING ENTERPRISES, INC.
51 EAST 10th STREET
NEW YORK 3, N. Y.

Miss Lilan Gee
Indian Brook Camp
W. Bridgewater, Vermont

3.5b Letter from Yun Gee to Li-lan at summer camp (verso), with envelope, July 30, 1956.

In contrast to her early schooling, Li-lan fared well at the High School for Performing Arts. There were many different kinds of students with an interest in the arts that was serious, as was Li-lan's. She studied acting there but turned to painting soon after graduation. Her formal art schooling was almost nil except for a four-month period at Pratt Institute in New York and a year of once-a-week private tutoring. The majority of her art training took the form of looking at art at the Museum of Modern Art (she often did her homework in the sculpture garden) and in New York galleries and hanging around with artists at parties, at art openings, and at the famous Cedar Bar when she was a teenager of fifteen or sixteen. She had little knowledge of early Renaissance art until 1964, when she spent some time traveling to Rome, Florence, and Paris; she was particularly taken with early-Renaissance painting and architecture. Looking at art and architecture in Florence was a formative experience. Except for painting and drawing with her father, and because of her sensitivity to the different creative environments in which she has lived, Li-lan was able to train herself. Most artists at that time went to art schools or entered the art programs that had been organized at colleges and universities in the 1950s, but Li-lan seems to have been able to profit from looking intensely at a lot of different kinds of contemporary and traditional art, and she had the good luck to be born in New York and to profit from the years when the new seemed to be continually happening. Closer to home, her father provided her with an openness to ideas and to the art of many cultures, simply because she was surrounded by it in his studio. His perseverance as an artist may also have provided her with a model that has fostered her tenacity and her desire to continually perfect her skills.

The United States in the post–World War II years, when Li-lan was growing up and becoming more aware of herself and the world, was a very different country than the one that was the environment for Gee's life and work. For the most part, the quest for regional community and a commitment to social solidarity, as pictured in the art of social realism, was over after the war; capitalism, hatred of Communism, and the desire for individual expression became the reigning ideologies. A growing zeal for what was believed to still be industrial capitalism enveloped even those whose leanings in the 1930s and early 1940s had been socialist. No longer isolated and regionalist in mentality, as in the prewar days, the country was fast becoming a major player on the world stage, but without the experience necessary to that role—a problem still haunting the United States today.

The country seemingly united in its anti-Communist, pro-capitalist stance, and yet it was also a hotbed of anxiety. And then there was the counterculture of the 1960s. Cultural practices mapped those dilemmas. Mass media and popular forms were emerging, and their rapid spread was obvious in the pronounced rage against them, as early as 1939, on the part of cultural guardians like Clement Greenberg.[15] In the art world, at first, political prestige was afforded by association with earlier movements of political abstraction like Russian constructivism and the German Bauhaus, and in the name of a radical departure from traditional art forms. In the aftermath of World War II and the destruction and destitution of Europe and its cultural center in Paris, almost all aspects of socialism and Communism were expunged from discussions about abstract expressionism.[16] As "art for art's sake" became the ruling premise in the late 1940s and the 1950s, narrative and figurative forms were almost obliterated in relation to the art world's exhibitions and discussions—a problem we saw affecting Gee's career. And then there was racism.

Gee had been the victim of obvious racism, particularly of a type engendered by the war and the attitude toward the Japanese (and, by extension, toward all

Asians). Li-lan's experience was somewhat different. The populations in major cities were becoming even more diverse, with immigration from Europe and then from many other countries, and with the relaxation, in the 1950s, of discriminatory laws that had blocked Asians from full citizenship. As a result, Li-lan was not subjected to the overtly racist practices that her father endured, although the everyday slights had their affect. As a youth, she did have friends, primarily Caucasian; but from her high school days on, many of her friends were African American, and Li-lan also participated in organizations like the Congress of Racial Equality, where she met many people from diverse backgrounds. As a young artist growing up in the 1960s, she was able to participate freely in the exhilaration that came from living in New York and meeting all kinds of people—and, in the early 1960s and the 1970s, many people of color.

For the most part, and as one result of the contributions of immigrants from Europe, New York was fast becoming the center of the art world and was exporting abstract expressionism everywhere. Li-lan remembers the excitement of being on the fringes of the scene, a witness to the talk from the growing antiexpressionist generation of 1960s artists she met there.[17] She was absorbing everything, from the lingering abstract expressionism, which she tried and found completely uncongenial, to color field painting, pop art, and minimalism, which were rapidly replacing abstract expressionism. Artists like Roy Lichtenstein and Andy Warhol may have been influences, but Li-lan's early work had an illusory, more personal quality, and the painter's touch was always primary; her 1960s painting, like some of her father's years earlier, was decidedly indebted to surrealism. She was also going to poetry readings, to Fluxus events, to storefront showings of the early works of Claes Oldenburg (at The Store on Avenue A), and to openings and happenings staged at the Greene Gallery by Allan Kaprow and others, and she was very involved with jazz and frequently went to jazz clubs. Li-lan was living the life of many a young artist growing up in New York.

If it was fortunate for Yun Gee to have been born at such an exciting time in China, it was equally fortunate for Li-lan to have been raised in New York during a period of rich cultural and political change. The country would soon become more politically conservative, but Li-lan's environment in her adolescent years was decidedly leftist. She went to the radical Downtown Community School from grades five through eight; Pete Seeger taught music there, and when the principal was called before the House Un-American Activities Committee, parents of the children who attended the school voted in favor of his retention. The summer camp that Li-lan went to was also leftist in orientation. Her consciousness as an artist and a person was formed in the 1960s, when civil rights and all forms of multicultural protest produced an environment congenial to her desires and formative in her creative quest. She met

YOUTH · ART · HYPE

A Different Bohemia

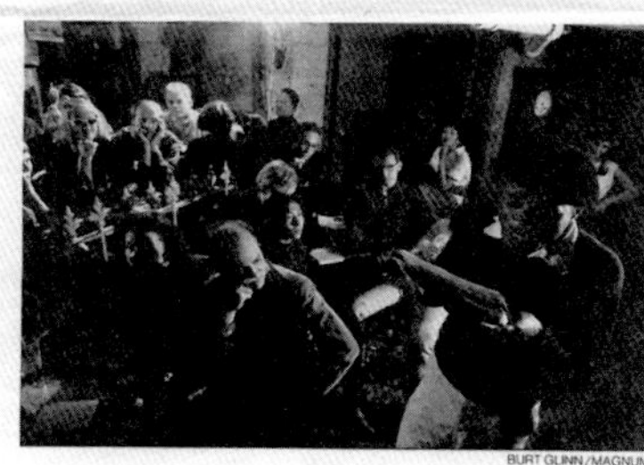

BURT GLINN/MAGNUM

a poetry reading, circa 1959, in Greenwich Village, a bohemian haunt of another decade.

By Maureen Dowd

ANN MAGNUSON SITS ON a worn couch in her East Village apartment, rummaging in the junkyard of American culture. She talks, with affectionate mockery, about icons and totems and slogans, past and present. Her allusions spill out like the contents of some crazed time capsule — Steve and Eydie, "The Beverly Hillbillies," Patty Hearst, Gidget, Wonder bread, Amway, TV evangelists, Lawrence Welk, Jim Morrison and the Doors, Chicken McNuggets, high-fiber diets, midstate pork princesses, Mantovani, Mr. Spock and "Beyond the Valley of the Dolls."

Recently christened "the Funny Girl of the avant-garde" by People magazine, the 28-year-old conjures up these spirits in her satirical skits for downtown clubs such as Area, Danceteria and the Pyramid. Her characters include Mrs. Rambo, who shoots her way through Bloomingdale's to save Nancy Reagan from getting a New Wave makeup job at the Yves St. Laurent counter, and Fallopia, Prince's new protégé, who is really Delores Jean Humpshnoodleburger, a graduate of the Rose-Marie School of Baton and Tap in Duluth.

In the past, Ann Magnuson, who had a bit part in the movie "Desperately Seeking Susan," would have been described as an aspiring actress and her territory would have been called the bohemian part of town. Now she is a performance artist with a cult following and the area where she lives and works is simply called downtown.

She is at the center of the vivid New York arts community that has captured international attention spinning what has come to be known as "the downtown style." The artists cannibalize high art and the mass culture of the last three decades — television, suburbia, pornography, Satur-

Maureen Dowd is a reporter for The New York Times.

3.6a Li-lan at a poetry reading in Greenwich village, c. 1959.

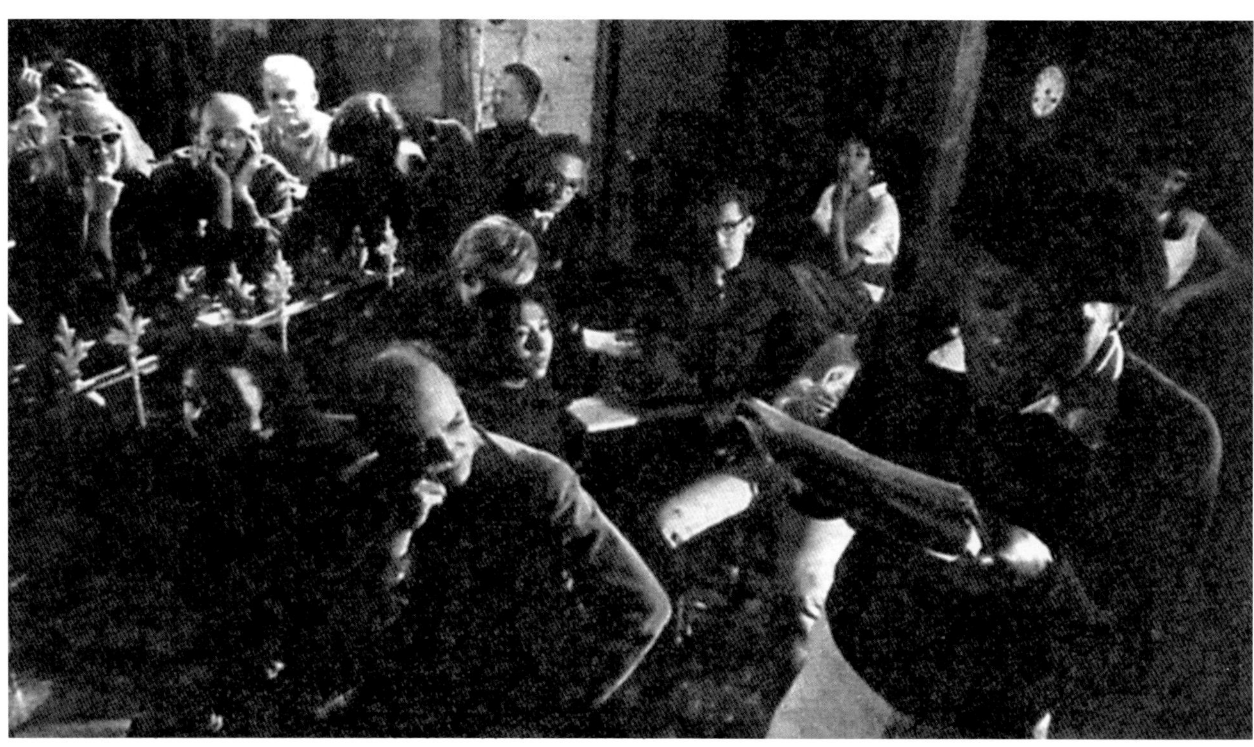

3.6b Li-lan at a poetry reading in Greenwich village (enlargement), c. 1959.

many artists, dancers, musicians, and writers, and in spite of her shyness, Li-lan made friends with many of them. When she speaks about her first trip to Mexico, she talks excitedly about traveling all over with a diverse group and meeting many artists, some of whom are still good friends today. Some of them were also instrumental in her meeting with Asian artists in New York. She loved Mexico and traveled there several times, two or three times with Masuo Ikeda. Her features, particularly her cheekbones and nose, often made Mexicans take her for a native. Li-lan had entrée into many Mexican homes, and at eighteen—she went to Mexico a year after graduating from high school—she lived the life of an artist vagabond, dressing in Mexican clothes, wearing Mexican jewelry, and singing and dancing to Mexican music. This trip was among her first ventures to other countries and cultures, and Li-lan was struck by the experience.

From her later teen years on, Li-lan had friends and acquaintances from all kinds of backgrounds, and she began to embrace that part of her that is Asian, which has continued to nurture her up to the present moment. She was close to Isamu Noguchi until he died, and he spent many summers visiting her in East Hampton. That friendship also stimulated her interest in Japan, and the fact of their both being biracial was a special aspect of their bond. She then met many Japanese artists in New York, such as On Karawa, who became a close friend, and Shusaku Arakawa, Ay-O, Yoko Ono, and Yayoi Kusama, among others; they were among the most radical artists of their time. Thus, even though the 1960s in New York were really formative years for Li-lan, personally and artistically, the time she spent in Japan, from the late 1960s through the late 1970s, was also of singular importance.[18]

Life in Japan

> If I want to imagine a fictive nation, I can . . . isolate somewhere in the world (*faraway*) a certain number of features . . . and out of these features deliberately form a system. It is this system which I shall call: Japan.
>
> Hence Orient and Occident cannot be taken here as "realities" to be compared and contrasted historically, philosophically, culturally, politically. I am not lovingly gazing toward an Oriental essence—to me the Orient is a matter of indifference, merely providing a reserve of features whose manipulation—whose invented interplay—allows me to "entertain" the idea of an unheard-of symbolic system, one altogether detached from our own. What can be addressed, in the consideration of the Orient, are not other symbols, another metaphysics, another wisdom . . . ; it is the possibility of difference, of a mutation, of a revolution in the propriety of symbolic systems.[19]

In spite of Barthes's declaration of creating a fiction, his picture has been taken almost literally and, as Alexandra Munroe suggests, has "led to the popular conception of Japan as the paradigm of postmodern culture," with a "highly-advanced information society and commodity culture" that "came to epitomize the postmodern condition whereby the real, the referent, no longer exist and all is simulation and pastiche."[20] Barthes, as a structuralist, described a sign system that he called "Japan"; it is the system itself that he finds intrinsic to Japanese culture and social behavior. In light of this system, he analyzes everything in contrast to the West, from preparing food, eating, and using chopsticks to bowing, playing Pachinko (slot machines), the theatrical face and theater itself, Bunraku dolls, and, of course, calligraphy. But it is also an outsider's invention, like the delightful but clichéd film *Lost in Translation*. In light of transnationalism and globalization, Barthes's intriguing semantic game may both apply to and caricature being Japanese today, or in the 1960s and 1970s, when Li-lan lived part of each year there. What his game misses entirely is bodily presence—what it feels like to live in modern Japan for long periods of time, with the senses synergistically in play—but that absence is natural in structuralism and in much of poststructuralist thinking. How did being present in Japan affect Li-lan's life and work?

Li-lan is a New Yorker and speaks about her love for the city and the great diversity of persons and social and cultural forms that make up this still great cosmopolitan center, but Tokyo is her second city. She embraced Japanese culture before she became acquainted with that of China, and many of her friends were Japanese. Until recent years, being Asian was identified with Japan more than with China. From about 1969 to 1979, Li-lan and Masuo Ikeda lived part of the year in Tokyo, part of the year in Soho, and, from 1972 on, part of the year in East Hampton. She speaks with joy about her life in Japan and still finds Tokyo one of the places she feels most at home. She earned a partial living there designing book covers and writing essays that she illustrated with photographs she had taken, and so she was also somewhat engaged with the business world. She talks about a felt equation between Japan and Mexico because she had an intuitive love for both countries, and traveling to the latter with Masuo, and earlier with her Japanese friend Shizue, added another personal connection.

As a professional woman, Li-lan had many artist friends in Japan—in particular, many women friends who were artists and whose lives were different from the stereotypical image of the Japanese woman's life. As a foreigner, Li-lan was not expected to conform to Japanese social mores; in fact, she was essentially outside the society except among artistic groups. Her husband had many friends who were writers, dancers, and actors, and Li-lan participated in a rich cultural life with him. It is important to understand that she was also well known as a painter in her own right; her first one-person show was in Tokyo, and several others followed there. She met people through those events, and so she had a circle of friends she had made on her own;

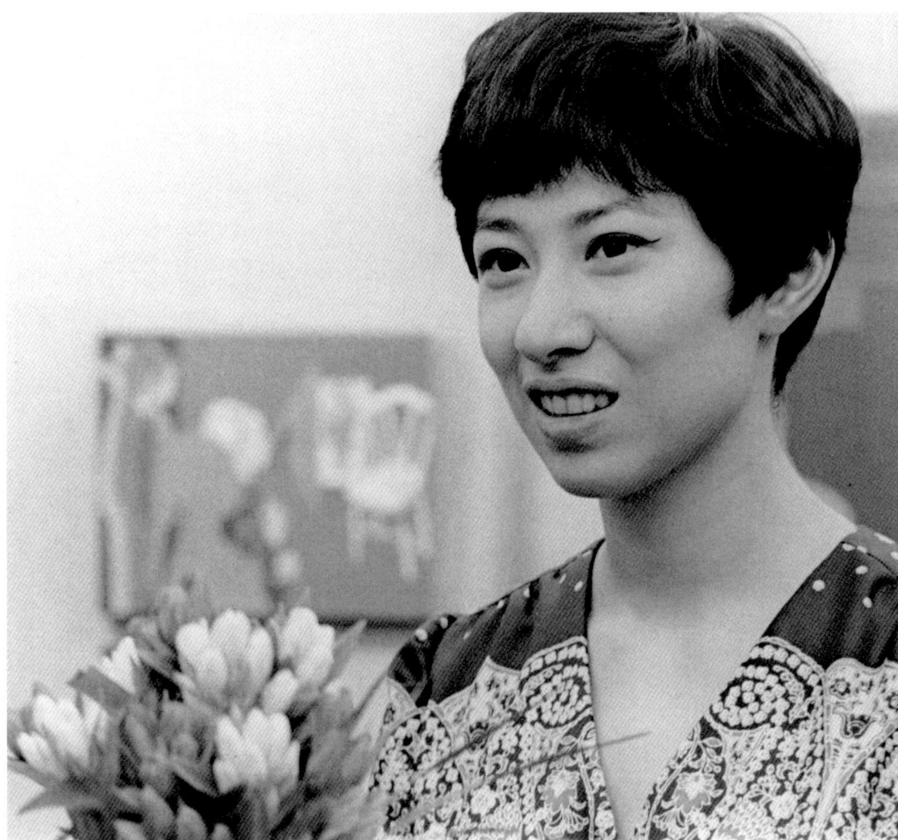

3.7 Li-lan at the opening of her first exhibition, Tokyo, 1969.

some of them later told her that younger artists there had been looking at and emulating her work. She was very free in Japanese society, in contrast to most other Japanese women (if they were not professional), although their lives were beginning to change.

Japan in the 1960s and 1970s was experiencing an economic miracle that also began to stimulate social change, and the country was also playing a crucial role on the international scene. These changes affected art as well, and the art scene in Japan at that time was as radical as it had been during the years when Li-lan was growing up in the United States. She was lucky to have experienced amazing changes in both countries. When I pressed Li-lan to describe what it was in particular about Japanese culture that she so admired, she emphasized its aesthetic nature. Unlike her husband, who was then immersed in contemporary culture, Li-lan also wanted to discover traditional Japanese customs and Japanese art. She visited many Buddhist temples and Shinto shrines, with their altars and painted decorations and screens, and, like the Japanese food she loves, they seemed to her beautiful and fulfilling through "a less is more" kind of aesthetic. Her own apartment in New York and her house in East Hampton reflect this approach. Japan also provided the type of contrast that she finds most nurturing for her life and work to the present day: between the intensity and visual glitz of a city like Tokyo, and the serenity of Kyoto and the Buddhist temples and monasteries, with their silent interiors and beautiful gardens. Li-lan talks about the lovely screens she saw in the temples, and which, along with contemporary Japanese art, had their impact. Then there were the traditional Noh plays; Kabuki theater, with music and dance; and the contemporary Butoh performances, particularly prominent in Japan from the mid-1950s to the present and internationally famous in the past three decades. Japanese culture in all its ramifications was exported along with Japanese financial know how.

Aside from the current interest in everything Asian, including its food, some artists who are known in Asia are beginning to become more recognized in the United States, even if they are American citizens like Yun Gee and Li-lan.[21] Li-lan had a reputation in Japan not only because of her painting but also because artists in Japan began to write about themselves instead of simply waiting for critics to review their work. In addition to the book about her early life that was published in Japan, Li-lan wrote an article about her first trip to China as well as several other pieces for newspapers and magazines. Her scrapbooks are filled with reviews and articles about her life and work when she lived in Japan, and that is true with respect to Taiwan more recently. Her reputation in Japan, the current interest in Asian artists, and the fact that galleries often owned by Asians are opening in the United States are all factors that have led to recent exhibitions of her work in New York and Los Angeles. This is also a sign of the globalization that is a large part of the contemporary art world almost everywhere, with the reverse happening to Yun Gee, since he is being discovered in China as an early modernist as that country recognizes the contributions of its overseas populations.

New York, East Hampton, Taiwan, and China

Like her father, Li-lan is a cosmopolite. Although she has spent parts of each year, first with her husband and then alone, in her other house and studio in East Hampton, she does so in order to work and to take a break from the intensity of New York City. She complains about the lack of ethnic diversity in East Hampton and about how few of her peers still live there among the wealthy and the art stars. What diversity there is comes, for the most part, from the Latino and Vietnamese populations that serve the upper middle class and the very rich. Although Li-lan is not a political activist, her association with persons of color is an intrinsic part of her social, political, and artistic life. Therefore, she needs big cities in order to survive, and New York, although less efficient and slower in tempo than Tokyo, provides the contemporary intellectual and creative energy she feeds on, just as it provides ease of communication: her native language is English, although she can communicate in Japanese. Both the meditative environment of East Hampton and the hectic nature of New York are necessary to fulfill her present needs and desires; in East Hampton she paints, swims, and practices tai chi, and in New York City her life is almost frantic as she paints, writes, promotes her father's work, exhibits her own, visits galleries, attends openings, and participates with her many friends in many of the cultural events that the city offers—and also keeps swimming.

When I started working with Li-lan on this book, she was living on Canal Street; about five or six years ago, she moved to the Wall Street area. In 1999 she painted *Wall Street, PM* (pl. 23). It shows the wall of her studio room with three shades drawn, and postmarks with numbers referring to times of day, the last being 11:12 P.M., which she reiterates, and the month, January. Perhaps these are ciphers that lead us to the feel of the interior at that time in that month. I am reminded of the privacy and quietude of her father's *Untitled (Nude)* (pl. 7). Her own painting is very sparse, mostly in grays and whites formed as a painting within a painting, and outside the shadowed edge is a small red-framed box with the letters STAMP. Although it was painted several years before the events of September 11, 2001, the picture is almost a prescient image of retreat from what is in the streets outside the studio now, with the effects of 9/11 everywhere. The noise of traffic and construction is always a problem in New York, as it was when she made this picture, but now it is deafening in that area of the city. Li-lan has moved again, to Twenty-fourth Street, in order to be free of the everyday ramifications of that nightmare and to be able to live and work in some kind of quietude.

Li-lan pursues her transnational life—Japan in the past, and now, more frequently, in Taiwan, since her father's exhibition there in 1992 and her own one-person shows from 1993 to the present. Formerly, many of her friends and acquaintances were Japanese, and she still travels to that country; now, as a result of the exhibitions, many of her friends are Chinese, and she says her life has been taken over by them. Li-lan's first visit to China was in 1980, on a specially planned artist's tour that traveled to five different cities.[22] She wrote about that trip for a Japanese magazine and took photographs for it, including one of her family in her father's village.[23] While the rest of the group stayed in Canton, she went with an interpreter to the village where Yun Gee was born. She had no idea where her father's house was, but from the moment she told people who she was, the whole village came out to greet her and to show her what was still the largest house in this still poor town: Gee's family home, which had framed announcements of his exhibitions hanging on the wall. There was also a postcard of the ship on which he sailed to the United States, and a picture of Li-lan's grandmother, which they gave her. Gee was still considered a hero, even among young people, because of the money he had sent home, particularly in the grim 1940s. In the end, Li-lan could not believe that her sophisticated father had come from a poor village like this one. She

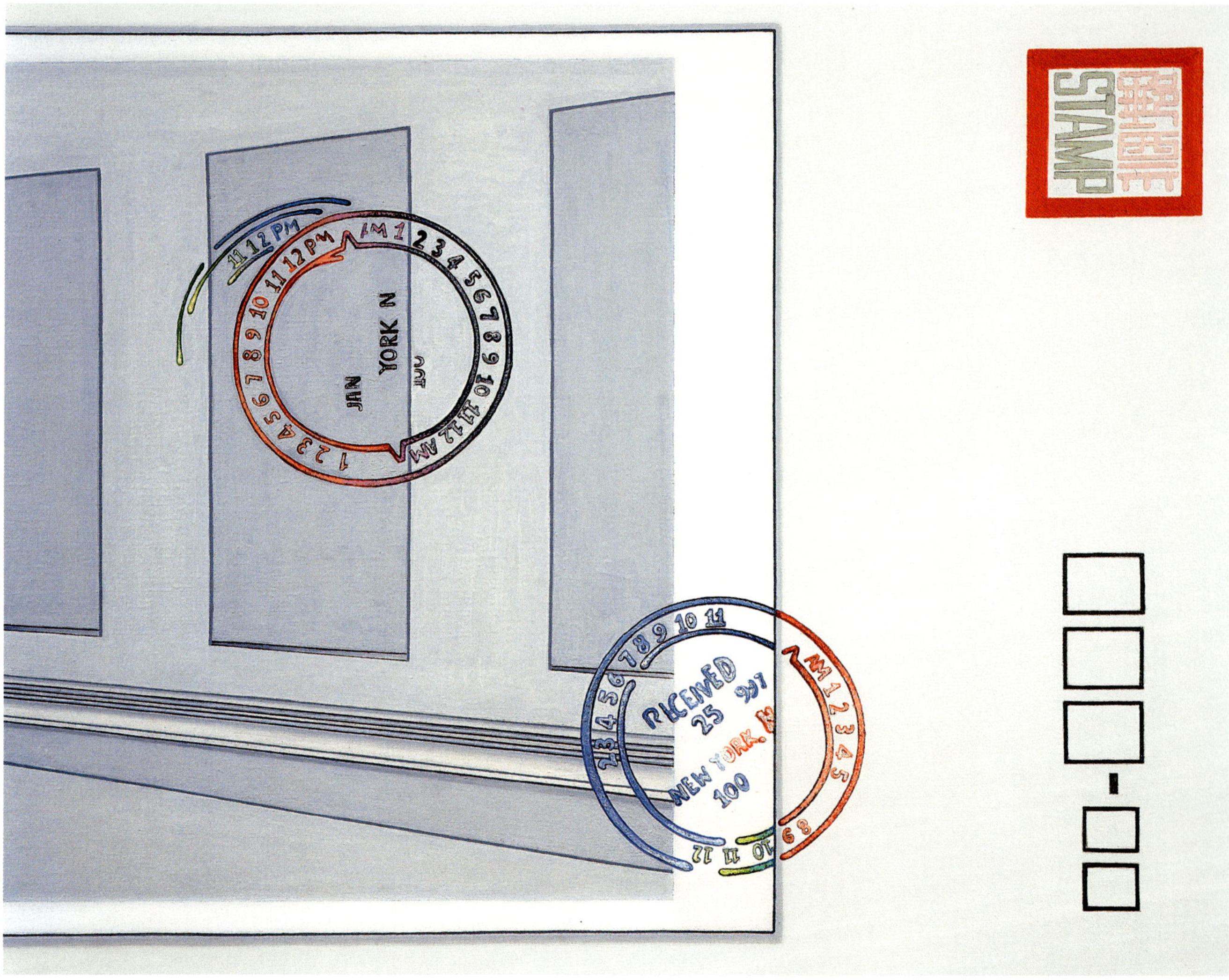

Plate 23 Li-lan, ***Wall Street, PM***, oil on linen (24 in. x 30 in.), 1999.

wondered whether he might have spent time learning in Canton, a city hours away, but although his family seems to have been the richest in the village, it is still questionable whether his family would have been able to afford to send him to school in Canton.[24]

When Li-lan went to China the second time, in 1995, she was invited to talk about her work by the Central Art Academy in Beijing. On the same trip, she visited her father's village as well as surrounding areas. She speaks vividly about a traditional practice in her honor: a family slaughtered a chicken in an ancestor-worship ceremony in which Li-lan participated; this event was captured on a video of that trip. Li-lan admits to a fondness for chicken feet that sometimes bewilders her dinner companions.[25] Her family members in China expressed their regard for Yun Gee and their delight in meeting her, but when Li-lan showed them a book about Gee's paintings, they were totally uninterested. They did show her a framed collection of photographs and exhibition announcements that Gee had sent home, and which they still kept. When I talked with Li-lan about the impact of this trip, she felt that it had not really been going to China and to her father's village that made her conscious of her Chinese background but rather the people she worked with on her own exhibitions, and on her father's in Taiwan, who engaged her in close relationships and made her more aware of Chinese contemporary art, literature, everyday customs, and mores. This immersion in that culture may account for the greater prevalence of Chinese stamps and images in her recent paintings.

It is revealing to compare the experiences of passage in the lives of father and daughter. Yun Gee easily folded aspects of the cultures of the United States and France into his worldview. Li-lan, brought up primarily as Caucasian, just as easily absorbed Japanese and Chinese (Taiwanese) cultural practices into her adult life. Her time spent with her father probably enabled her to embrace the part of her that was Chinese, even if she suffered from that identity in her youth. Perhaps she also learned from Gee to acknowledge the complexity that is the makeup of each of us, even if few of us choose to recognize our fundamental hybridism.

As a biracial woman, Li-lan lives as a transnational in the very flesh of her body and mind. Yun Gee literally crossed from nation to nation, with curiosity and openness as prime factors. While Li-lan shares that ability to cross boundaries, in a profound sense her experiences of passage also result from crossings in the genes that have been with her from the day of her birth. How one tunes in to that mixture—listening to both parts, or only hearing one or the other—can lead to the sensibility of a cosmopolite living in that critical "third space" that may open one to real diversity, or it can lead to a retreat into a ghetto of exclusions. Neither Yun Gee nor his daughter opted for the latter but instead embraced the complexities unleashed by the former. It could have been otherwise for Li-lan, given the social and environmental aspects of her upbringing, and some of the research on biracial persons suggest that Li-lan's is a test case for what not to do in relation to a child of mixed racial background.[26] As I have suggested, ethnic and racial complexity is a factor in everybody's constitution, but when difference is marked on the body—and particularly when the prominent features are those of a minority group—suffering is often entailed. It is the ability to live and work above that pain, and develop from it the complex awareness of other ways, that Li-lan shares with Yun Gee in the "in between" space they both have inhabited. It is that space that Li-lan paints, perhaps even more consistently than Gee did.

4 LI-LAN

Global Icons and Painting Practices

Butterflies,

ships,

sea shapes, corollas,

leaning towers,

dark eyes, moist and

round as grapes . . .

—PABLO NERUDA, "ODE TO A STAMP ALBUM"

Pablo Neruda's "Ode to a Stamp Album" is a perfect invocation with which to begin to experience Li-lan's floating images. They reveal a precise sense of contemporary location at the same time that they reflect nostalgic engagement with times past. Humor and plenitude sit upon a surface that *seems* empty and partially a result of what *appears* to be the coolness of her approach. Her work needs time to unveil visual meaning, and as a result it does not always engage contemporary viewers who are used to the immediacy of intense stimuli. For those who look closely, the brushed surfaces conjure up many aspects of paintings past, and the coolness disappears in the knowledge that only obsessive intensity in the act of painting could result in works like these. What is also important to her process is the serendipity that governs the practice that seems to be so conceptually ordered. Li-lan does not usually make drawings in preparation for paintings but works directly on the canvas: one form leads to another. Her pastel paintings are also not preparatory for the larger canvases but are completed works in their own right; the change in medium produces a perceptual experience very different from the oils, if sometimes very similar in content. Many private events are hidden in the visual signs offered; likewise, a quick look at the painting betrays

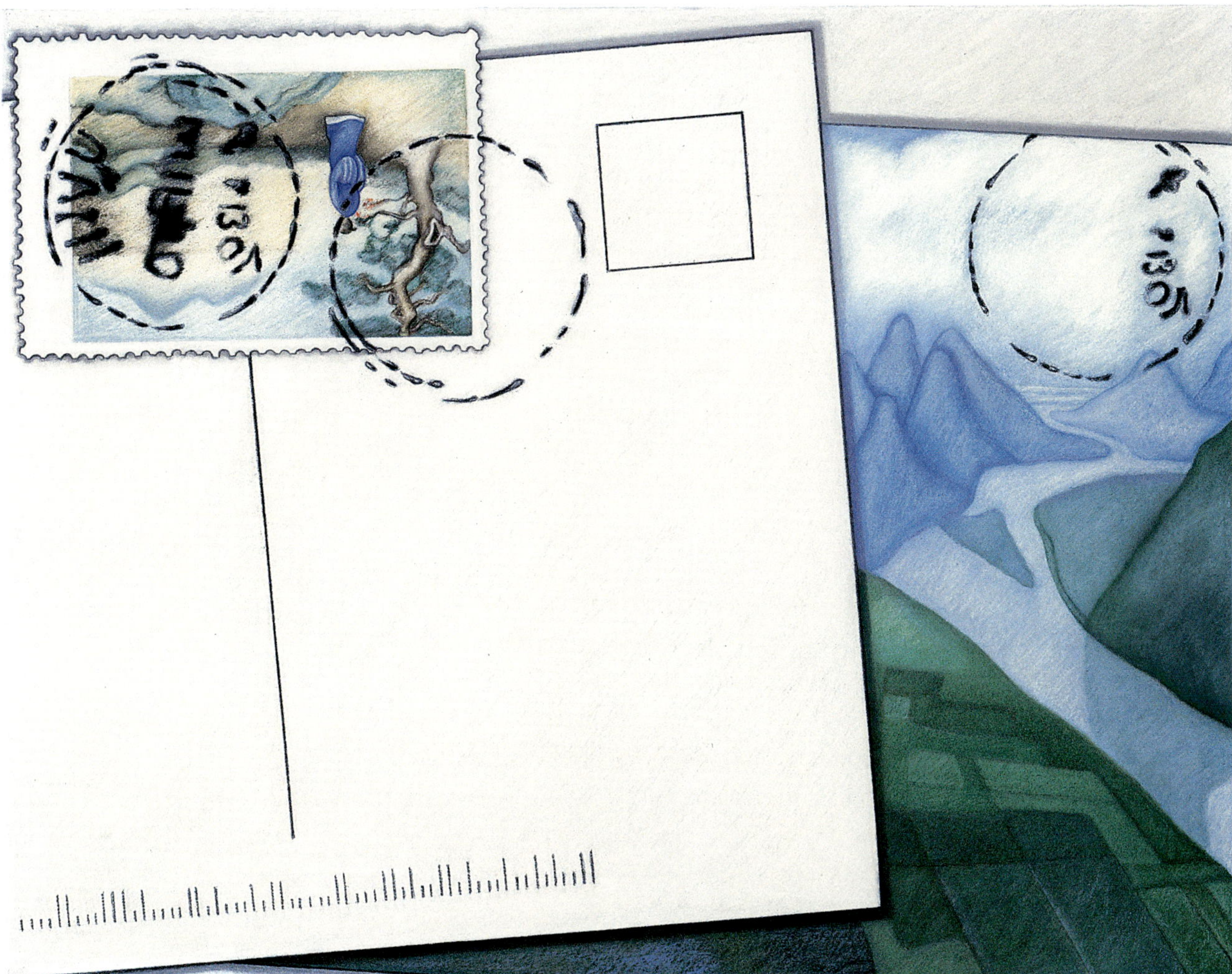

Plate 24 Li-lan, *Post Card: Landscapes of Guilin*, pastel on canvas (24 in. x 30 in.), 1994.

the process that makes them, which is anything but fast and conceptual.

What is most intriguing about Li-lan's work is the play between the individual sign, which can be read but often is not understood in conjunction with other signs (a semiotic issue), and the presence of the painterly mark that was always there but has become more prominent in her recent work and references the artist's physical practices. In addition, the surreal, if not in a form as dramatic as the Comte de Lautréamont's "chance meeting on a dissection table of a sewing machine and umbrella," is pervasive.[1] Replacing the implied cruelty in the writer's poetry is the artist's play between juxtapositions that are sometimes sober and sometimes ridiculous. Roland Barthes's description of a Japanese meal could also be an apt description of Li-lan's paintings:

> Entirely visual (conceived, concerted, manipulated for sight, and even for a painter's eye), . . . here everything is the ornament of another ornament: first of all because on the table, on the tray, food is never anything but a collection

> of fragments, none of which appears privileged by an order of ingestion; to eat is not to respect a menu (an itinerary of dishes), but to select, with a light touch of the chopsticks, sometimes one color, sometimes another.[2]

Over the course of her career, Li-lan's work has been identified with a multiplicity of styles: surrealism, minimalism, pop art, photorealism, and aspects of both Japanese and Chinese painting. Her ongoing closeness with intellectuals and artistic figures in New York who are associated with these styles, as well as with her Chinese and Japanese friends, may partially account for such attributions. What has been ignored are her connections to Japanese conceptualism and her friendships with some of the artists in New York and Tokyo who were also part of Fluxus. Nevertheless, the association of her work with any single mode precludes engagement with those richly painted "empty surfaces" that are replete with cross-cultural implications.

Li-lan's work represents a carefully developed and highly personal method of painting that alludes to her complex origins and to her extensive periods of living in Japan. Her particular blend of style and reference, as narrated in her more recent paintings through renditions of stamps, postmarks, and architecture from around the world, acts as a metaphor for the weave that encompasses her own diverse origins. Often the stamps and postmarks come from cards and letters sent by friends, as well as from places she has never visited, and they lead her to reflections on travel, history, geography, and forms of communication that are particularly relevant to contemporary sensibilities.

As in her father's case, a *fusion* of cultural sources critiques the approach that delineates the Asian from the Western parts. Li-lan responds to visual stimuli from all over the world, and Chinese elements are no more engaging than those from Africa or Latin America, although they seem more frequent recently, as a result of professional and cultural interests discussed in the previous chapter. As for the reception of her work when it was first shown, in the 1970s, the most responsive audiences were in Japan, where emptiness and cognizance of "the void" were still potent religious and philosophical concepts. Taiwanese viewers in the 1990s, when she began to show her work in Taiwan, were puzzled because the content was so ambiguous. Now it may be the case that her work is not activist enough, or that it is without sufficient universal appeal, or that it is not involved with installation, photography, and the electronic practices that are prominent in the work of artists from both Taiwan and China. For the most part, American audiences think her paintings are very Asian, and Asian viewers think her work is very American. It would be sadly ironic if Li-lan's career mirrors Yun Gee's in being out of sync with the times in spite of her transnational content. One reviewer has suggested that there will be a new audience for her work in Taiwan:

> Interests are changing. . . . The new wave of collectors is younger and more educated, and Li-lan's art . . . offers a fresh way of looking. . . . Stylistic pluralism has emerged as a special symbolism for the Taiwanese. Prof. Ming Ming Lee, who heads the Graduate Institute of Art Studies at the National Central University in Taiwan, emphasizes the need to demonstrate openness, tolerance, adaptability and the elimination of authority in a political climate that opposes the authoritarian cultural practices of mainland China. A conflict between the two Chinas has been escalating this year as the People's Republic regularly confirms its intention to absorb Taiwan. "Amid this stylistic pluralism," Professor Lee said, "the art community and society as a whole [prefer] to show that they are looking toward Asia and Asian blood ties rather than to overt internationalism."[3]

It may well be that taste is catching up with Li-lan, in a positive sense. Nevertheless, even though times have changed with respect to the art scene both in Taiwan and in mainland China, political tensions are still rampant, and how they may affect the art world in each country is anyone's guess. What is most intriguing is the emphasis "toward Asia and Asian blood ties," a political move in the East/West discourse.

In discussions of Li-lan's work, as in discussions of her father's, issues involving East and West often come into play (for example, in relation to Li-lan's manner of drawing). A prime element in all her work is the way in which the clear edges that define the shapes she creates are in accord with the seductive painterly marks that fill them and the surface of the picture plane. It is significant that Gee's training in calligraphy did not produce a linear style as refined as his daughter's drawing technique. So much has been written about his Chinese education in brush painting that it is taken for granted that this automatically produces fine draftsmanship. There are masters of calligraphy, and then there are the less proficient others. Gee was a marvelous colorist, but Li-lan is adept at both line and color, the former in spite of her inability to learn calligraphy. Differences in artistic backgrounds may be crucial here. Gee learned to draw with a brush in a fluid linear form, and I think he did not depart from that training after his few very accomplished "cubist" drawings made in San Francisco. While his paintings were radical, his later drawings were quite conservative.[4] Li-lan developed her drawing techniques in an atmosphere of hard-edged minimalism, in the comic-book environment of pop art in the United States and Japan, and through her love for the "realist" surrealist painters. There are few elements of Chinese calligraphy in her renderings; nevertheless, in the 1993 *China: 30 Yuan,* for example, she paints framed black cancellation marks that diminish in clarity from a rich black to a light gray and seem to resonate with calligraphy. This effect often happens

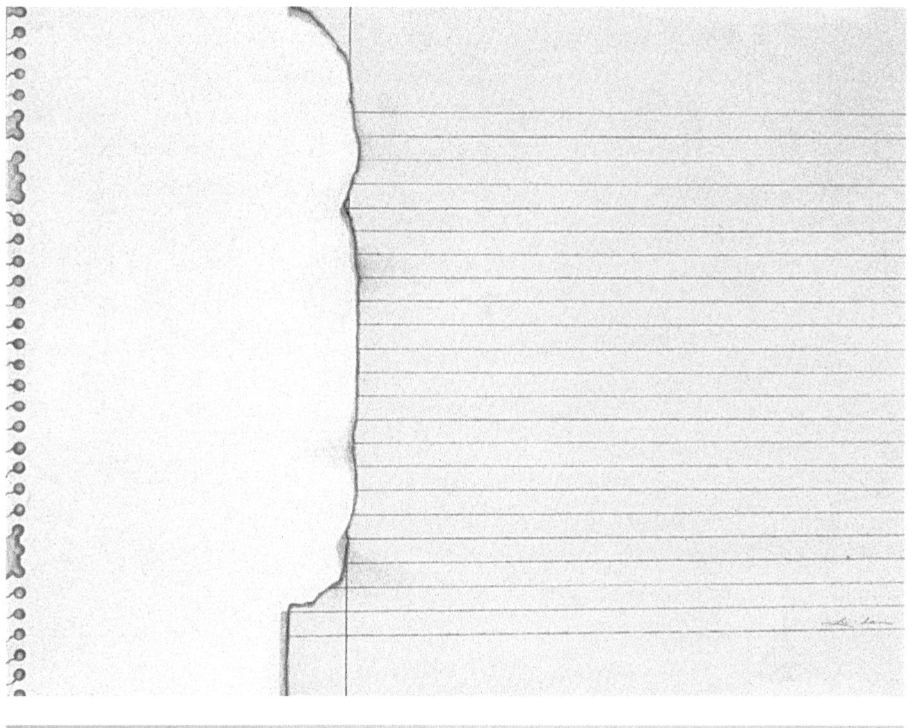

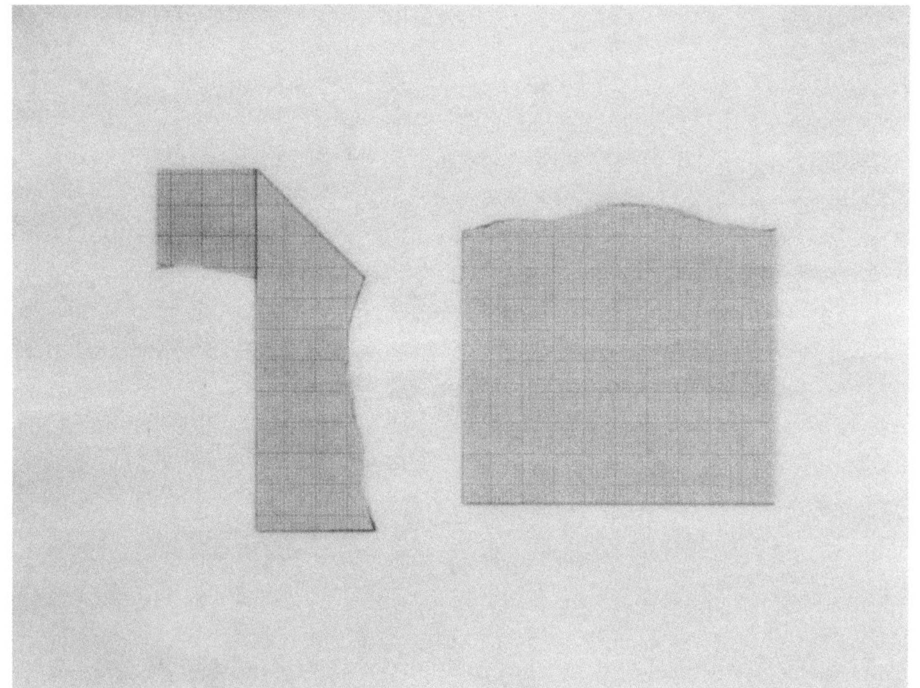

4.1 Li-lan, *Paper*, pencil, colored pencil, watercolor (11 in. x 14 in.), c. 1976.

4.2 Li-lan, *One Sheet of Graph Paper in Two*, watercolor and colored pencil (22 ½ x 30 in.), 1980.

when pressure is not applied equally during stamping, or during replication in the silkscreen printing process that Andy Warhol—an artist who probably made an impact on Li-lan's graphic style—loved to exploit. Li-lan often teases out meaning in her work, and because she is painting Chinese stamps, she may want to evoke the calligraphic association in spite of the fact that her drawing style is late modern and postmodern, with little of the fluidity that is intrinsic to Chinese calligraphy (and to the work of some early modern expressionists and abstract expressionists).

While Li-lan was maturing as an artist, late modernism was in vogue and postmodernism was emerging. Li-lan was able to meld aspects of both, the former through emphasis on the plane, controlled brushstrokes, and the "abstract" arrangement of the shapes. Alongside the hard-edged drawing style, Li-lan's "narrative" content is often related to breakdowns in communication, and to contemporary issues of alienation, discontinuity, and displacement that are key issues in postmodernism. Li-lan was never an ideological painter wedded to convictions about the "truth" of one way of painting in relation to another, and so she was able to slip effortlessly between both "isms," and that continues to be the case. She has her preferences, and refined technique and a minimalist orientation are two of them, but she is also able to engage many different kinds of visual imagery. She is rooted in the long history of the practices of painting, whereas her sensibility is allied to the present moment.

Early Years: Painting in New York, and Experiences of Travel

Li-lan is disdainful of her early paintings in the abstract expressionist mode, and so she has never shown them. She experimented with that "ism," among several others, in the early 1960s but found it ill suited to her instincts as a painter. The landscape and figural works from 1966 to 1968, which she still considers interesting, were constructed through the use of subtle expressionist brushwork. The painterly surface is relatively thick, and in a simple range of colors, shades of blue and red predominate; the shapes are abstract in the manner of the late cutouts of Matisse. The love of touch—what Richard Shiff labels the "indexical" mark left by the practices of painting—has been intrinsic to Li-lan's process, from these early works to the present.[5] As was also true of her father, the activity of painting is a major part of each day of her life.

In the next phase of her work, the areas of color are not as thickly applied as in the previous paintings, and they are contained by even more subtly stroked surfaces and clear outlines. In them Li-lan left any trace of expressionism behind. By 1968, Li-lan was introducing small representational figures and interior places sometimes culminating in dead ends, with furnishings like chairs, and frames surrounding empty spaces that would remain in her work for the rest of the decade. She exhibited these in several group shows in New York, but Li-lan's earliest solo exhibition was in Tokyo in 1969 at the Miyuki Gallery.[6] There she showed these new works, so different from the early paintings and yet unlike those to be painted in 1972, when she began her notebook pictures with a variety of light-colored grounds, which have become an element of her signature style.

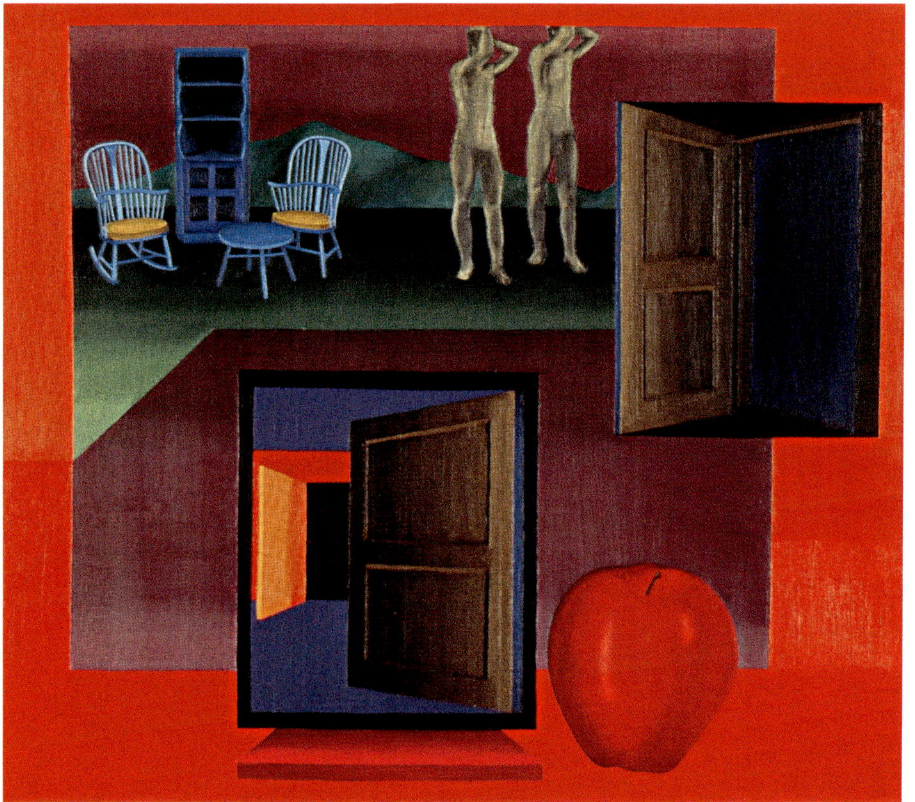

Plate 25 Li-lan, *Midday*, oil on canvas (30 ½ in. x 33 ¾ in.), 1971.

The relatively small paintings exhibited in 1969, and in 1971 in the Nantenshi Gallery in Tokyo, use a full range of contrasting colors and are brighter than the earlier work. In these pictures, profiles of women appear that recall Renaissance portraits, painted as flat silhouettes that enforce the plane, while little organic figures, often men, recede through open doorways or onto orthogonal pathways. Humor is evoked through the power of these female profiles in contrast with the little men. Eggs and apples abound alongside doors that open onto blocked spaces, framed pictures that exist within the picture, and bare rooms with few pieces of furniture. They seem to reference Li-lan's memory of the tiny room she and her mother lived in after Helen left Gee. In these paintings, the manner of floating objects and planes of color is already established, held in place by the relative flatness of the overlay. In *Midday* (pl. 25), the red ground meets the large red apple, and two open doors are set in rectilinear shapes, one framed in black. In the upper part, Li-lan has painted a little domestic group, two chairs, and a small table between them with a hutch behind; next to that are two nude male figures with faces covered by their raised arms. In *Evening Profile of a Lady (2)* (pl. 26), of 1971, the portrait of the woman and her blue shadow are flat counterparts to the picture plane, but the three tiny receding nude men are plastically rendered and, again, brushed in tones and shades of flesh color. Li-lan credits the photographer Muybridge for inspiring these little men.[7] This painting is an early example

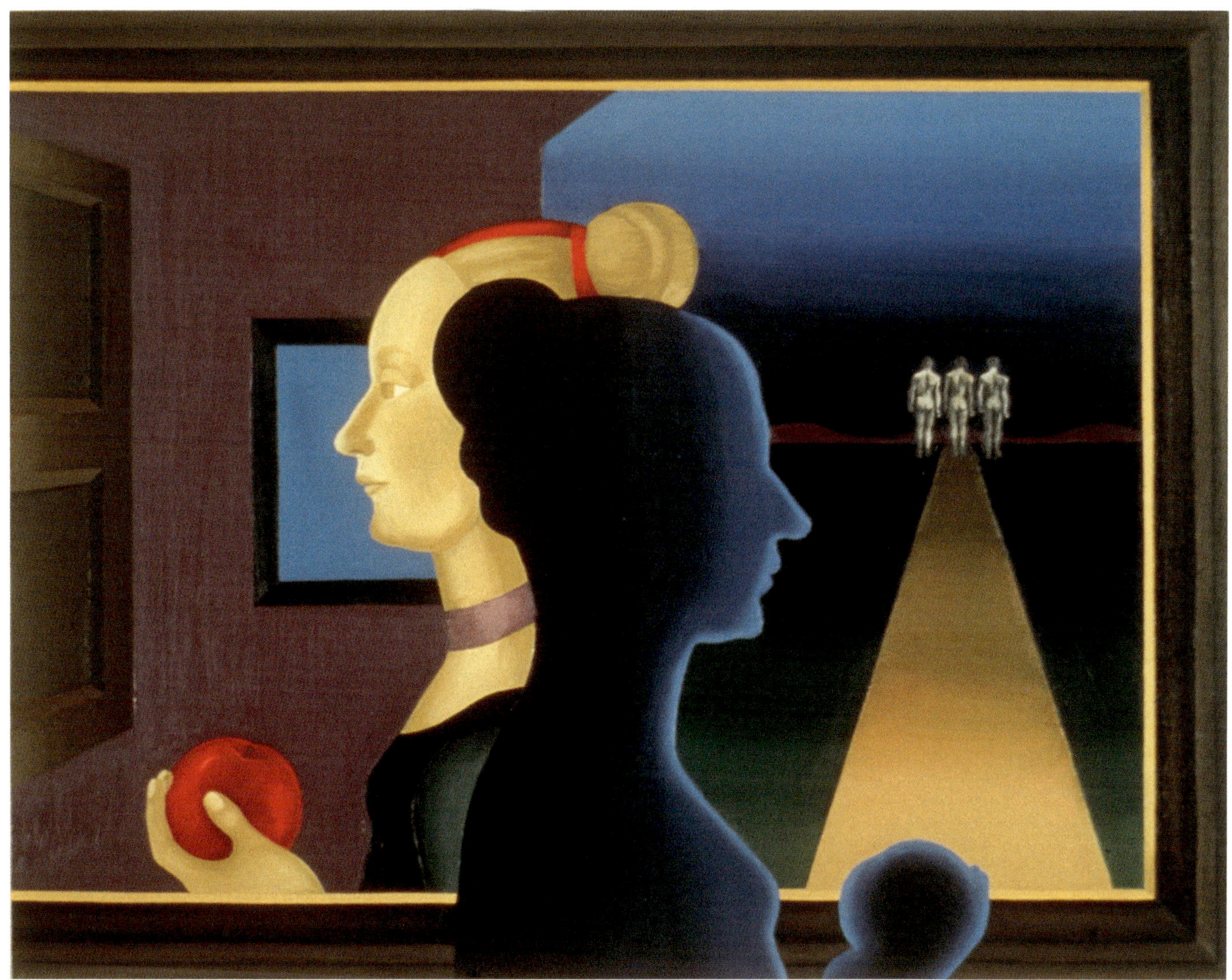

Plate 26 Li-lan, ***Evening Profile of a Lady (2)***, oil on canvas (28 in. x 35 in.), 1971.

of how her curiosity is manifested through the multifarious sources from which she plucks motifs that make their way into her paintings.

In these early works, the freedom of the modern artist to enjoy intense color harmonies is in tandem with content that resonates with desire gone astray, and perhaps even with abandonment, approached sometimes in sadness and at other times with humor; ambiguity in relation to content is already evident. An aspect of these small but powerful paintings can be understood in light of a creative woman's confrontations with choices about love, desire, mating, and procreating—in Li-lan's case, the life of an artist. The resolution of choices may lead through denial to loss. Nevertheless, in two small paintings, *Tuesday Landscape Green* and *Passing Night*, there is a comic moment as two men flee from a large hand holding an apple in the former, and a nude male runs out of the picture space from the huge eggs that may be rolling toward him. This element of the playful—sometimes even bordering on the goofy, which continues into the future—can sit side by side with the melancholy and the somber.[8]

Many of these works were also the result of impressions from her frequent travels: to Mexico in 1962 and 1963, to Italy in 1964, and to Berlin, in 1967–68. These encounters, rather than formal studies or readings in art history, were primary in her art education. The visual experience then stimulated the urge to learn more about the works she had seen. Her paintings, then, were probably more influenced by the European tradition, as well as by the muralists' paintings she saw in Mexico, than by what she was viewing at home. It may not have been the social and political content that impressed her as much as a certain monumental reserve in the figures of Rivera, which complemented what she was also attracted to in Renaissance painting. In Berlin, it was not the German expressionist art that excited her but the exhibitions she saw of artists like Kasimir Malevich and other Russians connected to constructivism. At the present moment, with the return of painting as a dominant form, and the revival of interest in minimalism and abstraction, works by these artists can be frequently seen in museums and galleries; they were less available in the United States when postmodern concerns dominated the art scene. Just as she had absorbed Italian Renaissance art and made it part of her 1960s paintings, her experience with the Russians would become an important factor in the paintings that Li-lan made in the 1970s. Her travel experiences were not unique, but what is important in her case is that passage from place to place would become an intrinsic component of Li-lan's entire body of work.

Another aspect of Li-lan's travels at this time was her looking at works that reinforced her predisposition toward fantasy and the surreal. The fanciful interiors just discussed are primarily indebted to the stagelike perspectives of early Renaissance painting that she saw in Italy. "I loved the fresco[e]s of Giotto, Piero della Francesca, Masaccio and Fra Angelico," she says. "I incorporated [their] . . . images in a collage- or montage-like way."[9] Modern artists, like the Italian Giorgio de Chirico and the French René Magritte, resonate as well: "I have always loved the Surrealists, and I do relate to the feelings of absence and solitude that I find in Surrealism."[10] The surrealism Li-lan is talking about is not the kind practiced by Picasso, Gorky, Matta, Masson, and the early de Kooning, which helped to form abstract expressionism in late 1940s and the 1950s. Instead, this body of Li-lan's work, while also indebted to other European sources, looks to the fantasy narratives of Magritte and de Chirico that are rooted in realist conventions, and to the modes of abstraction inherent in early modernism, from its inception in cubism and constructivism. The art critic Ichiro Hariu summed it up in a short paragraph he wrote in the brochure for the 1969 exhibition at the Miyuki Gallery:

> Shadows of men, women and animals rise from the streets of the city. The scenes are sharply cut by cubes or surrounded by frames, like a play within a

> play. Sometimes women appear on a stage as if painted by Giotto or Botticelli, sometimes men materialize as if documented in Muybridge's photographs, sometimes chairs and mountains emerge. "You present an intriguing montage. Simultaneously, the past and the present, fiction and reality, in which time has stopped—as in a vacuum of space or in the abyss of Eros. You seem to be groping beyond the fragments of a daydream for the archetypes of a treatise on happiness; indeed, a future arcadia."

While I am not sure that these early paintings picture the desire for a future arcadia, Hariu certainly perceives them in the context of desire, and he addresses elements that would remain part of Li-lan's oeuvre even as her format changed radically. The "vacuum of space" is also a prime element in the surrealist painters she was looking at, and it would become so for her as well.

If the combination of surrealism and modernist formalism that Li-lan was practicing at the time seems related to Gee, and particularly to his later work, the painting choices that each artist made were quite different. It is interesting that while Gee was in Paris, in the heyday of surrealist experimentation, he seemed indifferent to the irrational, the psychological, and the content of the unconscious embedded in much of that work. Rather, surrealism's impact on his painting emerged in a penchant for Chinese and symbolic subjects expressed through a linear fluidity that replaced the angularity of his cubist mode. In his later works, the sense of the surreal stems from the mystery that exudes from the relations among all the things that he placed in a single painting. He rarely left space empty. As for Li-lan, although surrealism had been absorbed into abstract expressionism by the 1950s, particularly the form of surrealism that had been brought by refugee artists to the United States, she was interested in those artists, respected more in Europe than in New York, who painted recognizable subjects but with irrational and psychological content. Again, in contrast to Gee, artists like de Chirico enabled her to strengthen her formalist proclivities. But the younger Li-lan also saw some of the 1950s works that Gee was painting; the union of the surreal, the real, and the still present undertones of formalism in his work may also have affected her desire to follow that path.

Her interest in Magritte, however, may have added another layer to her work that she could not have found in Gee's. Foucault has written about the insurmountable chasm between words and things, using Magritte's works as models.[11] Foucault's concerns are with discourse, not really with painting practices, but Magritte's pictures are full of recognizable images that can be named but not affirmed as representing the real.[12] Their interrelationship is one of pure similitude:

> Magritte knits verbal signs and plastic elements together, but without referring them to prior isotopism. He skirts the base of affirmative discourse on which resemblance calmly reposes, and he brings pure similitudes and non-affirmative verbal statements into play within the instability of disoriented volume and an unmapped space.[13]

Not until later would Li-lan use actual language, complicating interpretation even further, but these early paintings evoke that sense of similitude—one thing and another—equal in emphasis, floating in an unmapped space. Later on, she would play with pictures on stamps; those she copied were already also signs, and Li-lan would appropriate them—never representing them accurately—while making them into little pictures within the large paintings. Pictures on and within other pictures lose both material tangibility and, seemingly, personal reference through becoming signage. In some ways, this kind of transformation became even stronger in her later paintings, where she juxtaposed images, and sometimes words, that seem to have no interrelationship other than the one imposed by her idiosyncratic choices. From the beginning, her paintings have been filled with secrets that tease and tantalize. Yun Gee's paintings are rooted in the particular genre event, and in the material presence of the people portrayed, even if abstract devices are in play; Li-lan's images of the banal and ordinary have undergone a conversion from their association with the real and the personal to the artificial world of similitude. Yet they, too, resonate with the everyday events of a person's life. Most important, although they can be "read," as can all visual images, and although they enter the domain of discourse, they are also perceived as material events because the paint marks that compose the forms are entirely visible. With any artwork, it is crucial to understand the differences between reading the work and perceiving it as the result of carnal activity, but Li-lan's paintings lend themselves to slippage between the two realms, and that is a major factor in their particularity.

Painting in the 1970s and 1980s: New York, East Hampton, and Japan

The art scene in New York in the 1960s and 1970s has been more than well documented. One of the key texts from that period, Irving Sandler's *American Art of the 1960s*, is replete with illustrations that highlight the amazing proliferation of modes of working in those years. After discussing the painterly and postpainterly work of the early 1960s, and the sensibility of the art world in the whole of that decade, Sandler offers chapters on pop art, the new perceptual realism and photo-realism, op art and kinetic sculpture, minimal sculpture, construction sculpture, the artist as political activist, eccentric abstraction

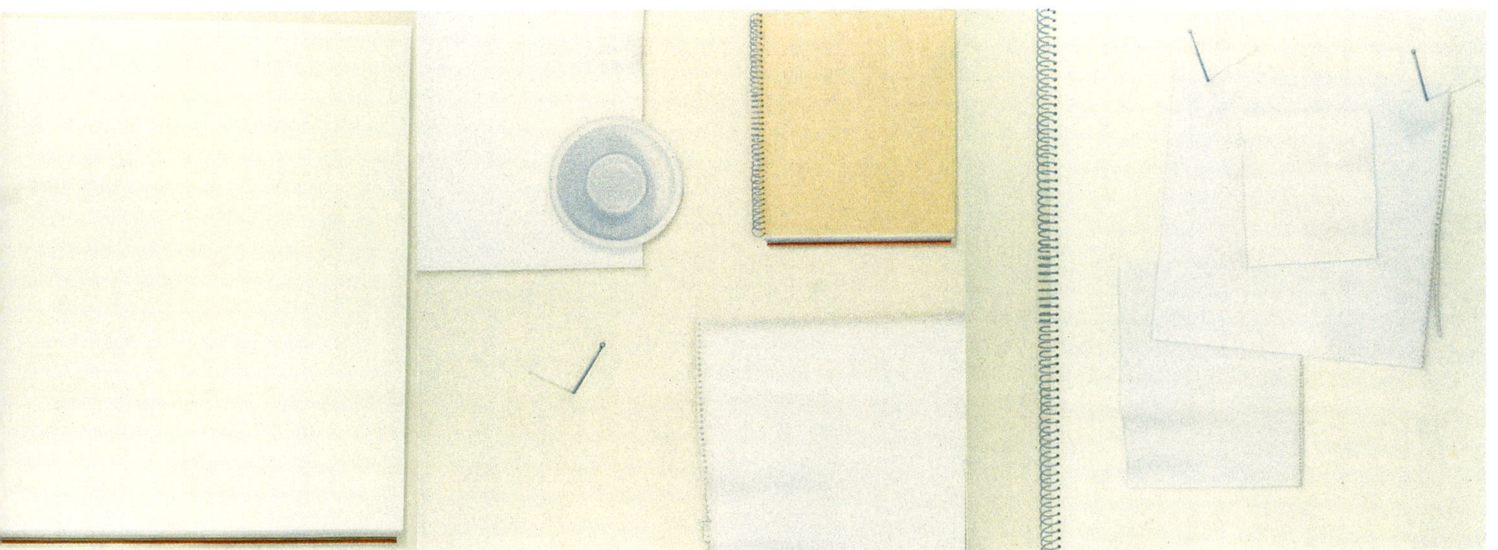

27a-c Li-lan, ***Autobiography*** **(triptych), oil on canvas (52 in. x 144 in., each panel 52 in. x 48 in.), 1974.**

and process art, earthworks, minimal environments, and performances and conceptual art. The book's epilogue, titled "1970—The Death of the Avant-Garde," indicates that this period of intense creativity, and this search for the new and the original, were superseded by the postmodern sensibility for conceptualism, appropriation, nostalgia, and the critique of modern art. Many have challenged Sandler's story since then, and these challenges include the current questioning of the divisions between modern and postmodern art in the later 1960s and early 1970s, but his book certainly covers the plethora of different ways of making and thinking about art that dominated the decade of the 1960s and are still providing artists with stimulating ideas. Li-lan was looking closely at all these "isms," and many of her friends and acquaintances were 1960s and 1970s artists. She exhibited with many of the well-known artists associated with these forms. It was therefore "natural" for her to empty out her paintings and concentrate on the banal things around her studio, particularly in light of the pop and minimalist sensibilities. Her hard-edged manner of drawing was also in keeping with many of the prevailing modes, but when she turned in the 1970s to her notebook paintings, and in the 1980s to her stamps and envelopes, I think Japan then provided an artistic environment that may have made an equally profound impact. In 1977 Li-lan wrote:

> Images that surround me in my studio grow larger than life: a blank paper torn from its spiral; a ripped or folded piece of notebook page; empty pads and books in subtle shades of white or various hues of yellows, violets, blues. A single red margin line must hold its own as it crosses a ruled page—as does an edge of the cardboard cover peeking out from under a mammoth sketchbook. Paper still without words, music sheets still without notes, canvas still without images—with their own space and mystery, with their shadows that cast spells on the walls—are fragments of dreams: part of my daily life.[14]

Plate 28 Li-lan, ***A Certain Song***, oil on canvas (50 in. x 60 in.), 1977.

Sometime around 1972, Li-lan's paintings became larger, and at first simple objects like nails, plates, and eggs overlapped the sheets of paper. In a review of her 1978 exhibition at the Robert Miller Gallery, she is quoted saying, "I used to have all those figures in my paintings. The figures got smaller and walked out of the paintings, they actually did. Then I started putting in eggs, cups, and pieces of paper nailed on walls. Then the nails fell down. Then *they* started to disappear."[15] Then everything disappeared but the papers, with their torn edges, and/or notebooks with different kinds of spiral bindings and sometimes a colored edge, all meticulously rendered. In *A Certain Song* (pl. 28)—as well as in other works from the 1970s, like *Legal Pad, 1* (pl. 29)—the torn edges of music sheets seem to retain an almost organic/bodily presence akin to that of the profile portraits of her earlier paintings and the ever-present egg shapes. The first of these paintings was done in East Hampton, but Li-lan's experiences in Japan nurtured the silence that was already a factor even in her

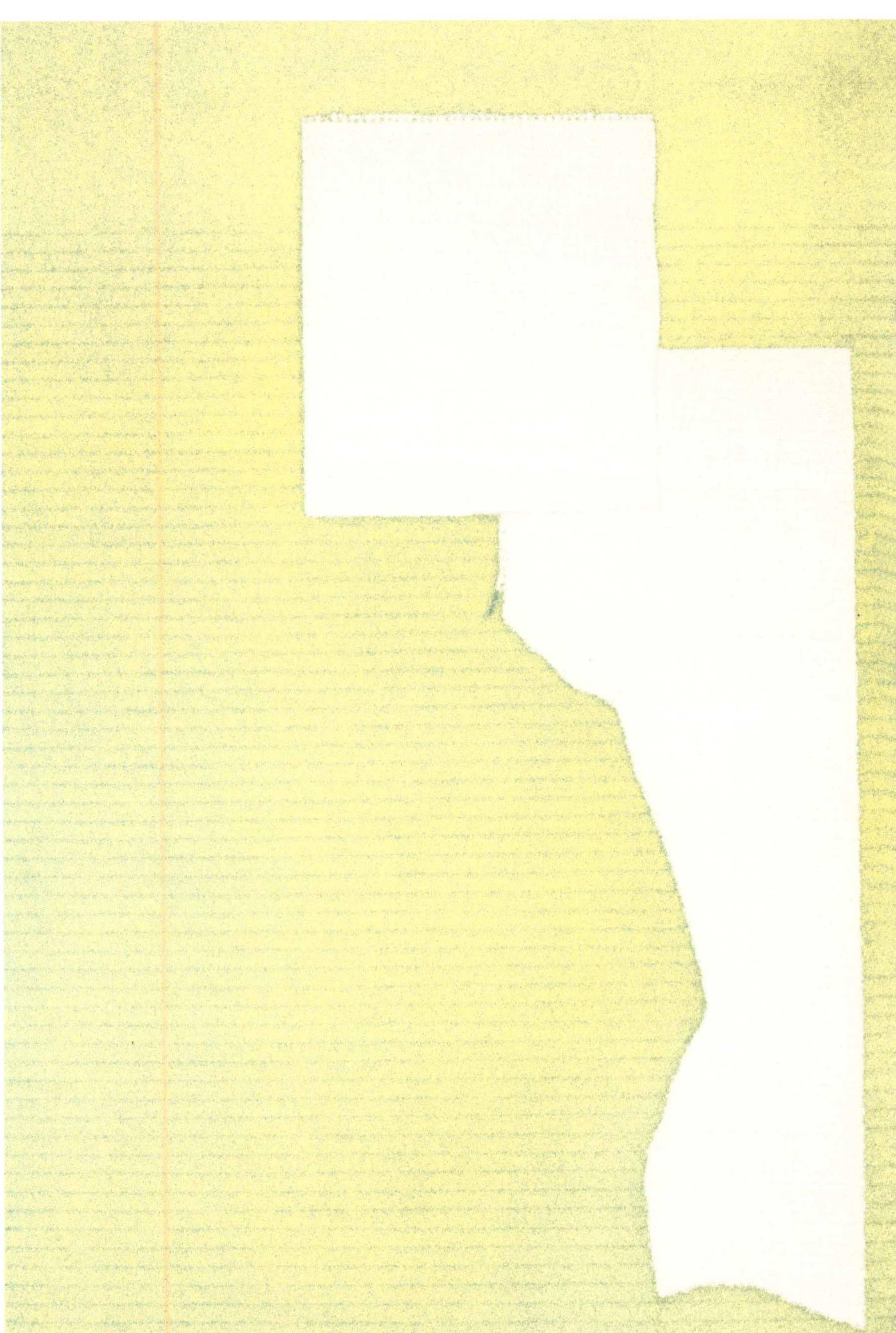

Plate 29 Li-lan, *Legal Pad, 1,* oil on canvas (70 in. x 50 in.), 1975.

high-intensity 1960s paintings. In an interview on the occasion of her solo exhibition in 1990 at the William Benton Museum of Art, she replied to a comment about her change of imagery:

> One day—it must have been in the early '70s—I was sitting in my studio in East Hampton, sketchbook in my lap. I was emptying out my mind, thinking about what I was going to paint or draw. At that moment I wanted to paint the sketchbook, so the sketchbook moved from my lap into a painting. At first I combined sketchbooks and notebooks with other images. Over time the notebooks themselves or blank pages from them grew larger and larger, and

> the other objects, such as cups and nails, began to disappear, or leave one by one. It was an emptying-out process. As the notebooks and blank pages grew larger and larger—larger than life—my paintings became more minimal and solitary. The images themselves had always been isolated from one another to create a sense of aloneness, and as time went on each image began to stand alone on the canvas.[16]

When I read this, I immediately thought about the cups in Shusaku Arakawa's fourth panel of the subdivision, "*Feeling of Meaning*"; he wrote beneath them, "Which Cup Will Be the First to Break?"[17] Arakawa's cups are real, indicating that it is the language that displaces the object, but Li-lan's elimination of the things that had filled her paintings, her replacing them with empty notebooks and ledgers, and her subduing of the brushstrokes discernible in her earlier works suggest a flirtation with conceptualism in the 1970s, and that is also a probable factor in the words and numbers that were to proliferate later on. Minimalism and pop art have been suggested as influences on her work, but Li-lan herself has mentioned, with some frequency, Japanese artists connected to conceptualism, and I will address that connection later on.[18]

First, however, is the question of minimal form and pop content. The response that people often have to Li-lan's empty-notebook paintings is that they are distancing. This reaction may be a result of the sparse formalism, but it may also emerge from the absence of what we usually associate with notebooks: handwriting and personal notations of all kinds. Li-lan seemed to be holding back just when the need to make present the ordinary events of a life—the personal made political—was the dominant mode, particularly in feminist art practices. Analogous to the emptying out of the surface is the fact that the actual distance that seems appropriate to the viewing experience is somewhat fixed—maybe about four or five feet from the canvas for the large works (the more intimate pastel paintings need closer viewing). At that distance, one can see the whole painting and its details, including the subtle brushstrokes. By contrast with the painterly development from impressionism on (particularly in abstract expressionism), and with the more interactive direction of art practices from the late 1960s on, Li-lan's work seems to necessitate neither closer observation nor further backward movement in order for the whole to be taken in.

A meditative mode, stimulated by both the sparseness of the surface and the fixed distance, with the body relatively still, may be the most appropriate response to these paintings. In terms of meditation, it seems obvious to link this aspect of Li-lan's work to Chinese religious practices, as in Buddhism, but Li-lan associates her form of meditation not with religious practices but with the meditative practice of painting itself. She also describes as meditative her experience in Matisse's chapel in Vence, and she has commented in particular

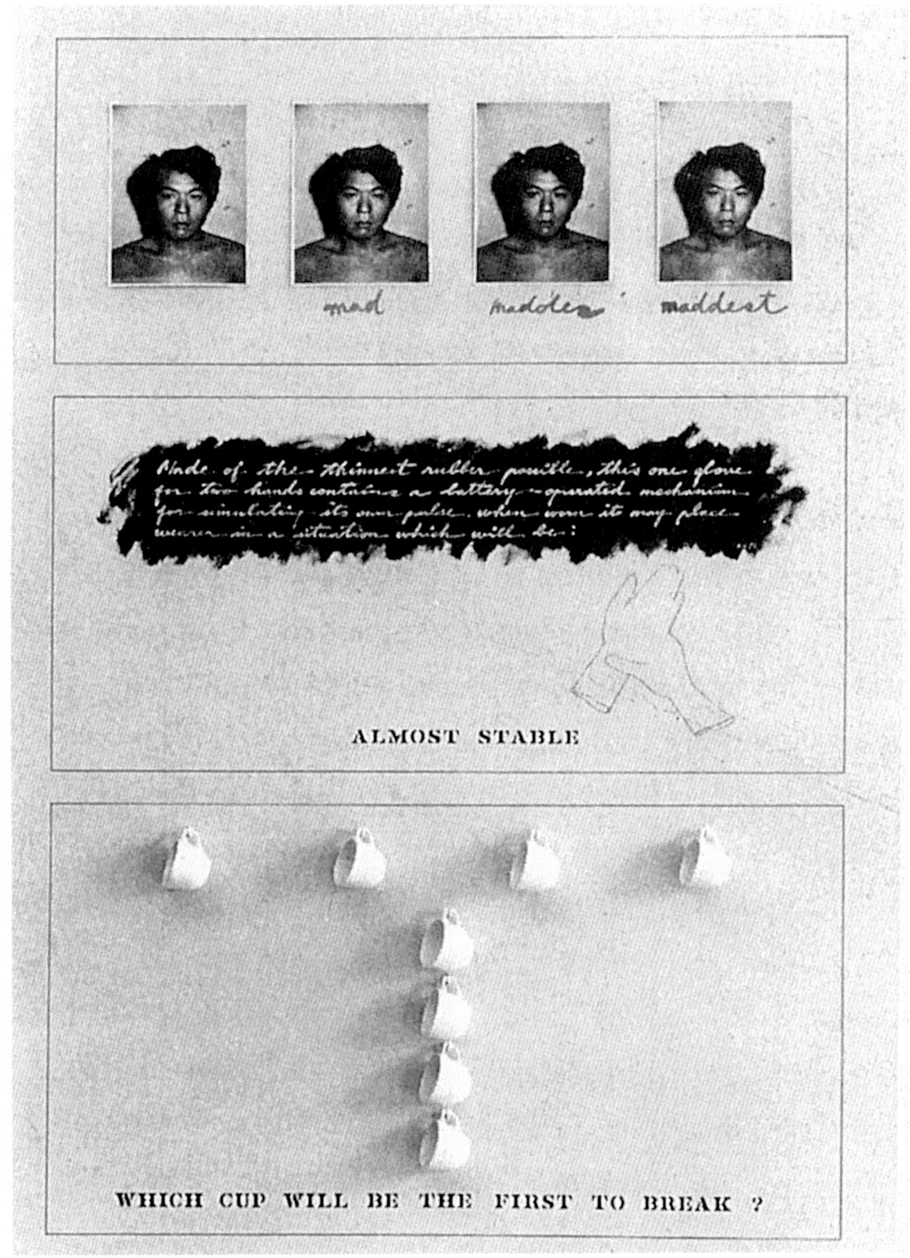

4.3 **Shusaku Arakawa,** ***Fourth Panel of the Subdivision "Feeling of Meaning,"*** **mixed media, 1978.**

on the effect of the relation between the white light engaging the vividness of color from the glass windows in that manner. *Eight Subject Divided* (pl. 30) of 1983 could stand as a kind of translation of that experience, through the luminosity that emanates from the surface. It is one of the most daring of this group, since the plane is filled only with the repetitious ruled lines of an open notebook, and it is also conceptually clever, with the eight color codes in the margin acting as the tabs for each section of the book. There is so little to look at, but then one fixates on the repetitious lines and the luminous, sensuous surface, the result of the finish that Li-lan produces by polishing layer after layer of paint with fine sandpaper.[19]

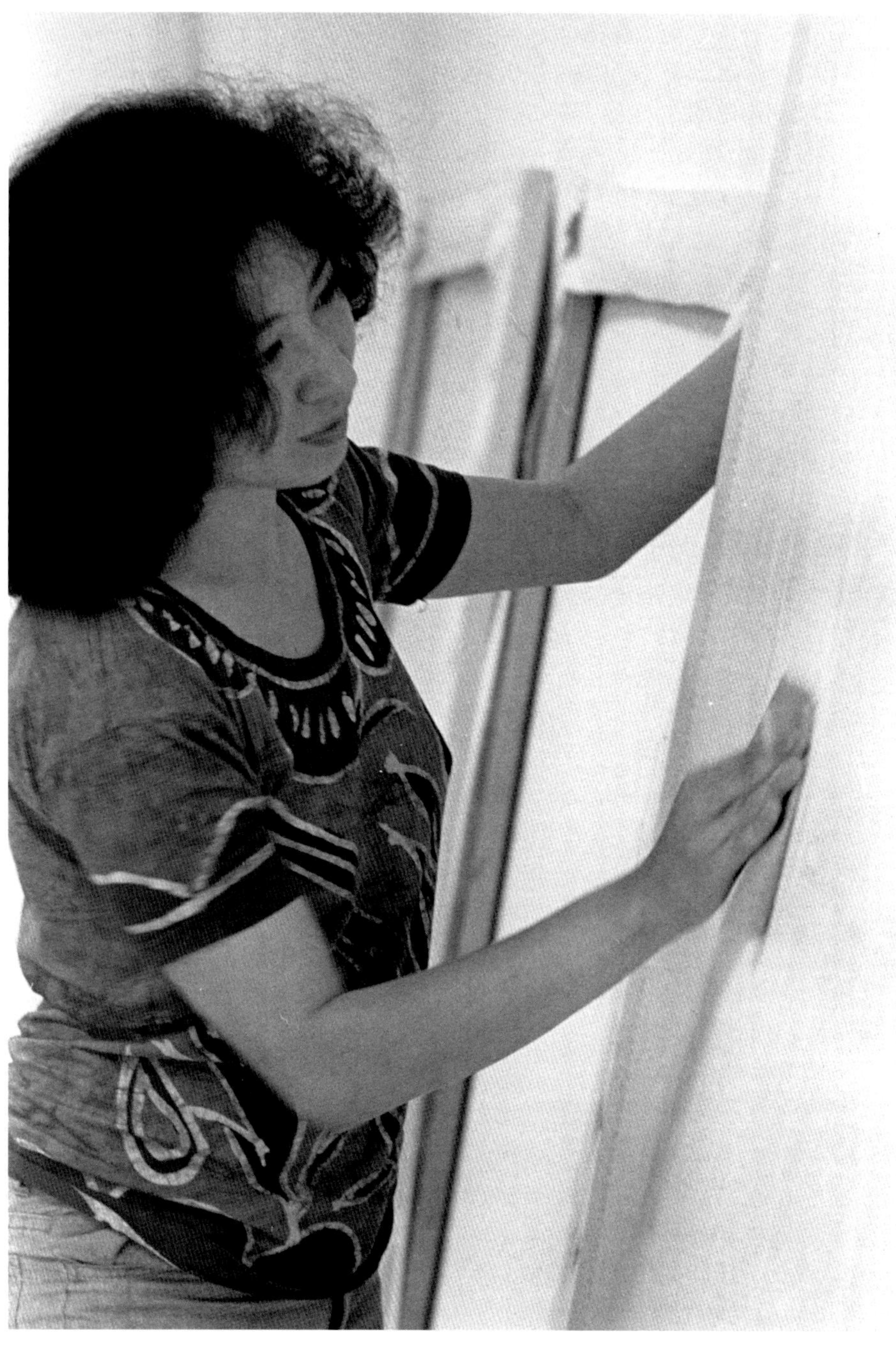

4.4 Li-lan in her East Hampton studio, sanding a painting, 1976. Photograph: Georgie Roberts.

Her paintings from this period are so contained that Michael Fried's ideas about absorption and theatricality—in vogue at the time these works were done—can usefully be introduced here in order to discuss them as examples of modernism.[20] In this classic Greenbergian text, Fried developed his understanding of the formalism in modern art as a distancing of the viewer so as to make the painting an entity in its own right—the "art for art's sake" discourse. Through the total exclusion of narrative theatricality and baroque devices that make the viewer an intimate and emotional part of the depicted

Plate 30 Li-lan, ***Eight Subject Divided***, oil on canvas (60 in. x 76 in.), 1983.

event, the beholder is now excluded, and the object is endowed with a contained sanctity. Li-lan's paintings from this time are reserved and also contained, but they are also too rooted in the ordinary—almost banal in their subject matter—to enter the discourse of metaphysical profundity often claimed for the content of modern and abstract art. These paintings have also been discussed as postmodern—the surfaces to be filled by the viewer in a kind of interactive mode—but the emphatic presence and completeness of these ruled notebooks and ledgers negates that kind of approach.

Li-lan describes her "ledger" paintings of the mid-1980s as very formal, and they are, but lines and overlapping planes proliferate, and they are more colorful. This whole body of work, whatever else it is about, seems to address the ordinary aspect of a person's life, both private and professional. If the notebooks imply private life, the ledgers are necessary for keeping track of one's work, taxes, and accounts of all kinds, and they play a real part in the life of someone as meticulous as Li-lan. The notion of keeping order—as she has done in organizing and maintaining the archives of her father's life and work—is a key factor in understanding the private and professional nature of her own life and work. It would not take complex analysis to find the roots of aspects of her desire to be surrounded by orderliness and stability in the disruptive events of her formative years. She works with a strong sense of physical location, and although she has traveled to many places, her day-to-day life takes place in an almost repetitive mode; she moves between New York and East Hampton and now travels only reluctantly.

Yet, as previously indicated, passage and travel are constant motifs in Li-lan's work. Stamps are the quintessential manifestations of both—they travel and pass from sender to receiver, both of whom remain stationary. Sometime in 1986, Li-lan began to draw single stamps, then paintings of whole sheets of stamps with their perforated edges straight from the post office. In some cases, only a few stamps are filled in, and the grid is left exposed. Again, the personal and the professional entered into these choices because Li-lan loves to write and to receive letters. Soon paintings of envelopes and then of postcards followed. Li-lan corresponds with friends and does business all over the world from her studio, where she spends most of her time, and she searches very little for things outside; she is not a collector, not even of stamps:

> In 86 I began doing drawings of stamps, and in 87, paintings. At first I painted whole sheets of 40, 50 or 100 stamps, or fewer if from a torn sheet. What initially intrigued me were not the stamps but the printer's color-separation key, which is on the edge of the sheet of stamps. In fact, I had torn a color key off one and had it on my desk for several months before using it. When I did paint it, I placed it at the bottom of 100 "Orchids Issues" stamps. I was intrigued by the grid layout of the sheet and its regular perforations. (So far, I must have painted thousands and thousands of dots by hand in this series.)[21]

The pages of stamps allow for a grid structure, in keeping with minimalist devices in painting and sculpture, akin to the paintings with ruled lines from notebooks and musical-score sheets. Li-lan's earliest trip to China, in 1980, produced two paintings based on graph paper that she had bought there, and grids and graphs are natural components of this phase of her work. Her paintings may have some affinities with minimalist practices, just as they do with pop imagery, but her work is more like that of Agnes Martin, whose paintings Li-lan did not engage until many years later, even after she was in a group show with Martin. For both artists, refined surfaces and repetitive systems are primary, as are the meditative responses that they activate.

The 1990 group show at the Ben Shahn Galleries, titled The Grid: Organization and Idea, included, in addition to Li-lan and Agnes Martin, the minimalist artists Sol LeWitt, Jennifer Bartlett, James Biederman, Robert Ryman,

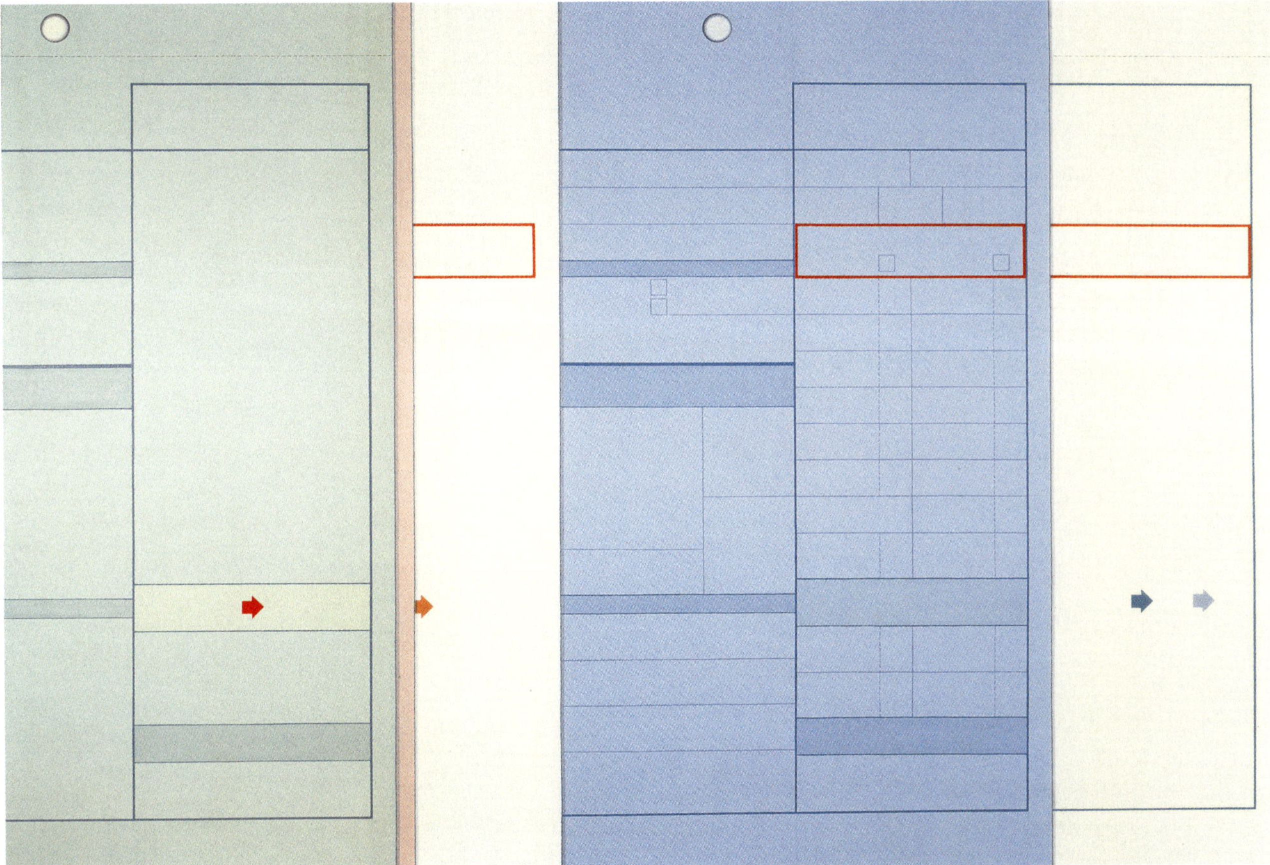

Plate 31 Li-lan, ***Invoice in Five***, **oil on canvas (53 in. x 77 in.), 1986.**

Tony Smith, and others identified with minimalism. Li-lan exhibited a painting there, *Posta Romana* (pl. 32), that she had made in 1989. The exhibition catalogue stressed the use of the grid as an ordering device—rational, stable, and able to generate abstract design. One of its contributors introduced the notion that "in a culture and time that exalts the individual artist, there are those who choose the grid as a corrective."[22] Another echoed that sentiment: "The grid, . . . as repetition, undermines the concept of the artist as originator. The grid is nobody's invention. It is not an original concept. It duplicates its own form endlessly. . . . The artist becomes, instead, the person who imposes a preconceived rigid form onto a canvas rather than an originator of style."[23] This conception of the use of the grid can be understood, in the context of its time, as a lingering reaction to the supposedly free form and individual expression that characterized abstract expressionism, although minimalism had already been around for more than a decade. Many artists who were called minimalists, such as Agnes Martin, Eva Hesse (who was not included in the exhibition), and Li-lan, were mistakenly so labeled.

Li-lan's use of the grid as a formal structure was subtly destabilized, as in the grid sculptures of Eva Hesse (Li-lan was looking at Hesse's work), by the seductive quality of the resins she was using.[24] Then there are the painted

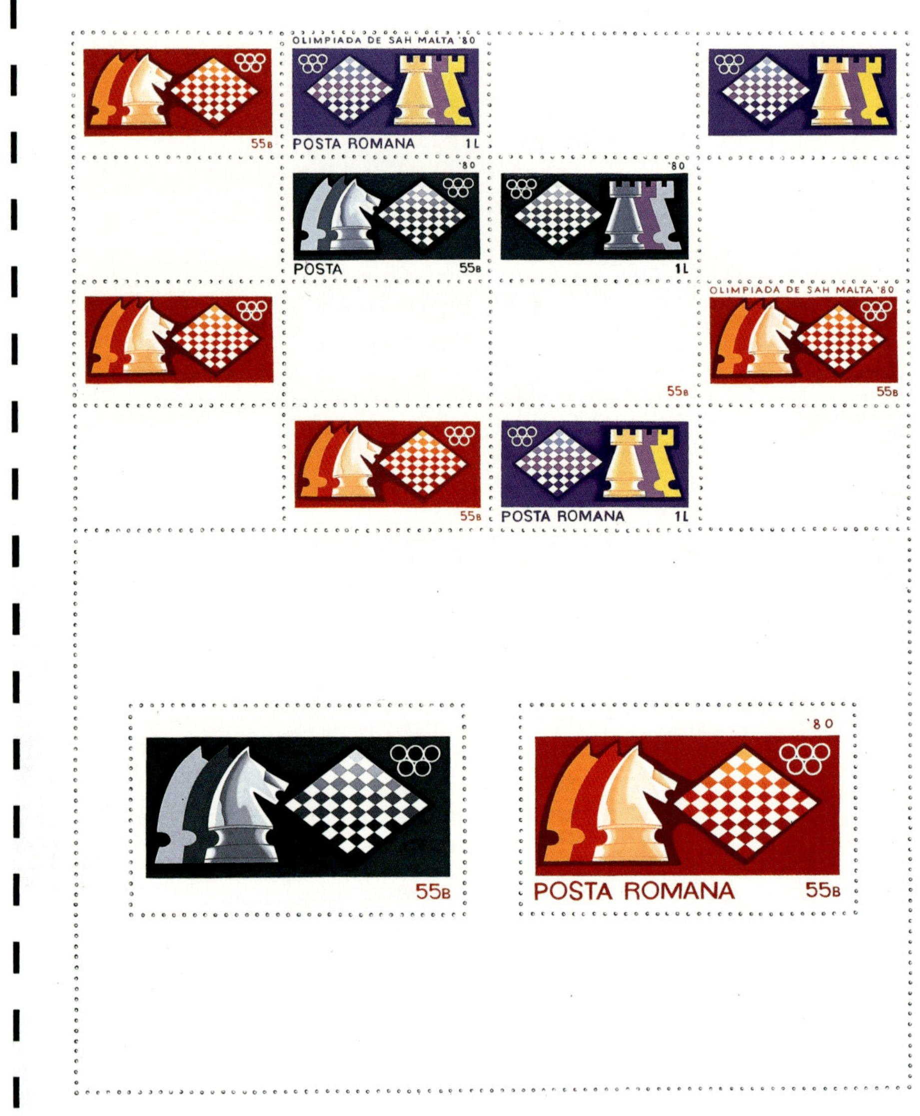

Plate 32 Li-lan, *Posta Romana*, oil on canvas (58 in. x 46 in.), 1989.

surfaces: instead of the flat colored areas in the work of some minimalists, like LeWitt, these artists cover the surfaces with brushstrokes and emphasize the hand and the concomitant physical actions involved in making the work, more in the manner of Robert Ryman, who is sometimes labeled a minimalist. Also, minimalism seems to be a more appropriate label for the industrial forms of Carl Andre, Tony Smith, and others than for the work of most of the painters who are called minimalists. Li-lan's paintings from the mid-1970s and 1980s are "cool," and the grid and the graph predominate, but they function as coherent items—pages of stamps, ruled notebooks, ledgers—and emerge from the personal use of these repetitive forms in the ordinary activities of life. That fact undercuts the use of the grid as expressive of a desire to counteract the individual presence of the artist. Li-lan is right to label her work minimal rather than minimalist.

In concert with the grids, the thousands of dots, perforated and torn paper edges, and loose-leaf bindings that Li-lan has painted obsessively inhabit the world of pattern. They cast an unnatural and dimensionless shadow and invite attention with an urgency not usually assigned to such mundane forms. Patterns do not often cast shadows and are usually associated with decorative art. In the context of these paintings, they seem surreal. Perhaps Li-lan's interest in Magritte and de Chirico, reflected in the early paintings, now falls on even more prosaic items and gives them full meaning. So-called Oriental art has been cited as another source of the decorative in these paintings—but why? For example, an exhibition of Li-lan's and Yun Gee's paintings at the art gallery on the Southampton campus of Long Island University was reviewed in the *Southampton Press* on July 7, 1988, by Alexander Russo, who compared Li-lan's work to Yun Gee's in a manner that reiterated the desire to categorize her work as Oriental:

> It is paradoxical that Li-lan's paintings seem more Oriental than her father's. . . . One would expect that Li-lan would be more "Westernized," having been exposed more totally to Western influences. However, this assumption is contradicted by her "visual coding." Imagery is treated in flat, simplified terms. A sense of two-dimensional space dominates, and the all-over effect is decoratively flat, perhaps like Chinese calligraphy, though less direct, and more like scroll painting.

It was appropriate for Russo to associate a 1987 vertical diptych by Li-lan, *International Letter Writing Week, 1 and 2* (pl. 33), with scroll-like forms; although such forms are not a frequent format in Li-lan's work, they are related to Japanese art. Flatness, however, is simply a component of work done everywhere by artists who engage modernism. Moreover, although it is true that use of the flat panel is a convention intrinsic to the discourse of modern art, it is also the case that hanging scrolls have been used as structural supports for paintings in many cultures, and for a very long time. It may be far-fetched to see Japanese and Chinese scroll painting as a factor in use of the flat panel over the long tradition of Western art, but it may be consequential to consider that association with respect to contemporary painting. Li-lan plays with broad connotations even when she seems to use a denotation system that excludes that kind of complexity—in the case of these panels, by using the vertical shape to echo the scroll format.

Again, Li-lan plays in relation to the signage in both panels, since they include very decorative stamps with strongly colored figures in Japanese costume. And yet again, what could be more obvious than to describe these images as Oriental in inspiration? Nevertheless, Li-lan was using decorative stamps from both East and West—from Rome, Paris, Mozambique, and San

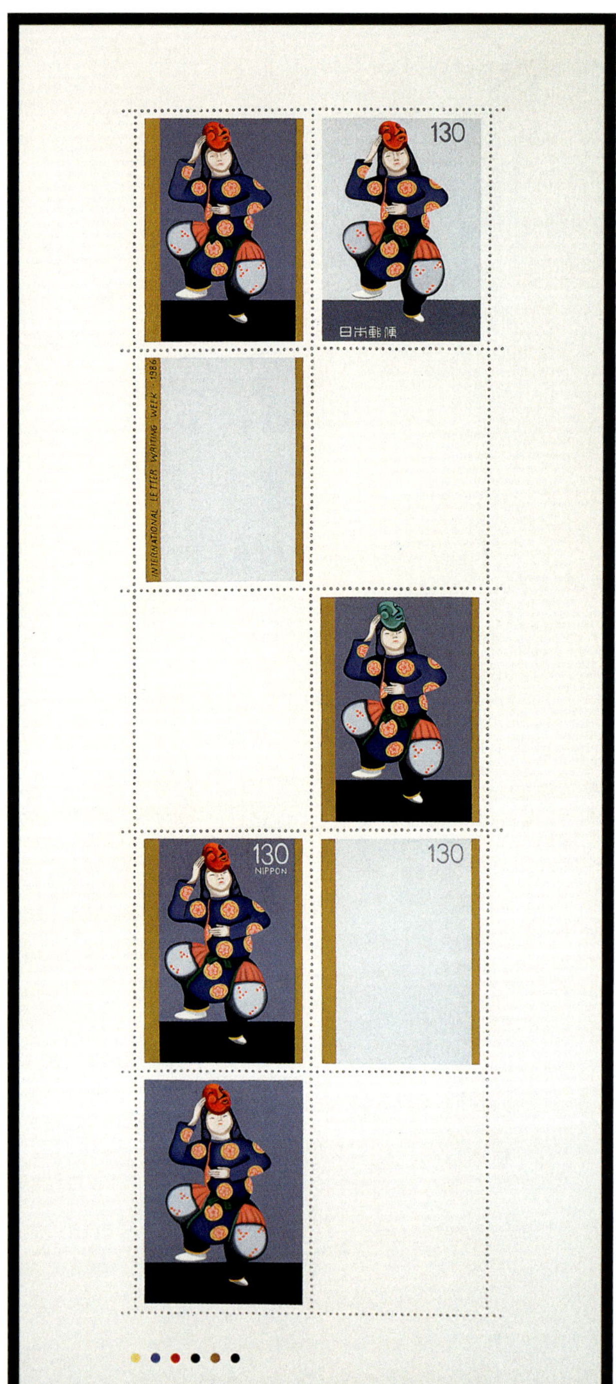

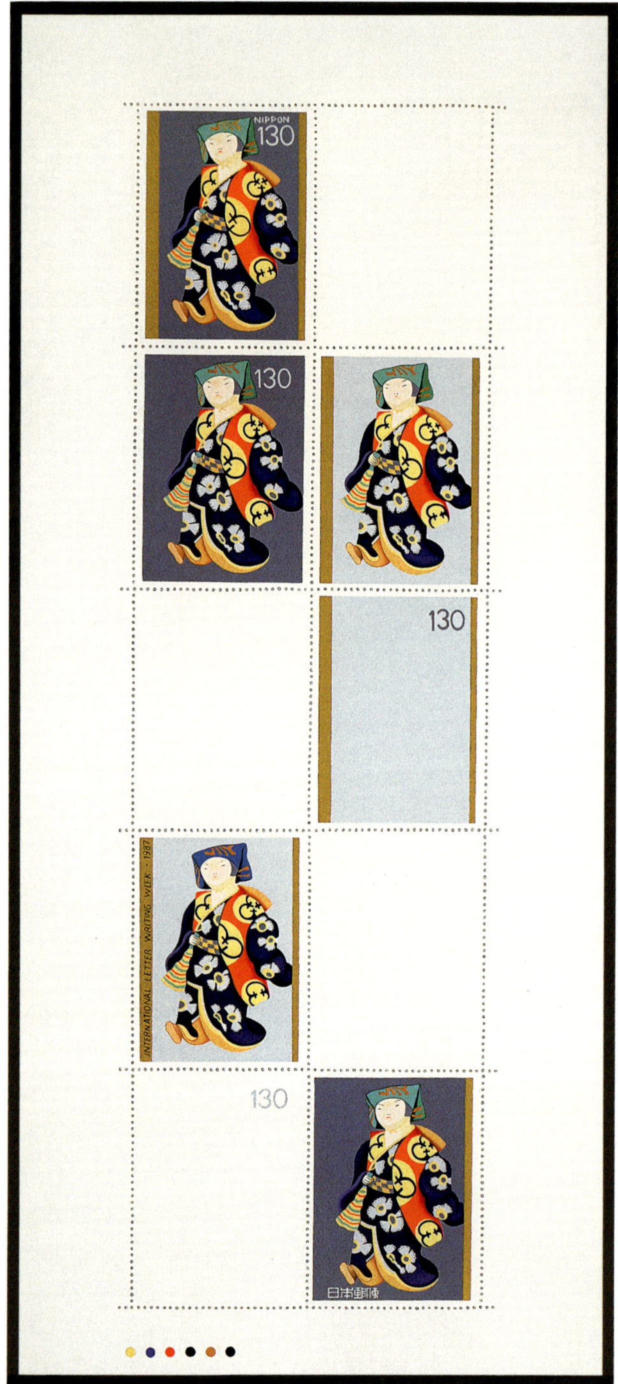

Plate 33a-b Li-lan, *International Letter Writing Week, 1 and 2* (diptych), oil on canvas (103 in. x 46 ½ in., each panel 51 ½ in. x 23 ¼ in.), 1987.

Marino, and from the Navaho Indians—and, in her later work, from anywhere in the world if she found an image intriguing. Usually the stamps have been on letters and postcards that friends either sent to her or kept for her from letters they had received. The use of a large vocabulary of signs from all over can be attributed to globalization, in a superficial sense, and a signifier with no connection to a signified is at the heart of contemporary experience. Li-lan paints stamps from many places that she knows only from pictures. Pictures engage her, and images in books are also sources for many of the architectural motifs that fill her later paintings. In the studio, through her painting practices, she transforms these signs into a visual travelogue constructed from painted brushstrokes and abstract arrangements. What is relevant here, then, is Barthes's aesthetic system of signs in relation to contemporary Japanese culture, not puerile notions of Japanese art, especially in light of whatever "Oriental" may mean. As we explore Li-lan's paintings in depth, we see how subtly the aesthetics of form (in this case, the grid and the pattern) and the easy appropriation of imagery from everywhere undercuts the assigning of a specific national, cultural, or ethnic identity to her practices. Questions about location with respect to any of these categories are particularly apt in an age of electronic messaging, a time when issues of presence and absence are crucial, as they are in Li-lan's work, in spite of her use of traditional painting media.

Li-lan was exhibiting these paintings with some frequency in the 1970s and 1980s in New York: at the Robert Miller Gallery in 1978, and then in three more solo exhibitions in the O. K. Harris Gallery in 1983, 1985, and 1987. She exhibited in two group shows in 1983, at O. K. Harris West, in Scottsdale, Arizona, and at the New York Gallery. It is evident from the brochures for these group exhibitions that her work was included with the work of artists engaged with every kind of painting then being practiced, but painting's heyday was over then, and the "death of art" rhetoric was in vogue. It was the time when photography, installations, happenings and performance art, earthworks, and conceptual art were prominent. It may also have been the case that finding the appropriate niche within which to place her work was difficult. If she was not really a minimalist or pop artist—and exhibitions of this kind of work were becoming more infrequent anyhow—the postmodern aspect of her imagery was not really understood, because it seemed to be embedded in modernist forms. She began to have fewer solo shows in New York, although she did exhibit in other cities in the United States (frequently in group shows) and, more regularly, in Taiwan.

An aspect of her career that she seems to share with her father's is that she shows her work regularly, as he did, but, as was also true of Yun Gee, her manner of working has not always been synchronous with the art world's preferred modes of painting. A perfect example of this lack of synchronicity involves the revival of figural and abstract expressionist styles of painting in the 1980s, just at the point when Li-lan began to include words and numbers, first in the field of the stamp, and then postmarks with words, in the field of the ledgers. Not only was Li-lan using conceptual symbols, they were, as always, carefully rendered, closer to pop-style drawing, in contrast to what was then the penchant for expressive brushstrokes. Li-lan's work progresses slowly; thus, when she arrived at the stage where she was ready to include this kind of signage, the fact that its heyday had been in the 1970s may have made her new work seem already out of date. But Li-lan's persistence in following her own path is evident in that these types of signs continue to float in her most recent paintings, often becoming complex statements that are both poignant and comic:

> Stamps and postmarks center around words and images about security and insecurity: moved; returned; protected; forwarded; received; expired; registered; cancelled; entered. Through these subtle strategies she images the anxieties hovering over the contemporary psyche.[25]

These signs of anxiety may also relate to the "in between" state, the "third space," that Homi Bhabha has theorized in speaking about the immigrant sensibility. In Li-lan's case, that space is internalized as the psychic condition that emerges from being biracial, but that kind of awareness also enables a response to differences that is perhaps even more enlightened then the actuality of physical relocation. Li-lan's early life experiences could almost be summed up in the stamped language that fills the field. But the "in between" space—either psychological or physical, biracial or transnational—can also be expressed in forms of humorous or satiric play. The passage just cited stresses anxiety but neglects humor—even the humor intrinsic to the process itself. In an interview in 1990, Li-lan remarked, "It is humorous—or ironic—to enlarge a mundane, mass-produced piece of printed material and transform it into a sensual icon for contemplation. Especially since I choose the most ordinary, most inartistic and prosaic subject matter."[26] And humor abounds in the particular choices and juxtapositions that also reveal stresses in communication. One of the earliest paintings, of an envelope marked PAR AVION, is titled *Returned to Sender* (pl. 34). It shows a pointing finger with "Returned to Sender" and "Forwarding Order Expired" rubber-stamped on it. Beneath both stamps is a yellow gum label with the letters and numbers LGO8648. (In the catalogue for the exhibition where this work was shown, the painting is dated 1991, although the postmark reads 31 Dec. 1990.) These are quirky elements—letters and numbers that have meaning only to Li-lan. And then the beautifully rendered Indian headdress is on the United States stamp in the corner, with cancellation lines over it. It is a fully realized image in the domain of the visual; it does not need the realm of discourse for clarification of its meaning; instead, it shows the power of iconicity. The stamps and postmarks multiply, and their meanings, inclusive of social and political views as well, are everywhere in Li-lan's paintings, but they are restrained; viewers need to make the subtlety work for them.

One of the most intriguing stamp paintings, *Postes 0,20* (pl. 35), was made

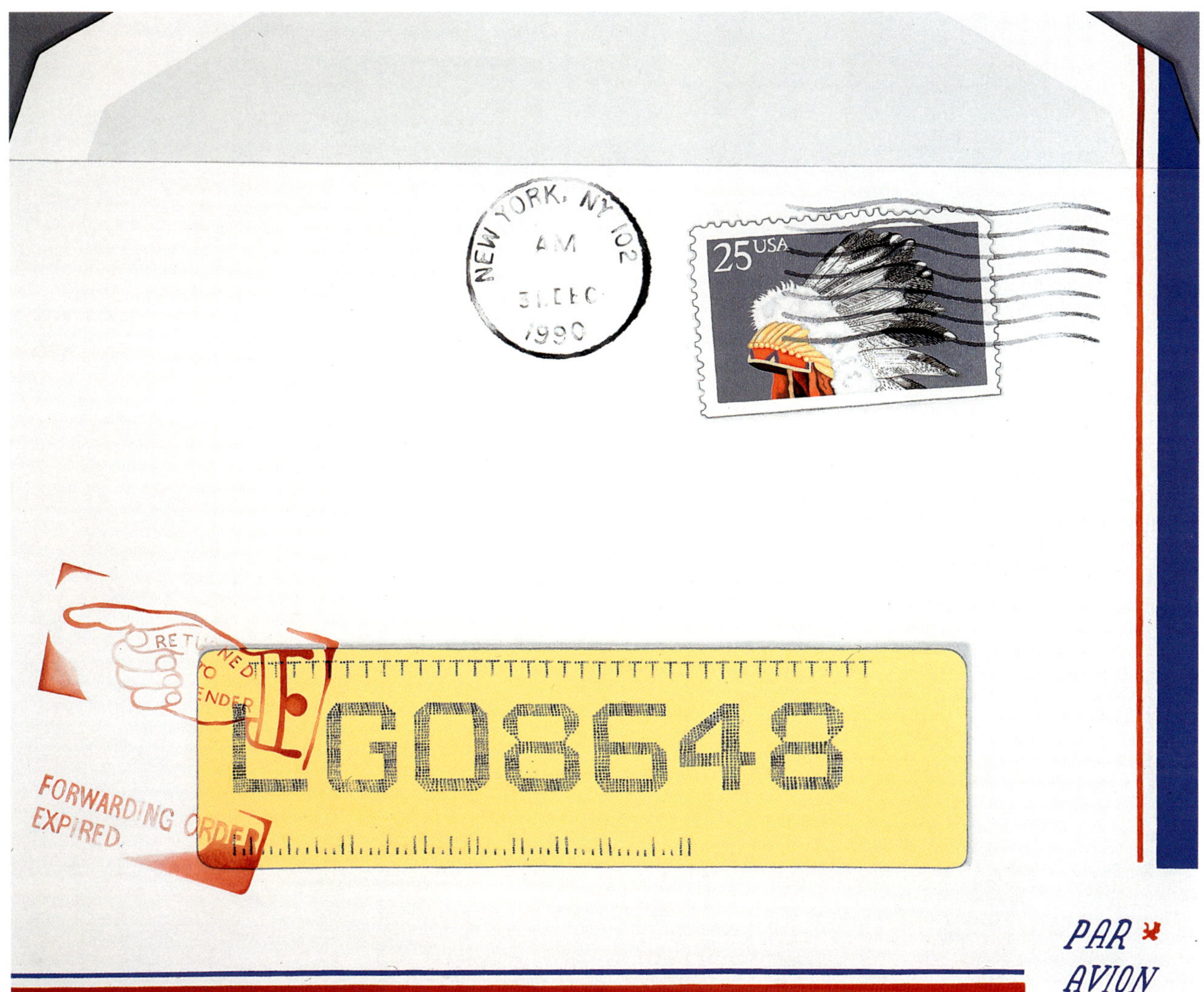

Plate 34 Li-lan, *Returned to Sender*, oil on canvas (41 in. x 48 in.), 1991.

in 1989, and again the canvas shows an envelope marked PAR AVION and bordered in blue and red on two sides. There are three stamps, two of them eyes done in Roy Lichtenstein-style halftones, with the enlarged benday dots that reflect the halftone process, and the third a beautifully rendered Saint Lo Republique Française issue with a golden fleur-de-lis. At the bottom, a comma floats in from the edge, followed by "New York 10013." A similar but larger painting from the same year, now with the partial address of the sender visible ("rue du Dragon"), has the same stamps, but Li-lan ends the stamped date with 1975. Li-lan tells me that *rue du Dragon* had nothing to do with Lichtenstein, and she thinks the eye stamps may have been made after another artist's work, perhaps Man Ray's photograph *Untitled (Lee Miller's Eye)*, taken in 1932.[27] They point to some of her more recent paintings that include eyes and lips and noses. The eyes in the "rue du Dragon" painting are little abstractions, but they are nevertheless quite startling as they directly confront the viewer. This kind of stark engagement is not usual in Li-lan's work, and

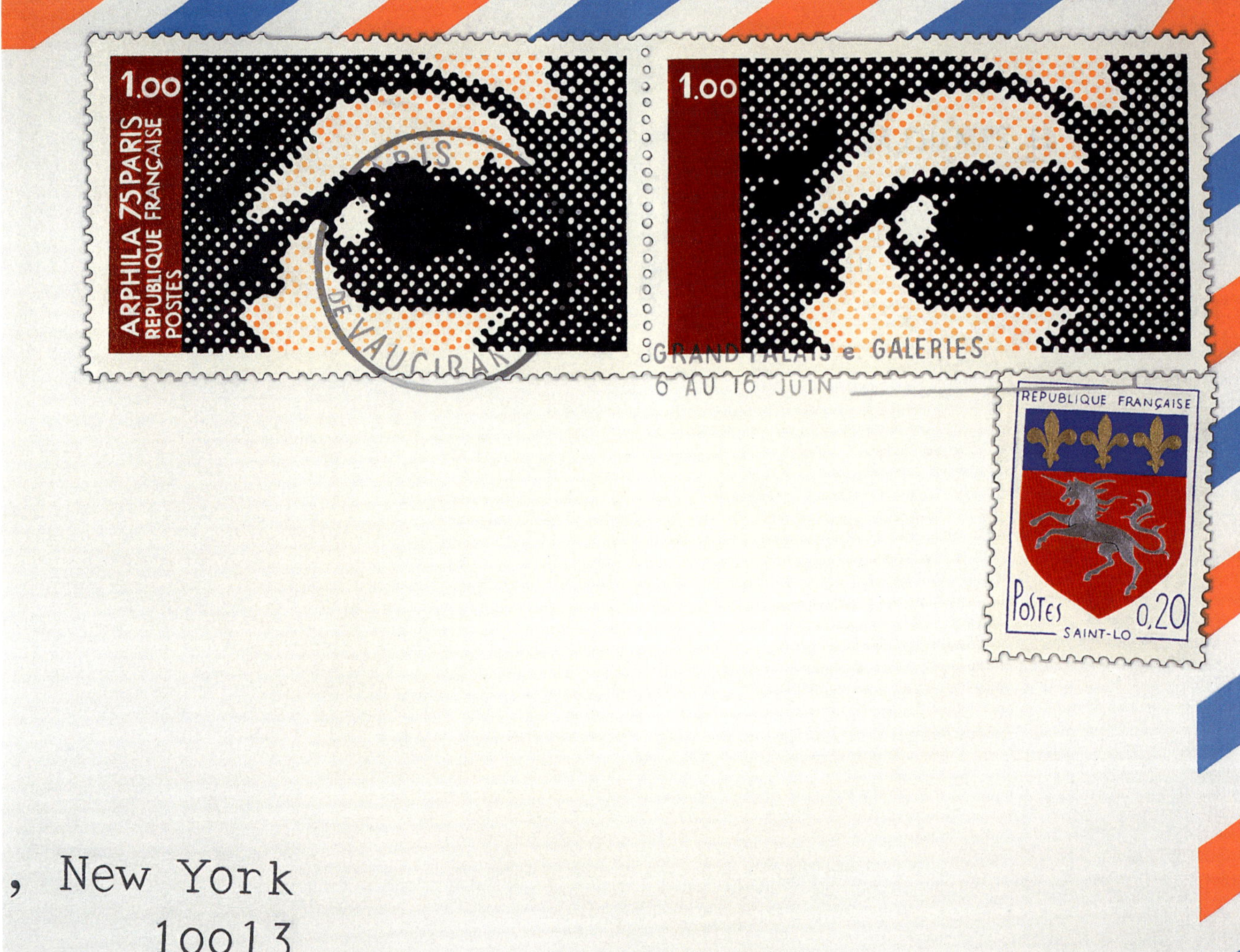

Plate 35 Li-lan, ***Postes 0,20,*** oil on canvas (20 in. x 26 in.), 1989.

perhaps it is her youthful experiences as a biracial person that surface in most of her 1970s and 1980s paintings, which are devoid of faces and figures.

To put the work from those years in context, if one looks at a cross section of the artists who were working in New York during that period, Li-lan's paintings of spreadsheets, notebooks, and stamps are unlike the work she was seeing then in studios and galleries. There are some obvious affinities with Lichtenstein's paintings of inflated banal imagery executed in benday format. Jasper Johns's soft encaustic grounds with overlay forms and subtle shadows from objects, like flags, that have little volume may also have played a part, as his target and a number of his other paintings may have done. Another influence may have been the general trend toward minimalist form and popular imagery. Li-lan's painting is different from Lichtenstein's, however, because her choices are always personal and filled with secrets, and her painting is also different from that of Johns, and it is distinct as well from Johns's tendency to make "the whole picture function . . . as an object—a flat thing—that was the exact image, shape, and size of a flag."[28]

In contrast, Li-lan's imagery floats on the surface. Her paintings always remain paintings, and she leaves many clues—color-coded bars, for example, and the transformation of machine-pressed stamps to icons bearing painterly imperfections—that reinforce her desire that they remain paintings. She also plays with the edge to reinforce the painting plane. Her work never achieves "objectness," in part because it always remains somewhat fragile and marked on the surface with the touch of the brush. When Li-lan makes the painted edge of an envelope contiguous with the edge of the canvas, it is not in order to make "the 'literal shape' of the canvas" identical with "the 'depicted shapes' within it"—not in order to produce "objectness," as in Frank Stella's late-1950s and early-1960s paintings—but to reinforce the picture plane as painterly surface.[29] A giveaway is that the envelope does not follow along all four edges; instead, the plane always peeks through. Maintaining the plane is sacrosanct.

Then there are the repetitions, the series, the witticisms, and the implied narrative that always escape interpretation, suggesting analogies with some of Warhol's paintings and silk screens. The feel of Li-lan's work, however, is very different, even though there is a trace of the surreal in both artists' work. Except for the early hand drawings and paintings, Warhol's pieces have the look of mass-media production and the correlative "dispassionate irony" that is never evident in Li-lan's paintings.[30] Li-lan's kind of humor is more satirical than ironic, and because it is filled with echoes from private events, it is never dispassionate. In addition to all these possible analogies, I am again reminded of certain conceptualist images, such as On Kawara's *I Got Up* of 1976, a series of twenty postcards addressed to John Perreault and bearing pictures, stamps, and postmarks.[31] But differences between that work and Li-lan's abound; to mention only two, Li-lan's are really paintings, and they are indeed oil paintings, with all the attention to the making of marks that the medium supports.

Painting While Living in Japan

> The native religion, Shinto, can be seen as the religious dimension of every Japanese group, but especially of the nation itself, with its divinely descended emperor. Part of the problem in defining Shinto, or indeed in defining purely Japanese culture, is that it seems to be contentless. This "contentlessness" led Nishida Kitaro to define Japanese culture as a "formless form" and Maruyama Masao to call Japanese tradition an "empty bag," or an "unstructured tradition." Japanese culture as the "container" is less easy to define than the heterogeneous "contents" of a largely foreign origin, but it is the container that tenaciously persists while ever-new contents are received and often later abandoned.[32]

This quotation about the "container" may be a generalization of the kind that plagues those who make assessments of Japanese culture, but it represents a notion tenaciously held by many Japanese intellectuals. The art critic Reiko Tomii has suggested that this is an internal, or indigenous, stereotype, but that transnational Japanese writers are seeking to find what is particularly Japanese in what fills the container. Tomii has indicated as well that in Japan there is pessimism about what has always been posited as the Japanese ability to absorb other cultures—like that of China in the past and, more recently, that of the United States—whereas transnationals like herself are much more optimistic about what is "original" in the culture.[33]

In Li-lan's paintings from the early 1970s through much of the 1980s, as mentioned earlier, color changes and a variety of very light tones were applied to the plane; the subjects of the earlier paintings disappeared, until only empty notebooks and ledgers were left. Then the grids with stamps emerged, while much of the plane was left bare. I spoke to Li-lan about these changes that seem to have begun while she was living part of the year in Japan. She agreed that being in Japan had been important for her work. I have mentioned those aspects of Li-lan's paintings that are indebted to her visual experiences during the 1960s, the 1970s, and the 1980s, in New York and abroad; in the 1970s, the impact of Japanese art reinforced some of the tendencies that seem to have been characteristic of her painting conceptions from the beginning. Although Li-lan was looking at traditional Japanese art while she was living in Japan, it seems to me that this experience also had effects that showed up in Li-lan's paintings of the late 1980s and that still belong to her repertoire. It may be that, at the time when she was living in Japan, aspects of Japanese contemporary art—particularly surrealism, minimalism, and conceptualism—furthered her early concerns, and in particular her emptying out of the objects and her painting only the vehicles that are usually used for transmitting information: the container rather than the contents. Before she lived in Japan, some of the Japanese artists she met in New York who made the most profound impressions on her were performance artists and conceptualists, and it is interesting that the work of these very artists who had emigrated to New York were the same ones whose work she was drawn to in Tokyo:

> Around [the late 1950s and 1960s] several younger painters crossed the Pacific Ocean for New York: Minoru Kawabata . . . , Kusama Yayoi . . . and Tadaaki Kuwayama . . . all arrived in New York . . . in 1958. . . . Not Paris, but New York—the "triumphant" center of postwar international painting—became increasingly the city of choice among migrating Japanese artists beginning in the fifties. Other artists who came to New York around 1960 include Ay-O in 1958, On Kawara in 1959 . . . and Shusaku Arakawa in 1961.[34]

The art that was most frequently exhibited in Tokyo when Li-lan lived there, from the late 1960s through the late 1970s, changed dramatically from the earlier twentieth century among the artists identified with the avant-garde. In the first part of the century, there were artists who emended aspects of traditional painting, those who were influenced by French impressionism and postimpressionism, and, later, those whose abstract painting was part of the international modern art movement.[35] With the Gutai group, starting in the mid-1950s, the work identified with what we now call postmodernism was as experimental as it was in the United States but even more conceptual in its orientation.[36] Li-lan had met Shusaku Arakawa and On Kawara in New York. The mixture of minimalism and conceptualism in the pencil drawings and mixed-media paintings of Arakawa seem to have impressed her, as did Kawara's *Today* series (begun on January 4, 1966), his earlier *Bathroom* series, and his other conceptual works. She knew Kusama's *Infinity Nets* series of sumptuous, all-over textured paintings in tones of white, and Yoko Ono's twenty-two ink-on-paper works titled *Instructions for Paintings* of 1961–62, which contained tiny rows of beautiful Japanese script floating on small sheets of paper. They were first exhibited at the Sogetsu Art Center in Tokyo in 1962, but Li-lan may have seen them later in New York or Japan. The Sogetsu Art Center was a place where many of the most progressive people in the arts in Japan showed and performed, as did such Western artists as Georges Mathieu.[37] The Fluxus group was wholeheartedly embraced by Japanese artists like Yoko Ono, and several of them had been leading members of this fluid group from the beginning. Whereas artists in China were discriminated against by the Chinese government—their exhibitions were closed down, and traditional art was upheld—Japan had been a hotbed of open activity from the early twentieth century, when Japanese artists experimented with Western modern art, up to and beyond the inception of the Gutai group in the 1950s, with its actions akin to "happenings."

Many artists also followed a more minimalist direction, as did Tadaaki Kuwayama and Yamada Masaaki.[38] Takamatsu Jiro's oil painting *Pressed Shadows* of 1965 is light in tone and repeats the same picture: the shadow of a woman and a chair that recedes into the distance, becoming smaller and smaller. A play between the planar and perspective systems engages issues of perception, as do the shadows, without portraying what casts them. Some of Li-lan's paintings from the later 1960s and early 1970s, with silhouettes, eggs, cups, plates, nails, and so on, against those luminous surfaces, engage similar concerns. A major difference is that, again, the objects that fill her painting world are those that surround her in everyday life.

Alexandra Munroe differentiates as follows the minimalism and conceptualism practiced by Japanese and Western artists:

> Where Euro-American Conceptual artists generally employed language, nonsense, process, minimalism and conceptualism to serve a theoretical end—to critique the art system and the definition of art itself—Japanese Conceptual artists have used identical means to probe more cerebral issues: the nature of perception, cognition, and being. Preoccupied by philosophy (rather than epistemology), their common means, in the words of critic Miyakawa Atsushi, were to "posit the mirror as a primary form of the imaginary . . . going beyond to include all art and thought."[39]

Li-lan's form of minimalism and conceptualism is neither Eastern nor Western, nor is it a fusion of the two; rather, it resides in the ambiguities of perception, reductionism, and emptying out of the space. Her paintings from this period have an affinity with aspects of Japanese art, but only the art that appealed transnationally. It is probable that she would have moved in this direction even if she had not lived in Japan but had only encountered the work of these Japanese artists in the United States.

Kusama has called her own work "obsessional art." I do not think that the legacy of dada and surrealism—so pervasive in Japanese art in the earlier part of the twentieth century, and continued in the dark and obsessive work of many others in the 1960s—is an obvious component of Li-lan's paintings, but she frequently talks about Ankoku Butoh and the works of Kusama as inspirational. The effects of the postwar era stirred up, according to Munroe, "a carnal darkness at the foundation of the Japanese psyche":

> Images of physical deformity, self-obliteration, and spiritual violence dominate the sculptures of Miki Tomio, the objects, environments, and Happenings of Kusama Yayoi and Kudo Tetsumi, and the performances of Hijikata Tatsumi, originator of Ankoku Butoh or the "Dance of Utter Darkness." Independent of established genres, and heirs to the legacies of Dada, Surrealism, and Existential thought in the Japanese avant-garde, these artists shared a peculiar sensibility that was rooted in personal trauma and societal crises.[40]

It may well be that, for Li-lan, some identification between these works and aspects of her own life, in particular the abandonment and fear she felt in her childhood, triggered her empathy with this dark side of Japanese art. But it does not emerge in images of violence; rather, a disturbing sense of the void emanates from these works, alongside the obsessively repeated patterns, and yet this edge of darkness is held in check by the ordinariness of the things being painted.

The works of the Japanese artists who have engaged Li-lan's interest—like the works of those artists of Chinese background who are surveyed in the epilogue—are works produced by just those artists who are transnational and engaged in the international art world. Their lives seem to be unsettled, and they move from one cosmopolitan center to another. In the process, they often explore or are unconsciously impacted by the art environment in the cities in which they live. Because they are flaneurs of the avenues of the world, it is certainly understandable that several of them were engaged in the Fluxus movement, that worldwide flow of events rooted in the ordinary sights and sounds of everyday activities. Li-lan is more rooted in her own life, but her paintings are responsive to the fluidity between art and life, and to the playful, even goofy, humor that was characteristic of many Fluxus events. Her later paintings resonate with that kind of sensibility, but they also include aspects of her immersion in traditional Japanese art forms.

Painting from the 1990s On

Many Japanese paintings on scrolls and screens leave large areas void, in contrast with most Chinese painting, which seems to fill the whole surface. I was recently reminded of that when I saw an exhibition of seventeenth- and eighteenth-century painting at the Japan Society in New York.[41] In Japanese painting, a single branch can fill a screen many feet wide on an almost completely empty surface that is sometimes gilded—if of silk, stained—and sometimes simply left the same color as the paper. Li-lan visited many temples and shrines when she was in Japan, and she saw numerous screens and paintings in them, although she did not consciously choose motifs on the basis of those experiences. What she also saw there were narrative devices different from those used in the painting tradition that had made an impact on her work after she saw Renaissance art in Italy, and that perhaps had more in common with the narrative systems of medieval art. Early Renaissance narrative, while still planar, was cohesive and linear in how it proceeded from scene to scene; Giotto's Arena Chapel frescoes are a prime example. In the contemporary art that Li-lan engaged in in New York and Germany, a pervasive formal harmony and unity resolved the sections into a coherent whole, whether the work was abstract expressionist or postpainterly, and narrative elements were eliminated. In minimalism, the repetition of parts can be infinite in its extension, thus obviously denying the closure of traditional narration. In both Chinese and Japanese traditional painting, when a story is being told, its different parts are scattered all over the painting, and the flow from event to event is often propelled by aspects of the natural world—trees and mountains, rivers and pathways—that direct the viewer from part to part. If one knows the story before hand, one knows how to proceed, but the visual experience is complicated by all the details that the artist paints to tempt you along the way, and often these details are more enticing than the actual scenes, which can often be quite small in relation to the vastness of the natural surroundings. Architectural elements, pavilions, and domestic interiors are also ubiquitous. Both

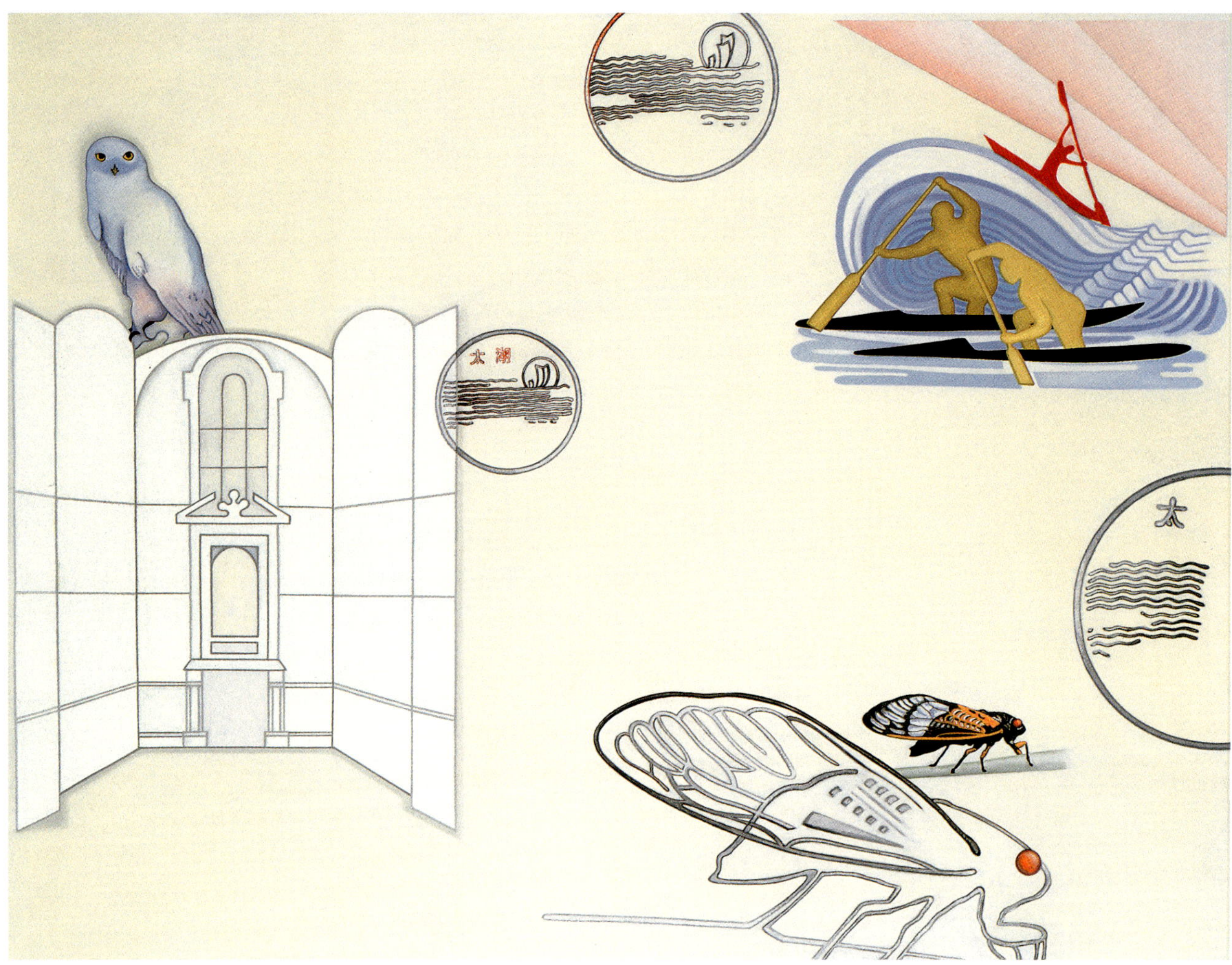

Plate 36 Li-lan, *Sea of Silence,* oil on linen (42 in. x 54 in.), 2005.

emptying out and the scattering of narrative juxtapositions over the surface became stable elements of Li-lan's painting practices; her experiences in Japan may have helped her refine her particular manner of presenting her "narration." I have addressed issues concerning the luminosity of those large expanses of "empty" space, but it is the form of narrative that has become more developed in Li-lan's later works. At the same time, these works also provide places for the juxtaposition of the scattered "narrative" elements that emerged in full force and are still visible in her present work.

Li-lan's paintings seemed somewhat sparse in the 1970s and 1980s, but in the 1990s many of them have given up their minimal structure and become filled with images that are often askew; they dance away from the formality of the horizontal and vertical axes, although they are bound by the rigor of its grip. Architectural motifs are everywhere, and although in the past they were usually depicted within the boundaries of stamps, envelopes, or postcards, now they stand on their own in the main field. The postmarks have become more and more ridiculous—featuring alligators, cartoon animals, and strange alien creatures drawn with less precise edges—and they bring to mind the comic

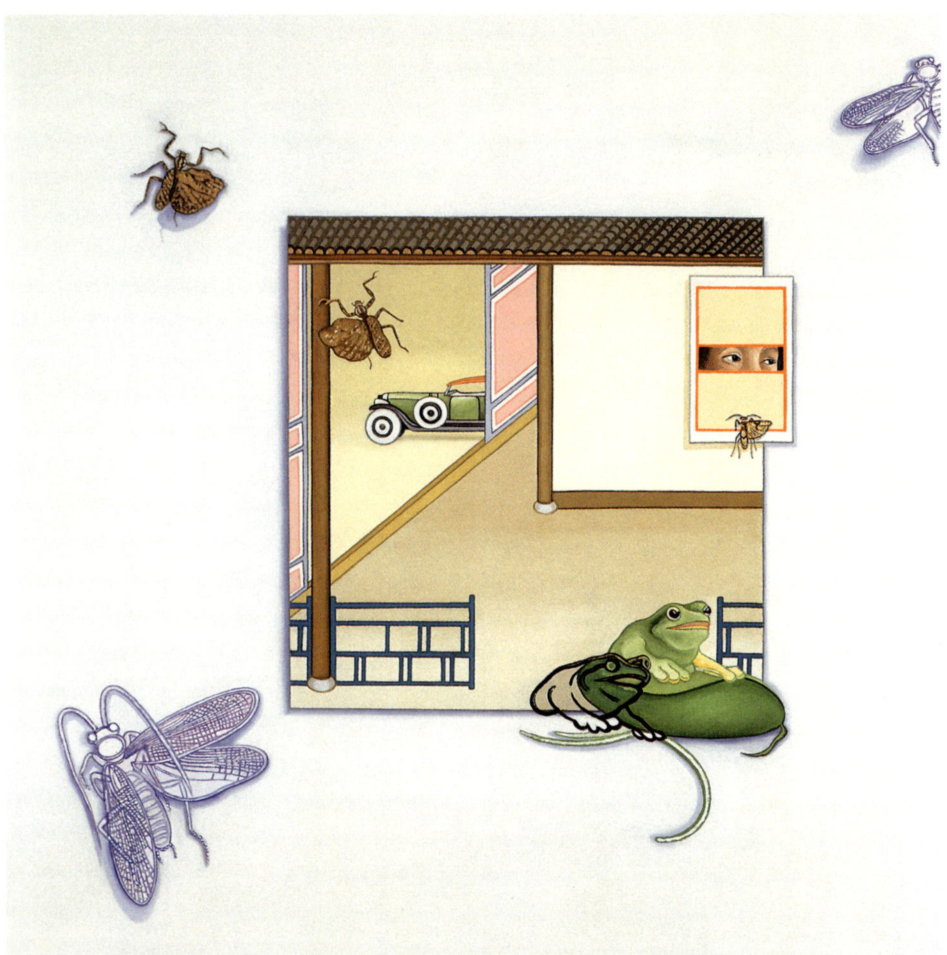

Plate 37 Li-lan, *Withindoors,* oil on linen (34 in. x 32 in.), 2006.

books that are so widely a part of contemporary Japanese culture. Many of the postmarks are more painterly, while meticulously illustrative bugs crawl over the surfaces and seem almost photorealistic or, better, create a trompe l'oeil effect. Humor abounds, as in the 2003 *Fly On*, in which "air" is stamped, one "scientifically" drawn fly crawls toward an ancient Chinese pavilion, and another casts its more than realistic shadow at the corner of a blank postcard. For the first time, real volume exists, the kind that might suggest actually picking these flies out of the painting, but their shadows are too strong for little bugs.

Wonderful creatures of nature appear in Japanese paintings, as in *Flowers and Birds by a Pond*, a stunning scroll by the eighteenth-century painter Yamamoto Bautsu, which was included in the 2004 Japan Society exhibition: in this scroll, not only are the ever-present birds depicted, but an enlarged insect also crawls across the field. Perhaps Li-lan was stirred by looking at works like this in Japan; before she lived there, nature had not been an obvious subject in her paintings, although birds did appear with frequency. Perhaps she was inspired by the many birds her father had in his studio, and insects appear in the book illustrations she is always looking at.

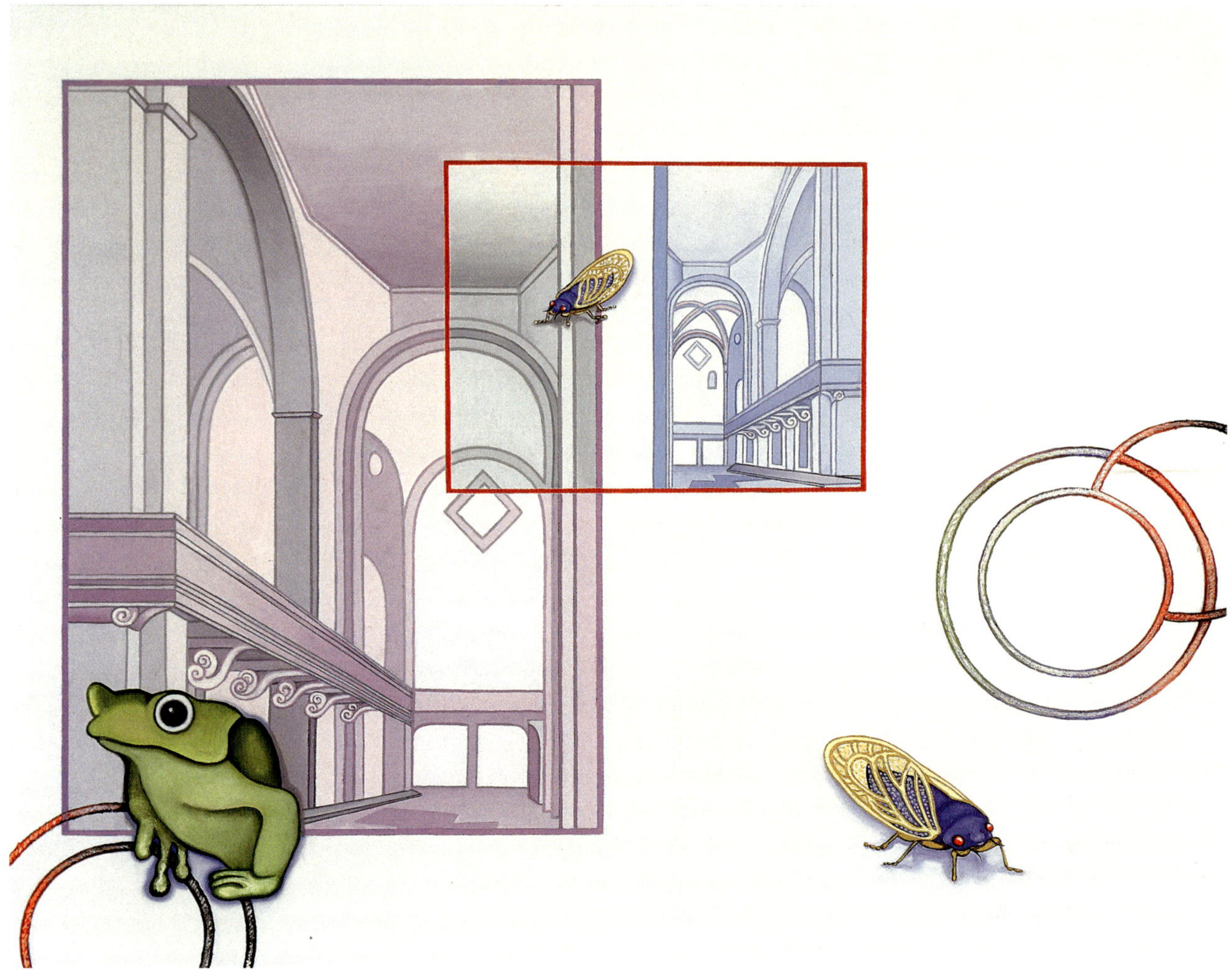

Plate 38 Li-lan, ***Reflections,*** oil on canvas (24 in. x 30 in.), 2006.

Dinosaurs inhabit the stamps in the 1990 *First Class Mail,* and in *Malaysia 10c* from the same year, on an envelope marked PAR AVION, two stamps from Malaysia are beautifully rendered; the one that costs a dollar shows a mosque or a palace and those elegantly carved stone windows and doorways that are hallmarks of Islamic architecture. A Jordanian stamp depicts a turret in the 1991 *Historic Site,* and two swimmers are on Chinese stamps in the 1993 *China: 30 Yuan.*[42] Figures have seldom been included in Li-lan's paintings until very recently, and although Li-lan swims a lot and has always enjoyed it, perhaps her present inclusion of the swimmers and other figures simply reflects her chance encounters with the Chinese stamps that she receives more frequently as a result of her contacts and exhibitions in Taiwan. These images may also have been chosen for secret reasons; they may be the type of content that exists for the artist in the private realm that often makes the practice of painting so absorbing.

A small intaglio/collagraph—*Correspondence: Between Two*, one of the few prints Li-lan has made—is from the same year as her second trip to

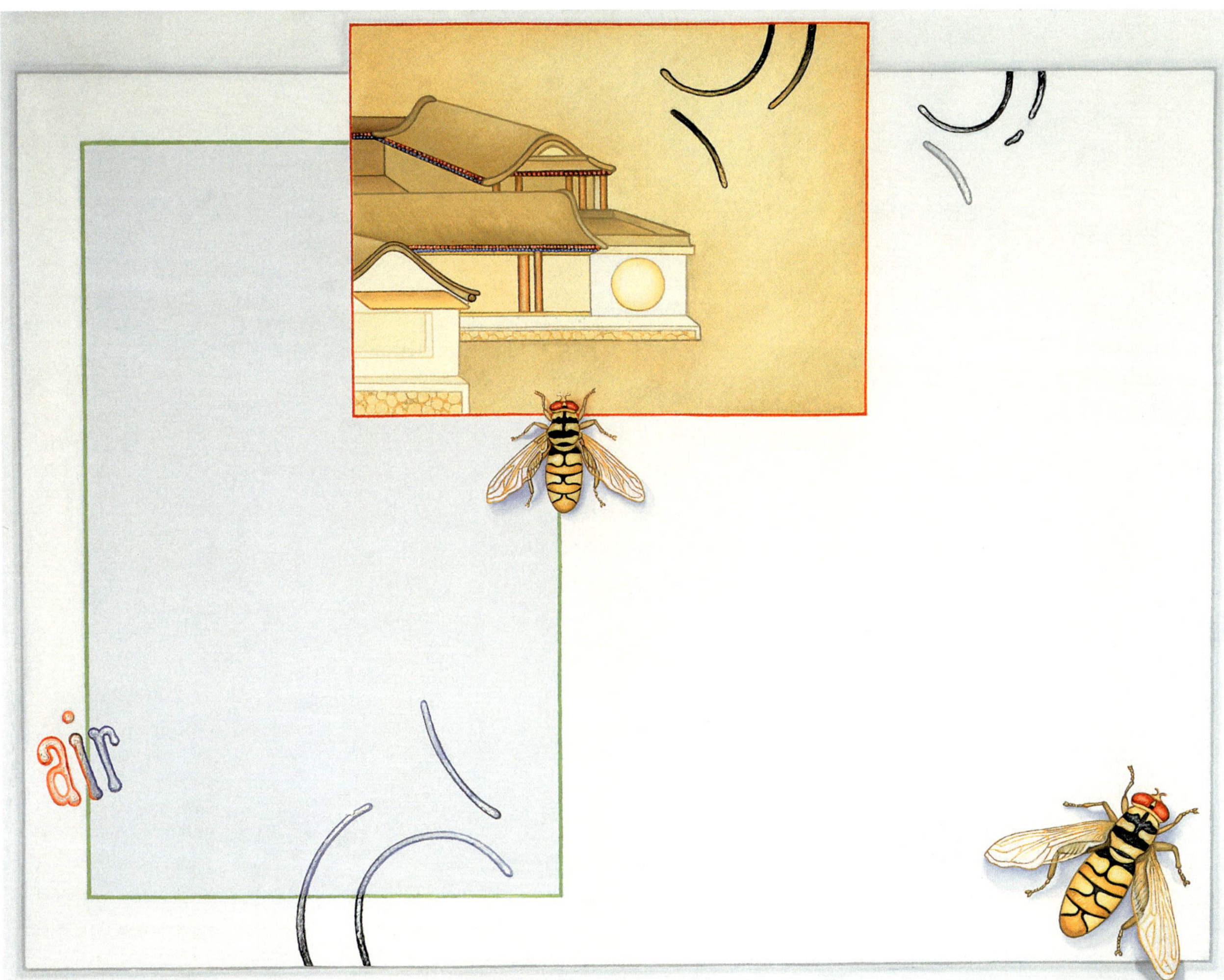

Plate 39 Li-lan, *Fly On*, oil on linen (24 in. x 30 in.), 2003.

mainland China and her father's village.[43] On two manila envelopes, two stamps depict Chinese scrolls and folded books, and the postmarks are in Chinese; David Ebony translates them as meaning "printed matter." It is particularly apt for the intaglio, however, that the print followed from a five-by-nine-foot canvas with the same title, painted in 1994. As was also the case with Yun Gee, when something Chinese is introduced into one of Li-lan's paintings, even as smart a reviewer of her work as David Ebony succumbs to the East/West pairing; he writes of this painting that it "is a spare and elegant composition that recalls the infinite landscapes found in Chinese painting of the Northern Sung Dynasty."[44] There is a pastel, *Post Card: Landscapes of Guilin* of 1994, that he describes in the essay for a 1997 exhibition of her work in Taipei as "a record of an apparently personal exploration. Here a mountain scene . . . is an homage to the misty landscapes of the Sung Dynasty."[45] This is certainly an appropriate description because two Chinese-like landscapes are rendered in the pastel. To return to *Correspondence: Between Two,* however, Ebony writes:

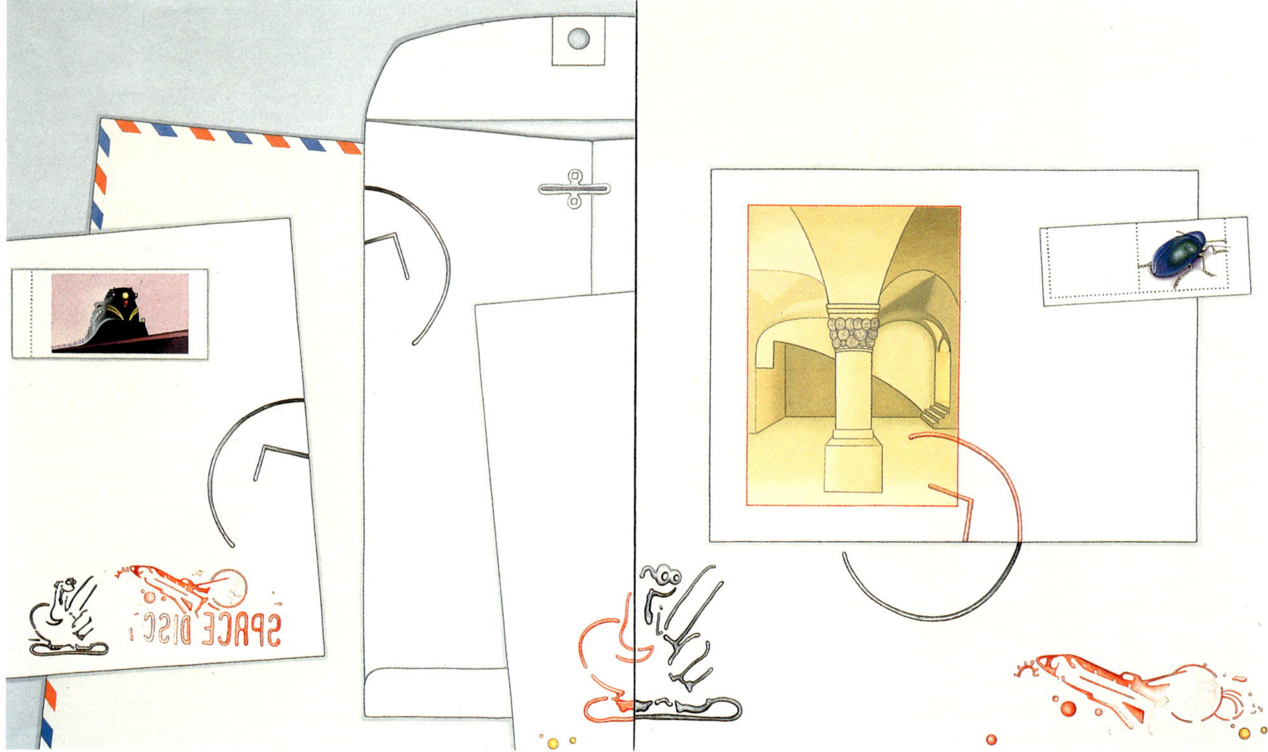

Plate 40 Li-lan, *Space Disco* (diptych), oil on linen (60 in. x 100 in., each panel 60 in. x 50 in.), 2002. Photo credit: Kevin Ryan

> The stamp on the left features a partially unrolled scroll, the kind traditionally used in the East for writing and painting. The stamp on the right is similar but features a more modern-looking Western-style book. In this work, as in a number of other works in the show, Li-lan sets up subtly opposing elements that are deeply personal but also seem to have sociopolitical implications.[46]

The notion that sociopolitical implications exist in this work is overdetermined, and not just because there are no Chinese landscapes; moreover, the division between East and West in the identification of the books is out of place. The one on the right is a folded book that opens up like a small screen and can be almost as traditional a form as the scrolls used for writing. I think that both of these Taiwanese stamps show surfaces to write and paint on, and they raise an enigma—who sent them to whom?—that is the personal mystery which Li-lan often hints at but never reveals. Li-lan's discovery of mainland China, but particularly of Taiwan, has added a series of images to her album that now complicate and enrich her life as well as her iconic collection. Yet this discovery, coming relatively late in her life, has not brought about fundamental change but instead has become part of a complex mixture that surely bypasses distinctions between East and West.

Ebony's discussion of Li-lan's postcard paintings is most illuminating in his citation of Jacques Derrida. From the mid-1990s on, postcards and envelopes have abounded in Li-lan's work, and *Space Disco* (pl. 40) of 2002 has it all.

Ebony quotes Derrida's essay "Envois": "The postcard is no longer a simple metaphor, and is even, as the site of all correspondences, the 'proper' possibility of every possible rhetoric," and in an earlier part of the essay Derrida says, "What I prefer, about postcards, is that one does not know what is in front or what is in back, here or there, near or far . . . nor what is the most important, the picture or the text, and in the text, the message or the caption, or the address."[47] Li-lan's postcard paintings seem to be visual echoes of these citations.

Li-lan has not traveled to many of these sites, so why does she include them in her paintings? These places are flattened representations of a reality that exists only in the discourse of images. Li-lan does paint some motifs from places where she has been, but most of the sites represented in her paintings are known to her only from the hundreds of postcards she receives with their stamps, their partial addresses, and their postmarks, and from the illustrations in books from which she copies insects, architectural motifs, and other images that pop up in her work. And everything seems to have the same emphasis, as Derrida suggests is the essence of the postcard. Elements are chosen to play a part when the circumstances are right, but the proper circumstances seem serendipitous. Do these images speak of her desires, or are they only wonderful to paint? She can put one image next to another, and a possible narrative is formed, but what constitutes narrative "meaning" in these paintings? And the postcards, like her notebooks and ledgers without inscriptions, never contain personal messages, only the pictures, marks, and stamps that demarcate the institutions of communication. And yet Li-lan, in her copy of Derrida's *The Postcard*, has marked a page, and I am only guessing at what part of it she is noting; perhaps it is this one: "Finally the post office is the place of all *affairs,* all negotiations; through it the absent become present; it is the consolation of my life."[48] Li-lan may be wedded to the postcard, with its pictures of sites from all over the world, but through the act of painting she makes present what for Derrida are only *cites*. What she does with images of the faraway and the exotic is to capture them in a surreal web of personal fantasy and desire, where they are fixed through her act of painting them. At the same time, they do register as images of sites, pictures that the tourist pastes into a scrapbook or album upon returning home, as a reminder that he or she was were really there. But a crucial difference remains: Li-lan's painting practice keeps these sites vividly present, whereas the tourist's images are simply stale evocations of a past that is often hardly remembered. The tourist skims the surfaces: one site or another, in the form of an image on a photo or a postcard, is just as easily discarded as remembered, and each is easily displaced by the next. Li-lan's sites can never be so displaced, because they have been re-presented through meticulous renditions. In the play between sites and *cites*, she images contemporary instances of the dialogue between absence and presence that the most sophisticated theories engendered by electronic media are now engaging.

Apart from their role in the play between site and citation, Li-lan's freehand stamp copies can be classed as appropriations of already existent paintings, prints, photographs, and graphic illustrations. Many are copies of tourist sites taken from books and photographs: the Red Door of the Forbidden City; a Chinese villa; the pyramids of Giza; the theater at Spoleto; the bridges, domes, arcades, and vaults of Roman, Romanesque, and Renaissance architecture; scenes from Liberia; and, as mentioned earlier, Jordan, Malaysia, and Mozambique.[49] Others are copied from more literal signs related to travel, both past and present: old-fashioned toylike biplanes resembling those her father painted; jets; old-fashioned locomotives and high-speed express trains; automobiles; and parachutes. Li-lan's practice of copying from stamps and printed reproductions is different from the tradition of artists borrowing motifs from other artists' work in that most of the images she copies, with the exception of the architectural images, come from popular art and illustration, not from the major works of high art that were her sources in earlier paintings. And her copies truly are copies, even when they are subtly tinkered with; they are not just the parts or motifs that it is the business of art history to detect. Hers is a peculiar form of pop art: rather than depicting the banal objects of the consumer world (which fill the prints of Andy Warhol, as a prime example), Li-lan juxtaposes things from different visual cultures; her copies jumble together visual sites and their citations, across borders and categories, in a fashion that once would have been considered surreal but that now signifies the world many of us really inhabit.

Like sound bites, these visual images float in and out of the realm of recognition. Sometimes the place being depicted can be identified; at other times. the postmarks and writing on the stamps are smeared. *Post Card: Landscapes of Guilin* is just such an example, with a figure in a painted "Chinese" landscape turned upside down and overlying another landscape, both with blurry postmarks. At the same time that communication is sometimes blurry, Li-lan's copies of the structures of arches and vaults are meticulously rendered, as are those quasi-scientific illustrations of bugs that have recently appeared and sometimes crawl near them. These creatures are often on stamps; occasionally they have crawled out of the frame and are colored to match the architecture. *Fly On*, mentioned earlier, is quite sparse, with the postcard field empty, the marks "air" and a few stamped lines, and two beautifully painted flies colored like the section of Chinese architecture framed in an enlarged stamp above, in a pale yellow rectangle.[50] In contrast, images cohabit in the more cluttered environments of the 1997 *Endangered Species* and the 1998 *& Protect Endangered Species* (pl. 41), with its marvelous stamp renditions of old-fashioned jukeboxes. The former is a small oil painting with a New York postmark

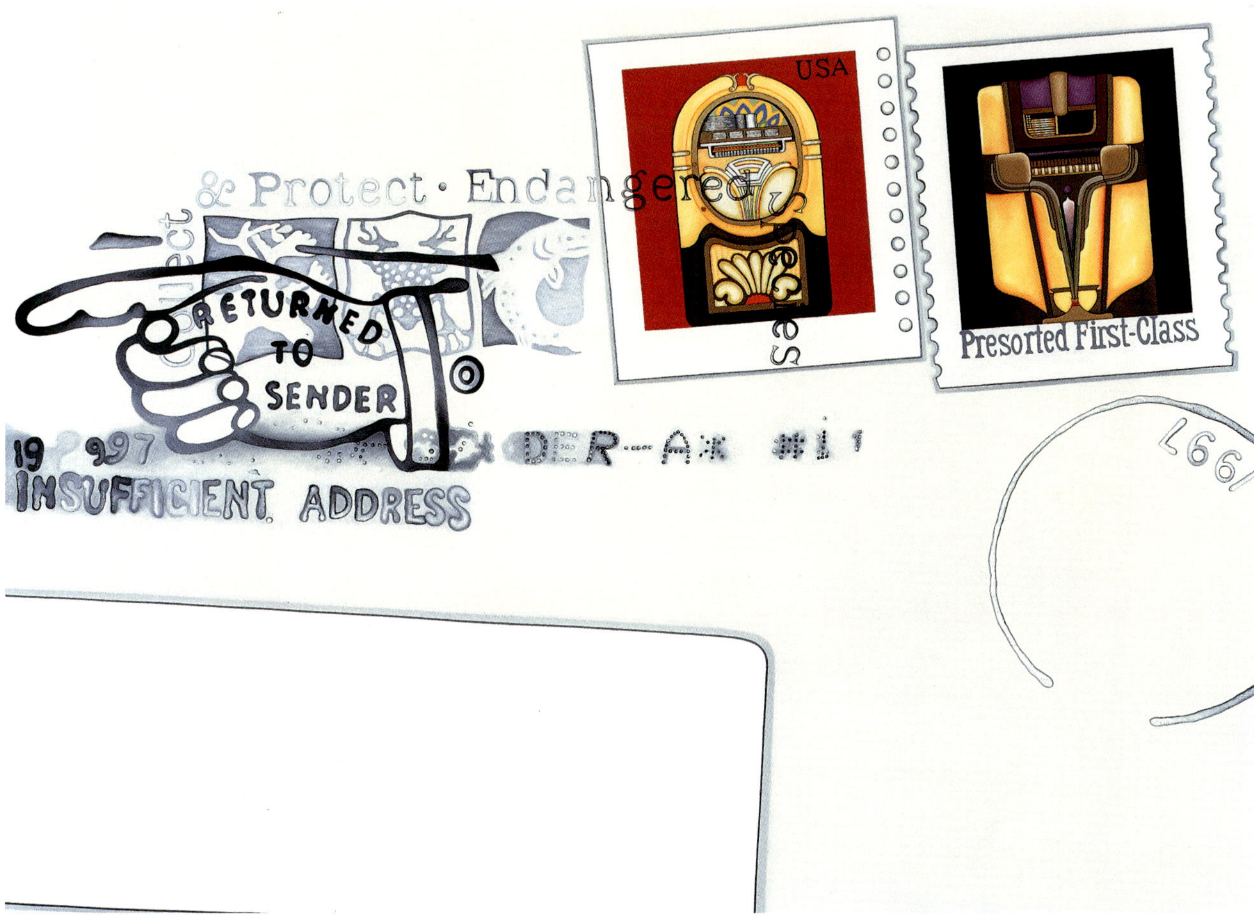

Plate 41 Li-lan, ***& Protect Endangered Species***, **oil on linen (42 in. x 57 in.), 1998. Photo credit: Kevin Ryan**

(14 Oct. 1997), bar codes, and stamped notices that resonate with nostalgia, secret yearnings, and the social/political references that the stamps engender: returned to sender, collect and protect endangered species (with goofy gray paintings of a fish, a frog, and an endangered animal with horns), insufficient address, and blurred words and numbers or parts of messages, like "national," whose reference is indistinct. Many of the images that Li-lan chooses belong to the world of ordering and to legal and institutional practices, which she then subverts through blurring and through juxtapositions that are sometimes ludicrous. Indistinct meanings come to mind again and become visual symptoms of the loss of communication, with meaning obfuscated and finally completely lost. Vacillations among the surreal, the semiotic, and the real are constantly in play.

Somewhere—I don't remember where—a reviewer once suggested that there is an erotic dimension to Li-lan's painting; and, indeed, the stages of arousal, which often involve teasing, are analogous in some ways to Li-lan's use of vacillation. The seduction is partly an effect of the sensuous surfaces, which Li-lan makes by rubbing the layers down with sandpaper, meticulously building them up with strokes of paint, and adding wax to the oil medium.

The sinuosity is even more intense in her many pastel paintings, since she layers the surfaces over and over again, as she does in the oils. As she builds from the plane, stroke by stroke, the individual marks of her performance are more visible than in her oil paintings. Then there is the conceptual arousal that stems from teasing the viewer with what seem to be clues that frustrate closure, often because they are only partially rendered or make no semantic sense. And then there are the eye paintings—a few with lips and noses, and one without eyes at all—which are becoming more frequent and are also very seductive. There is never a whole face—again, only a part is presented, and when it is only the eyes, arousal is most intense. Are they Li-lan's eyes, and how can we tell?

In *Postes 0,20* (pl. 35), with the two eyes formed with benday dots, the eyes are almost absorbed in the Lichtenstein-like pattern. When Li-lan painted eyes again, ten years later, the treatment of the theme became decidedly representational. In 1999, she painted two small oils, *Overbridge: Crossing,* and *Chinese Bridge,* which were probably triggered by the eye surgery she underwent in 1999, and also by her acquisition of German stamps; the eyes in *Overbridge: Crossing* are not hers but are purely Caucasian.[51] It is usually the eyes that identify Asians, so Li-lan gives us all kinds. In the eight or nine paintings with eyes or lips or the bridge of the nose, it is impossible to be certain whose features are represented, and issues around being biracial and the contingent "orientalism" are floating about.[52] The titles are a subset of that interpretive direction, since they also seem to refer to biracial and transnational themes about bridging and crossing. *Bird of Passage* (pl. 42) is among the most captivating, not only because of its vividly colored bird but also because the three Asian eyes are treated in separation overlays that are about color differences as well as about being different. The play between color as a formal element and color as social stereotype is left ambiguous, particularly because the painting is so humorous. One of those "alien" creatures is loosely drawn in the upper field, and the words "comics class (ic?) collection" overlap the bird. Below, a postmark of an airplane is drawn in red. Thus, if on one level there is a serious social concern, on another level its absurdity is put in play. In the 2001 *Journey: Round Trip*, the yellowish cast of the Asian eyes contrasts with the fleshy pink of the nose and lips—biracial indeed! If eyes are supposed to be the windows to the soul, one would never be able to make that leap from Li-lan's eye paintings.[53] Almost as a play on words, in the last to date of this series, *Look Out* (pl. 43) of 2004, a "Geisha" identified only by her eyes and her white painted skin looks out seductively from behind a rectangular screen that masks all but the upper part of her face; insects, postmarks, and two stamps with "Oriental" architectural motifs are randomly placed in the remaining field. Li-lan copied the eyes from a Japanese postcard that was potentially capable of sending the sign of the Oriental stereotype anywhere and everywhere.[54]

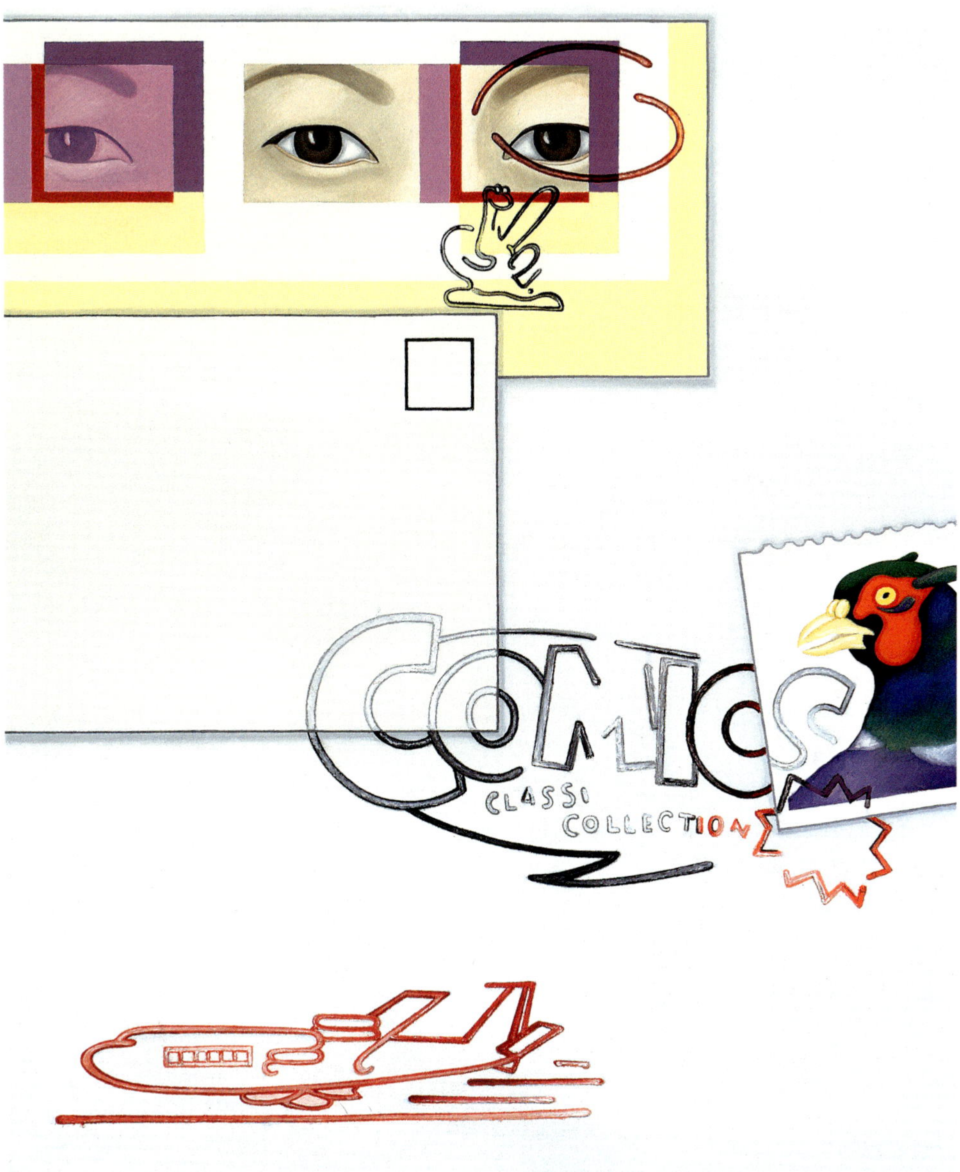

Plate 42 Li-lan, *Bird of Passage*, oil on linen (30 in. x 24 in.), 2001.

In another direction, the sign of crossing worlds is ever present. Sometimes this sign is literally the subject, as in the 1995 pastel *Two Cards: Three Worlds*—New York and its skyline in subtle tones of gray, a gently askew postcard with Chinese letters, and an even more skewed bright-red stamp from Helvetia (Switzerland). The larger oil on canvas of 1996, *One Arch: Two Cards, Three Worlds*, depicts a Gothic-type stone bridge as background, again in grays, with two orchid stamps from Africa on a blank postcard with a Chinese postmark that overlaps it. Other ciphers more mysteriously reference the crossing of boundaries, as does *Open Immediately*, which contains a stamp with a bridge (the stamps are from China) and another with what looks like a computer and keyboard marked over with words and numbers and "Please Open Immediately" and then again "Open Immediately," with numbers that seem to have no reference and the words "Mailed from Zip

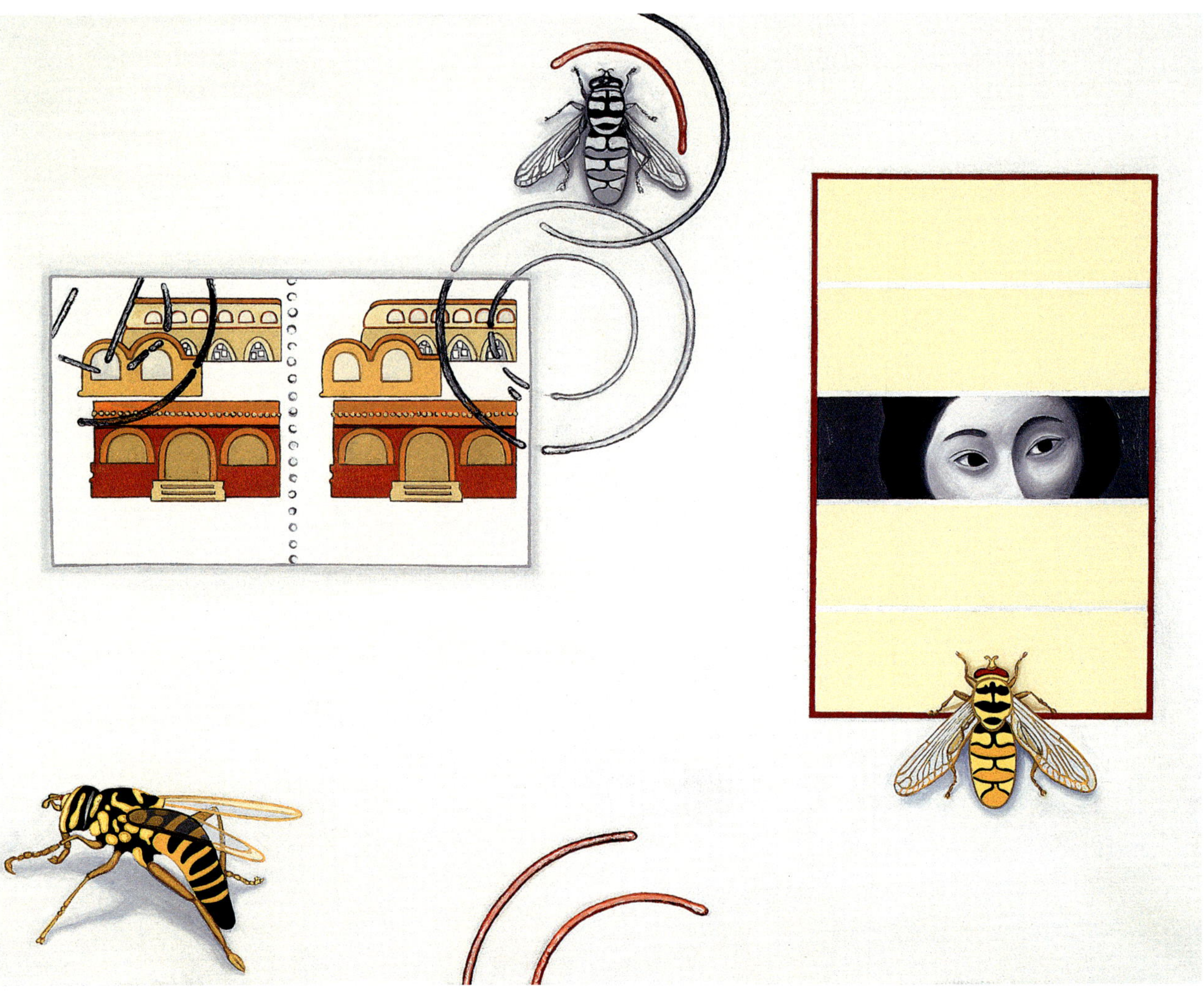

Plate 43 Li-lan, *Look Out*, oil on linen (24 in. x 30 in.), 2004. Photo credit: Kevin Ryan

Code." What seems like a desperate need to communicate with someone somewhere has been thwarted.

In some of the paintings of the last few years, Li-lan has sometimes returned to the sparser format of the earlier work and included blank pages, blank postmarks, and even blank stamplike shapes that are Asian postmarks or that have no particular reference to any specific locale. Words are partially obliterated, so semantic meaning is more insistently frustrated, and often words do not appear at all.[55] But there are also paintings from 2003 with figures doing wushu, such as *Fable* (pl. 44), and *Legend* has a drawn silhouette of a falling figure and a small running man. Figures have been missing from Li-lan's work since her 1960s paintings, and these figures, unlike the earlier ones, are not representational but rather signs of figures in action, more like advertising logos. Architecture abounds, carefully structured, and the insects seem to be crawling around everywhere. *Court* (pl. 45), for example, is a little frightening because the beautiful Chinese pavilion seems vulnerable to the enlarged insects roaming about. Everything seems to be endangered. These

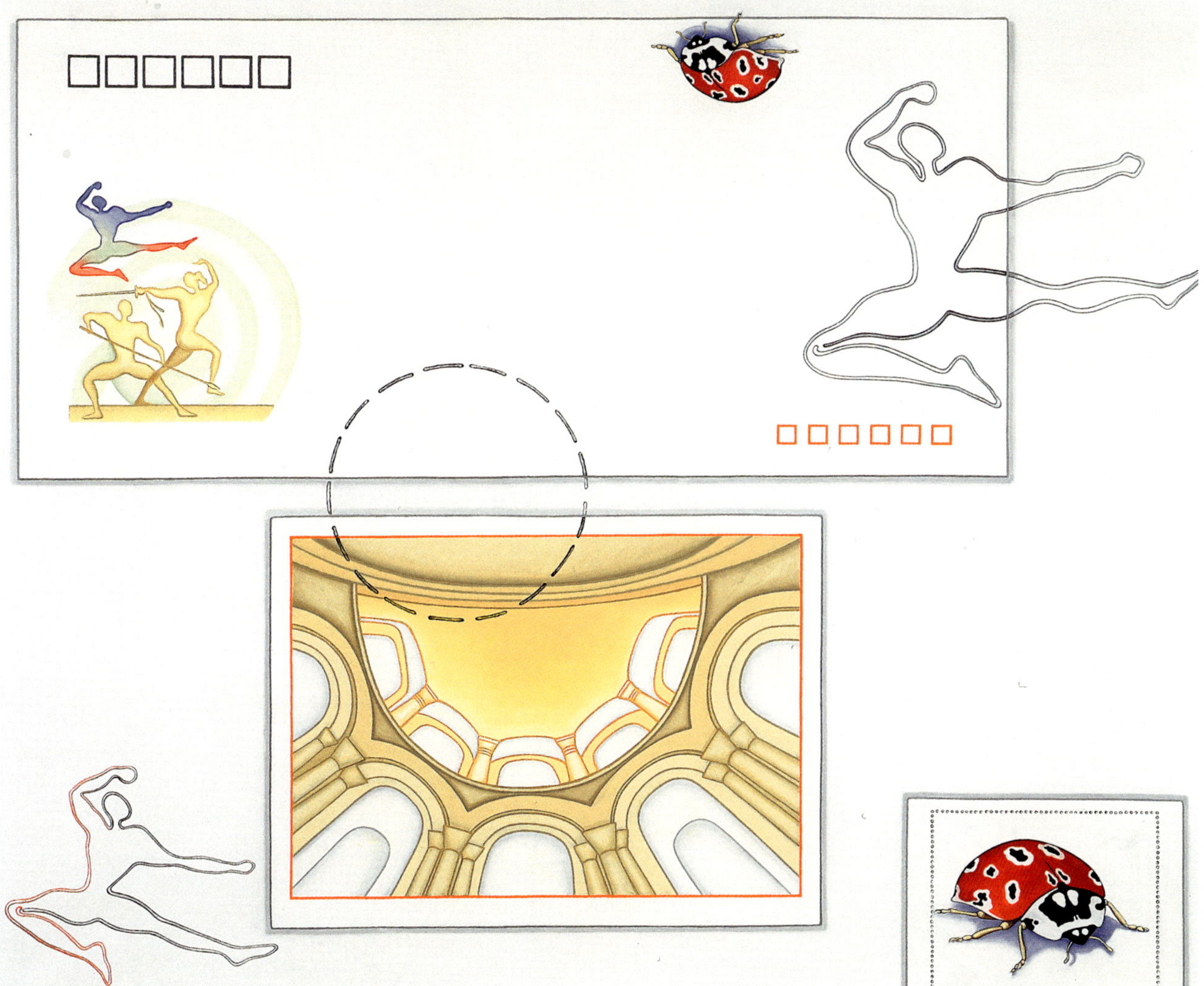

Plate 44 Li-lan, *Fable,* oil on linen (50 in. x 60 in.), 2003. Photo credit: Kevin Ryan

paintings are at the same time more sinister and more mischievous, with their up-to-the-minute perspective on the anxieties we live by.

One of the more complex paintings pushes at the limits of those anxieties. In the large diptych *Labyrinth* (pl. 46) of 2003 with the difficult-to-read "endangered" at the upper right-hand corner, the stamp and postcard format, while still present, seems to be disappearing. The postmarks are mere shadows of their former strong imprint, and alligators, fish, and birds are fading away. At the same time, a refined architectural rendering of what could be Renaissance or Cistercian corridors, painted in pale yellow and violets, dominates the lower part of the upper panel. The lower panel depicts the old-fashioned automobile that Li-lan has painted before, and two pop-style images of alligators emerging from the water. The one in pale mauve and green looks like a silly paint-by-numbers alligator, and the one all in grays seems to be taking a last gasp. Everything in this painting, even communication, seems endangered, but Li-lan's loose style of rendering some of the images, along with her

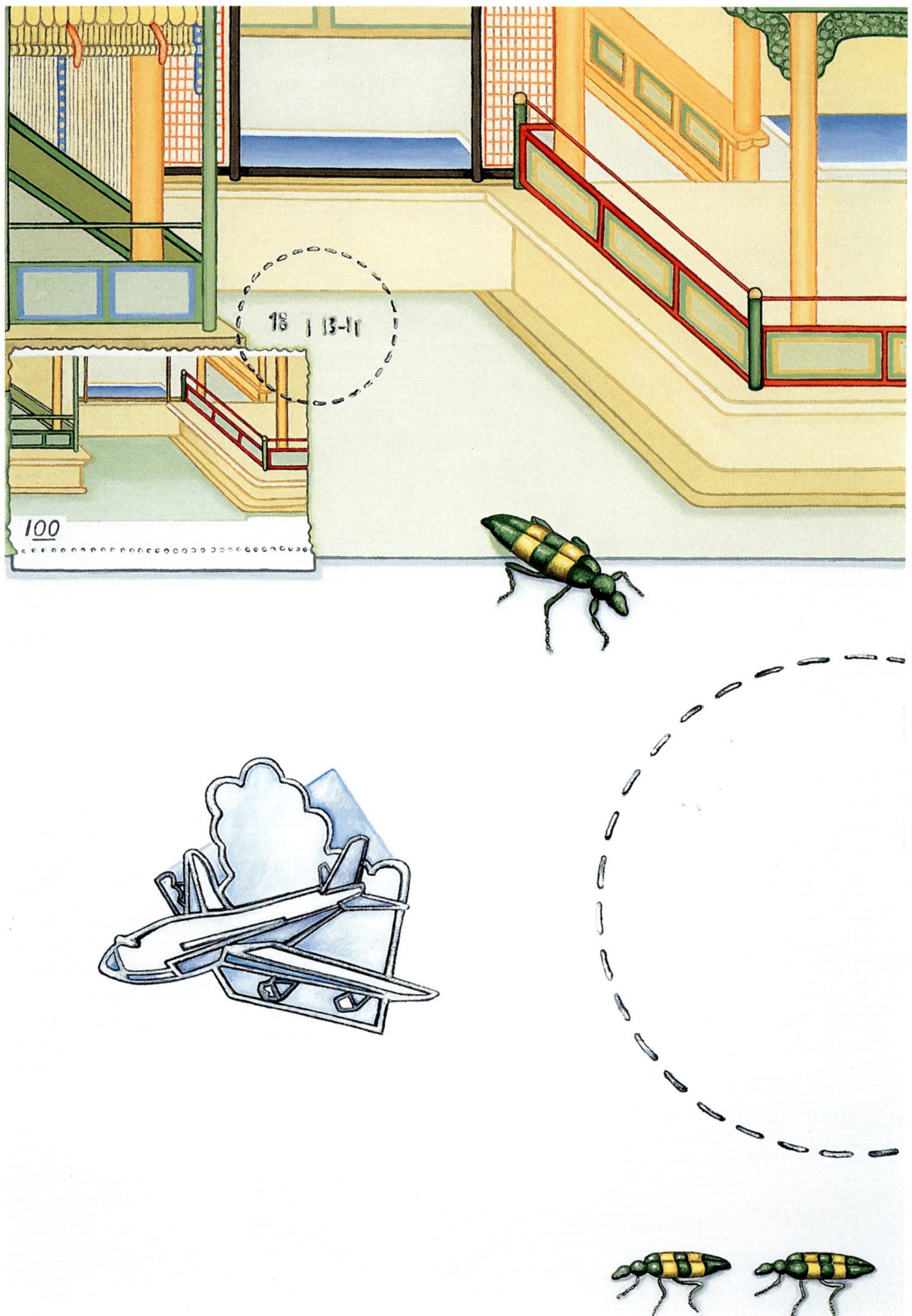

Plate 45 Li-lan, *Court*, oil on linen (30 in. x 20 in.), 2003.

more illustrative technique in painting others, adds the moment of ambiguity that undercuts the seriousness of aspects of the content. Perhaps the title *Labyrinth* should be the guide to the tangles and snares of ambiguous communication. This loose array of images adds up to what seems a creepy echo from a world already past being endangered, and it resonates with a kind of shrug-of-the shoulder, postdespair apathy toward all that is lost and that will soon be gone.

In the single catalogue for two exhibitions of Li-lan's work that took place in 2003, Peter Frank's essay amplifies the element of teasing as a primary one

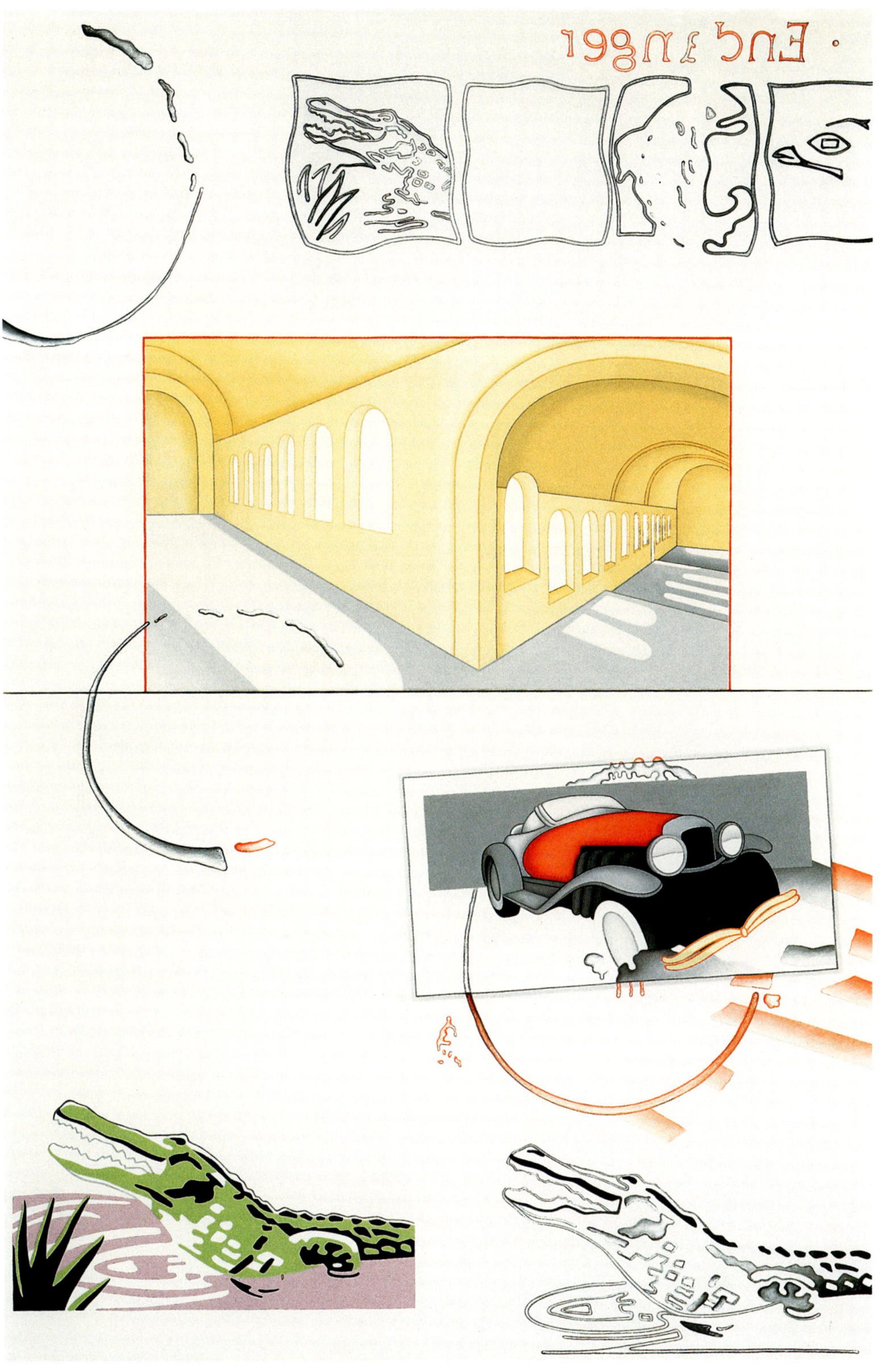

Plate 46 Li-lan, ***Labyrinth*** **(diptych), oil on linen (84 in. x 54 in., each panel 42 x 54 in.), 2003. Photo credit: Kevin Ryan**

in her painting, and he finds "so much provocative information in Li-lan's pictures that she tricks us into 'reading' rather than seeing them." He also emphasizes the formal elements while addressing the postmodern condition of continuous discontinuity that he finds reflected in her work:

> Li-lan's program is not the description of place, nor the account of going places, but the sensation of being many places at once—the meta-cubist condition of comprehending the world as a spannable, available site of tangentially related experiences, a continuous discontinuity if you will. This is a—the—post-modern condition, which in the digital (post-post-modern) age has become much more acute. These are paintings, however, of an individual whose consciousness was shaped before the condition pertained.[56]

He ends the essay by suggesting that Li-lan's identification with surrealism is apt because her juxtaposition of images unlikely both in their scale and in their spatial positioning is related to shifts that are happening all the time in our lives: as a condition of modernism, Frank says, "we're all living surreally."[57] Frank's encounters with Li-lan's paintings are all very perceptive. Nevertheless, her consciousness was also shaped by being both biracial and transnational, and sometimes her experiences as a biracial person were deeply injurious. The more playful game of postmodern discontinuities functions in tandem with the unifying themes of a personal nature formed from the life lived. It is visually exciting to see Li-lan's work in all its dimensions, including its playful one, but this should not diminish the significance of her experiences of passage, which resonate so poignantly.

EPILOGUE

I would like to close this book, and open up possibilities for future research, by referencing a few of the many biracial and transnational artists of Asian background who, like Yun Gee and Li-lan, have forged a singular mode from the cultural mix that has been an outcome of their complex lives. Only recently have the contributions to modernism made by Asian and other neglected artists in the United States and other Western countries become a topic of study; artists like Isamu Noguchi, who was Japanese and Caucasian, and Wilfredo Lam, whose father was Chinese and whose mother was of mixed African, Indian, and European descent, are only now becoming the subjects of writings that emphasize their biracial and transnational lives. Contemporaries of Gee, both of them continued to work into the 1980s and enjoyed international attention throughout their careers. Lam, again like Gee, was very successful in Paris in the 1920s and 1930s for what Jean-Paul Sartre considered his "Africanisation of western art."[1] And although Noguchi labeled himself one of the "not exactly belonging people,"[2] he nevertheless became one of the most famous and sought-after of modern artists, developing a reputation that grew stronger as he produced sculpture, furniture, sculpture gardens, memorials, stage sets, and other works worldwide.[3] Noguchi perfected a form of abstraction that he could apply to these many kinds of art and design, in a manner that seemed to engage the essence of postwar modernism. Gee seems to have started out on similar trajectory but was unable to achieve the same kind of success, for the many reasons I have explored.

Where the contemporary scene is concerned, although Homi Bhabha is certainly an appropriate guide in approaching artists like Yun Gee and Li-lan, Asian artists and scholars provide the kind of "situated knowledge" that is pertinent to discussions of transnationalism in the second half of the twentieth century and into the twenty-first. Reflections on the current scene may provide insights with which to enrich the study of artists who lived and worked before the current discourse about transnationalism emerged, and such reflections may also help in highlighting those artists' similarities and differences with respect to historical contexts. Thus an exciting part of my research for this book has been my discovery of the writings of Asian artists, curator/historians, and theoreticians of contemporary Chinese art, in particular the late Alice Yang, Gao Minglu, and Wu Hung, among others. That said, as many of these writers are also transnational, works by authors like Homi Bhabha are often part of their intellectual baggage as well. As Gao Minglu has said in an interview with Hou Hanru, "Now I think that Chinese artists overseas are becoming objects of a kind of 'post-orientalism.' Homi Bhabha uses the term 'third space' to turn what Edward Said considered as the opposition between the East and the West into a kind of interactive 'in-betweeness.'"[4] It is the discourse about this kind of positioning that runs through the writings of these authors.

In a book by Alice Yang, published after her untimely death, a selection of very important reviews and critical essays reveals her sensitivity to experiences of passage that flow from her own transnational status:

> Because art is viewed in this context [the closed circuit of negation identified with identity politics in opposition to the norm] as a kind of corrective to misrepresentation, the development of identity politics . . . has also tended to institutionalize particular styles of artmaking. What is often mandated is a style that can easily be read as encoded by race, one that I would characterize as primarily descriptive or illustrative.[5]

Yang goes on to suggest that contemporary exhibitions that bring together artists of a particular race view them as an "artifact of difference."[6] Her approach would be to shift the emphasis away from race alone, "towards positions of greater complexity and specificity that encompass race as only one of the many components that both shape artistic practice and are addressed by it."[7] A recent exhibition included examples of that complexity and specificity in the work of artists practicing today.[8]

With respect to artists whom Yang discusses as transnational, such as Xu

Bing, the differences between those who remain in their native countries and those who emigrate are apparent but are becoming less so today. Those like Xu, neither political pop artists nor obviously expressive of personal agendas in the context of the social and political environment of China, deconstruct cultural signs directed to diverse national audiences. Yang, discussing Xu's stunning installation *A Book from the Sky* (1987–91)—an installation of massive sheets of Chinese characters on the walls and the floor of a gallery and suspended from the ceiling, a work that has been considered an extension of the Chinese calligraphic tradition—suggests that "while he constructed a symbolic text fully resonant of this tradition, he did so only to evacuate all meaning from the text."[9] Xu, trained in the calligraphic tradition, spent three years hand-carving the individual printing blocks for four thousand totally unintelligible Chinese characters that had the appearance of traditional symbols. When I saw this work as part of an exhibition in San Francisco, it and several other artists' contributions were prime factors in stimulating my thinking about issues surrounding the transnational.

Xu Bing, born in China in 1955, has been a resident of the United States since 1990 and has exhibited in major art centers here and abroad. *A Book from the Sky,* like his other complex works, is open to numerous interpretations, given the context of the showing, but it is nevertheless independent from the "reading" of assembled parts that plays such a strong role in the interpretation of hybrid works, and the aesthetic dimension, rooted in technical refinement, is everywhere visible. Xu Bing is not unique in the contemporary scene; many other Chinese transnationals, whatever else characterizes their work, appeal through polished craftsmanship to many viewers around the world. The same can be said of Li-lan's paintings, and refined technique seems to be once again in ascendance today, by contrast with the basic conceptualism that dominated postmodernism with its critique of "aesthetic" practices.

Wu Hung and Gao Minglu write about and form exhibitions of contemporary Chinese art practices in China and abroad.[10] Minglu also refers to Bhabha's notion of the "third space" to speak about artists who live abroad and who "may play the most important role in confronting and communicating with an international cultural mainstream. Rather than being part of a 'diaspora,' the identity and visual world of recent émigrés may be shaped by, and may be shaping, a 'third space' that truly is between East and West."[11] Minglu discusses two transnational artists who now live in the United States, Cai Guo-qiang and Wenda Gu. Both artists were more radical and nationalist before they left China. Cai was a member of an avant-garde group, the 85 Movement. He emigrated to Japan in 1987 and then to the United States in 1995. He has performed his gunpowder explosions and his *Projects for Extraterrestrials* in South Africa, the Netherlands, Japan, the United Kingdom, and the United States, among other places.[12] Minglu writes that these projects transcend Cai's "early oriental ideal by asking the audience to realize a dimension of art that is transcultural and transpolitical, perhaps even universal."[13] Wenda Gu belonged to the Rationalist school of painting in China and then created installations inspired by Asian mysticism; like Xu Bing, he also deconstructed Chinese calligraphy.[14] Since his move to the United States, in 1987, he has been working on a project called *United Nations,* using hair collected from all kinds of people and places. Minglu says of this work, "Unlike [the work of] many Euro-American contemporaries whose art deals with bodily substances and the crises of the human body, Gu's work doesn't address specific social, political, religious, or sexual issues. Rather, he explores the eternal human verities and the general human condition."[15] Like Cai, he has exhibited all over the world.[16]

Wu Hung has written about and formed exhibitions of the most radical aspects of art in China and abroad. His catalogues for two recent exhibitions that took place at the David and Alfred Smart Museum of Art, in Chicago, are models of theory and practice.[17] The first exhibition, held in 1999, featured work done between 1979 and 1999, and the second, held in 2000, was a re-creation of two works from a show that had been canceled in 1998 in Beijing. Of the twenty-one artists included in the 1999 exhibition, most were living and working in Beijing, and four are in New York. Perusal of the catalogue for that exhibition shows that recently there have been fewer differences between artists who have remained in China, particularly those living in major cities, and those who have emigrated to New York; the internationalization of current art styles, from painting and printmaking and photography to installation, performance art, and the use of electronic media, is pervasive. If the content that was prevalent from the 1980s to the mid-1990s was often critical of Mao and his regime, and if political pop art seemed ubiquitous, more recent work emphasizes issues of personal identity, as in the installations and performance art of Qiu Zhijie, or as in the works of Xu Bing and Wenda Gu, which Wu Hung labels "demystification."[18] The visual formulations, while still involved in critique, are subtle and engage broader cultural and social concerns. Hung thinks that many artists, beginning around the mid-1990s, "finally bid farewell to the Cultural Revolution and its visual mental baggage. A related change is that these artists also disengaged themselves from *yun dong,* the Chinese term for large-scale political, ideological, or artistic campaigns or movements."[19] A provocative early example, Xu Bing's *Ghosts Pounding the Wall* of 1990—executed at the Great Wall in Beijing, but exhibited only when he emigrated to the United States, in 1991—calls into question not only the received history of the "Chinese" tradition but also inherited notions of tradition in general, particularly as they form nationalist sensibilities.[20] It is probably the case that artists working abroad have played an inspirational part in the work of local artists, who have thereby been enabled to exhibit on the international scene.[21]

To compare Yun Gee's life and work with the life and work of Li-lan, and to compare their lives and work with those of these contemporary artists, is to note the similarities as well as the differences that are constitutive of the transnational situation in the first and second halves of the twentieth century and in the early twenty-first century.[22] Gee was transnational and cosmopolitan, a citizen of the world, and his philosophy embraced universalism; these were major factors in how he lived, and what he painted was related to the times in which he worked. Interestingly enough, he can be compared with contemporary transnational artists who seem also at the moment to be striving for a certain universal approach that undercuts multiculturalism as well as particular political agendas.[23] Li-lan is also committed to cosmopolitanism in her work and convictions, in part because of the impact of her father intellectually, emotionally, and perceptually. She is not interested in modernist universality or transcendence; her postmodern concerns are imaged in paintings formed of the fragments of a rootless contemporary sensibility. Her life is not as literally transnational as Gee's was, but I believe I have shown that her work is conceptually transnational, as she is in her very being.

The profound similarity between Gee and Li-lan, and between them and contemporary artists living and working in the "third space," renders the labels "national," "Oriental," and "exotic" hollow, challenging the creation of the Other, an enterprise that has been dominating the social and political agendas of nations ever since nations have existed. The artists discussed here embody cosmopolitanism and transnationalism, and in reaching for a new kind of vision, they are perhaps leading us toward a postnational future world that may be supported by free movement, economic equity, and ease of communication. At this time, however, that is only a vague hope. In his review of a 2003 exhibition, Peter Schjeldahl wrote, "Cosmopolitan may be the world's destiny, and even its best hope for redemption, but there's no end of loss and pain in the phenomenon."[24]

COLLECTIONS AND EXHIBITIONS

YUN GEE

Public Collections

Hirshhorn Museum and Sculpture Garden, Washington, D. C.
Los Angeles County Museum of Art, Los Angeles
Musée d'Art Moderne, Centre Pompidou, Paris
Oakland Museum of California
Weatherspoon Art Museum, University of North Carolina, Greensboro
Whitney Museum of American Art, New York
Wolfsonian Museum, Florida International University, Miami Beach

Selected Solo Exhibitions

1926	Modern Gallery, San Francisco
1929	Galerie Bernheim-Jeune, Paris
1931	In Tempo Gallery, New York
1932	Balzac Galleries, New York
1933	San Francisco Art Center, San Francisco

1936	Galerie à la Reine Margot, Paris
1938	Galerie à la Reine Margot, Paris
1940	Montross Gallery, New York,
1942	Milch Galleries, New York
1943	Milch Galleries, New York
1945	Lilienfeld Gallery, New York
1946	Lucien Laubaudt Gallery, San Francisco
1947	China Institute in America, New York
1948	Jersey City Museum, Jersey City, New Jersey
1962–1963	Gudenzi Galleria, New York
1968	Robert Schoelkopf Gallery, New York
1979–1980	**The Paintings of Yun Gee:** William Benton Museum of Art, University of Connecticut, Storrs; Weatherspoon Art Museum, University of North Carolina, Greensboro; Oakland Museum of California; Bowdoin College Museum of Art, Brunswick, Maine
1983	Vanderwoude Tananbaum Gallery, New York
1991	Jan Holloway Gallery, San Francisco
1992	**The Art of Yun Gee:** Taipei Fine Arts Museum, Taipei, Taiwan
1995	Lin & Keng Gallery, Taipei, Taiwan
1998	Lin & Keng Gallery, Taipei, Taiwan
2002	Chambers Fine Art, New York
	Lin & Keng Gallery, Taipei, Taiwan
2003–2004	**The Art and Poetry of Yun Gee:** Pasadena Museum of California Art, Pasadena

Selected Group Exhibitions

1928	Salon des Indépendants, Paris
1929	Salon des Indépendants, Paris
1930	Salon des Indépendants, Paris
1931	**Paintings, Sculpture, and Drawings by American and Foreign Artists:** Brooklyn Museum of Art, Brooklyn, New York
1932	**Murals by American Painters and Photographers:** Museum of Modern Art, New York
	The Social Viewpoint in Art: John Reed Club, New York
1934	18th Annual Exhibition of the Society of Independent Artists, New York
1936	**Peinture Nouvelle:** Galerie Le Niveau, Paris
	Fleurs Et Paysages: Galerie Carmine, Paris
1938	**L'Exposition du Prix Paul-Guillaume:** Galerie Bernheim-Jeune, Paris
	Salon des Indépendants, Paris
1941	**Art for China:** Ritz Tower, New York

	Paintings by Fifty Oncoming Americans: Boston Institute of Modern Art, Boston
1944	**Portrait of America:** Metropolitan Museum of Art, New York
1974	**Inaugural Exhibition:** Hirshhorn Museum and Sculpture Garden, Washington, D.C.
1975	**Art on Paper:** Weatherspoon Art Museum, University of North Carolina, Greensboro
1977	**Selections from the Lawrence H. Bloedel Bequest and Related Works from the Permanent Collection:** Whitney Museum of American Art, New York
1983	**The Great East River Bridge:** Brooklyn Museum of Art, Brooklyn, New York
1988	**Empire City and the Age of Urbanism (1875–45):** Grand Central Galleries, New York
	Yun Gee and Li-lan: Paintings by a Father and Daughter: Fine Arts Gallery, Long Island University, Southampton, New York
1993	**The Art Works of Sanyu and Yun Gee:** Lin & Keng Gallery, Taipei, Taiwan
1994	**New Chinese Painting:** Lin & Keng Gallery, Taipei, Taiwan
1995	**Facing Eden: 100 Years of Landscape Art in the Bay Area:** M. H. de Young Memorial Museum, San Francisco
	With New Eyes: Toward an Asian American Art History in the West: San Francisco State University, San Francisco
1998	**Changing Perspectives on Modernism:** University of Oregon Museum of Art, Eugene
2000	**Made in California: Art, Image, and Identity, 1900–2000:** Los Angeles County Museum of Art, Los Angeles
2000–2001	**The Pacific Makes Us Neighbors:** Residence of the U.S. Ambassador to Beijing, Art in Embassies Program, Beijing, China
	On Gold Mountain: A Chinese American Experience: Autry Museum of Western Heritage, Los Angeles
2002	**On-Ramps: Transitional Moments in California Art:** Pasadena Museum of California Art, Pasadena
	From Emperors to Hoi Polloi: Portraits of an Era, 1851–1945: Wolfsonian Museum, Florida International University, Miami Beach
2003–2004	**The Not-So Still Life: A Century of California Painting and Sculpture:** San Jose Museum of Art, San Jose, California
2004	**The Not-So Still Life: A Century of California Painting and Sculpture:** Pasadena Museum of California Art, Pasadena
	Art Singapore: The Contemporary Asian Art Fair: Lin & Keng Gallery, Singapore

2005 **China International Gallery Exposition:** Lin & Keng Gallery, Beijing, China

Sanyu & Yun Gee, 1926–1960: Lin & Keng Gallery, Taipei, Taiwan

International Asian Art Fair: Seventh Regiment Armory, New York

Landscape—Cityscape: Marlborough Gallery, New York

Art Singapore: The Contemporary Asian Art Fair: Lin & Keng Gallery, Singapore

Yun Gee: A Modernist Painter, Marlborough Gallery, New York

2006 **The International Asian Art Fair,** Seventh Regiment Armory, Marlborough Gallery, New York

Art Basel 37, Miami Beach, Florida

2007 **Art in America: 300 Years of Innovation,** Guggenheim Museum, Venues: National Art Museum of China, Beijing; Shanghai Museum of Contemporary Art, Shanghai, China

Inaugural Exhibition, Lin & Keng Gallery, Beijing, China

Cubism in Asia, The Japan Foundation, Venue: La Maison de la culture du Japon à Paris, Paris, France

LI-LAN

Public Collections

Arkansas Arts Center, Little Rock
Art for Peace Collection, Fischer Pharmaceuticals Ltd., Tel Aviv
Atlantic Richfield Company, Dallas
Best Products, Richmond, Virginia
Chermayeff and Geismar Associates, New York
Estée Lauder, Inc., New York
Gap, Inc., Oahu, Hawaii
Guild Hall Museum, East Hampton, New York
Heckscher Museum, Huntington, New York
Jacobs, Visconsi & Jacobs, Cleveland, Ohio
Lifetime TV, New York
Marion Corporation, Mobile, Alabama
Mobil Oil Corporation, New York
Modern Art Museum, Toyama, Japan
Ohara Museum of Art, Kurashiki, Japan
Parrish Art Museum, Southampton, New York
Seattle First National Bank
Security Pacific National Bank, Los Angeles

Sezon Museum of Modern Art, Karuizawa, Japan
Sydney and Frances Lewis Foundation Collection, Richmond, Virginia
Vassar College Art Gallery Collection, Poughkeepsie, New York
Virginia Museum of Fine Arts, Richmond
Virlaine Foundation, New Orleans
Weatherspoon Art Museum, University of North Carolina, Greensboro
Werner Kramarsky Collection, New York
Westfield State College Art Gallery Collection, Westfield, Massachusetts
William Benton Museum of Art, University of Connecticut, Storrs

Selected Solo Exhibitions

1969	Miyuki Gallery, Tokyo
1971	Nantenshi Gallery, Tokyo
1974	James Yu Gallery, New York
	Nantenshi Gallery, Tokyo
1976	Benson Gallery, Bridgehampton, New York
1977	Nantenshi Gallery, Tokyo
1978	Robert Miller Gallery, New York
1980	Asher/Faure Gallery, Los Angeles
	Nantenshi Gallery, Tokyo
1982	Asher/Faure Gallery, Los Angeles
1983	O. K. Harris Gallery, New York
1985	Nantenshi Gallery, Tokyo
	O. K. Harris Gallery, New York
1987	O. K. Harris Gallery, New York
1989	Franz Bader Gallery, Washington, D.C.
1990	William Benton Museum of Art, University of Connecticut, Storrs
1991	New Arts Program, Kutztown, Pennsylvania
1992	Amelia A. Wallace Gallery, State University of New York, Old Westbury
	Benton Gallery, Southampton, New York
1993	**Correspondence: Between the Lines:** Benton Gallery, Southampton, New York; Lung Men Art Gallery, Taipei, Taiwan
1994	**Post Marks: Recent Paintings and Pastels:** Art Projects International, New York
1995	Lin & Keng Gallery, Taipei, Taiwan
1996	**Correspondences: Recent Paintings:** Art Projects International, New York
1997	Lin & Keng Gallery, Taipei, Taiwan
2001	Lin & Keng Gallery, Taipei, Taiwan

2002 — **Mary H. Dana Women Artists Series:** Rutgers University, New Brunswick, New Jersey

2003 — DoubleVision Gallery, Los Angeles

2004 — **Labyrinths:** Nabi Gallery, New York

2006 — **Silent Journey,** Jason McCoy, Inc., New York

Unfinished Journey, Lin & Keng Gallery, Tapei, Taiwan

Selected Group Exhibitions

1970 — Albright-Knox Art Gallery, Buffalo, New York

1973 — Guild Hall Museum, East Hampton, New York

1975 — Guild Hall Museum, East Hampton, New York

1976 — Guild Hall Museum, East Hampton, New York

1977 — Guild Hall Museum, East Hampton, New York

1979–1980 — **The East Hampton Art Colony: Selections from the Guild Hall Museum Collection:** Fort Lauderdale Museum of Art, Fort Lauderdale, Florida; Mississippi Museum of Art, Jackson; Pensacola Museum of Art, Pensacola, Florida

1979–1985 — **Late-Twentieth-Century Art from the Sydney and Frances Lewis Foundation Collection:** Anderson Gallery, Virginia Commonwealth University, Richmond; Institute of Contemporary Art, Philadelphia; Worcester Art Museum, Worcester, Massachusetts

1981 — Sheldon Memorial Art Gallery, University of Nebraska, Lincoln

1983 — **Paintings and Sculpture by Candidates for Art Awards:** American Academy and Institute of Arts and Letters, New York

1984 — **May I Have Your Attention, Please!:** Wing Luke Asian Museum, Seattle, Washington

Photographs/Politics: P.S.1 Contemporary Art Center, Long Island City, New York

1987 — **Art Against AIDS:** DIA Art Foundation, New York

The Hot Centre: Contemporary Art: Norton Center for the Arts, Centre College, Danville, Kentucky

Paintings and Sculpture by Candidates for Art Awards: American Academy and Institute of Arts and Letters, New York

1988 — **Yun Gee and Li-lan: Paintings by a Father and Daughter:** Fine Arts Gallery, Long Island University, Southampton, New York

1989–1991 — **Lines of Vision: Drawings by Contemporary Women:** Blum Helman Gallery, New York; Grand Rapids Art Museum, Grand Rapids, Michigan; Hillwood Art Gallery, Brookville, New York; University Art Gallery, University of North Texas, Denton; University of Oklahoma Museum of Art, Norman

1990 — Albright-Knox Art Gallery, Buffalo, New York

	The Grid: Organization and Idea: Ben Shahn Galleries, William Paterson College of Art, Wayne, New Jersey
	No Trends: Nahan Contemporary Gallery, New York
1991	**Encore: Reviewing the Past:** William Benton Museum of Art, University of Connecticut, Storrs
	Show of Strength: Anne Plumb Gallery, New York
1992	**SLOW ART: Painting in New York Now:** P.S.1 Contemporary Art Center, Long Island City, New York
	Soho Twenty Strikes Gold: Soho 20, New York
1993	**New Expressions in Asian American Art:** Graduate School, University Center, City University of New York
	Taipei Art Fair: 1993 International: Taipei World Trade Center, Taipei, Taiwan
	Women's Art, Women's Lives, Women's Issues: Tweed Gallery, New York
1994	New Museum of Contemporary Art, New York
1995	**75 Years of Collecting:** Heckscher Museum, Huntington, New York
	Taipei Art Fair: 1995 International: Taipei World Trade Center, Taipei, Taiwan
1996	**Artists—Messengers of Peace:** Eretz Israel Museum, Tel Aviv
	Paperworks: 20th-Century Works on Paper from the Permanent Collection: Heckscher Museum, Huntington, New York
1997	**Taipei Art Fair: 1997 International:** Taipei World Trade Center, Taipei, Taiwan
1998	**The Centennial Open:** Parrish Art Museum, Southampton, New York
	To Extend: Contemporary Art of Overseas Chinese: Galerie Pierre, Taichung, Taiwan
1998–2000	**Artists—Messengers of Peace:** Art for Peace Foundation, Tel Aviv
1999	**Hsinchu Science-Based Industrial Park Art Fair:** Lin & Keng Gallery, Hsinchu, Taiwan
2000–2001	**Chinese American Artists:** Residence of the director of the American Institute in Taiwan, Art in Embassies Program, Taipei
	Figuration: GOCAIA (Gallery of Contemporary and Indigenous Art), Tucson, Arizona
	The Likeness of Being: Contemporary Self-Portraits by 60 Women: DC Moore Gallery, New York
	The Nature of Seeing: Works from the Collection: Parrish Art Museum, Southampton, New York
	We the People of the United States: Residence of the U.S. Ambassador to the European Union, Art in Embassies Program, Brussels, Belgium

2001 **Fifteen Asian American Artists:** University Art Gallery, SUNY, Stony Brook, New York

Finely Drawn: Weatherspoon Art Museum, University of North Carolina, Greensboro

On Gold Mountain: A Chinese American Experience: Arts and Industries Building, Smithsonian Institution, Washington, D.C.

2003 PaceWildenstein, New York

2004 Guild Hall Museum, East Hampton, New York

2007 Jason McCoy, Inc., "Options within Realism," New York, NY

Jason McCoy Inc., Art Chicago, The Mart Center, Chicago, IL

Lin & Keng Gallery, Inaugural Exhibition, Beijing, China, Lin & Keng Gallery, Taipei, Taiwan

NOTES

Preface

1 See Joyce Brodsky, "Curator's Statement." The exhibition, titled *Dis-placements and Anxious Objects*, took place in 2000 at the Mary Porter Sesnon Gallery of the University of California, Santa Cruz.

2 Joyce Brodsky, *The Paintings of Li-lan.*

3 Thane Rosenbaum, "The Shadow of the Holocaust," 26.

4 This book does not directly engage diasporic issues, although studies of them have influenced my work. For example, I have always been interested in the paintings of R. B. Kitaj, the Jewish artist who was one of the first to write about his art and diaspora; see R. B. Kitaj, *First Diasporist Manifesto*, a portion of which is also included in Nicholas Mirzoeff, ed., *Diaspora and Visual Culture*, along with studies of other aspects of diaspora, among them Stuart Hall, "Cultural Identity and Diaspora," one of many crucial writings by Hall that deal with issues of identity and difference and with notions of the "other" that are essential components of diasporic research. Another important text is Arjun Appadurai, ed., *Globalization*. Ideas about the Diaspora originated in relation to the wanderings of the Jews, and with respect to Jewish history, particularly in light of the Holocaust, but the meaning of the term "diaspora" has expanded and is now used in connection with any individuals or groups of people who have been forced from their native lands or have left by choice

to live elsewhere. The bibliography includes a number of writings that, although not in themselves central to the life of either Yun Gee or Li-lan, have their origins at least partly in postcolonial issues and are related to the problems of racism that are explored in this book.

5 This concept has been explored, for example, by Donna Haraway, *Simians, Cyborgs, and Women,* 111.

6 Trinh T. Minh-ha, *When the Moon Waxes Red,* 230.

7 See Joyce Brodsky, *The Paintings of Yun Gee.* That catalogue is out of print and not easily accessible, but I will use material from it when I think my interpretations still hold. This book, as already mentioned, builds on my earlier research about the painter Yun Gee and my more recent close study of the work of his daughter, Li-lan.

8 Homi Bhabha, *The Location of Culture,* 5.

9 For some examples of Zarina's work, see Theresa Harlan, "Zarina," 173–75, and the exhibition catalogue *Weaving Memory,* which includes my essay "The Imprint of a Transnational Life."

10 Anthony Lee, ed., *Yun Gee: Poetry, Writing, Art, Memories.*

11 See Tunghsiao Chou, "Yun Gee's Early Paintings and Life Journey." By consulting this article as well as Gee's own writings in English and Chinese from the Yun Gee archives, which Tunghsiao helped organize with great care, I was able to correct some of my earlier errors concerning the artist's life.

Introduction

1 The epigraph is taken from the introduction to *Displacement, Diaspora, and Geographies of Identity*, ed. Smadar Lavie and Ted Swedenburg, p. 1. It continues: "The essays in this volume are concerned with the undoing of one particular, old certainty—the notion that there is an immutable link between cultures, peoples or identities and specific places. The confidence in this permanent join between a particular culture and a stable terrain has served to ground our modern governing concepts of nations and cultures."

2 I use the term "world citizen" with caution, and only because Yun Gee thought of himself that way. It is a loaded concept that maps Western ideas about the Greek polis onto a contemporary world of incredible diversity, wherein the very concept of citizenry is open to scrutiny.

3 The term "hybridity" is usually found in the context of writings about postcolonialism, the subaltern, and diasporas, as in the work of Homi Bhabha, Edward M. Said, and Gayatri Chakravorty Spivak. It was picked up by critics in connection with the work of artists like Tomie Arai, Hanh Thi Pham, Sung Ho Choi, Hung Liu, and others. These artists have produced exciting work in a manner that postmodernism embraces, and that the art world still encourages. Works by these artists have important political agendas, and for émigré artists who were working under repressive regimes—for example, in China, which until recently has favored socialist realism—it would have been logical to use aspects of that form of imaging in their visual cri-

tiques; see Kim, Machida, and Muzato, *Fresh Talk, Daring Gazes*. Parallel to this form of hybridism is another manner of practice that some of these artists have now adopted. It is rooted in a global "cosmopolitanism" similar in kind to that of artists like Xu Bing, who have emigrated more recently to urban art centers in all parts of the world, to share in the artistic life of cultural transnationalism. These artists arrive well versed in contemporary art styles that are practiced in major art centers all over the globe. The paintings of Yun Gee and Li-lan embody uses of such styles from a period before the contemporary notion of transnationalism took form. See the epilogue of this book for a discussion of some of these artists.

4 See Jane C. Ju, Li Lundin, and David Teh-yu Wang, *The Art of Yun Gee,* 53.

5 Discussions of these issues reveal their complexity; see, for example, Sheldon Pollock, "Cosmopolitan and Vernacular in History," where the author pluralizes the terms "hybridity," "transnationalism," and "cosmopolitanism" and in so doing undercuts aspects of the homogeneity and universality that permeate a good deal of the literature on these subjects.

6 Smadar Lavie and Ted Swedenburg, eds., *Displacement, Diaspora, and Geographies of Identity,* 10.

7 Homi Bhabha, "The Third Space." There are critiques of his position; see, for example, Ioan Davis, "Negotiating African Culture," 129, where the author suggests that Bhabha's model is essentially elitist in its concern to create "a transnational culture from an anti-nationalist space." See also Geeta Kapur, *When Was Modernism,* which also questions Bhabha's thesis on these grounds but concedes that "the Bhabha legacy functions best in the cosmopolitan world of the 'twice-born,' the immigrant intelligentsia from the third world lodged within the first world whose identity is ambivalent, restless, interrogative—though hardly in this age diasporic." As I suggest in this book, issues concerning the global and the local are very complex; one that needs to be explored is the homogeneity that may result from transnationalism as a global style, with concomitant claims to universality and transcendence that must also be critiqued.

8 Bhabha, "The Commitment to Theory," 25 (emphasis in original).

9 Defining transnationalism has become a very complicated matter. For example, many artists who have remained in China have also had recent exhibitions in other countries; see Wu Hung, *Exhibiting Experimental Art in China,* and Wu Hung, *Transience,* both of which introduce some of the artists whose work cannot always be distinguished from that of transnational artists. And a city like Beijing is a vital center of international artistic activity, as are Shanghai and others. The terms "globalization," "internationalization," and "transnationalism" are becoming synonymous.

10 Edward M. Said, *Reflections on Exile and Other Essays*, 173, 186.

11 Irit Rogoff, *Terra Infirma: Georgraphy's Visual Culture,* 5–6.

12 The late Nathan Knobler raised this question along with other issues in the extensive notes that he drew up after reading the abstract for this book. I am very grateful for his effort.

13 Interestingly enough, Arshille Gorky, who arrived earlier, and whose style was eclectic, was second only to Jackson Pollock in being influenced by those modern artists

who had emigrated to the United States. This country, and particularly New York, obviously played a crucial role in becoming home to these émigrés as well as affording them access to one another's work.

14 In the first part of the twentieth century, there were Chinese and Japanese artists in the United States as well as in other Western countries, such as France, who participated in the modernist enterprise. Yasuo Kuniyoshi was one such artist; he arrived in the United States when he was a teenager and went to art school in New York. Gee always belittled the work of the Japanese artist Foujita, who was very popular in France and did cater to Western tastes for modernist "orientalia." Gee also felt that the Parisian preference for Japanese artists was due to France's high regard for Japan in those years. In 1929, when Gee saw the exhibition of Japanese works in Paris, he found it "somewhat annoying" that "most of [the] pretended Japanese works" were "no more than imitations of the Chinese masters," according to Arthur A. Young, "Yun Gee, Chinese Interpreter of East to West," *China Weekly Review*, n.d.; see reviews, Yun Gee archives. Traditional Chinese art forms, particularly calligraphy, influenced several West Coast modernist artists, such as Mark Tobey and Bradley Tomlin.

15 Xu Bing, for example, discussed in the epilogue of this book, left China because the ruling party criticized his work, but he was not in danger, although his freedom to pursue his creative desires was limited by the government. The 1985–86 period was a fairly liberal one until the government crackdown resumed, first in 1986 and again in 1989. In 1989, Xu Bing and Wu Shanzhuan left China, as many other activists had done before and as many have done since then; see Julia F. Andrews and Gao Minglu, *Fragmented Memory: The Chinese Avant-Garde Exile*, 15–18. The latter catalogue discusses the work of Xu Bing and three other transnational artists—Huang Yongping, Wenda Gu, and Wu Shanzhuan—all four of them still among the best-known contemporary Chinese artists.

16 Cosmopolitan artists like these are similar to artists like Otis Oldfield, Gee's teacher, who went to Paris to seek out the cubist international style and took it back to San Francisco. In the case of Otis's trip, however, Paris, as a world center of art, was a more common destination and was still within the Western arena. Artists today travel to the United States from every country in the world, often only after having developed their international styles in their native countries. They also exhibit at the international annuals and biennials that take place in major cities all over the world, and they use the World Wide Web both to encounter artwork on a global basis and to show their own work.

17 He also made a visit to Spain in 1928, and his self-portrait *The Blue Yun* may have been influenced by some of the paintings he saw there.

18 Yun Gee, "East and West Meet in Paris," unpublished manuscript, Sept. 1944; see reviews, Yun Gee archives.

19 Li-lan, "Memories of My Father," 192.

20 See books on this issue by Judith Butler, *Bodies That Matter*; Donna Haraway, *Simians, Cyborgs, and Women*; and Amelia Jones, *Body Art*.

21 See *Maya Lin: A Clear Strong Vision*.

1 Experiences of Passage in the Life of Yun Gee

1 See Anthony Lee, ed., *Yun Gee: Poetry, Writing, Art, Memories,* 3.

2 Sometimes Gee says he was born in 1907; see biography, Yun Gee archives.

3 Yun Gee's brochure on the Diamondism School was probably written in the early 1950s; see writings about and by Yun Gee, Yun Gee archives.

4 See Lee, ed., *Yun Gee: Poetry,* plate 4.

5 There is a wonderful painting of Velma Aydelott in Li-lan's collection.

6 See *The Art of Yun Gee*; the retrospective was followed by exhibitions in Taipei in 1995 and 1998.

7 I wish to thank Nancy Bing, whose mother was Yun Gee's niece, for setting the record straight about many aspects of Gee's life; see Nancy Bing, "Reclaiming Yun Gee," which contains information similar to that given to me by Li-lan and is a realistic but tender evocation of Bing's uncle once removed.

8 See the fine essay by David Teh-Yu Wang, "The Art of Yun Gee before 1936." See also the important essays of Anthony Lee and Paul Karlstrom in Lee, ed., *Yun Gee: Poetry*. Wang's essay is well researched, for the most part, and quite thorough in its discussion of Gee's life and work until 1936; Lee, both in Lee, ed., *Yun Gee: Poetry,* to which he contributed several essays, and in Anthony Lee, *Picturing Chinatown,* 201–36 (the chapter titled "Revolutionary Artists"), investigates aspects of Gee's life and work from the viewpoint of radicalism and racism.

9 See Lee, ed., *Yun Gee: Poetry,* 7–8.

10 Li-lan, interview with the author, June 2003; Bing, "Reclaiming Yun Gee."

11 Lee, ed., *Yun Gee: Poetry,* 82.

12 Joyce Brodsky, *The Paintings of Yun Gee,* 9. Helen Gee says that Gee had a bad depression from 1933 to 1935 and stopped painting, although there are signed drawings from this time as well as many poems, and he was otherwise active. There are many undated paintings, too, that may belong to this period. Li-lan also speaks of her father's moods and suggests that his relationships with both his wives seem to have been tempestuous. Gee was a complicated man, very passionate and sometimes quite angry.

13 The marionette show, in four acts, was called *Kuan Kung's Generosity (The Chinese Wars of the Three Kingdoms)* and seems to have been done in 1933 for the Works Progress Administration Theatre Project; see Helen Gee, *Helen's World of Yun Gee,* 29.

14 See Lee, ed., *Yun Gee: Poetry*. See also Lee, *Picturing Chinatown,* 201–36, which also provides, as background for Gee's early years in China, a summary of the revolutionary events in China in the first and second decades of the twentieth century.

15 See Brodsky, *The Paintings of Yun Gee,* 13, 15–16.

16 Yun Gee kept almost everything written about him, in addition to letters that he and others had written, exhibition catalogues, reviews, and his own writings. His autobiographical writings are undated, fragmented, and often more novelistic then factual. He sometimes repeated portions of these partial autobiographies as if he were starting again at different times in his life. There is no pagination, for the most part, and the length of the writings varies from two or three pages to more than twenty; see Gee autobiography, in biographical writings, Yun Gee archives.

17 According to Li-lan's notes taken from a telephone conversation with Nga Lai Bing, Sept. 6, 2002, and relayed to the author, Winston emigrated to the United States before World War II but went back to China and got married there. He seems to have managed some kind of airplane factory in Guang-xi. Gee's sister married in China and went to Canada in 1947. Gee's niece also mentioned many other family members as well as a family tree apparently put together in the late 1980s or early 1990s.

18 Ibid.

19 See Gee autobiography. This is a long section titled "Biography and Criticism of Yun Gee" written about 1949. It reads as if written from the point of view of someone else, and it is filled with editorial corrections that cannot be dated. In all citations of Gee's unpublished writings, minor errors have been allowed to stand except where their correction will aid the reader's understanding.

20 Ibid.

21 The work of the Lingnan School artists is briefly discussed in chapter 2, this volume.

22 See *Between the Thunder and the Rain*, 171.

23 Ralph C. Croizier, *Art and Revolution in Modern China: The Lingnan (Cantonese) School of Painting, 1906–1951*, 62–64.

24 Ibid., 88–89.

25 His other brother had already been to San Francisco; see Gee autobiography.

26 Ibid.

27 Ibid.

28 Croizier, *Art and Revolution in Modern China*, 187.

29 Yun Gee quoted this from Jehanne Biétry-Salinger, "Is Glory Awaiting This Steerage Passenger?"

30 See Gee autobiography.

31 Gee taught art all through his life, when he was able to do so, and particularly in New York. While he needed to teach in order to support himself, and his teachings were not revolutionary in this sense, he did try to promulgate his theories about art, which he did think were revolutionary in a spiritual as well as an artistic sense.

32 The photograph is published in many places. See, for example, Brodsky, *The Paintings of Yun Gee*, 23; Lee, *Picturing Chinatown*, 202. There are other photographs of Gee, from his later days in New York, teaching a group of students in what appears to be his apartment; see photographs, Yun Gee archives.

33 Karen Higa, *Some Notes on an Asian American Art History*, 14; this scroll was identified by Wang, "The Art of Yun Gee before 1936," 21.

34 Lee, *Picturing Chinatown*, 213–16.

35 Ibid., 217.

36 Much has been made of this visit, and there is a lively description of it in Lee, *Picturing Chinatown*, 201–4. We do not know whether Gee was acquainted with Rivera's work, because he left before the mural project at the San Francisco Art Institute; see Paul J. Karlstrom, "Yun Gee: A Modernist Painter's Journey in America," 21–34.

37 Reuben H. Menken, "Yun Gee, American Chinese Artist," *China Weekly Review*, n.d.; see writings about and by Yun Gee, Yun Gee archives.

38 Lee, *Picturing Chinatown,* 218.

39 Ibid.

40 To give one example, in a letter to Paul Bird of *Art Digest*, Gee claimed that there was prejudice against him because he was supposedly considered to be a revolutionary. As proof that he was not, he wrote that he had turned down a contract because the person "demands I should stop criticizing the Communists"; letters in English, Yun Gee archives.

41 Ibid.

42 Lee, ed., *Yun Gee: Poetry,* 57.

43 Lee, *Picturing Chinatown,* 218.

44 "Noted Chinese-American Artist Sets Painting Aside for War Work," *Sperry News,* n.d.; see writings about and by Yun Gee, Yun Gee archives. This article identifies Gee as among the personal friends of Madam Chiang Kai-shek and says that he was invited to be on the committee to welcome her.

45 Lee, ed., *Yun Gee: Poetry,* 56.

46 Anthony Lee, "The Painting and Poetry of Yun Gee."

47 Biétry-Salinger, "Is Glory Awaiting This Steerage Passenger?"

48 Ibid.

49 Yun Gee, "East and West Meet in Paris," unpublished manuscript, Sept. 1944; see reviews, Yun Gee archives. Li-lan says her father tried to teach her French, but she was hopeless at it.

50 For reproductions of some of these photographs, see Brodsky, *The Paintings of Yun Gee*, 8, 26.

51 See slides for this painting, Yun Gee archives.

52 Lee, ed., *Yun Gee: Poetry*, 59.

53 For a fairly good reproduction of the painting, see Wang, "The Art of Yun Gee before 1936," 202.

54 Arthur A. Young, "Yun Gee, Chinese Interpreter of East to West," *China Weekly Review*, n.d.; see reviews, Yun Gee archives.

55 We have *Confucius (Chinese Sage)*; *Butterflies: Dream of Chuang-Tze*; *Landscape in Chinese Style*; *Figures from a Chinese Legend*; *Harmonie universelle (Lao-tzu)*; *One Who Loves Himself*; and a second *Lao-tzu. Yang Kuei-fei,* one of four scroll paintings, also had a Chinese subject. Gee did paint *Chinese Musicians* in San Francisco, but it was more a genre subject in his cubist style and not recognizably Chinese except for the title. He also wrote a poetic essay—"Confucius," dated April 15—that may have been written in 1927 before he left for Paris; see Lee, ed., *Yun Gee: Poetry,* 143. Because Gee painted over some of these works later on, they are difficult to reproduce; they can be seen in slides, Yun Gee archives.

56 See Wang, "The Art of Yun Gee before 1936," 25.

57 See Tunghsiao Chou, "Yun Gee's Early Paintings and Life Journey," 263, where the author compares a reproduction of the self-portrait with a small resin bust of himself that Gee made in 1928. Li-lan had this bust cast in bronze. It resembles the portraits in every respect except the hat.

58 Lee, ed., *Yun Gee: Poetry*, 63.

59 See Paul Goldberger, "Shanghai Surprise," 145: "Streets in Chinese cities have tradi-

tionally been used for transport and commerce, not for social encounters. . . . Nothing seems less Chinese than the notion of the flaneur, of the street as a place in which to observe other people." Yet being a flaneur was exactly what Gee was, from the days of his early desires in China to the days of their actualization in San Francisco, Paris, and New York.

60 Li-lan told me that Raymond Duncan, a friend of Gee's in Paris (Gee had met his future wife at Duncan's salon), told her that in 1961 or 1962 Paule de Reuss jumped or fell from a window to her death. Gee seems not to have been able to finance Paule's trip to America, and because her family had disowned her when she married him, she could not afford the journey to be with him.

61 Menken, "Yun Gee, American Chinese Artist."

62 See Lee, ed., *Yun Gee: Poetry.*

63 Ibid., 143.

64 Ibid., 61.

65 Ibid., 60. Paule had already published three books and seems also to have been somewhat accomplished in drawing, as seen in her portrait of Yun signed and dated Feb. 2, 1930; see Brodsky, *The Paintings of Yun Gee*, 67.

66 Lee, ed., *Yun Gee: Poetry*, 38.

67 Poems, among them "Falling Leaves," that are not published in Lee, ed., *Yun Gee: Poetry* can be found in poetry, Yun Gee archives.

68 The poem "Coincidence"—playful in a less serious sense, yet with a touch of sadness because it is about a beggar—is not dated, but the words conjure up a typical poor Paris neighborhood like the one Yun pictured in the genre painting *Place Maubert.*

69 See Brodsky, *The Paintings of Yun Gee*, 51; Ju et al., *The Art of Yun Gee*, 119.

70 Fu Chau Fa was an editor of a Chinese-ink newspaper *La Tinta China*; see Chinese materials, Yun Gee archives. Anthony Lee states that *Chinese Man in Hat* may be a portrait of a member of the Revolutionary Artists' Club; see Lee, *Picturing Chinatown,* 230. Lee doesn't give reasons for that suggestion, but it is an instance of his reading paintings to enhance the revolutionary image of Gee that he wants to construct.

71 Lee, *Picturing Chinatown*, 231.

72 Wang, "The Art of Yun Gee before 1936," 24–25.

73 Ibid., 25.

74 Gee indicates in one version of his poem about Lao-tzu that some of this writing was on the painting. There are several copies, variously dated 1927, 1929, and 1932. One copy is in French and is perhaps the original. See poetry A-M, Yun Gee archives.

75 The poem appears in Yun Gee, "The Charm of Music," unpublished manuscript, n.d.; see writings about and by Yun Gee, Yun Gee archives.

76 Lee, ed., *Yun Gee: Poetry,* 113–14, dates the poem to 1951.

77 Yun Gee, "Yun Gee Speaks His Mind," unpublished manuscript, n.d., New York Museum of Modern Art archives. This was part of a brochure that Gee put together to publicize his Diamondism School in the 1950s; it contains a reproduction of *Room with a View* dated (on the painting) 1951. A typed version of the piece exists, with editorial changes; it may have been written in the 1940s and expanded for the brochure.

78 See n. 13, above.

79 Wang, "The Art of Yun Gee before 1936," 31, 35. (Wang was unable to find figures reflecting the total count of the Chinese population in 1930.)

80 Gee lived at 461 Sixth Street; see reviews, Yun Gee archives.

81 Helen Gee, "Yun Gee: A Reminiscence," 8.

82 Ibid.

83 Lee, ed., *Yun Gee: Poetry*, 84.

84 Ibid., 65, 68.

85 Ibid., 73.

86 Letters, Yun Gee archives.

87 See Lee, ed., *Yun Gee: Poetry*, 66; see also Gee, "A Reminiscence," 8.

88 Lee, ed., *Yun Gee: Poetry*, 76.

89 Ibid., 85.

90 Ibid.

91 Gee, "Yun Gee Speaks His Mind."

92 Among the dated ones are "Philosopher's Dream," "Repeating Lover's Memory," "Abstraction a Picture," "Rain," "Why So Proud," "Abstraction," "Abstraction Who," "Abstraction Color," "Abstraction En-Act," "Pessimist," "1.2.3.4. Rumble Clock," "Interior Soul," "Abstraction Eat," and "Wo Woo Wooo (Lao-tzu)"; see Lee, ed., *Yun Gee: Poetry*, 96, 98, 99, 100, 101.

93 Gee, "Yun Gee's World: A Reminiscence," 9.

94 Li-lan, "A Journey Home," 12.

95 Ibid.

96 This information is in letters in English and in writings about and by Yun Gee, Yun Gee archives. Several letters are addressed to people who bought paintings from his collection and neglected to finish paying for them, and to students who had not paid their bills.

97 Helen Gee, "Yun Gee: A Reminiscence," 9.

98 Mary Braggiotti, "He Paints the Inner Man."

99 Lee, ed., *Yun Gee: Poetry*, 4.

100 See Erika Doss, *Benton, Pollock, and the Politics of Modernism: From Regionalism to Abstract Expressionism*.

101 Gee painted Powell's portrait and presented it in 1944 to the School of Journalism at the University of Missouri (Powell was a graduate of that institution); see *School of Journalism Bulletin* 45:10 (May 1944), in writings about and by Yun Gee, Yun Gee archives. Other poems probably from this time are "A Very Bad Man's Death," "Song," "The Bend of the Hour," "Memory of Paul Valéry," "Leaving Chicago," "The Critic" (a sarcastic lampoon against criticism), and "Li-Po Drinking Alone in the Moonlight"; see Lee, ed., *Yun Gee: Poetry,* 112, 115–16, 118.

102 Lee, ed., *Yun Gee: Poetry*, 115.

2 Yun Gee's Paintings

1 By using the terms "internationally" and "global," I am essentially referring to artists in Western countries, some artists in Latin America, and some artists in Japan who were familiar with cubism and its reverberations. As mentioned previously,

these were Gee's aims, and in some ways they were in compliance with aspects of modernism's creed of universality.

2 See George Kubler, *The Shape of Time*. Some of the same issues are addressed in Joyce Brodsky, "Continuity and Discontinuity in a Theory of Style: A Problem in Art Historical Methodology."

3 See Yun Gee's brochure on the Diamondism School, in writings about and by Yun Gee, Yun Gee archives; see also Brodsky, *The Paintings of Yun Gee*, 15.

4 Woodward's review is of Max Kozloff, *New York: The Capital of Photography*; see Richard B. Woodward, "Beyond a Century of Photos, Was there a Jewish Eye?"

5 See David Teh-Yu Wang, "The Art of Yun Gee before 1936," 18. Wang writes that Gee mentions Kao Chien-fu (Gao Jianfu) as a painter depicting contemporary subjects, such as railroads and industrial buildings. Gee refers to him many years later; see Yun Gee, "Art in the Chinese Republic," unpublished manuscript, n.d., collection Helen Gee. Lee thinks that Gee "very likely trained as a painter in the studio of the famous Gao brothers," although the only indication of such training is Gee's mention of Gao Jianfu in "Art in the Chinese Republic"; see Anthony Lee, *Picturing Chinatown*, 211. But if Gee had actually studied with him, I imagine that he would have mentioned it. Gee's family seems not to have had the kind of money that would have allowed him to study art in Canton, however, and in any case I think Gee was probably too young to have studied with Kao Chien-fu, who did not return from Tokyo in 1916, as Wang suggests, but, according to Ralph C. Croizier, *Art and Revolution in Modern China: The Lingnan (Cantonese) School of Painting, 1906–1951*, returned in 1908, left for Shanghai in 1912, and got back to Canton in 1918.

6 See Robert E. Harrist Jr., *San Francisco, Paris, and New York: Works by Yun Gee, 1926–1933*.

7 Croizier, *Art and Revolution in Modern China*, 56.

8 Yun Gee, "Yun Gee Speaks His Mind," unpublished manuscript, n.d., New York Museum of Modern Art archives.

9 See Joyce Brodsky, *The Paintings of Yun Gee*, plate 69. There is also a drawing that Gee did as an illustration for Chinese newspapers to raise money for "the Forerunner Team of the Flight School for Chinese Overseas"; it is signed by Gee in English and Chinese, but there is no date (Tunghsiao Chou, personal communication with the author, March 18, 2003). The painting referred to in the present volume as *Wheel "Industrial New York"* is conventionally called *Wheels: Industrial New York*, but Helen Gee informed me in 1977 that the title *Wheel "Industrial New York"* is the one written in Gee's hand on the back of a photograph of the painting, and so that is the title I use here.

10 Gee's daughter, Li-lan, has continued this tradition by including a biplane in several of her own paintings.

11 Wang, "The Art of Yun Gee before 1936," 15; Croizier, *Art and Revolution in Modern China*, fig. 16.

12 Yun Gee "Art in the Chinese Republic."

13 Ibid.

14 See Brodsky, *The Paintings of Yun Gee.*

15 Ibid.

Gee: Poetry, fig. 2. He sent ten paintings to a 1931 Brooklyn Museum show titled Paintings, Sculpture, and Drawings by American and Foreign Artists: the four paintings on silk; *Lao-tzu Taking a Sunbath*; *Emperor Chu (Ming Dynasty)*, a watercolor; *The Pantheon and the Workmen*; *Notre Dame*; *Temptation*; and *The Resurrection*. *The Blue Yun* was exhibited on September 28 in a self-portrait show at the College Art Association and was included in the fifteenth annual exhibition of the Society of Independent Artists. In the same month, Gee donated a seventeen-foot mural to the Chinese Public School at 16 Mott Street to raise money for Chinese flood relief. The following year, at the sixteenth annual exhibition of the Society of Independent Artists, he showed the San Francisco painting *My Conception of Christ* and the Paris painting *The Hundred Beauties*. Also in 1932, he was invited to submit work to the Museum of Modern Art's exhibit titled Murals by American Painters and Photographers and sent *Wheel "Industrial New York"* (pl. 4) and three oil studies (*Merry-Go-Round, Sun Bathers*, and *Modern Apartment*) done over a period of two or three months in that year; see Ju et al., *The Art of Yun Gee*, 125, 128, 132. In May 1932, he also had a two-person show at the Balzac Gallery, where he showed mostly Paris paintings but also a still life and a few city scenes that were probably painted in New York. In June, he had a one-person exhibition at the Milch Gallery on behalf of Democracy in Action, a group affiliated with the British and American ambulance corps; admission proceeds went toward the purchase of ambulances and equipment for the United Nations. Of the thirty paintings shown there (more than half of them done in Paris), the only one from Gee's San Francisco days was *Where Is My Mother* (pl. 2). There were two political paintings, several cityscapes and views of Central Park, several nudes, and a few paintings of horses done in a somewhat romantic mode, as were the last three paintings listed in the exhibition catalogue: *Sisters, Dancers at the Lake*, and *Persephone*. Gee's linear style prevailed in many of the newer paintings, and some were more like colored drawings. Gee showed a political painting, *The Tanaka Memorial*, at the John Reed Club in an exhibit titled The Social Viewpoint, which also took place in 1932. He was also honored by a solo exhibition of twenty watercolors at the San Francisco Art Center (formerly the Modern Gallery, which he and Otis Oldfield had cofounded in 1926). Gee discussed these watercolors in terms of his new theories (probably related to Diamondism) regarding geometry and color. His last solo show in New York, in 1934, was an exhibition of sixty of his paintings, accompanied by a dance recital, at the National Musical Benefit Society in New York, and he continued to show his work, through 1936, at the annual exhibitions of the Society of Independent Artists.

81 These studies are all that are left; see Lee, ed., *Yun Gee: Poetry*, 14–16.

82 See *The New York Times* of June 25, 1933, and *The Parish Visitor* (publication of St. Peter's Church), both in reviews, Yun Gee archives.

83 Erika Doss, *Benton, Pollock, and the Politics of Modernism: From Regionalism to Abstract Expressionism*. Thomas Hart Benton becomes a key figure in Doss's story, and she thinks that Benton profited from his early involvement with abstraction. Her thesis—that Benton remained a modernist in his regionalist mural work as well—may reflect what is perhaps too loose a use of the term "modern." I agree with Doss that Benton's framing and compartmentalizing of various sections to interrupt a

linear progression effected a dynamic fracture in the structure of his narrative, particularly in his *America Today* of 1930, and yet his figures, even though elongated, were painted realistically, and the overwhelming impact of the work flowed from the representational content. With respect to social issues, Doss suggests that abstractionists like Stuart Davis, in works like *New York Mural*, painted in 1932, had many things in common with the regionalist Benton, such as "bright palettes and energetic forms," and that both artists similarly composed their works "to embody the sense of dynamism inherent in the industrialized world of the twentieth century" (116). The same thing could be said about many other painters who were working at the time, including Gee, but the "modern," particularly in the 1930s, was identified with foreign influences, and that meaning persisted after World War II as well, when many immigrants brought a new wave of European modernism to the United States. Doss, developing her very interesting thesis in chaps. 4 and 5, links Jackson Pollock with social issues in painting that had been inherited from Benton; thus Benton becomes more modern as Pollock's work becomes more political. But this thesis disregards the fact that the subjects of Benton's murals were "the people," whereas for Pollock the complete emphasis on postwar individualism and self-expression was intrinsic to the "political" meaning of the work. Benton, representing his Americans in all their positive activities, in work and at play, intended to revitalize a despairing country, and as he became more conservative in that endeavor, the form of his work retained few traces of his experiment with modern art. Throughout the United States, regionalism prevailed, and many artists were employed by the Federal Arts Project and the Works Progress Administration to produce murals and paintings with uplifting themes. Even the archsynchromist Stanton MacDonald-Wright was painting in a realist style in California; witness his commissioned mural *Moving Picture Industry* of 1934–35 for the Santa Monica Public Library. Doss thinks that the major difference between Davis and Benton was that Benton was only a liberal and therefore appeared conservative in the minds of most leftists (and the art community was leftist at the time), whereas Davis, a leftist, was considered avant-garde in those circles, and so he was the preferred artist. Davis remained radical, both in his politics and in his devotion to abstraction. Many other artists in the 1930s were also leftist in their political affiliations, but most painted and drew in a realistic style. A few, Davis among them, used abstraction in a manner that had been inherited from Russian constructivism to encourage a Marxist social program. Even though Davis had little to do with abstract expressionism, he and others like him were considered heroes in the 1950s, whereas Benton was denigrated. At any rate, the divide between regionalism and abstract expressionism was not only over politics but also over the differences in an art that had been influenced by decadent Europe and one that represented what the New World was to become: vital, industrial, capitalist, and free of European cultural domination. If one can use the term "transnational" in connection with the spread of cubism and its offshoots to many countries in the first quarter of the twentieth century, then the 1930s and 1940s ushered in a return to nationalism (for example, social realism in the United States, socialist realism in Russia, and pseudoclassicism/romanticism in Fascist Germany).

84 See also Serge Guilbaut, *How New York Stole the Idea of Abstract Expressionism*, for an interesting view of the politics of abstract expressionism.

85 The letter from Lincoln Kirstein is in letters, Yun Gee archives.

86 Edward Alden Jewell wrote this for the *New York Times*, May 8, 1932; see reviews, Yun Gee archives.

87 Although Helen Gee, as we have seen, points to the depression that Gee suffered over his work's lack of recognition, she also recalls that Gee received a stipend of $300, which was a lot of money in 1932; see Helen Gee, *Limelight: A Greenwich Village Photography Gallery and Coffeehouse in the Fifties*, 190, 191.

88 There was a story circulating that when Pierre S. DuPont (most famous as chair of General Motors) was asked to sponsor a particular radio program, he refused because "at three o'clock on Sunday afternoons everybody is playing polo"; see Robert Bendiner, *Just Around the Corner: A Highly Selective History of the Thirties*, 49. Adding to the irony here is DuPont's notion of "everybody." His comment, made during the Depression years, represents the ultimate in power's arrogance.

89 The photograph is in the files of the Museum of Modern Art, New York.

90 See Lee, ed., *Yun Gee: Poetry*, fig. 3.

91 Wang, "The Art of Yun Gee before 1936," 27, thinks that they belong together and should be viewed from left to right—from *Merry-Go-Round*, on the left, to *Sunbathers*, in the center, and *Modern Apartment*, on the right—and that they show "a progressive modernism in style: from the loose figurative depiction in the left panel to the complex balance of spatial relationship and the distorted figures in the central panel to the almost total disintegration of spatial relationships and figures in the right panel."

92 Ibid., 28.

93 Joseph Mitchell, "Apostle of the New Cubism Teaches Art in a Tenement," *New York World-Telegram*, n.d. (c. 1930s); see writings about and by Yun Gee, Yun Gee archives. Gee claimed that his theory of Diamondism had been formed in San Francisco, but there is no evidence to suggest such an early date.

94 This is from Gee's very detailed brochure advertising his Diamondism School and probably put together in the early 1950s; see writings about and by Yun Gee, Yun Gee archives.

95 Patricia Kolk Connor, "Toward the Iconographic Meaning of Crystals and Glass in Cubism and Expressionism," lecture delivered at 66th annual meeting of the College Art Association, New York, Jan. 25–28, 1978.

96 Wang, "The Art of Yun Gee before 1936," 28.

97 *Temptation* resembles the backdrop for a Chinese play, with the two actors in costume painted in Gee's Paris style. *The Tanaka Memorial* and *Dance: Hitler and Hirohito* are strong political caricatures, like several cartoons with anti-Japanese themes that Gee did during this period. *The Tanaka Memorial* predicts the order of conquest—China, Russia, and the United States—that would supposedly lead to Japan's achieving world domination. *Dance: Hitler and Hirohito* shows the two leaders in cahoots, dancing over their dead adversaries. For reproductions of all these paintings, see Ju et al., *The Art of Yun Gee*, 126, 127. The density of the buildings

in *Houses in the Bronx* fills the panel to the edges in a complex network of abstract planes painted with soft brushstrokes in colors like those in *Wheel*. In *Morning in the Bronx*, the apartment buildings are recognizable, but the canvas is more dynamic, and linear elements interlock with the more abstract passages.

98 For examples of drawings and watercolors, see Wang, *Yun Gee*.

99 Ibid., 86, 87. Some of these watercolors are in Li-lan's collection, and she has verified the style.

100 Gee's comments were originally included in a letter to the writer of an article titled "Undeterred by Depression Watercolors of Yun Gee on View," *San Francisco Examiner*, Feb. 26, 1933; see writings about and by Yun Gee, Yun Gee archives.

101 See Ju et al., *The Art of Yun Gee*, 134, 135.

102 Lee, ed., *Yun Gee: Poetry*, 14.

103 There is mention of a *Crucifixion* having been exhibited at the Sanino Music and Arts Club in Flushing, New York, in April 1935. In the *Gazette de Lausanne* of December 1936 there is an announcement that Gee's painting will be shown in a Christmas exhibition; the writer says, "On trouve du tout au Lion d'Or, jusqu'à un artiste Chinois, Yun Gee. Une *Sensation* exposée par ce *Fils du Ciel* ressemble de façon impressionnante . . . des Fils de la terre: elle n'est pas plus nouvelle pour cela"; see reviews, Yun Gee archives. There is also some mention of a stay in London, but I have been unable to track it down.

104 I don't know what was exhibited, since I cannot locate any reviews.

105 See reviews in *La Tribune des Nations*, Nov. 25, 1937, and in *Les Nouvelles des Expositions*, Nov. 1937, both in reviews, Yun Gee archives.

106 I can account for about half the paintings shown at La Reine Margot. Some were newly painted portraits: *Edouard Champion*; *Paul Valéry*; *Pierre Mille*; *Mme Gabriel Perreux* (pl. 14); *The General (Fan-Cheng-Wu)*; and one of Mme Yvonne Serruy, called *Le Sculpteur*. *Portrait of My Father*, from Gee's first Paris trip, was also included along with *Lao-tzu Taking a Sunbath, Yang Kwei Fei at the Bath, Resurrection, Pantheon in the Rain, My First Impression of Paris*, and *Rue Pétrarque (House with Gate)*. A few paintings from New York—*Meditation, Radio Street (Pelham Bay)*, and some other city scenes—were also included. Achille Murat and Pierre Mille wrote short pieces for the catalogue that illustrated *Confucius (Chinese Sage)* (pl. 3) and a self-portrait. *Big Robbers and Little Robbers*, which may have been painted in San Francisco, was also in the group, and perhaps other early paintings were included as well. *Big Robbers and Little Robbers* is illustrated in *L'Art Vivant,* June 1938. *Alley in Bilancourt*, of which there are two versions, was a genre scene painted in this second Paris period, as was *Cluny at Night*. This exhibition was mentioned in many newspapers and magazines, although there were no extensive reviews.

107 Gee was living at 3, rue des Carmes, on the Left Bank, in the fifth arrondissement.

108 I have seen the portrait of Valéry; other portraits are available only as reproductions, either because they are lost or because they are in private, inaccessible collections in Paris and Asia.

109 There are studies like these that were drawn earlier in New York. For these drawings and watercolors, see Gee, *Helen's World of Yun Gee*, 46, 47, 49, 50, 51, 91,

92. For some of the earlier and more fluid brush drawings, see Wang, *Yun Gee*, 76, 77.

110 Pierre Mille, "Yun Gee." Mille wrote this short essay in 1939 for the government-sponsored exhibition in Paris that ultimately was cancelled when war broke out.

111 See, for example, the scathing review by Melville Upon, *New York Sun*, Oct. 15, 1943, in reviews, Yun Gee archives.

112 The reviews appeared in the *Nationalist Daily*, March 22, 1940, and in the *Chinese National Daily*, n.d. These notices mention a cross section of Gee's work from both Paris periods and from his first New York sojourn. I cannot identify all of them, either because they are lost or because their titles are different in translation.

113 Mille, "Yun Gee."

114 Catalogue for the Milch Gallery exhibition, 1943 (emphasis added); see exhibition catalogues, Yun Gee archives. The "pagoda . . . skyscraper" characterization is taken from Duncan, "Exposition of the Works of Yun Gee." It is not known whether Gee provided the information that he was the son of an American-born Chinese.

115 Gee was among 150 artists chosen from a field of 5,000. In 1945, Gee exhibited twenty-two paintings at the Lilienfield Gallery, many of which would have been included in the previously mentioned Paris exhibition, and Pierre Mille's short essay, as we have seen, played a part. Alongside the paintings made in Paris were scenes more recently painted in New York. On the cover of the catalogue was that almost satiric portrait of Paul Guillaume as connoisseur, smoking a cigarette with an aureole of linear smoke circling his head, standing in front of Picasso's *Pure Joy*. This painting is either lost or in some private collection in Paris. In some ways, Guillaume could have been a stand-in for Gee's self-image at the time. In photographs of him, that bohemian youth with hair standing on edge has become a sophisticated cosmopolite. Short reviews and notices of the show, sometimes with a reproduction of one of the paintings, appeared in *Art Digest, Art News,* and *Picture*, so Gee did receive some coverage, but no extended review.

116 The date of Lucien Laubaudt's death was communicated to me in notes written by an anonymous reviewer of the manuscript for this book, whom I thank for this information.

117 See exhibition catalogues, Yun Gee archives. I visited the Lucien Laubaudt Gallery, still in existence in 1978, when I was doing research on my earlier writing about Gee. The gallery was in a wonderful wooden San Francisco house, which, unfortunately, has been torn down.

118 Stephanie Lieber, *Paintings of Yun Gee*.

119 Gee's small sculptures included *Couple Walking*, from his early cubist phase; *Confucius (Chinese Sage)*; and *Self-Portrait*, possibly made in Paris and now in the collection of Li-lan.

120 One sentence from the exhibition catalogue suggests a level of sensitivity to Gee's work: "Over the years his style has varied greatly, changing with the times and his personal development, so that his [current] exhibition[,] . . . including works of several of his periods, exhibits a range not usually covered in a one-man show"; see Stephen Haff, *An Exhibition of the Work of Yun Gee*.

121 In a letter, Gee says that he visited Jehanne Biétry-Salinger on a trip to San Francisco in 1958; see letters, Yun Gee archives.

122 From this period of work, as far as I can tell, there are more than fifty paintings that are dated (or to which dates can be attributed on the basis of subject and style) and many drawings. This number excludes works not yet documented, and those in private collections that are coming to the market with frequency. About a dozen or more are genre scenes, many in Central Park; about the same number are portraits (four of them are of Li-lan), and the rest are nudes. There are also some twenty undated paintings (which I think were made during this time) that are also scenes; a few portraits and still lifes; some color-theory studies; some works with Chinese and mythical themes; a few paintings of animals; and many more nudes. Given Gee's propensity to work in many styles at the same time, it is difficult to know if they were painted in New York or in Paris. I am excluding from discussion paintings from earlier periods that were redone, mostly in diamond patterns.

123 See *Yun Gee, 1906–1963*, 31; Wang, *Yun Gee*, 30. The most "expressionist" of the works are a series of nudes that seem to have been painted in the late 1930s and early 1940s but that were rarely exhibited. *Dancing Nudes*, dated 1939, was shown in New York but could have been painted in Paris, since its subject is nudes in nature, as in other pictures that Gee painted and drew there. It still feels more French than the darker and more Germanic *Seated Nude* of 1942, which was probably painted in New York. The figures are confronted directly; sometimes only the upper body is painted, and the color range is almost as bright as in some of the San Francisco paintings. One of the most colorful nudes is painted on paper in bright oranges and yellows against a blue-green background, whereas *Seated Nude* is on canvas, heavy and dark, with black against a yellowish green. I think these paintings are awkward if not somewhat grotesque, but they are strangely powerful and very different from Gee's usual and more lyrical treatment of nudes. It is interesting to see him utilize that manner of painting in Central Park landscapes, in green and blue framed by buildings, with people going about summer activities. The paint is more thinly applied, and line accentuates trees, figures, and animals in an almost paradisiacal setting. *Swan Lake, Central Park* is like them, although the scene is in winter, and the ground is painted a light ocher.

124 See Wang, *Yun Gee*, 31, 56, 57, 63; *Yun Gee, 1906–1963*, 44, 46, 47, 77.

125 See Wang, *Yun Gee*, 40, 41, 45.

126 Ibid., 33, 43, 47.

127 Gee's ability to switch his manner of painting at different times is clearly demonstrated by two versions of the same scene: a fountain (probably the one sculpted by Alexander Calder's father) with river gods and nymphs in a small park, which I believe was painted in Philadelphia in the winter, perhaps while Gee was visiting his brother who lived there. One is in the manner of the School of Paris and impressionism, with short diagonal strokes and light colors, rather blurry; the other is a winter snow scene, more hard-edged realistic, and heavier in the application of paint; see Wang, *Yun Gee*, 32, 33. Did Gee visit his brother earlier, perhaps the first time he was in New York after returning from Paris, and then again in the 1940s,

and would that account for the radical differences in conception? For the most part, his hard-edged, more realistic scene paintings are later works.

128 See Wang, *Yun Gee*, 39.

129 *Bridge in Winter*, which depicts the same scene, is more painterly; see slides, Yun Gee archives.

130 Li-lan has a small painting on wood, undated, that is the one copied on the easel. It seems to me a late work; see *Yun Gee, 1906–1963*, where *Seven Nudes in Central Park* is reproduced. In such paintings of women in nature, it seems that Gee wedded a landscape motif with nudes, formed in a linear manner that recalls the fluidity of Chinese ink drawing; perhaps a combination of Eastern and Western ways of painting was intended in this case. The subject matter is decidedly Western, however.

131 Gee was photographed working on a bust while teaching his class in San Francisco. Li-lan has that plaster bust, which can be seen in photographs of Gee's New York apartment, and in one photomontage he puts part of a photograph of his body under it; see photographs, Yun Gee archives.

132 *Yun Gee, 1906–1963*, 57.

133 See Wang, *Yun Gee*, 75.

3 The Life of Li-lan

Chapter epigraph: Isamu Noguchi, *Li-lan: Tokyo 1980* (Tokyo: Nantenshi Gallery, November 8–22, 1989), 2.

1 Unless otherwise noted, the information about Li-lan's life comes from these and past discussions and interviews with her. I had several discussions with Helen Gee in the late 1970s, but this book pays close attention to Li-lan's perspective, which was entirely missing from my earlier writing about Yun Gee.

2 I am unable to translate the many reviews of Li-lan's exhibitions or the other writings about her in Japanese and have relied on Li-lan's interpretations of this material. Some of the more recent catalogues have been printed in both English and Japanese. Li-lan has also written some essays about herself and her memories of her father as well as a book in Japanese about her life; see for example, Li-lan, *Canvas with an Unpainted Part: An Autobiography.*

3 See Scarlet Cheng, "Postcards from the Edge," 1. Cheng's article is a profile on Li-lan, written in connection with an exhibition of Li-lan's paintings at Arts Projects International, New York, in 1996.

4 Li-lan, interview with the author, March 3, 2003. Unless an interview date is important for some reason, I will not continue to cite as sources my interviews with Li-lan.

5 See Helen Gee, *Limelight: A Greenwich Village Photography Gallery and Coffeehouse in the Fifties.*

6 Li-lan recently showed me a group of photographs kept by her mother's sister, Ellen Berland, that show Li-lan as a little girl playing and smiling. Li-lan learned that it was this aunt who nurtured her from the time she was two until she was six years old. Li-lan and her mother lived with her after Helen's separation from Gee, and both sisters and Ellen's husband, Charles Berland, owned the Limelight until they had a falling

out; they were estranged from that time on. It was only after her mother's death that Li-lan was reunited with her aunt and her cousins; sadly, her aunt died only a little over a year after they came together again.

7 Helen writes about the time she and Li-lan won a trip to Europe by participating in a game show on television. (Helen had tried to resist buying a TV set, but Li-lan insisted, since all her friends had one.) Li-lan was twelve or thirteen at the time, and this was her first experience abroad. She was too young for Europe to make much of a lasting impression, but the trip was a good experience for her because Li-lan had her mother all to herself. See Gee, *Limelight*, 27–29.

8 Li-lan told me that her parents kept her in a better school, even though it was out of her mother's school district, by giving her father's address in the Village as Li-lan's home. Her mother put her on the bus, and her father picked her up and brought her back to the bus every day (as he continued to do later on, after Li-lan was placed in private school). Unfortunately, however, the ruse was discovered, and Li-lan had to go to a school where there were no other Asian students or students of color. She was ostracized and teased and remembers coming home crying every day, and so Helen put her in private school. Li-lan received one of three ethnic scholarships, and although this was a better school, she still suffered from the spotlight on her as one of the impoverished three.

9 Li-lan's contribution, an excerpt from *Canvas with an Unpainted Part*, was published in *Heresies*, Feb. 8, 1979.

10 She describes Gee's illness as incapacitating; see Helen Gee, "Yun Gee: A Reminiscence." Elsewhere, she says that Gee was diagnosed with schizophrenia in the early 1940s; see Helen Gee, *Helen's World of Yun Gee*, 35. She has also referred to "Yun's breakdown, which occurred within a few years after our daughter Li-lan was born"; see Helen Gee, "Yun Gee's World: A Reminiscence," 10. At the time when Helen wrote the latter comment, I did not know of Yun's later work in the 1940s and 1950s, since I had not been shown any of it, nor was I aware of his various moneymaking enterprises in those years, efforts that belie the story of his incapacitation.

11 Li-lan, *Canvas with an Unpainted Part*, 56.

12 Helen, too, died recently, and so the loss is now irrevocable.

13 Li-lan, *Canvas with an Unpainted Part*, 57. The joining of memory with psychological factors often produces distorted pictures of the past; recently Li-lan revisited her aunt's old home, still owned by the family, and said it really was a very nice apartment.

14 Ibid.

15 See Clement Greenberg, "Avant-Garde and Kitsch." As is well known, this article became one of the classic texts of modernism.

16 It is postmodernism's distinction to have unveiled the irony of joining elitist forms with the leftovers of socialist doctrines. Erika Doss writes about that irony when she says that Greenberg "did not reflect on the inherent fallacy that elites could be expected to support a revolutionary culture whose function, as he had made explicit, was to generate social change and pave the way for Marxism. By stressing that elites alone were responsible for keeping the avant-garde alive, Greenberg further isolated a potentially revolutionary art form"; see Erika Doss, *Benton, Pollock, and the Politics of Modernism: From Regionalism to Abstract Expressionism*, 373.

17 Li-lan mentions having met John Chamberlain, Neil Williams, Eva Hesse, Tom Doyle, Elaine de Kooning, Alfred Leslie, LeRoi Jones, AB Spellman, Archie Shepp, Omar Rayo (from Colombia), Rodolfo Abularach (from Guatemala), and Luis López Loza (from Mexico) at the Cedar Bar and at Dillon's. At parties and openings she met Mark di Suvero, Chuck Ginnever, Jack Whitten, Bob Thompson, Emilio Cruz, Ay-O, On Kawara, Shusaku Arakawa, Kate Millett and Fumio Yoshimura (she met Masuo Ikeda at their wedding party), Nam June Paik, and many others in the art, music, and literary worlds. Li-lan was also interested in poetry and went to readings by Allen Ginsberg, Gregory Corso, Ray Bremser, Ted Jones, and others when she was in high school.

18 Li-lan had hated wearing Chinese dress when she was a child but enjoyed wearing Japanese dress in Japan.

19 Roland Barthes, *Empire of Signs*, 3.

20 Alexandra Munroe, *Japanese Art after 1945: Scream against the Sky*, 21.

21 It is also a sign of the times that Yun Gee had a one-person exhibition in New York's Marlboro Gallery in October 2005.

22 Her traveling companions included Sol LeWitt, Lucy Lippard, Charles Simmons, Steve Gianokos, Dorothy Lichtenstein, Betty Asher, and others.

23 She wrote it in English, but it was translated and published in Japan. Li-lan took wonderful photographs for it, and some were included in exhibitions along with her paintings. Li-lan told me that the cut-and-paste originals are hidden in boxes somewhere. For my birthday, she presented me with a photograph of shoes on a sill, a picture she had taken on that trip while in Beijing. It is reminiscent of the shoes in Gee's *The Red Chair*.

24 A relative in Chu Village suggested during an interview with Li-lan in 1995 that Yun Gee had gone to school in Canton. Interviews were with a few relatives who were very old, and since so much time had passed, it is difficult to trust the reliability of memory. Perhaps this relative was speaking about Yun Gee's having been there to study English before he left for San Francisco. In Gee's autobiographical writings there is no mention of his having studied there; since he embellished every aspect of his "elitist" education in China, presumably he would have referred to any schooling he had undertaken in that sophisticated city.

25 I share it, and I ate chicken feet particularly when I was little and living with my very orthodox grandparents—another related or just coincidental custom, both Chinese and Jewish.

26 There is a rich literature about the effects of being a biracial person, particularly in relation to blacks and whites, but there are few studies about mixed Asian and Caucasian persons. Interesting works are published by Carter and Associates; for a list of recent articles and books, see http://roberttcarterassociates.com.

4 Li-lan: Global Icons and Painting Practices

1 Comte de Lautréamont, *Maldoror and the Complete Works of the Comte de Lautréamont*, 14.

2 Barthes, *Empire of Signs*, 22.

3 Phyllis Braff, "Minimalist from Springs with Chinese Roots Exhibits Envelopes in Taiwan."

4 See *The Art of Yun Gee*, 138–62.

5 See Richard Shiff, "Cézanne's Physicality: The Politics of Touch."

6 There is no listing of the paintings Li-lan showed at her first exhibition, which took place at the Miyuki Gallery, Tokyo, September 16–21, 1969. The brochure reproduces *6:00 One Evening*, which is similar to the works she showed in 1971 at the Nantenshi Gallery.

7 Li-lan has always been interested in photography and is an accomplished photographer. Her works in that medium were published with her early writings in Japan.

8 These paintings are reproduced in Isamu Noguchi, *Li-lan* (exhibition catalogue for the show that took place November 15–27, 1971, in Tokyo).

9 *Li-lan: Stationary Images*, 4 (exhibition catalogue for the show that took place November 5–December 23, 1990, at the William Benton Museum of Art, University of Connecticut).

10 Ibid., 9.

11 Michel Foucault, *This is Not a Pipe*. Originally published in French in 1968, this was one of the formative texts of structuralism and postmodernism, although it can be read as a defense of issues in modern painting because its subject is the total divide between words and pictures.

12 It is interesting that surrealism has recently emerged as a source for contemporary art and theory; a case in point is an exciting book by Hal Foster, *The Return of the Real: The Avant-Garde at the End of the Century*.

13 Foucault, *This Is Not a Pipe*, 54.

14 Li-lan, cited in Noguchi, *Li-lan*.

15 Jerry Tallmer, "The Nails Fell Down."

16 Robert Berlind, interview, *Li-lan: Stationary Images*, 4.

17 Li-lan saw many works by this artist and others in the exhibition titled The New Japanese Painting and Sculpture (for which there is a catalogue), which took place in 1966 at the Museum of Modern Art, New York.

18 Li-lan exhibited works like these in solo exhibitions in 1974, 1977, 1980, and 1985 at the Nantenshi Gallery, and in one-person shows in New York and Los Angeles from 1974 through the mid-1980s as well as at the O. K. Harris Gallery in 1983 and 1985.

19 Most of these works have not been reproduced. Only a pale idea of what these paintings look like comes across in Noguchi, *Li-lan*, and in the brochures for her 1977 and 1985 exhibitions at the Nantenshi Gallery. It is next to impossible to reproduce Li-lan's work, particularly from this period, because of the subtlety of the light and the luminous colors.

20 See Michael Fried, *Absorption and Theatricality: Painting and Beholder in the Age of Diderot*.

21 Berlind, "Li-lan at Nabi," 119.

22 David Raymond, "Why the Grid?," 3.

23 Karl Lunde, "The Grid," 2.

24 Sometimes this use of materials in Hesse's work is related to feminism, but Hesse was no more a proclaimed feminist in her work than is Li-lan. In light of, for example, Jasper Johns's seductive, encaustic surfaces, it is too easy to emphasize gender difference in the use of materials. Nevertheless, Li-lan has been actively feminist, both in her life and in her participation in shows that were clearly feminist in orientation.

25 Joyce Brodsky, *The Paintings of Li-lan*, 5.

26 Berlind, "Li-lan at Nabi," 119.

27 The words "Grand palais e Galeries" and the dates "6 Au 16 Juin" overlap one of the eye stamps in the painting. I wonder whether she bought the stamp there, or whether there was an exhibition of his work there and someone sent it to her. The eye is cut out and added to the metronome in Ray's well-known *Indestructible Object* of 1965; see both Ray images in the interesting article by Janine Mileaf, "Between You and Me: Man Ray's Object to Be Destroyed."

28 See Irving Sandler, *American Art of the 1960s*, 21.

29 Ibid., 35. The conception of "objectness," particularly in relation to Stella, was formulated by Michael Fried, "Shape as Form: Frank Stella's New Paintings."

30 The phrase "dispassionate irony" is from David Ebony, "Li-lan at Art Projects International."

31 See Alexandra Munroe, ed., *Japanese Art after 1945: Scream against the Sky* (New York: H. N. Abrams, 1994).

32 Robert N. Bellah, *"Imagining Japan": The Japanese Tradition and Its Modern Interpretation*, 189.

33 Reiko Tomii, interview with the author, May 5, 2004. An essay by Tomii is included in Alexandra Munroe, ed., *Japanese Art after 1945*, to which I am indebted for much of my information about Japanese contemporary art, since Japanese critical writings are only now beginning to appear in English translation; this volume is devoted to a number of compelling issues, among them the tension in Japan between absorbing other cultures and discovering what is particularly Japanese.

34 Reiko Tomii, "Infinity Nets: Aspects of Contemporary Japanese Painting," 311.

35 See Shuji Takashina, Thomas J. Rimer, and Gerald D. Bolas, *Paris in Japan*; John Clark, "Artistic Subjectivity in the Taisho and Early Showa Avant-Garde"; Alexandra Munroe, "Circle: Modernism and Tradition."

36 Alexandra Munroe, "To Challenge the Mid-Summer Sun: The Gutai Group."

37 Nam June Paik, "To Catch Up or Not to Catch Up with the West: Hijikata and His Red Center," 77.

38 See Munroe, ed., *Japanese Art after 1945*, plates 177–79.

39 Ibid., 220.

40 Munroe, ed., *Japanese Art after 1945*, 189.

41 The exhibition, titled An Enduring Vision, took place March 9–June 20, 2004.

42 For reproductions of these works, see the 1995 Lin & Keng exhibition catalogue, *Li-lan*, 13, 14.

43 Ibid, 6.

44 Ebony, "Li-lan at Art Projects International," 92–93.

45 David Ebony, *Li-lan: Recent Paintings and Pastels*, 5.

46 Ebony, "Li-lan at Art Projects International," 92.

47 Ebony, *Li-lan: Recent Paintings and Pastels*, 7; see also Jacques Derrida, *The Postcard: From Socrates to Freud and Beyond*, 65, 13.

48 Derrida, *The Postcard*, 69–70.

49 For reproductions of some of these paintings, see Lin & Keng, *Li-lan*, 1995; see also Brodsky, *The Paintings of Li-lan*.

50 For more recent examples, see *Li-lan: Silent Journey*, which includes an essay by Carter Ratcliff in addition to several paintings from 2005, among Li-lan's best works to date.

51 For an excellent reproduction of *Chinese Bridge*, see ibid., plate IX.

52 Li-lan was invited to participate in a group exhibition, held in New York in 2000, titled The Likeness of Being: Contemporary Self-Portraits by Sixty Women. She contributed *Chinese Bridge*, using a representation of her own eyes. In 2000, she painted *Two Views Bridged*, again using representations of her eyes, and a pastel titled *Fly By*, which shows Asian eyes along with the lower part of a nose and full red lips (the latter are not Li-lan's). *Marked: Classic Collection* is another pastel with all kinds of eye types. The painting *Bird of Passage* of 2001 shows Asian eyes. A small pastel, *Passenger*, shows no eyes at all, only earlobes and lips; a version painted in 2002 is titled *Journey*, and representations of Li-lan's eyes appear in it along with likenesses of the bridge of her nose and a visible hairline.

53 For reproductions of some of these paintings, see *Li-lan* and *Li-lan: Silent Journey*.

54 As previously indicated, Li-lan finds motifs in books, postcards, stamps, and the like; every kind of illustrative material is grist for the mill. Recently she purchased a book that reproduces nineteenth- and twentieth-century postcards from Japan and has borrowed a few motifs from it, as in *Look Out* (on the postcard Li-lan consulted, a woman is looking out from behind a bamboo shade); see Anne Nishimura Morse, J. Thomas Rimer, and Kendall H. Brown, *Art of the Japanese Postcard: The Leonard A. Lauder Collection at the Museum of Fine Arts, Boston*, 201, 209. My perusal of this book indicates that Li-lan was not particularly influenced by the postcard tradition while she was in Japan. Although she has purchased and received postcards from almost everywhere, Japanese postcards seem not to have played a particular role in her paintings.

55 See *Li-lan: Silent Journey*, plates III and IX.

56 Peter Frank, "Li-lan: The Game of Seeing Life," 4.

57 Ibid., 5.

Epilogue

1 Jean-Paul Sartre, cited in an excellent essay by Lowery Stokes Sims, "The Post-Modern Modernism of Wifredo Lam," 88. Sims challenges the notion of primitivism that attached to Lam's work through a sophisticated understanding of the manner in which he unified Afro-Cuban spiritual symbolism with Western cubism and surrealism.

2 Isamu Noguchi, *Li-lan*, 2.

3 By contrast with the case of Yun Gee, who suffered racism, particularly in his mature years, even Noguchi's identification with the internment of Japanese Americans dur-

ing World War II, a confinement he voluntarily shared for several months in 1942, did not detract from his international fame; see Bruce Altshuler, *Isamu Noguchi*.

4 Gao Minglu, "Strategies of Survival in the Third Space," 183–89.

5 Alice Yang, "Asian American Exhibitions Reconsidered," 96.

6 Ibid., 97.

7 Ibid. In another essay in the same volume, as background to more complex viewing, she discusses several artists practicing nonofficial art in China in the 1990s and characterizes their work in two ways. One group practices political pop, reworking "the popular imagery of the Socialist revolutionary era in an ironic commentary on the symbols of collective hope and unity," sometimes even by introducing Western consumer logos; see Alice Yang, "Beyond Nation and Tradition: Art in Post-Mao China." In the first group, she mentions Wang Guanyi and Yu Youhan; in the second and more numerous group, she lists Cai Jin, Zhang Huan, Song Dong, Fang Lijun, Yin Xiuzhen, Zhu Fadong, Zhang Xiaogang, Zhang Peili, and Geng Jianyi. Another group reacts to the socialist legacy by focusing on the "individual and the intensely personal" to emphasize subjectivity over collectivity. It is the latter group that particularly interested Yang.

8 See the exhibition titled Pop Vision 5: Contemporary Artists from Mainland China, curated by Ming Fei Gao and Patrick Merrill, at http://www.csupomona.edu/~kellogg_gallery/PopVision/default.html, accessed Oct. 12, 2006. These artists were all painters, but both groups employ a variety of media, including installation, performance, and video. It is also interesting that the use of forms of hybridism in the sense of assemblage, mentioned earlier, is, in a somewhat different manner, a current practice in China. The contemporary painter Wang Yigang, one of the artists in Pop Vision 5, works this way, combining wonderful painted Chinese traditional fabrics with propaganda imagery from the Cultural Revolution for both ironic and nostalgic purposes. See Patrick Merrill's essay for the exhibition at http://www.csupomona.edu/~kellogg_gallery/PopVision/popvision.html, accessed Oct. 12, 2006.

9 Yang, "Beyond Nation and Tradition," 110.

10 Minglu, *Inside/Out*, 20, discusses Chinese artists who work in mainland China, Taiwan, Hong Kong, and overseas, suggesting that each of these regions "reflects its own context of identity: nationalism in the Mainland, 'nativism' in Taiwan, regionalism in Hong Kong, and the third space for Chinese overseas."

11 Ibid., 19.

12 Ibid., 21. It is interesting to consider that gunpowder seems to have been invented in China and was first used for pleasurable events, such as displays of fireworks; only later, in the West, was gunpowder turned into an instrument of death. I think Cai is consciously working out of the indigenous tradition, now adopted worldwide.

13 Ibid., 34.

14 Ibid., 21, 35. Minglu identifies the Rationalist school as one that was positive and spiritual, with a utopian desire to purify society.

15 Ibid., 35.

16 Wu Hung, *Transience: Chinese Experimental Art at the End of the Twentieth Century*, 181. Although I am partial to work that does address those specific issues, I am also attracted to the installations and performances of many contemporary

Chinese artists and to those of artists from many other countries in which the aesthetic appeal is foregrounded. I am and have been an advocate for many of the more conceptual and aesthetic-resistant forms practiced in postmodernism but must admit that it is a real pleasure to be looking once again at beautifully crafted work.

17 See ibid.; see also Wu Hung, *Exhibiting Experimental Art in China*.

18 See Hung, *Transience*, 168–74.

19 Ibid., 23.

20 Ibid., 33–34.

21 See the work of Vivan Sundaram in Chaitanya Sambani, *Edge of Desire: Recent Art in India*, 100–101. This volume is the catalogue for the exhibition of the same name, cosponsored by the Asia Society and Queens Museum in New York in 2005. The exhibition's first venue was in Australia, and it was scheduled to travel to Mexico City and Monterrey and then on to New Delhi before ending in Mumbai—certainly a transnational set of showings.

22 An interesting difference between Yun Gee and Li-lan is that he spoke about eternal human verities, even if they were embodied in the everyday activities of ordinary human beings, whereas Li-lan's paintings may appeal to many people from different cultures but make no claim to universality. In this way, Gee may be closer than Li-lan is to some contemporary transnational artists. The postmodernist critique of the essentialism that was at the core of some aspects of modernism may also be applicable to the contemporary scene.

23 Fereshten Daftari, *Without Boundary*, the catalogue for the 2006 exhibition of the same name, contains many references by transnational artists to the notion of universal appeal. For example, Shirazeh Houshiary and Pip Home write in their artists' statement, "We want the work not to relate to any particular place or religion. Our interest is to discover and reveal our common origins and humanity and to transcend the confines of name and nationality." Is this a full-circle return to the essentialism that modernism proclaimed?

24 Peter Schjeldahl, "Target America," 83.

BIBLIOGRAPHY

Altshuler, Bruce. *Isamu Noguchi*. New York: Abbeville Press, 1994.

Andrews, Julia F., and Gao Minglu. *Fragmented Memory: The Chinese Avant-Garde Exile*. Exh. cat. Columbus: Wexner Center for the Arts, Ohio State University, 1993.

Appadurai, Arjun, ed. *Globalization*. Durham, N.C.: Duke University Press, 2001.

The Art of Yun Gee. Exh. cat. Taipei: Taipei Fine Arts Museum, 1992.

Barthes, Roland. *Empire of Signs,* trans. Richard Howard. New York: Hill and Wang, 1982.

Befu, Harumi, ed. *Cultural Nationalism in East Asia: Representation and Identity.* Berkeley: Institute of East Asian Studies, University of California, 1993.

Bellah, Robert N. *"Imagining Japan": The Japanese Tradition and Its Modern Interpretation*. Berkeley: University of California Press, 2003.

Bendiner, Robert. *Just around the Corner: A Highly Selective History of the Thirties.* New York: Harper & Row, 1967.

Berger, Joseph. *Displaced Persons: Growing Up American after the Holocaust*. New York: Scribner, 1998.

Berlind, Robert. "Experimentation in Still Lifes." *New York Times,* May 6, 1990.

———. "Interview." *Li-lan: Stationary Images*. Exh. cat., 4–10. Storrs: William Benton Museum of Art, University of Connecticut, 1990.

———. "Li-lan at Nabi." *Art in America*, Jan. 2005, 119.

Between the Thunder and the Rain: Chinese Paintings from the Opium War through the Cultural Revolution, 1840–1979. Exh. cat. San Francisco: Echo Rock Ventures/ Asian Art Museum, 2000.

Bhabha, Homi. "The Commitment to Theory." In Homi Bhabha, *The Location of Culture*. New York: Routledge, 1994.

———. *The Location of Culture*. New York: Routledge, 1994.

———, ed. *Nation and Narration*. New York: Routledge, 1990.

———. "The Third Space: Interview with Homi Bhabha." In Jonathan Rutherford, ed., *Identity: Community, Culture, Difference*. London: Lawrence and Wishart, 1990, 207–31.

Biétry-Salinger, Jehanne. "Is Glory Awaiting This Steerage Passenger?" *San Francisco Examiner*, July 17, 1927.

Bing, Nancy. "Reclaiming Yun Gee." *Art & Collection*, March 2000, 232.

Bourdieu, Pierre. *The Field of Cultural Production*. New York: Columbia University Press, 1993.

Braff, Phyllis. "Five-Part Harmony: Five Artists." *New York Times*, Sept. 19, 1999.

———. "Journeys through Time and Space." *New York Times*, Dec. 13, 1992.

———. "Li-lan, Lin & Keng." *ARTnews*, Jan. 1996, 138.

———. "Minimalist from Springs with Chinese Roots Exhibits Envelopes in Taiwan." *New York Times*, Oct. 29, 1995.

———. "Point, Line and Plane: Drawing and Sculpture." *New York Times*, Sept. 6, 1998.

Braggiotti, Mary. "He Paints the Inner Man." *New York Post*, Oct. 24, 1943.

Breckenridge, Carol A., Sheldon Pollock, Homi K. Bhabha, and Dipesh Chakrabarty, eds. *Cosmopolitanism*. Durham, N.C.: Duke University Press, 2002.

Brodsky, Joyce. "Continuity and Discontinuity in a Theory of Style: A Problem in Art Historical Methodology." *Journal of Aesthetics and Art Criticism* 39 (1980), 27–37.

———. "Curator's Statement." In Joyce Brodsky, *Dis-placements and Anxious Objects*. Exh. cat. Santa Cruz, Calif.: Mary Porter Sesnon Gallery, 2000.

———. "How to 'See' with the Whole Body." *Visual Studies* 17 (2002), 99–112.

———. *The Paintings of Li-lan*. Exh. cat. Taipei: Lin & Keng Gallery, 2001.

———. *The Paintings of Yun Gee*. Exh. cat. Storrs: William Benton Museum of Art, University of Connecticut, 1979.

———. "The Imprint of a Transnational Life." In *Weaving Memories*. Exh. cat. Mumbai: Bodhi Art, 2007.

Butler, Judith. *Bodies That Matter*. New York: Routledge, 1993.

Carver, Mabel MacDonald. "Retrospective of Yun Gee Works." *The Villager*, Dec. 6, 1962.

Cheng, Chung-Ying, and Nicholas Bunnin, eds. *Contemporary Chinese Philosophy*. Oxford: Blackwell, 2002.

Cheng, Scarlet. "Border Crossings." *Asian Art News* 3 (1993), 54–55.

———. "Li-lan at Lin & Keng," *Asian Art News* 5 (1995), 6.

———. "Postcards from the Edge." *Asia Times* 1 (1996), 230.

Chou, Tunghsiao. "Delicate Self-Contained Universe: Li-lan at Nabi Gallery." *Artist Magazine* 348 (May 2004), 485–86.

——— "Yun Gee's Early Paintings and Life Journey: Special Exhibition a Minimal Vision of His Portraits' World." *Artist Magazine* 325 (June 2002), 256–69.

Clark, John. "Artistic Subjectivity in the Taisho and Early Showa Avant-Garde." In Alexandra Munroe, ed., *Japanese Art after 1945: Scream against the Sky*. New York: Harry N. Abrams, 1994.

Clarke, David. *Hong Kong Art: Culture and Decolonialization*. London: Reaktion Books, 2002.

———, ed. *Modernity in Asian Art*. Broadway, New South Wales, Australia: Wild Peony, 1993.

Clifford, James. *The Predicament of Culture*. Cambridge, Mass.: Harvard University Press, 1988.

Cogniat, Raymond. "De M. Yun Gee à feu M. Degas." *Beaux-Arts,* March 25, 1938, 4.

Coombes, Annie. "Inventing the 'Postcolonial': Hybridity and Constituency in Contemporary Curating." *New Formations* 18 (1992), 39–52.

Croizier, Ralph C. *Art and Revolution in Modern China: The Lingnan (Cantonese) School of Painting, 1906–1951*. Berkeley: University of California Press, 1988.

Daftari, Fereshten. *Without Boundary*. Exh. cat. New York: Museum of Modern Art, 2006.

Davis, Ioan. "Negotiating African Culture: Toward a Decolonization of the Fetish." In Frederic Jameson and Masao Miyoshi, eds., *The Cultures of Globalization*. Durham, N.C.: Duke University Press, 1998.

de Courtivron, Isabelle, ed. *Lives in Translation: Bilingual Writers on Identity and Creativity*. New York: Palgrave Macmillan, 2003.

Delatiner, Barbara. "Art of Two Cultures and Two Generations." *New York Times,* June 26, 1988.

Derrida, Jacques. *The Postcard: From Socrates to Freud and Beyond,* trans. Alan Bass. Chicago: University of Chicago Press, 1987.

Dompierre, Louise. *The Age of Anxiety*. Exh. cat. Toronto: Power Plant Gallery, 1995.

Doss, Erika. *Benton, Pollock, and the Politics of Modernism: From Regionalism to Abstract Expressionism*. Chicago: University of Chicago Press, 1991.

Dreyfus, Herbert L., and Paul Rabinow. *Michel Foucault: Beyond Structuralism and Hermeneutics*. Berkeley: University of California Press, 1984.

D'Souza, Aruna. "Surrealism and the Visual Arts." *Encyclopedia of Aesthetics,* vol. 4. New York: Oxford University Press, 1998.

Eagleton, Terry, Frederic Jameson, and Edward Said. *Nationalism, Colonialism, and Literature*. Minneapolis: University of Minnesota Press, 1990.

Ebony, David. "Li-lan at Art Projects International." *Art in America*, Feb. 1995, 92.

———. "Transmissions: Recent Work by Li-lan." In *Li-lan: Recent Paintings and Pastels*. Exh. cat., 4–7. Taipei: Lin & Keng Gallery, 1997.

Emerling, Susan. "Li-lan at DoubleVision, Los Angeles." *ARTnews,* Apr. 2004, 124.

Erickson, Britta. *The Art of Xu Bing: Words without Meaning, Meaning without Words*. Exh. cat. Washington, D.C./Seattle: Arthur M. Sackler Gallery, Smithsonian Institution/University of Washington Press, 2001.

Errington, Shelly. *The Death of Authentic Primitive Art and Other Tales of Progress.* Berkeley: University of California Press, 1998.

Fanon, Frantz. *Black Skin, White Masks.* New York: Grove Press, 1967.

Foster, Hal. *The Return of the Real: The Avant-Garde at the Turn of the Century.* Cambridge, Mass.: MIT Press, 1996.

Foucault, Michel. *This Is Not a Pipe,* ed. and trans. James Harkness. Berkeley: University of California Press, 1983.

Frank, Peter. "Li-lan: The Game of Seeing Life." In *Li-lan.* Exh. cat. Los Angeles/New York: DoubleVision Gallery/Nabi Gallery, 2003.

Fried, Michael. *Absorption and Theatricality: Painting and Beholder in the Age of Diderot.* Chicago: University of Chicago Press, 1980.

———. "Shape as Form: Frank Stella's New Paintings." *Artforum,* Nov. 1966, 18–27.

Fusco, Coco. *English Is Broken Here: Notes on Cultural Fusion in the Americas.* New York: New Press, 1995.

Gee, Helen. *Helen's World of Yun Gee.* Exh. cat. Taipei: Sotheby's, 1999.

———. *Limelight: A Greenwich Village Photography Gallery and Coffeehouse in the Fifties.* Albuquerque: University of New Mexico Press, 1997.

———. "Yun Gee: A Reminiscence." In Jane C. Ju, Li Lundin, and David Teh-yu Wang, *The Art of Yun Gee.* Exh. cat. Taipei: Taipei Fine Arts Museum, 1992.

———. "Yun Gee's World: A Reminiscence." In Joyce Brodsky, *The Paintings of Yun Gee.* Exh. cat. Storrs: William Benton Museum of Art, University of Connecticut, 1979.

Gemeinboeck, Petra. "Virtual Reality: Space of Negotiation." *Visual Studies* 19:1 (2004), 52–59.

Global Conceptualism: Points of Origin, 1950s-1980. Exh. cat. New York: Queens Museum of Art, 1999.

Goldberger, Paul. "Shanghai Surprise." *The New Yorker,* December 26, 2005–January 2, 2006, 144–45.

Gómez, Edward M. "When East Came West: Asian Americans Are Finding Their Places in the History of Modern Art." *Art & Antiquities,* February 2003.

Gramsci, Antonio. *Selections from Cultural Writings.* Cambridge, Mass.: Harvard University Press, 1991.

Greenberg, Clement. "Avant-Garde and Kitsch." *Partisan Review,* Autumn 1939, 34–49.

Guilbaut, Serge. *How New York Stole the Idea of Abstract Expressionism.* Chicago: University of Chicago Press, 1983.

Haff, Stephen. *An Exhibition of the Work of Yun Gee.* Exh. cat. Jersey City, N.J.: Jersey City Museum/Museum Galleries of the Bergen Branch Library, 1948.

Hailey, Gene, ed. *California Art Research Monographs,* vol. 19. San Francisco: Works Progress Administration, 1937.

Hall, Stuart. "Cultural Identity and Diaspora." In Nicholas Mirzoeff, ed., *Diaspora and Visual Culture: Representing Africans and Jews.* London: Routledge, 2000.

Hanru, Hou. "Towards an Un-Unofficial Art: Deideologicalization of China's Contemporary Art in the 1990s." *Third Text* 34 (Spring 1996), 37–52.

Haraway, Donna. *Simians, Cyborgs, and Women: The Reinvention of Nature*. New York: Routledge, 1991.

Harlan, Theresa. "Zarina: Embodiments of Home/Imprints of Existence." In Elaine Kim, Margo Machida, and Sharon Muzato, *Fresh Talk, Daring Gazes*. Berkeley: University of California Press, 2003.

Harrison, Helen. "Exhibits Showcase: Four Women Artists." *New York Times,* March 14, 2004, 12.

——— "Filling In Between the Artist's Lines." *New York Times,* March 8, 1992.

Harrist, Robert E. Jr. *San Francisco, Paris, and New York: Works by Yun Gee, 1926–1933*. Exh. cat. New York: Chambers Fine Art, 2002.

Haw, Jane, ed. *The Grid: Organization and Idea*. Exh. cat. Wayne, N.J.: Ben Shahn Galleries, William Paterson College of Art, 1990.

Henry, Gerrit. "Li-lan at O. K. Harris." *Art in America,* Apr. 1986, 191.

Higa, Karen. *Some Notes on an Asian American Art History*. Exh. cat., 9–14. San Francisco: Art Department, San Francisco State University, 1995.

"History of Modern Art." *Art & Antiques,* Feb. 2003, 60–65.

Hung, Wu. *Exhibiting Experimental Art in China*. Exh. cat. Chicago: David and Alfred Smart Museum of Art/University of Chicago Press, 2000.

———. *Transience: Chinese Experimental Art at the End of the Twentieth Century.* Chicago: University of Chicago Press, 1999.

Hutchinson, Linda. "Immigrant Bias, Artistic Freedom." *San Gabriel Valley Newspaper,* Jan. 9, 2004.

Jameson, Frederic, and Masao Miyoshi, eds. *The Cultures of Globalization*. Durham, N.C.: Duke University Press, 1998.

Jewell, Edward Alden. "In the Realm of Art: Museum of Modern Art Is 'at Home.'" *New York Times,* May 8, 1932.

Jones, Amelia. *Body Art: Performing the Subject*. Minneapolis: University of Minnesota Press, 1999.

Ju, Jane C., Li Lundin, and David Teh-yu Wang. *The Art of Yun Gee*. Exh. cat., 53–64. Taipei: Taipei Fine Arts Museum, 1992.

Kapur, Geeta. *When Was Modernism: Essays on Contemporary Cultural Practice in India*. New Delhi: Tulika, 2000.

Karlstrom, Paul J. "Yun Gee: A Modernist Painter's Journey in America." In Anthony Lee, ed., *Yun Gee: Poetry, Writing, Art, Memories*. Seattle: University of Washington Press, 2003.

Kato, Shuichi. "Li-lan." In *Good Day in the High Land: Memories from the 20th Century,* 174–76. Nagano: Shinano Mainichi Shimbun-sha, 2004.

Kim, Elaine, Margo Machida, and Sharon Muzato. *Fresh Talk, Daring Gazes*. Berkeley: University of California Press, 2003.

Kitaj, R. B. *First Diasporist Manifesto*. London: Thames and Hudson, 1989.

Kozloff, Max. *New York: Capital of Photography*. New Haven, Conn.: Yale University Press, 2002.

Kubler, George. *The Shape of Time: Notes on the History of Things*. New Haven, Conn.: Yale University Press, 1962.

Kuczynski, Alex. "In New York, Midas Fever Rises." *New York Times*, May 9, 2004.

Lang, Berel, ed. *The Death of Art*. New York: Haven Publications, 1984.

Lattimore, Owen. *The Mongols of Manchuria*. New York: John Day, 1934.

Lautréamont, Comte de (Isidore Lucien Ducasse). *Maldoror and the Complete Works of the Comte de Lautréamont*, 2 vols., trans. Alexis Lykiard. Cambridge, Mass.: Exact Change, 1994.

Lavie, Smadar, and Ted Swedenburg, eds. *Displacement, Diaspora, and Geographies of Identity*. Durham, N.C.: Duke University Press, 1996.

Lee, Anthony. "The Painting and Poetry of Yun Gee." In Anthony Lee, ed., *Yun Gee: Poetry, Writing, Art, Memories*. Seattle: University of Washington Press, 2003.

———. *Picturing Chinatown: Art and Orientalism in San Francisco*. Berkeley: University of California Press, 2001.

———, ed. *Yun Gee: Poetry, Writing, Art, Memories*. Seattle: University of Washington Press, 2003.

Levin, Gail. *Synchromism and American Color Abstraction, 1919–1925*. New York: George Braziller, 1978.

Lieber, Stephanie. *Paintings of Yun Gee*. Exh. cat. New York: China House, 1947.

Lieberman, William S. *Painters in Paris, 1895–1950*. Exh. cat. New York: Metropolitan Museum of Art, 2000.

Li-lan. "A Journey Home." In Jane C. Ju, Li Lundin, and David Teh-yu Wang, *The Art of Yun Gee*. Exh. cat. Taipei: Taipei Fine Arts Museum, 1992.

———. *Canvas with an Unpainted Part: An Autobiography*. Tokyo: Asahi Shimbun, 1976.

———. "Memories of My Father." In Anthony Lee, ed., *Yun Gee: Poetry, Writing, Art, Memories*. Seattle: University of Washington Press, 2003.

"Li-lan: Labyrinths." *Asian Art Newspaper*, March 2004.

Li-lan. Exh. cat. Los Angeles/New York: DoubleVision Gallery/Nabi Gallery, 2003.

Li-lan. Exh. cat. Taiwan: Lin & Keng, 1995.

Lloyd, Fran, ed. *Consuming Bodies: Sex and Contemporary Japanese Art*. London: Reaktion Books, 2002.

Long, Robert. "Mystery and Skyline." *East Hampton Star*, Oct. 18, 2001.

Lunde, Karl. "The Grid." In Jane Haw, ed., *The Grid: Organization and Idea*. Exh. cat. Wayne, N.J.: Ben Shahn Galleries, William Paterson College of Art, 1990.

Machida, Margo, with Vishakha N. Desai and John Kuo Wei Tchen. *Asia/America: Identities in Contemporary Asian American Art*. Exh. cat. New York: Asia Society Galleries/New Press, 1994.

Maya Lin: A Clear Strong Vision, directed by Frieda Lee Mock. Santa Monica, Calif.: Sanders + Mock Productions, 1994.

Mercer, Kobena, ed. *Cosmopolitan Modernisms*. Cambridge, Mass.: MIT Press, 2005.

Mileaf, Janine. "Between You and Me: Man Ray's Object to Be Destroyed." *Art Journal*, Spring 2004, 5–23.

Mille, Pierre. "Yun Gee." In *Paintings by Yun Gee*. Exh. cat. New York: Lilienfeld Galleries, 1945.

Minglu, Gao. "Strategies of Survival in the Third Space." In Gao Minglu, ed., *Inside/Out: New Chinese Art*. Exh. cat. Berkeley: University of California Press, 1998.

Minh-ha, Trinh T. *When the Moon Waxes Red: Representation, Gender, and Cultural Politics*. New York: Routledge, 1991.

———. *Woman, Native, Other*. Bloomington: Indiana University Press, 1989.

Mirzoeff, Nicholas, ed. *Diaspora and Visual Culture: Representing Africans and Jews*. London: Routledge, 2000.

Morse, Anne Nishimura, J. Thomas Rimer, and Kendall H. Brown. *Art of the Japanese Postcard: The Leonard A. Lauder Collection at the Museum of Fine Arts, Boston*. Boston: MFA Publications, 2004.

Moure, Nancy Dustin Wall. *California Art: 450 Years of Paintings and Other Media*. Los Angeles: Dustin, 1998.

Munroe, Alexandra. "Circle: Modernism and Tradition." In Alexandra Munro, ed., *Japanese Art after 1945: Scream against the Sky*, 125–37. New York: Harry N. Abrams, 1994.

———, ed. *Japanese Art after 1945: Scream against the Sky*. New York: Harry N. Abrams, 1994.

———. "To Challenge the Mid-Summer Sun: The Gutai Group." In Alexandra Munro, ed., *Japanese Art after 1945: Scream against the Sky*, 83–100. New York: Harry N. Abrams, 1994.

Munsterberg, Hugo. *The Art of Modern Japan from the Meiji Restoration to the Meiji Centennial, 1868–1968*. New York: Hacker Art Books, 1978.

Neruda, Pablo. "Ode to a Stamp Album," trans. Margaret Sayers Peden. Cited in Mark Strand, "The Ecstasist: Paul Neruda and His Passions," *The New Yorker*, Sept. 8, 2003.

The New Japanese Painting and Sculpture. Exh. cat. New York: Museum of Modern Art, 1966.

Noguchi, Isamu. *Li-lan*. Exh. cat. Tokyo: Nantenshi Gallery, 1980.

Noye, Harry. "Three California Painters." *American Magazine of Art*, Apr. 1925, 199–204.

Ogawa, Masataka. "Delicate Paintings: Li-lan." *Asahi Shimbun*, May 18, 1974.

Paik, Nam June. "To Catch Up or Not to Catch Up with the West: Hijikata and His Red Center." In Alexandra Munroe, ed., *Japanese Art after 1945: Scream against the Sky*, 77–81. New York: Harry N. Abrams, 1994.

Pollock, Sheldon. "Cosmopolitan and Vernacular in History." In Carol A. Breckenridge, Sheldon Pollock, Homi K. Bhabha, and Dipesh Chakrabarty, eds., *Cosmopolitanism*. Durham, N.C.: Duke University Press, 2002.

Ratcliff, Carter. "Silent Journey." In *Li-lan*, exh. cat. New York: Jason McCoy, 2006.

Raymond, David. "Why the Grid?" In Jane Haw, ed., *The Grid: Organization and Idea*. Exh. cat. Wayne, N.J.: Ben Shahn Galleries, William Paterson College of Art, 1990.

Rogoff, Irit. *Terra Infirma: Georgraphy's Visual Culture*. London: Routledge, 2000.

Rosenbaum, Thane. "The Shadow of the Holocaust." *New York Times Book Review*, May 6, 2001.

Said, Edward M. *Culture and Imperialism*. New York: Vintage Books, 1994.

———. "Intellectuals in the Post-Colonial World." *Salmagundi* 70/71 (1986), 54–64.

———. *Orientalism*. New York: Pantheon, 1978.

———. *Reflections on Exile and other Essays*. Cambridge, Mass: Harvard University Press, 2000.
———. *The World, the Text, and the Critic*. Cambridge, Mass.: Harvard University Press, 1983.
Sambani, Chaitanya. *Edge of Desire: Recent Art in India*. Exh. cat. London: Philip Wilson, 2005.
Sandler, Irving. *American Art of the 1960s*. New York: Harper and Row, 1988.
Schaarschmidt-Richter, Irmtraud, ed. *Japanese Modern Art: Painting from 1910 to 1970*. Zurich: Editions Stemmle, 2000.
Schjeldahl, Peter. "Target America." *The New Yorker*, Aug. 4, 2003, 82–83.
Shiff, Richard. "Cézanne's Physicality: The Politics of Touch." In Salim Kemal and Ivan Gaskell, eds., *The Language of Art History*. Cambridge: Cambridge University Press, 1991.
Sims, Lowery Stokes. "The Post-Modern Modernism of Wifredo Lam." In Kobena Mercer, ed., *Cosmopolitan Modernisms*. Cambridge, Mass.: MIT Press, 2005.
Sloterdijk, Peter. *Critique of Cynical Reason*. Minneapolis: University of Minnesota Press, 1987.
St. John, Terry. *Society of Six*. Exh. cat. Oakland: Oakland Museum of California, 1972.
Sullivan, Michael. *Art and Artists of Twentieth-Century China*. Berkeley: University of California Press, 1996.
Takashina, Shuji, Thomas J. Rimer, and Gerald D. Bolas. *Paris in Japan*. Tokyo/St. Louis, Mo.: Japan Foundation/Washington University in Saint Louis, 1987.
Tallmer, Jerry. "The Nails Fell Down." *New York Post*, May 20, 1978.
Tannenbaum, Judith. "Li-lan." *Arts*, Sept. 1978, 2.
Terada, Toru. *Japanese Art in the World Perspective*. New York: John Weatherhill, 1976.
Three Installations by Xu Bing. Exh. cat. Madison: Elvehjem Museum of Art/University of Wisconsin-Madison, 1991.
Tomii, Reiko. "Infinity Nets: Aspects of Contemporary Japanese Painting." In Alexandra Munroe, ed., *Japanese Art after 1945: Scream against the Sky*, 307–19. New York: Harry N. Abrams, 1994.
Trenton, Patricia. "Before the World Moved In: Early Modernist Still Life in California, 1920–1950." In Susan Landauer, William H. Gerdts, and Patricia Trenton, eds., *The Not-So-Still Life: A Century of California Painting and Sculpture*. Berkeley: University of California Press, 2003.
Tsutakawa, Mayumi, ed. *They Painted from Their Hearts: Pioneer Asian American Artists*. Seattle: University of Washington Press, 1994.
Wang, Chia Chi Jason. *Yun Gee*. Exh. cat. Taipei: Lin & Keng Gallery, 1998.
———. "Ceci n'est pas une Chinoise." *Artist* (Jan. 1996), 214–16.
Wang, David Teh-Yu. "The Art of Yun Gee Before 1936." In Jane C. Ju, Li Lundin, and David Teh-yu Wang, *The Art of Yun Gee*. Exh. cat., 18–52. Taipei: Taipei Fine Arts Museum, 1992.
Woodward, Richard B. "Beyond a Century of Photos, Was There a Jewish Eye?" *New York Times*, July 7, 2002.

Yang, Alice. "Asian American Exhibitions Reconsidered." In Alice Yang, *Why Asia? Contemporary Asian and American Art*, 94–98. New York: New York University Press, 1998.

———. "Beyond Nation and Tradition: Art in Post-Mao China." In Alice Yang, *Why Asia? Contemporary Asian and American Art*, 107–18. New York: New York University Press, 1998.

———. "Introduction." In *Li-lan Correspondences.* New York: Arts Project International, 1996.

Yun Gee, 1906–1963. Exh. cat. Taipei: Lin & Keng Gallery, 1995.

Zha, Jianying. *China Pop*. New York: New Press, 1995.

Zhang, Xudong. "On Some Motifs in the 'Chinese Cultural Fever' of the Late 1980s: Social Change, Ideology and Theory." *Social Text* 39 (Summer 1994), 129–56.

INDEX

C

D

N

O

P

Q

R

S

T

U

V

W

X

Y